THE PESSIMIST'S GUIDE TO HISTORY

Other Books by
Doris Flexner

THE OPTIMIST'S GUIDE TO HISTORY

THE PESSIMIST'S GUIDE TO HISTORY

UPDATED EDITION

STUART FLEXNER
WITH
DORIS FLEXNER

Quill
An Imprint of HarperCollins*Publishers*

HarperCollins books may be purchased for educational, business, or sales promotional use. For information please write: Special Markets Department, HarperCollins Publishers Inc., 10 East 53rd Street, New York, NY 10022.

FIRST QUILL EDITION 2000

The Library of Congress has cataloged the previous edition as:
Flexner, Stuart Berg.
The pessimist's guide to history / Stuart Flexner with Doris Flexner.
p. cm.
Includes bibliographical references and index.
1. Disasters. 2. Chronology, Historical. I. Flexner, Doris. II. Title.
D24.F55 1992 92-3829
902'.02—dc20 CIP

ISBN 0-06-095745-X (Quill ed.)

00 01 02 03 04 RRD 10 9 8 7 6 5 4 3 2 1

For
Jennifer, Geoffrey, Erin,
and Peanut
with love
MOMOX

ACKNOWLEDGMENTS

I am grateful to Stephen Power for asking me to update the catastrophes, fiascoes, and general mayhem that are occurring in the world as we slog into the next millennium. My sincere thanks to my editor, Bret Witter, for his sage editorial comments and for remaining an optimist after reading this somber tome.

Many people have contributed to the pessimistic view of history detailed in this book. Bruce Wetterau played a large part as project coordinator for the first edition. His crew of assistants included Ann Marr, Bruce Beasley, Katherine Somervell, Bill Wenthe, Suzanne Paola, Leila Finn, Sandra Neuse, and Mary St. John. A special thanks to all of them for the long hours spent in libraries tracking down source material and compiling entries. Laurel Adams deserves added appreciation for keyboarding all the draft entries and making editorial corrections. My thanks also to my original editor, David Highfill, for his many astute suggestions that added to the success of this endeavor.

For assistance on this millennium edition, I am indebted to my neighbor, Phil Hall, for the occasional use of his faster computer, and to my daughter, Jennifer, who took time out periodically from her law school studies to do research for me. I would also like to thank my son, Geoff, for supplying me with my new computer, which now takes me instantaneously into the chaos of the twenty-first century.

Pax vobiscum.

PREFACE

As celebrants around the world gathered to ring in the new year, the new century, and herald the next millennium, it was time to reflect on where we have been and to wonder where we are going. The last millennium came and went with no great worldwide celebration. In fact, most of earth's population scarcely noticed. We lived an agrarian life and continued to do so, for the most part, until the last couple of centuries.

A thousand years ago we were emerging from what historians refer to as the Dark Ages in European history. The Norse explorer Leif Ericsson discovered what later would be called America and what he called Vinland. The Chinese were using sulfur, charcoal, and potassium nitrate to make fireworks, the same components later used as gunpowder. The Crusades to wrest the Holy Land from the Muslims began in 1096 and would continue for two hundred years. As we progressed through the Middle Ages dynasties came and went, empires rose and fell, the Renaissance with its emphasis on humanism and intellect sprang forth, and once again America was discovered, this time by Columbus. And all during this period we suffered from war, massacres, famines, droughts, and plagues.

During the three-hundred-year-long Renaissance period, emphasis was on education and the study of the classics, helped by the invention of the printing press with movable type about 1440. The rebirth of intellectualism produced great artists, architects, writers, philosophers, and scientists. It was also the time of religious persecution, in particular the Spanish Inquisition, massacres, revolts, floods, famines, and plagues.

The years following the Renaissance brought us into the modern era. Ships plowed the seas opening up new worlds and ports of call; trains enabled us to go faster and farther; automobiles gave us individual freedom to travel; airplanes brought the world closer to our door. A period of great scientific discoveries and advancements ensued. Medicine brought us vaccinations, anesthesia, antiseptics, X rays, electrocardiograms, pacemakers, and the human genome project. Architecture and engineering gave us St. Paul's Cathedral, the elevator, subways, the telephone, the Brooklyn Bridge, the Panama Canal, skyscrapers, and the Chunnel. By the time we reached the technological age we now live in we had walked on the moon. But these were also the years of great wars in which millions died, religious persecution prevailed, especially in the horror of the Holocaust, massacres and revolts killed hundreds of thousands, famine killed countless more, floods and earthquakes doomed whole cities and the plague of AIDS began decimating populations.

Where will we be at the end of the next thousand years? Will our technology doom us? Will we obliterate ourselves in an explosion of atoms? Or will Mother Nature slowly erode us by floods, earthquakes, tidal waves, and volcanic explosions? Will we be bogged down in constant wars led by narrow-minded ego-driven personalities with their petty grievances?

Or will we soar to great heights, explore other galaxies, settle other planets? Will great minds discover cures for all our ailments? Will we feed and house the poor and starving and educate everyone? Will we finally understand that, despite our differences, we can all get along?

As Shakespeare wrote, "What's past is prologue."

THE PESSIMIST'S GUIDE TO HISTORY

DESCRIPTIONS OF EVENTS

18 Billion Years Ago: The Big Bang. The first and greatest natural catastrophe imaginable was the Big Bang, the cataclysmic event that scientists believe created virtually the entire universe we know today. The true pessimists among us might find it a less than desirable event, as the calamities that follow would never have occurred had it not been for the Big Bang.

While no one knows what really took place, scientists today believe the universe before the Big Bang was a single, super-cooled energy field no bigger than a speck that floated in a dark, limitless vacuum. Then, for some unknown reason, the energy field was disturbed by a random fluctuation.

Suddenly the field started expanding rapidly; then gravity, light, and subatomic particles formed from the original energy field. In a fraction of a second, the Big Bang blasted matter and energy outward at incredible speeds, and even today, billions of years later, the universe continues expanding outward. During the eons following the Big Bang, great clouds of gases and dust formed and gradually condensed into the galaxies, stars, planets, and everything else we see around us today.

65 Million Years Ago: Extinction of the Dinosaurs. For 160 million years dinosaurs roamed the earth, evolving into a multitude of species that could be found on land, in the sea, and in the air. They survived the massive upheavals of primeval continents breaking up and shifting about the face of the earth, all the while thriving in a climate that was much like a continuous temperate summer. Suddenly, sixty-five million years ago, they disappeared.

The mystery of their abrupt extinction has left scientists baffled. There are numerous theories, of course, some of them postulating rather improbable causes. One theory holds that the dinosaurs may have died of constipation after eating newly evolved forms of plant life that they could not digest. Others suggest there might have been a change in climate or even a sudden burst of radiation from a not too distant supernova. Increasingly, though, the evidence points toward a cosmic catastrophe—most likely a huge asteroid or comet that collided with the earth.

A layer of clay containing the heavy metal iridium (often found in asteroids) has been discovered in sites around the world, and in 1987 researchers located a twenty-eight-mile-wide crater in the floor of the Atlantic Ocean that is also rich in iridium, suggesting that the earth was hit by a big asteroid at about the time of the dinosaurs' extinction.

It could have ended that quickly. A fiery asteroid, six miles in diameter, falls out of the sky at forty-five thousand miles per hour, smashing into the earth with tremendous force. Great clouds of debris explode up into the atmosphere, shrouding the earth in darkness for months and lowering temperatures on the surface enough to kill off the majority of the plant life. Dinosaurs that fed on plants died first, while the carnivores succumbed soon afterward. This may have been the earth's first major ecological disaster.

6 Million Years Ago: Mediterranean Sea Dries Up. The Mediterranean's connection with the Atlantic Ocean, what is known today as the Strait of Gibraltar, was closed off about six million years ago by the drifting together of North Africa and Europe. Mediterranean waters rapidly evaporated, leaving nothing but salty pools of water until, on a number of occasions, the continents parted briefly, allowing Atlantic waters to again flow into the Mediterranean. The Strait of Gibraltar has remained open continuously for the last five million years.

85 Thousand Years Ago: The Last Ice Age? The change probably began with a barely perceptible cooling of the climate that lasted for thousands of years. Then, some eighty-five thousand years ago, temperatures finally dropped so low that a great ice age began. Slowly the thick sheets of ice covering the north polar region advanced southward.

As the cold worsened, some eighteen million cubic miles of water froze, and sea levels dropped by 425 feet. North America, Europe, and northern Siberia were largely buried under nearly two miles of ice and Asia and North America were joined by a massive bridge of ice. In the southern hemisphere, the south polar ice cap spread northward to cover New Zealand and the Andes Mountains. By the time the Ice Age reached its peak about eighteen thousand years ago, ice in the northern hemisphere extended as far south as southern Illinois. In New Hampshire, the sixty-three-hundred-foot Mount Washington was buried in ice up to its peak. Some areas not covered by ice became vast deserts. Regions of Africa that are now rain forests were covered by sand dunes. By about ten thousand years ago, the ice had largely receded from western North America, and by seven thousand years ago, the Ice Age was over.

The drastic climatic changes during the long Ice Age devastated the world's animal species. Competition for reduced food supplies and other factors drove half of the species in Europe and North America into extinction within twenty thousand years. Most of the world's large land mammals died out, including the saber-toothed cat, a twelve-foot-tall kangaroo, a three-ton ground sloth, and a fourteen-foot tusked mammoth. Only in parts of Africa did the large mammals survive. As zoologist Alfred Wallace put it, "We live in a zoologically impoverished world from which all the hugest, and fiercest, and strangest forms have recently disappeared."

While it was certainly the latest, this Ice Age was by no means the only one experienced over the millennia. In fact, there have been four separate Ice Ages in the last two million years, the other three lasting from approximately 1.6 to 1.3 million years ago, 900,000 to 700,000 years ago, and 550,000 to 400,000 years ago respectively. One can only wonder if this latest Ice Age is really the last.

10 Thousand Years Ago: Making of the Sahara Desert. At one time the area now known as the Sahara Desert was green and fertile. Tree-covered mountains towered over rivers and lakes, while wildlife, including hippos, rhinoceroses, elephants, and other animals thrived in the area. Tribes of primitive people flourished, too, raising crops and tending herds of animals. What happened to transform this bountiful region of Africa to the barren desert it is today?

Shifts in climate and geology over a period of hundreds of millions of years had already changed the area's environment many times. There were periods when ice covered parts of the area, and others when it was submerged under enormous seas. Continental drift gradually positioned North Africa at the equator, where high atmospheric pressure prevented the formation of clouds and rain. Ten thousand years ago, the rivers and lakes gradually began drying up. As lack of water killed off plant life, winds eroded the land, eventually leaving only fine, dry sand that could neither sustain crops nor hold moisture.

This is one example of what drastic atmospheric changes can do. Is the greenhouse effect an acceleration of such change?

5000 B.C.: Volcanic Eruption Creates Crater Lake. A spectacular eruption of the volcano Mount Mazama, located in what is today the Cascade Mountain Range in Oregon, blew away the upper portion of the volcano cone. The remnants of the volcano filled with water, creating the six-mile-wide Crater Lake. The area is now an ecologist's and vacationer's delight. Some scientists think it may be only temporarily dormant, however.

5 Thousand Years Ago: Giant Meteor Hits Arizona. The desert of present-day Arizona is scarred by a circular crater some four-fifths of a mile across and 550 feet deep, with a rim 150 feet high. It was dug in less than a second sometime between five thousand and fifty thousand years ago by a massive nickel-iron meteorite that may have been as big as a ten-story building or even larger.

Hurtling toward the earth at a speed of ten miles per second, the meteorite began to burn as soon as it hit the earth's atmosphere. White-hot chunks of nickel-iron as large as houses probably broke off, burning up in the atmosphere behind it. A column of compressed, superheated air was pushed in front of the falling meteorite, fanning out as it approached the earth's surface, and scorching to cinders everything on the ground within a hundred-mile radius.

When the meteorite struck, it drove through a quarter mile of solid rock, smashing it to dust. The impact is believed to have blasted three hundred million tons of rock into the air, scattering fragments of rock and meteor for six miles.

Ca.2400 B.C.: The Great Deluge. The Book of Genesis tells the story of a great flood that covered the earth in ancient times. While archeologists have looked for evidence of a disaster that may have inspired the biblical account of the deluge, it has so far eluded them.

Nevertheless, the story of Noah and the flood remains one of the most memorable accounts in the Bible. In it, the great cataclysm had a purpose—to punish man for his wickedness—and before unleashing the flood waters, God instructed Noah to build an ark large enough to carry his family and pairs of animals to repopulate the world.

Then the rains began: "All the fountains of the great deep burst forth, and the windows of the heavens were opened." For forty days and forty nights it rained, and before it was over, the ark floated on waters that rose above the tops of the mountains. The ark drifted for 150 days more as the waters receded. Noah and his cargo were fortunate. Future generations of humankind were periodically punished for their wickedness by the same means.

Ca.1628 B.C.: The Great Volcanic Eruption on Thera. The Minoan civilization, based on the island of Crete, was the center of a thriving Bronze Age culture that had existed for centuries on the islands of the eastern Aegean. One of those islands, located about seventy miles from the Minoan capital on Crete, later came to be called Thera. Ten miles in diameter, Thera was dominated by a great volcano towering a mile above the sea.

Though no historical records exist, archaeologists, geologists, and other scientists have established that in about 1628 B.C. the volcano on Thera exploded in one of the most massive eruptions ever known. Excavations show that a severe earthquake rocked the island first, collapsing houses and forcing the people of Thera to evacuate the island. The earthquakes ceased some time later, allowing at least some of the island's residents to return and begin clearing away rubble.

But the worst was yet to come. The great volcano rumbled to life, showering the island with ash and rock even before debris from the earthquake had been cleared away. Then suddenly the volcano blew open at the top in a massive explosion. It is probable that burning gases poured from the broken volcanic peak; the sky was blackened for hundreds of miles around as ash, dust, and pumice blocked the sun. More terrible explosions followed, blasting away some thirty-two cubic miles of the island and leaving a string of five small islands now known as Santorini.

Massive tidal waves between two hundred and three hundred feet high crashed ashore at many points in the Mediterranean, but it is likely the Minoan civilization on nearby Crete was especially hard hit. Though it is far from certain, archeologists believe the ill effects of the great eruption probably severely weakened the Minoans on Crete, after which their culture declined and disappeared altogether.

In 350 B.C. the Greek philosopher Plato wrote of the legendary civilization of Atlantis he had heard stories about. It was "a great and marvelous power, which held sway over all the island and over many other islands." According to Plato's account, Atlantis had been destroyed by "violent earthquakes and floods, then disappeared in the depths of the sea." Some now believe the legend of Atlantis refers to the great eruption on Thera in 1628 B.C. and the subsequent decline of the Minoan civilization.

1490 B.C.: Biblical Plagues in Egypt. Plagues of locusts, hail, and other calamities in Egypt as described in the Bible probably occurred about this time. The Exodus of the Hebrews from Egypt took place soon after. A wise move.

1226 B.C.: First Known Eruption of Mount Etna. Though the 1226 B.C. eruption of Mount Etna, located on the island of Sicily, was the first on record, it was by no means the last. Europe's largest volcano erupted again in 1170 B.C., 1149 B.C., 525 B.C., and at intervals thereafter up to the present day.

612 B.C.: Destruction of Nineveh. The ancient Assyrian capital, Nineveh, was surrounded by massive walls said to have been sixty feet thick and one hundred feet high. From this imposing fortified city, Assyrian kings ruled over a great empire—until the reign of Sardanapalus. During this period a coalition of Babylonians, Medes, and Chaldeans began a rebellion against Sardanapalus to end Assyrian rule.

For two years the rebel armies fought against the Assyrian

forces, but could not penetrate the walls of Nineveh. Sardanapalus felt safe, because an oracle had assured the Assyrian king that Nineveh would not fall unless the River Tigris became its enemy. As luck would have it, the Tigris overflowed, and its floodwaters knocked down a portion of the great wall surrounding the city.

The rebels poured in through the breach, and in despair Sardanapalus burned himself alive on a massive pyre in his palace. The fate of the oracle is not known.

The victorious armies sacked and pillaged Nineveh, and then, out of hatred for Assyrian rule, systematically destroyed and burned the city, including its magnificent temples, palaces, and homes. A shining example of the ravages of war.

Ca. 600 B.C.: The Terrible Price of Disobedience. When the Median ruler Astyages dreamed that his grandson would one day take over his throne, he ordered his servant Harpagus to kill the boy. (It would appear that Astyages was a little lacking in self-confidence.) Harpagus took pity, however, and gave the child to a herdsman whose own son had just died; he brought to the king the corpse of the herdsman's son as proof that the deed had been done.

But at the age of ten, the king's grandson was seen taking part in a game with other children in which he playacted the part of a king. He was noticed and brought to his grandfather, who recognized him immediately.

Practiced in the art of swift judgment, the king punished Harpagus in the most horrific way he could imagine. He invited the servant to dinner at the palace and, unknown to Harpagus, had Harpagus's own thirteen-year-old son killed and cooked. The king then served Harpagus his son for dinner.

When the meal ended, the king presented Harpagus with a basket containing the boy's hands, feet, and head. One can easily imagine the shock, horror, and anger the servant must have felt. But so absolute was the obedience commanded by this king that Harpagus merely bowed, saying that whatever the king did must be right. Astyages could have given Attila the Hun lessons in management by intimidation.

586 B.C.: Babylonian Conquest of Jerusalem. The kingdom of Judah had rebelled against Babylonian rule before, but ironically, this revolt was led by Zedekiah, the uncle of Babylonian King Nebuchadnezzar II. For sixteen months the city of Jerusalem in Judah withstood the siege of armies led by Nebuchadnezzar II, but gradually famine and pestilence began to ravage the rebels from within the city.

On July 9 the Babylonians finally breached the wall and stormed into the city. Zedekiah and his troops escaped, but they were later captured and brought before Nebuchadnezzar. The soldiers, together with eighty or so citizens, were put to death before the vengeful king, but Zedekiah was not to get off so lightly. He was forced to watch his sons killed before his eyes, and then to have his eyes put out.

The remaining population of Jerusalem, some forty-six hundred Jews, were rounded up and forcibly resettled in Babylon, thus beginning the Babylonian captivity. The soldiers looted and destroyed Jerusalem, knocking down the city's walls and setting fire to the temple, the palaces, and public buildings. Just as at Nineveh not too many years before, an army once again practiced no-holds-barred destruction.

538 B.C.: Babylon Burns in Great Fire. The magnificent Mesopotamian city of Babylon was leveled by fires that broke out after Persian King Cyrus the Great conquered it in 538 B.C. Many of its citizens died in the conflagration, and the city's famed Hanging Gardens, one of the seven wonders of the world, were destroyed. Thus Babylon, in turn, suffered defeat. And they say there's no justice.

490 B.C.: Battle of Marathon. From their vantage point on a hill overlooking the plain of Marathon, ten Athenian generals surveyed the massive Persian army threatening Athens, which was located just twenty-two miles away. Some one hundred thousand Persian troops stood in vast formations on the plain, not far from the shore where six hundred galleys that had brought the invaders to Greece lay at anchor. The Persians' reputation for being invincible no doubt gave the generals pause for thought. The fact that Persian soldiers outnumbered the Greeks ten to one would have convinced any reasonable tactician that it was time to withdraw to fight another day.

The Persians had launched their invasion of Greece to avenge the Athenians' burning of a Persian city nine years before. Some one thousand Plataeans joined the ten thousand Athenians who now commanded strong defensive positions in the hills between the Persian force and Athens. Sparta also promised to send troops to help fight the Persian invaders, but Spartan religious observances prohibited marshaling troops except during the full moon. So the eleven thousand Greeks were faced with the terrible choice of how best to defend Greece—to attack the far superior Persian force or to remain in defensive positions.

The Athenian generals split evenly on the question. Some generals denounced attack as suicidal folly. It remained for overall commander Callimachus to cast the tiebreaking vote. The general Miltiades said to him, "It now rests with you either to enslave Athens or, by assuring her freedom, to win yourself an immortality of fame." Callimachus voted to attack. Then came word that the much-dreaded Persian cavalry had disappeared from the plain, leaving the main body vulnerable to attack.

At dawn on September 21, ten thousand Greeks charged down the hillside on foot, a sight that Persians watched with stunned disbelief. The historian Herodotus wrote that the Persians "thought them a set of madmen rushing upon certain destruction." He called the Athenians "the first Greeks of whom I have heard who ever beheld without dismay the garb and armor of the Medes; for hitherto the very name of Mede excited terror."

The Athenians had the advantage of attack, and their bronze breastplates actually gave them better protection than the Persians' armor. But what the Persians could not know was that the Athenians had deliberately put more men on the left and right flanks of the line now charging the Persians.

The Persian center held against the weaker Greek forces, but the Persian flanks collapsed as the Athenian charge drove forward in furious hand-to-hand combat. Suddenly the Persians found themselves being enveloped by the smaller Greek force and had no choice but to flee to their ships. The Athenians pressed their attack, hacking away at the disorganized Persians and attacking the galleys as they prepared to flee. Though the Athenian leader Callimachus died in the battle, the Athenians had delivered a smashing blow to the superior Persian force. The plain of Marathon was strewn with bodies of about 6,400 Persians, while only 192 Greeks had died.

Athenian general Miltiades knew the war was not yet over, however. Realizing the Persians would probably try to attack

Athens again, he led an all-night march back to Athens, just in time to meet the Persian fleet as it arrived. On seeing the Greek army already in position, the Persian fleet turned back and sailed home.

464 B.C.: Spartan Earthquake. The Greek city-state of Sparta, famous for its long-standing tradition of strict military discipline, was shaken to its foundations by a devastating earthquake one afternoon in 464.

The youths of the Spartan nobility were at their regular exercise in the gymnasium when the violent shaking began and the building caved in on them. Houses toppled everywhere, killing men, women, and children under heavy stone blocks. Gaping fissures opened up in the earth, and boulders hurtled down on Sparta from mountains surrounding the city.

When the shaking finally ceased, it is said that only five houses remained standing, and that as many as twenty thousand people had died. Meanwhile the slaves in Sparta seized the opportunity to revolt, and overtook the city amidst the confusion. But Spartan leaders responded by sounding a call to arms, and the Spartans, in true military fashion, obeyed. The sudden muster of armed forces forced the rebel slaves to retreat to the countryside, where they successfully resisted capture until 461.

453 B.C.: Plague Ravages Rome. Rome, just about to enter a period of rapid expansion, was suddenly struck by a devastating plague that wiped out much of the city's populace.

Expansion policies have worked against many empires over the centuries. This Roman example was not the first or the last.

430–427 B.C.: Thousands Die in Plague at Athens. The Greek city-state Athens had enjoyed a long period of prosperity when war with its archrival Sparta broke out in 431. Athenians, then ruled by the great leader Pericles, decided to avoid fighting Sparta's superior armies by withdrawing inside the city's great defensive walls, while using the strong Athenian navy to engage in coastal raids. But as refugees flooded into the city at the first appearance of the Spartans outside Athens in 430, the populace fell victim to an unexpected enemy within the city's walls—plague.

The sickness was probably eruptive typhoid fever brought by

an infected traveler from North Africa. Crowded conditions and poor sanitation helped spread the infection. According to the historian Thucydides—himself a survivor of the plague—the sickness began with "violent heats in the head, and redness and inflammation of the eyes; and the internal parts, both the throat and the tongue, immediately assumed a bloody tinge, and emitted an unnatural and fetid breath." The plague moved inexorably through the victim's body, working its way into the lungs and finally to the stomach.

In the seven to nine days it took to kill, the plague tormented its victims. Deep despair accompanied the beginning of the illness, so that the sick lost all desire to recover. Then came the burning fever; the sick often could not bear to wear any clothing and threw themselves into fountains "in the agony of their unquenchable thirst, yet it was the same whether they drank much or little." As the plague reached victims' lungs, they coughed violently and retched uncontrollably. Sores broke out on their bodies.

The plague ravaged the city for two years, continuing long after the first Spartan army had withdrawn. Thucydides described the bodies "lying on one another in the death agony, and half-dead creatures rolling about in the streets and round all the fountains, in their longing for water." Not even birds of prey would go near the corpses; the few dogs that fed on the corpses supposedly died almost immediately. Funeral pyres for the dead burned throughout the city; in the haste to dispose of infected corpses, some people dumped the bodies onto other families' pyres and ran away.

Most of those who became sick died, while the few survivors often lost use of their fingers, toes, or eyes, or suffered complete amnesia. Those who recovered were immune to a second infection, however, and became the only nurses for the thousands of sick.

Amid all this tragedy, those who had not yet been infected became determined to spend their last days in wild revelry before the plague struck them. They feared retribution from neither the gods nor the law. The gods had apparently deserted them anyway, and no one feared the law because "no one expected to live till judgment should be passed on him," as Thucydides wrote.

Finally, after two long years, the plague abated for a year, only to strike again in 427. By the time the plague ended later that year, it had killed as many as a third of the one hundred thousand people living in Athens. Among the many dead was the great Athenian leader Pericles.

426 B.C.: Earthquake Shakes Greece. Shortly after twenty-five girls in Alponus, Greece, had raced to the top of the harbor tower in order to get a view of holiday festivities below, a massive earthquake ripped through eastern Greece, sending the tower and the girls plunging into the sea below.

The deadly quake tossed buildings off their foundations, churning and shaking the earth throughout a wide region. Many villages and cities were completely destroyed, and rivers changed their courses or dried up altogether.

The peninsula of Euboea, separated from mainland Boeotia by a river, was wrenched eastward by the powerful quake. Within minutes Euboea was an island, and the small river had expanded into the Euripus Strait.

Thousands died in the devastating quake, and thousands more were left injured or homeless.

399 B.C.: Tragic Death of Socrates. Socrates, one of the three most important philosophers of ancient Greece, whose teachings eventually became central to Western culture, was condemned to die in 399 after being convicted for "corruption of the young" and "neglect of the gods."

The very greatness of Socrates made the mean circumstances of his death that much more tragic. His indictment was in large part a result of the political instability of Athens after the Peloponnesian War. Furthermore, when accused, Socrates responded contemptuously to the charges against him and refused to request banishment rather than execution as his penalty. Unfortunately, he had his way and was condemned to poison himself with hemlock.

On the day appointed for his death, possibly in the spring or summer, Socrates' friends arrived at the prison as the jailers were removing his chains.

"How singular is the thing called pleasure, and how curiously related to pain," the philosopher mused as the leg chains he had worn for a month were loosened.

Socrates, who taught that death would only liberate the soul from its bodily fetters, faced his own death calmly. He told his friends that the soul "adorned in her own proper jewels, which are temperance, justice, courage, nobility, and truth . . . is ready to go on her journey to the world below."

The philosopher smiled ironically when asked how he wanted to be buried. "When I have drunk the poison I shall leave you and go to the joys of the blessed," he answered. "Be of good cheer, and say that you are burying my body only, and do with that as is usual, and as you think best."

Socrates then bathed, saying he wanted to spare the women the trouble of washing his body once he was dead. Then he met, for the final time, with his children and the women of his family. As sundown came, he prepared to accept the poison, scorning those who urged him to delay his death a few more hours.

The jailer who brought the cup of poison broke into tears, calling Socrates "the noblest and gentlest and best of all who ever came to this place."

Socrates asked for permission to make a libation to the gods with the poison, but was told there was only enough for him to drink. He raised the cup and prayed "for the gods to prosper my journey from this to that other world," and drank without resistance.

Instructing his weeping friends to be quiet and patient so that he could die in peace, Socrates walked around his prison cell until his legs felt heavy. He lay down and felt the numbing effect of the poison working its way up his legs, saying, "When the poison reaches the heart, that will be the end." His last words were simply "I owe a cock to Asclepius [the god of healing]; will you remember to pay the debt?" Then the philosopher who had spent his life preaching the immortality of the soul fell silent, his eyes glazed over in death.

390 B.C.: Gauls Burn Rome. Roman armies had been virtually undefeated for 360 years when the Gauls, led by Brennus, overcame them outside Rome. "There was a great slaughter in the left wing on the banks of the Tiber," wrote the historian Livy, "and many, overweighted by their armor, were drowned." Most of the defeated Romans retreated to nearby Veii, while some soldiers and citizens barricaded themselves in the citadel of Rome.

When the Gauls entered Rome, they found the city largely deserted, except for the wealthy patricians who, dressed in their finery, sat in stony silence in front of their mansions. Confused by the patricians' regal appearance, the Gauls made no move against them until one Marcus Papirius hit an inquisitive Gaul in the head with an ivory scepter. Not a good move, Marcus.

The Gauls promptly slaughtered him and the other patricians and began to sack the city. Attempts to take the citadel failed, though the Gauls destroyed the rest of the city.

373 B.C.: Earthquake Submerges Helice, Greece. The Greek geographer Strabo gave an account of the destruction of a city believed to be Helice, which sank into the Gulf of Corinth during a great earthquake in 373. Another installment in the continuing saga of the Mediterranean earthquakes which keep rearranging the Greek islands.

331 B.C.: Battle of Arbela. Persia's King Darius was determined to stop the advancing Macedonian Greek armies led by Alexander the Great before they could conquer his kingdom. To that end, King Darius assembled an army of 250,000 men, including 40,000 cavalry, fifteen war elephants, and two hundred chariots with scythes mounted on their wheels.

Undaunted by the far superior numbers arrayed before him at Arbela in Mesopotamia, Alexander attacked the Persians on October 1 with only a forty-thousand-man infantry and a seven-thousand-man cavalry. With a terrifying roar, Alexander's men attacked the huge Persian army, though Alexander did hold back a reserve force from the battle. Darius sent his two hundred chariots into the fray, but Alexander's men bravely ran ahead of the whirling blades and cut the traces of the horses, while other soldiers attacked drivers and horses with javelins.

The fierceness of the fighting on the right flank finally drew off so many troops that the Persian center became vulnerable. Alexander then led his reserves in the attack on the Persian center, turning the battle into a bloody rout. Darius fled on horseback, and soon the Persians were being slaughtered remorselessly. For fifty miles Alexander's army chopped down the fleeing Persians, thousands of whom died as they tried to force their way over a narrow bridge across the River Zab. Though estimates of the death toll vary widely, some put the Persian losses as high as ninety thousand men. Macedonian losses were less than five hundred. Often studied as an example of the tactics of penetration, the battle upheld Alexander's genius as a general and overthrew the Persian Empire.

224 B.C.: Quake Topples Colossus of Rhodes. A great bronze statue of the Greek god Apollo, one of the seven wonders of the world, stood at the entrance to the island of Rhodes until it was toppled by an earthquake in 224. Efforts to restore the one-hundred-foot-high statue to an upright position failed.

218 B.C.: Hannibal Crosses the Alps. Rivalry between Carthage and Rome again erupted into war in 218, in what came to be called the Second Punic War. At its outset, the great Carthaginian general Hannibal decided on an ingenious and dangerous plan for attacking Rome. He would invade Italy by landing his forty-eight-thousand-man army in Spain and marching through Gaul and across the Alps.

Hannibal lost many men due to attacks by hostile peoples and during such natural difficulties as fording swollen rivers. But his troubles multiplied as he reached the Alps towards November, when snow was already falling in the higher passes.

Hannibal's soldiers, all from the warm climes of North Africa, were neither accustomed to, nor clothed for, the brutally cold Alpine winter. Still, they began the treacherous ascent, leading packhorses, mules, and even elephants up narrow, icy paths. On the way up, thousands of men and animals fell to their deaths. Meanwhile, the Carthaginians also had to defend themselves against attacks by barbarian hordes.

Near exhaustion from the climb and the cold, the Carthaginians began their descent on their eleventh day in the Alps. But that same day they came to a spot where landslides had destroyed the path. Men and pack animals slipped and fell into the ravine below before Hannibal at last ordered that the army make camp and rebuild the road. For three days the weary soldiers worked valiantly until, finally, the trail was repaired.

Hannibal lost some twenty thousand men during this now famous march, many of them in the final days in the Alps. He still commanded a formidable army, however, and soon successfully attacked Roman positions in Italy.

This escapade is one of the early examples of the egotistical general hell-bent on victory, with equipment or without. Excellent idea about the elephants, Hannibal.

217 B.C.: One Hundred Cities Destroyed by Killer Quake. A deadly quake rocked much of North Africa in 217 B.C., demolishing one hundred cities and killing more than fifty thousand people.

216 B.C.: Hannibal Decimates Roman Army at Battle of Cannae. While Hannibal's Carthaginian army raged through Italy during the Second Punic War, the Romans assembled a massive army of ninety thousand men to oppose him. The great Roman army finally met the smaller fifty-thousand-man Carthaginian army at Cannae in southern Italy. Despite being outnumbered, the great general Hannibal remained confident of victory. According to Plutarch, before the battle he remarked to his general Gisgo, "In all that great number of men opposite, there is not a single one whose name is Gisgo."

By skillful maneuver the Carthaginians managed to surround the superior Roman forces before they realized what was happening. The Carthaginians then closed in on the helpless Romans and massacred them as they stood in their tracks. Between fifty thousand and seventy thousand Romans perished in one of the worst defeats ever suffered by a Roman army. Only six thousand Carthaginians died in the fighting. Hannibal, songs of victory ringing in his ears, later sent back to Carthage three bushels of gold rings taken from the fingers of slain Roman troops. That averages twenty thousand dead Romans per bushel, or five thousand per peck.

164 B.C.: Deadly Smallpox Epidemic Kills Thousands. Soon after Roman armies returned from the eastern Mediterranean, a smallpox epidemic broke out in Rome. The disease also spread throughout Europe and Persia, killing unknown thousands for over ten years after the initial outbreak.

Ca. 88 B.C.: Massacre of One Hundred Thousand Romans. Mithridates VI Eupator, ruler of the kingdom of Pontus along the Black Sea, took advantage of unrest in Rome to conquer Roman territories in Asia Minor and modern-day Syria. Deciding that the only way to control his newly won territories was to kill all Romans living in them, he orchestrated the massacre of some one hundred thousand men, women, and children. An early example of genocide. More to come.

87–80 B.C.: More Romans Die. Soon after the three-year Social War had drawn to a close, Rome found itself plunged into a series of bloody massacres as Roman generals Lucius Cornelius Sulla and Gaius Marius fought for control of the city.

The trouble began when Sulla, promised command of the campaign against Mithridates in the East, discovered that the command had been transferred to the aged Marius instead. Infuriated, Sulla marched on Rome with thirty-five thousand men, drove Marius from the city, and took his men off to fight Mithridates.

Marius took advantage of Sulla's absence to return to Rome with six thousand soldiers and thousands of volatile slaves he had freed from prison. An orgy of violence erupted when Marius ordered the slaves to massacre Sulla's supporters. Blood ran in the streets during the five-day slaughter, and thousands of butchered bodies littered the city, Marius having refused them burial.

A year after Marius's death in 86 B.C., Sulla and his army marched back into Rome. Merciless in his reprisals against those who had sided with Marius, Sulla called for the immediate execution of thousands, including senators, businessmen, and prisoners. Hundreds of severed heads were prominently displayed around town during the bloodbath, and Sulla's proscription list became longer each day. More than forty-seven hundred Roman citizens were killed in Sulla's reign of terror, which finally ended with his retirement from dictatorship in 80 B.C.

This may be the only time in history that a dictator ever resigned of his own volition. In all fairness, Sulla did carry through a constitutional reform program to restore the supremacy of the Roman Senate. Maybe he just decided to quit while he was ahead.

73 B.C.: Roman Gladiators Revolt. The Roman gladiators were prisoners of war who were compelled to fight and kill each other as public entertainment. In 73 B.C. Spartacus, a Thracian soldier of noble birth, broke out of a training camp for gladiators in Capua with about seventy followers and began a general uprising among gladiators and slaves.

By the following year Spartacus had organized a ragtag army of over one hundred thousand escaped gladiators, slaves, and outlaws that rampaged through what is now Italy. Spartacus's men fought well in battle, defeating Roman armies sent to recapture them. They avenged themselves by pillaging and raping their former Roman captors. Any prisoners they took were crucified, or forced to slaughter each other in combat, just as the gladiators themselves had been compelled to do. Though Spartacus apparently hoped to lead his men back to their homelands, he was ultimately unsuccessful in persuading them to lay down their swords.

After many victories, Spartacus was finally trapped in a desperate battle in southern Italy. Thousands of his men were killed in battle by armies under the Roman consul Crassus, who devised a cruel mass punishment for the thousands of rebels he took prisoner.

Crassus lined both sides of the road from Capua to Rome with some six thousand crucifixes, binding a captured rebel on each one of them. The sight of so many crucifixes stretching into the distance, a man slowly dying on each, satisfied the Romans that their slaves would not dare revolt again.

44 B.C.: Julius Caesar Assassinated. On March 15, despite warnings and omens of impending misfortune, Julius Caesar made his way through the streets of Rome to a meeting of senators at Pompey's Theater. Along the way, a passerby thrust a petition into Caesar's hand and implored him to read it, but Caesar received scores of petitions every day and decided this one could wait. That proved to be a fatal mistake.

Before Caesar's rise to supreme power, Rome had been a republic, run by a senate of wealthy patricians who often passed laws designed to protect the privileged status of the wealthy. Though a patrician by birth, Julius Caesar aligned himself with populist factions, eventually sharing the rule of the empire with two other consuls in the First Triumvirate. Caesar's conquest of Gaul made him a hero in Rome, and he eventually made himself sole ruler of the empire. Caesar then enjoyed widespread popularity, both for his military achievements and the reforms he pushed through the senate, but many of the senators resented his arrogance and his control over them. They longed to regain their power.

After five years of Caesar's autocratic rule, his enemies in the senate formulated a plot to kill him and restore the republic. The primary conspirator was Gaius Cassius, who soon recruited several other senators to the cause, among them Publius Servilius

Casca, Lucius Tillius Cimber, Decimus Brutus, and Marcus Junius Brutus, rumored to be Caesar's illegitimate son. News of the plot spread rapidly, and within two weeks, more than sixty senators knew of it. Only a few, however, knew that the deed was to occur at a meeting of the senate on March 15.

When the appointed day arrived, Caesar's wife, Calpurnia, begged him not to leave the house because she had dreamed of his death the night before, and reminded him that a fortune-teller had predicted that the Ides of March (the fifteenth) would be fatal to him. Moved by his wife's entreaties, Caesar had just decided to remain at home when Decimus Brutus arrived and chided him for yielding to such nonsense, finally persuading him to attend.

On the way to the meeting, a passerby stopped Caesar and begged him to read a petition. The parchment warned Caesar of the assassination plot against him, and had he read it, Caesar might well have lived. But he merely took the petition and went on his way to Pompey's Theater.

Meanwhile, the conspirators had already assembled there, armed with daggers in their stylus cases. They had managed to prevent the senators loyal to Caesar from attending the meeting, so that no one present would interfere with their plan.

Caesar entered the chamber of Pompey's Theater shortly after noon, still holding the unread parchment, and sat in a recessed area below a statue of Pompey. As Tillius Cimber pretended to petition Caesar for the return of his brother from exile, Casca slipped behind Caesar and stabbed him. Caesar jabbed back at Casca with his stylus, but the other senators quickly closed in around him, their daggers raised. In the frenzy of stabbing that followed, the conspirators hacked mercilessly at Caesar, wounding each other in the process. Then they abandoned Caesar's lifeless body, riddled with thirty-five stab wounds, at the foot of Pompey's statue.

Their treacherous deed was done, but its result was not what they had planned. The republic was not restored, and Rome suffered years of instability and civil war before Caesar's great-nephew Octavian became sole ruler of the empire as Augustus Caesar.

This infamous assassination did, however, provide William Shakespeare with the plot for one of his most famous plays and the immortal line, "Et tu, Brute?"

19 B.C.: Earthquake Destroys Syria. A wide area of what is modern-day Syria was rocked by a severe earthquake in 19 B.C., killing over one hundred thousand people.

27: Stadium Collapses in Rome. Expecting to be entertained by grisly gladiatorial combats, the Romans who packed a newly constructed wooden amphitheater had no idea they themselves would become part of a grim spectacle. They had no way of knowing the huge wooden theater in Fidenae, a town located just outside Rome, had been built by an unscrupulous speculator who tried to save money by failing to install a proper foundation.

Some fifty thousand people eagerly crowded into the raised structure before the combat was set to begin. As the seats filled, the pressure on the weak foundation increased, until finally the structure collapsed. The sound of screams and cracking timbers filled the air as tens of thousands fell into the crumbling structure. Some spectators were killed as they struck the ground, others were crushed under the weight of timbers, and still others were battered and crushed by the bodies falling on top of them. Estimates of the casualties vary, with the total dead and injured ranging from twenty thousand to fifty thousand.

Things haven't changed much. This still happens today—for the same reason.

Ca. 30: Jesus Crucified. It was a Friday morning in Jerusalem, and Jesus of Nazareth stood before the Roman procurator of Judea, Pontius Pilate, awaiting his sentence. He had been found guilty of blasphemy and condemned to death for allegedly calling himself the King of the Jews, and now awaited the order of execution. Following tradition, Pilate offered to free one of the condemned prisoners, asking the crowd to choose between Jesus and Barabbas, an insurrectionist and murderer. Many of Barabbas's cohorts were in the crowd, however, and after they cried loudly for his release, Pilate reluctantly ordered Jesus to be crucified.

Roman soldiers took Jesus to a courtyard, where they whipped him until he could barely stand, and then mockingly placed a robe over his shoulders and a crown of thorns on his head, derisively hailing him as "King of the Jews." Jesus was led into the streets with two thieves who were to be crucified as well, and made to carry a thirty-pound crosspiece to which his wrists would later be nailed.

While the crowd surrounding them jeered, Jesus and the thieves began the slow one-thousand-yard walk to the crucifixion site outside the city walls. About halfway, the exhausted Jesus fell to the ground, and a bystander, Simon of Cyrene, was made to carry the crosspiece the rest of the way. The procession continued to a hill outside Jerusalem's walls known as Golgotha, or the place of the skull, where the crucifixion was to take place. There a group of compassionate women brought Jesus some drugged wine—offered out of mercy to the condemned—but he refused to drink.

Without further delay, the executioner placed Jesus' arms on the crossbeam and drove heavy nails through his wrists. Four soldiers then hoisted Jesus and the crosspiece onto a six-foot post already planted in the ground, and nailed his feet, knees bent, to the post. Over his head an inscription in Latin, Greek, and Aramaic read: "The King of the Jews."

The two thieves were crucified to either side of Jesus, and one is said to have joined the soldiers and chief priests in mocking him, demanding that he prove himself to be the King of the Jews by saving himself. But the other thief turned to Jesus and said, "Jesus, remember me when you return in your glory." And Jesus comforted him, saying, "Today you shall be with me in Paradise."

Suddenly the sky began to darken, and soon the early afternoon appeared as if it were twilight. This unexplained darkness was reported by contemporary historians to have occurred in all parts of the known world. Gazing at the people below him in the darkness, Jesus prayed, "Father, forgive them, for they know not what they do."

Time passed as Jesus fought against the slow asphyxiation brought on by the physical strain of crucifixion. His breathing was labored, and with a great deal of effort, he cried out in despair: "Eli, Eli, lama sabachthani"—"My God, my God, why hast thou forsaken me?" Some in the crowd thought he was calling to Elijah, and gazed around expectantly to see if the prophet would come to save him. Instead, however, Jesus merely uttered, "I thirst." A Roman soldier stuck a sponge on the end of his spear, dipped it in the sour wine provided to the soldiers, and held it to Jesus' lips.

After three hours on the cross, it was evident that death was near. Jesus summoned the strength to pray, "Father, into thy hands I commit my spirit," and then uttered his last words: "It is finished."

It is reported that at the moment of Jesus' death, an earthquake shook Jerusalem, splitting the ground and walls of buildings. One of the Roman centurions guarding the scene was so moved by the spectacle that he exclaimed, "Assuredly, this man was the Son of God." Another soldier, though, was determined to make certain Jesus was not feigning death, and thrust his spear into Jesus' ribcage, releasing a trickle of blood.

The life and death of Jesus marked the beginnings of Christianity, a religion professing peace on earth and good will toward men. For these tenets of brotherly love, millions would fight, die, and be martyred.

37–41: Blood and Power: Caligula's Cruel Reign. A fortune-teller once told Caligula that he had as much chance of becoming emperor of Rome as he had of riding dry-shod over the Bay of Baiae. Upon becoming emperor in 37, Caligula ordered ships anchored across the three miles of the bay, had them covered with wood and dirt, and triumphantly rode his horse over them.

Within a year of taking power, however, Caligula declared himself a god and justified his incest with his sisters by citing Jupiter's liaison with his sister Juno. Along with this bizarre behavior, Caligula also became increasingly obsessed with killing for pleasure.

He referred to Rome as "the city of necks waiting for me to chop them," and his favorite method of execution was killing victims slowly by inflicting countless small stab wounds. At a banquet, Caligula once burst into laughter, saying, "It just occurred to me that I only have to give one nod and your throats will be cut."

Finally, in A.D. 41, Caligula's guards assassinated him and his wife, and beat his infant daughter to death.

One of the world's most famous sociopaths, Caligula is a prime example of Lord Acton's statement "Power tends to corrupt, and absolute power corrupts absolutely."

64: Great Fire of Rome. According to Roman historian Suetonius, in the summer of A.D. 64 the emperor Nero's adviser Tigellinus quoted lines from a Greek play: "When I am dead, may fire consume the earth." Nero corrected him: "While yet I live." Every contemporary Roman source blames Nero for instigating the fire that broke out the evening of July 19, two days after Nero had left Rome for Antium twenty-seven miles away. Motives ascribed to the emperor range from desire to rebuild the city for his own glory to simple desire for dramatic entertainment.

But whether or not it was deliberately set, the fire that consumed ancient Rome began in one of the shops that surrounded the Circus Maximus, a giant sports arena in the center of the city. Strong winds spread the blaze rapidly across the entire Circus Maximus area, where it fed on the flammable goods for sale in the shops and moved inexorably through the narrow streets crowded with wooden buildings.

The historian Tacitus, who witnessed the panic in the streets, described the "terrified, shrieking women, helpless old and young, people unselfishly supporting invalids or waiting for them, fugitives and lingerers alike—all heightened the confusion." Mobs of people rushed to escape the advancing flames, but the fire seemed to follow them everywhere they went. Many finally fled the city altogether, though some lay down to die in despair after losing their families or all their possessions.

The most ancient monuments of Rome—temples, shrines, and mansions—went up in flames. Gone were Nero's palace and the Temple of Jupiter, supposedly built by Romulus, one of the founders of Rome. Nero, awakened by messenger with the news, journeyed back to the burning city that night. Legend has it that the mad emperor stood in the tower of his gardens, gazing at what he called "the beauty of the flames." He then supposedly watched the city burn to ruins while playing the lyre and singing of the destruction of ancient Troy. Thus originated the saying "Nero fiddled while Rome burned."

For six days the fire roared on, unchecked. Tacitus reported that "menacing gangs" roamed the streets, threatening anyone who tried to put out the fire, and throwing torches to spread its devastation. "Perhaps they had received orders," he wrote, "or they may just have wanted to plunder unhampered."

After six days, the fire sputtered out at the foot of Equiline Hill.

But new fires then broke out, reportedly on the estate of the emperor's adviser Tigellinus on the other side of Rome. The rumor spread that Nero had ordered the city burned because, as Tacitus put it, he was "ambitious to found a new city to be called after himself."

Despite this alleged villainy, Nero opened his own gardens to those made homeless by the fire and even had emergency shelter built for them. He brought shipments of food from nearby Ostia and ordered a reduction in the price of corn to feed the hungry masses.

Of the city's fourteen districts, three were burned completely to the ground, and seven others were "reduced to a few scorched and mangled ruins," according to Tacitus.

Tacitus wrote that Nero blamed the fire on the Christians and used it as an excuse for horrendous persecutions, including having them torn apart by dogs or covered in pitch and used as human torches in his gardens.

Nero built himself a grandiose new palace called the Golden House of Nero, which had a 120-foot statue of himself at its entrance. "At last," he said, "I can begin to live like a human being."

64: Nero Persecutes the Christians. In the aftermath of the great fire that destroyed Rome, many blamed the Roman emperor Nero for setting the fires. Nero knew well enough that Roman citizens were "cruel, by their sports to blood inured. . . ." They wanted revenge, and Nero was said to have cleverly planned to put the blame on Christians and to divert the Romans' attention from the tragic fire by "mixing games and gaiety with spectacles of refined and atrocious cruelty. . . ."

Nero no doubt found Christians to be the perfect scapegoats. Christianity at this time was unpopular and little understood by many in Rome, and the sect was not officially sanctioned within the empire. Christians were rumored to have held orgies, killing small children to provide the "blood" and "body" they consumed during their services. Furthermore, the faith welcomed what Romans considered inferior beings, women and slaves. Christian beliefs that all other religions were false offended those who practiced them, while Roman rulers who depended on absolute obedience from their subjects also felt threatened by Christian tenets.

Ordering all Christians in Rome rounded up, Nero had all who confessed to their beliefs convicted on charges of setting the deadly fires and of "hatred to mankind." Then came the cruel and bloody spectacles, in which a "vast multitude" of Christians was put to death. Thus began the first great mass persecution of the early Christians.

A historian writes that "various forms of mockery were added to enhance their dying agonies." Many were publicly crucified, to the cheers of the Roman crowds. Others were covered with the skins of wild beasts, then set upon and mangled by dogs, as thousands of approving Roman citizens watched on. Children and elderly Christians were mauled and torn to pieces by tigers in the open theaters of the city. Nero also held chariot races in the gardens of the royal palace after twilight, illuminating the festivities with human torches. Christians were smeared with pitch and tar, then set ablaze to throw light on the races.

Persecutions of Christians in the Roman Empire continued sporadically over the next centuries, often brought on by a calamity, such as an earthquake, flood, or even a loss in battle, for which the Christians were then held responsible. The Edict of Milan in 313 finally granted official sanction to Christianity within the empire, putting an end to the persecutions.

70: The Siege of Jerusalem. It was spring in Jerusalem when Titus, heir to the Roman imperial throne, arrived with an army of eighty thousand men to lay siege to the city. The Jews had been in revolt against Roman rule since 66, and Titus now intended to force the city into submission. He had not counted on the city's heavily fortified walls, however, nor on the huge number of devoted Jews from the surrounding countryside who were now inside the Jewish holy city and fiercely determined to protect it.

Nevertheless, the Romans began their siege and chose Passover as the day to attack the city's walls, believing that the devout Jews would not fight on that day. To their surprise, the Jews vigorously repulsed the attack, killing hundreds of soldiers and destroying many Roman battering rams. Even the women of the city took part, pouring boiling oil on the heads of their attackers.

But the Jews were unable to break the siege as fighting continued in the following weeks. The Romans closed off all access to the city and proceeded to wear down the defenders in any way they could. In one case, Titus crucified five hundred prisoners and sent still others back into the city after cutting off their hands. But the Jews continued to resist.

Then famine overtook the besieged city. Starving, people ate grass, bits of leather, anything. Gangs roamed the streets, breaking into homes in search of food or eating horrid refuse from the streets. According to the historian Josephus, "No respect was paid even to the dying; the ruffians searched them, in case they were concealing food somewhere in their clothes, or just pretending to be near death." In one horrible case, a woman killed her own baby to eat its body. Unburied corpses littered the streets. Still, the Jews would not surrender their city.

Finally the Romans dislodged Jerusalem's zealous defenders from the city's outer wall, thereby gaining entrance to the city. But the Jews refused to surrender and took up new positions behind the massive walls surrounding their sacred Temple.

For six days the Romans tried to break through the Temple's outer walls with battering rams. In another attack, they scaled the walls with ladders. The Jews, determined to save the Temple, fought fiercely and beat back the Romans time and time again.

Titus finally ordered soldiers to set fire to wooden gates leading to the Temple, and after the fire had burned almost two days, he launched his final attack. As the furious onslaught began, a Roman soldier hurled a burning firebrand through one of the Temple's golden windows. A huge fire erupted within, quickly spreading to the wooden beams.

Roman soldiers raced wildly into the courts of the Temple, killing all who stood in their way. More fires were set; desperate Jews fought bravely but were outnumbered. Cries of despair rose together with the sounds of crackling flames in one dreadful roar. As the flames rose higher and the building began to crumble, many devout Jews hurled themselves into the conflagration, unwilling to live without their sacred Temple. Thousands of others, believing that a miracle would spare them, stood resolutely in the Temple's inner court. The Romans slaughtered some six thousand of them.

The Temple was burned to the ground, but the taking of Jerusalem was not yet over. Some rebel leaders escaped the inferno and took up positions in the fortified upper city. After eighteen days of preparations, the Romans scaled the walls and took this fortress, too. With this final victory, the Romans sacked the city, set it afire, and tore down the walls.

Talk about overkill.

79: Vesuvius Destroys Pompeii and Herculaneum. Romans living in the busy port towns of Pompeii and Herculaneum believed that the nearby volcano called Mount Vesuvius was extinct. Vesuvius actually had not erupted for thousands of years, and in A.D. 79, farmers cultivated the mountain slopes with olives and grapes.

But that was about to change. On the afternoon of August 24 the mountain exploded, blasting a column of pumice twelve miles into the air. Pliny the Younger, who was staying at a villa across the bay, saw it as "a cloud of unusual size and appearance, like an umbrella pine." His uncle Pliny the Elder, who commanded a Roman fleet, took some galleys to rescue friends who lived near the volcano at Stabiae, not far from Pompeii. As the ship headed toward the roaring volcano, "ashes were already falling, hotter and thicker as the ships drew near, followed by bits of pumice and blackened stones, charred and cracked by the flames." The rain of pumice descended at the rate of six inches an hour, and by late afternoon, roofs of houses near the volcano began to collapse under the weight.

By this time many of Pompeii's twenty thousand citizens, along with thousands from Herculaneum and other towns near the volcano, had fled the area. But some six thousand people in Pompeii and Herculaneum either refused to go or could not leave.

The elder Pliny was forced to land some miles from Stabiae, and traveled the rest of the way by land. By nightfall he saw "broad sheets of fire and leaping flames" blazing on the mountaintop. To reassure his companions, he insisted that it was only bonfires abandoned by the peasants when they fled the mountain in terror. But as the night wore on, terrible tremors emanated from Vesuvius. While resting at a friend's villa before attempting to return to his ship, Pliny noted "the buildings were now shaking with violent shocks, and seemed to be swaying to and fro as if they were torn from their foundations." Then, about midnight, a burning avalanche of hot gases, rocks, and pumice poured down the mountainside.

Daylight never arrived on the morning on August 25. Instead, the morning was "blacker and denser than any ordinary night," according to Pliny. The air was so thick with ash and sulfurous gases that it choked Pliny the Elder to death before he could reach his ships.

Meanwhile, Pliny the Younger described the "fearful black cloud rent by forked and quivering bursts of flame, and parted to reveal great tongues of fire, like flashes of lightning magnified in size." In the darkness the people panicked: "You could hear the shrieks of women, the wailing of infants, and the shouting of the men. . . . There were some who prayed for death in their terror of dying. Many besought the aid of the gods, but still more imagined there were no gods left, and that the universe was plunged into eternal darkness forevermore."

By eight-thirty on the morning of August 25, a centuries-long darkness had in fact descended upon Pompeii and Herculaneum—the two cities were now completely buried beneath a layer of ash some fifteen to twenty feet thick. And when light finally came on the morning of August 26, Pliny the Younger wrote, "We were terrified to see everything changed, buried deep in ashes like snowdrift." The top of Mount Vesuvius had been blasted completely away, and some sixteen thousand people living in cities and towns around the base of the volcano had been killed.

Pompeii and Herculaneum were all but forgotten until 1748, when systematic excavations of the two cities began.

79–88: Plague Ravages Roman Empire. Soon after the destruction of Pompeii and Heraculaneum by the eruption of Mount Vesuvius, a terrible plague swept through the Roman Empire. The pestilence reportedly killed upwards of ten thousand people a day at its height.

115: Antioch Demolished by Earthquake. Roman Emperor Trajan, then visiting the great city of Antioch in modern-day Syria, was among those lucky enough to escape from collapsing buildings during the violent earthquake of 115. Unknown thousands were killed, and the city was severely damaged.

125: Plague of Orosius. Plague swept through much of North Africa, killing eight hundred thousand in Numidia and some two hundred thousand in the region around Carthage. The plague is named after the Spanish theologian Orosius, who wrote a full description of it in the fifth century.

164–180: Plague of Antoninus. Roman legions returning from Syria brought back a plague, possibly smallpox or black plague, that had begun in the eastern reaches of the empire in 164. The pestilence, which followed the prosperous reign of Roman Emperor Antoninus, quickly spread throughout the empire, depopulating whole cities.

That's the army for you, always being blamed for bringing back strange diseases from foreign lands.

184–204: Yellow Turban Rebellion. During an epidemic in China, the traveling magician Chang Chueh reportedly healed many by giving them water over which he had said a magical incantation. The apparent success of his remedy earned him hundreds of followers, and Chang Chueh decided to exploit his success by beginning a rebellion against the corrupt eunuchs who actually controlled the Han Dynasty government. The emperor ruled China at this time in name only.

Chang Chueh assured his followers immortality on the battlefield by giving them potions, and in 184 he and his followers, all wearing yellow turbans, took up arms against the government. Chang Chueh himself was killed in 184, but his revolt continued for years afterward, thus setting in motion events that later led to the downfall of the Han Dynasty.

To suppress the revolt, the ruling eunuchs were forced to form large armies at great expense to the government treasury. Some of the corrupt eunuchs took bribes from the rebels, causing a rift between the eunuchs and the military that soon resulted in the massacre of the eunuchs. While the Yellow Turban revolt was ended by 204, anarchy reigned in the empire, and the ineffectual emperor became nothing more than a pawn in the hands of the power-hungry generals. The emperor finally abdicated in 221, ending the long reign of the Han Dynasty.

Future dynasties continued to use eunuchs as political advisers. Western governments of the period never required castration as a prerequisite for civil service.

186: Massive Volcano Erupts in New Zealand. Taupo, a volcano in New Zealand, erupted explosively in 186, blowing away four-fifths of its cone and leveling six thousand square miles of the surrounding countryside. The eruption was possibly the most powerful in history.

Third Century: War Destroys Library, Alexandria, Egypt. The most famous research library and museum in antiquity was destroyed during a civil war late in the third century A.D. Founded in the year 290 B.C. by Ptolemy Soter and maintained by a succession of Ptolemies, the library contained nearly three-quarters of a million volumes of scientific knowledge, all known Greek literature, and translations from other languages.

Although damaged by fire in 47 B.C., when Julius Caesar besieged the city, the central library had remained intact. A daughter library, established about 235 B.C. in the temple of Serapis, was later destroyed by the Christians in A.D. 391.

The destruction of these libraries eradicated most of the knowledge that had accumulated over the centuries. This loss and the political and social upheavals that followed plunged the Western world into the Dark Ages.

250–265: Black Plague Strikes Roman Empire. At the height of this plague, deaths in Rome numbered five hundred per day, and before it ended, much of the empire was depopulated.

Mother Nature keeping population growth under control again.

365: Earthquake Shakes Alexandria. Dawn had just broken over the magnificent city and seaport of Alexandria on July 21 when furious thunder and lightning erupted. The disturbance in the sky probably awakened many living in the city, located near the mouth of the Nile River in Egypt. Then, with only that warning, the whole city suddenly started to shake.

Historian Ammianus Marcellinus described the quake as a "horrible phenomena . . . such as are related to us neither in fable nor in truthful history. . . . The whole of the firm and solid earth was shaken and trembled." Indeed, much of the Roman Empire was being shaken at that very moment. Tremors were later reported to have occurred in Sicily, Greece, Egypt, and Dalmatia (in modern-day Yugoslavia).

In Alexandria, people shaken from their sleep raced into the streets as buildings trembled and threatened to collapse. Suddenly the ground became still, and the panicked citizens experienced a moment of calm. But Alexandrians out along the waterfront noticed something very strange taking place.

The sea was fast disappearing, pulling back as though receding after a massive wave. Suddenly the sea floor all the way out beyond the great port of Alexandria lay exposed. Marcellinus wrote that "in the abyss of the deep thus revealed, men saw many kinds of sea creatures stuck fast in the slime; and vast mountains and deep valleys, which Nature, the creator, had hidden in the unplumbed depths . . . first saw the beams of the sun."

Apparently the quake's epicenter lay beneath the sea and had violently disturbed the Mediterranean waters. Knowing none of this, amazed Alexandrians rushed out into the exposed seabed, grabbing fish with their hands.

Then they heard the roar as the sea returned in a massive tidal wave hurtling toward shore so rapidly, there was no time for anyone to escape. The wave struck Alexandria with astonishing force. Saint Jerome wrote that it "seemed as though God was threatening a second deluge, or all things were returning to original chaos."

As the enormous wave rushed into the city, buildings crumbled and were washed away into the sea. The streets of Alexandria flooded for miles inland. Some ships riding the onrushing waves crashed into the tops of buildings two miles away from the shore. Some fifty thousand people were drowned or crushed by the collapsing buildings. Bodies floated everywhere.

The tidal wave threatened many other coastal areas around the Mediterranean, though some were spared. At Epidaurus in Greece, the people ran to the monk Saint Hilarion for protection when the earthquake struck. He is said to have looked out over the sea as a tremendous wave approached. He marked the sign of the cross three times in the sand and lifted his hands toward the wave. It then withdrew and spared the town.

410: Visigoths Sack Rome. The fall of the Roman Empire from greatness was nearly complete when the Visigoths, invading barbarian tribes led by King Alaric, threatened the city of Rome itself. Appearing before the city, the Visigoths arranged a conspiracy whereby certain Roman slaves and servants secretly opened a gate to the city for them at midnight on August 14. An early example of fifth columnists in action. Thus the Visigoths entered Rome without striking a blow.

Once inside, the Visigoths roamed the city at will, burning, looting, raping, and killing unarmed citizens in cold blood. Remarkably, Alaric's order not to disturb Christian churches was heeded by his men, but elsewhere chaos reigned.

Bodies of slaughtered Romans filled the streets as thousands of Roman servants and slaves joined the Visigoths' rampage. The palaces and homes of wealthy Romans were stripped of treasures and furnishings. The Visigoths tortured anyone suspected of hiding valuables until the location was revealed. Many precious artworks were smashed or melted down for their valuable metals.

The pillage of Rome lasted six full days, and while churches and many public buildings were spared, the destruction and loss of life was enormous. But this was not the end of Rome's agony: The once proud city was soon sacked again, by the Vandals in 455.

Barbarians do not live by turning their swords into plowshares.

472: Vesuvius Erupts. While not nearly as destructive as the eruption of A.D. 79 that buried Pompeii, this one nevertheless collapsed buildings and killed scores of people in the area surrounding the volcano. Volcanic ash from the eruption spread over much of Europe.

A few more cities hit the dust.

526: Hundreds of Thousands Die in Antioch Earthquake. Thousands of visitors crowded into Antioch on May 29, one day before Ascension Day, for the annual religious festivals held there. Antioch, located in present-day Syria, was a thriving commercial city and an important Christian religious center complete with grand churches, marketplaces, theaters, public baths, and monuments.

At six o'clock that evening most people were indoors when a massive earthquake struck. There was no time to escape; screams of terror mingled with the great roar of buildings collapsing as they crushed or trapped thousands of victims. An eerie silence followed as the first violent shocks suddenly ended. Those trapped in the rubble waited in fear for the aftershocks, which soon came, adding to the death and destruction of the first shocks.

A blazing inferno soon engulfed what was left of the city, burning to death many of those trapped in the rubble, or asphyxiating them in the heavy, black smoke. Sparks and flying cinders filled the air. The flames moved so quickly throughout the city that one survivor described fire falling "down from heaven instead of rain." Almost every structure spared by the earthquake was destroyed by fire. "Except for the soils of the field, the fire surrounded everything in the city, as if it had received a command from God that every living thing should be burned."

Two centuries before, the Roman emperor Constantine the Great had built Antioch's Great Church, a splendid structure with golden domes. It seemed that perhaps some miracle would spare the magnificent building, but a few days after the fires began, the church burst into flames and burned to the ground.

Among the incredible tales of survival is one about a pregnant woman buried in the rubble. She was found alive days later, along with the healthy baby she delivered, despite the tons of debris piled above her.

Some 250,000 people died as a result of the deadly earthquake and fires that followed in its wake. But even those who survived and tried to flee the city with a few belongings became victims of the chaos created by the quake. As usual, thieves attacked them at will for their valuables, killing anyone who resisted. Hordes of robbers roamed through the city, looting the ruins. Legends tell of "divine retribution" visited upon these looters, however, many of whom supposedly died suddenly after taking treasures from the ill-fated city.

Though most everyone in Antioch had died or fled during the disaster, those survivors who remained began the work of rebuilding the city. But just two years later, another massive earthquake struck the city, destroying all the new buildings and claiming five thousand more lives.

Maybe they should have tried a new neighborhood.

532: Nika Revolt in Constantinople. On January 11 a festival was under way in the Hippodrome, Constantinople's giant open-air sports arena. Most of the city's population had assembled to watch the races and games, but the amusements were repeatedly disrupted by bickering and shouting from one of Constantinople's political factions, a group called the Greens.

Finally the emperor Justinian became impatient and demanded order and respect from the discontented faction, but they only became more antagonistic. The Greens yelled that they were renouncing their allegiance to the emperor, calling him a murderer, a fool, and a tyrant. At this, a group loyal to Justinian, the Blues, rose angrily from their seats and charged furiously toward the Greens. The clamor in the Hippodrome became deafening, and the fighting spilled out into the streets of the city.

In their enthusiasm, soldiers sent to quell the riot knocked down priests who were also trying to restore order. In the scuffling, religious relics were dropped and smashed, and the rioters now fought with renewed anger and strength, adding sacrilege to their complaints against Justinian's rule. Women joined in the commotion, throwing stones from open windows onto the heads of soldiers in the streets. Protestors also threw firebrands, starting fires that soon raged out of control through Constantinople and reduced nearly the entire city to ashes. Meanwhile, the warring factions roamed the streets yelling "Nika!" (victory), thus giving the deadly insurrection its name.

When Justinian resolved to punish the factions by executing seven of their leaders, the two groups joined forces against the emperor, and the fighting continued with increased bitterness. The insurgents now demanded the release of Hypatius, a nephew of the former emperor who was in the royal palace at that time. Hypatius was reluctant to place himself in the hands of the angry mob, but Justinian, hoping to appease the rioters, forced him to leave the palace. The insurgents then seized Hypatius, marched him to the Hippodrome, and crowned him their new emperor.

At this point, Justinian was more than ready to flee with his riches, his ships, and his consort, Theodora. But she refused to let him give up, insisting that he defend his reign. He managed to assemble three thousand loyal men, and while the unsuspecting mob celebrated at the Hippodrome, Justinian's forces quietly approached the arena.

Justinian's soldiers took the insurgents completely by surprise and brutally hacked them to death with swords. The Hippodrome ran red with blood before the soldiers finished their gruesome massacre of thirty thousand rioters. Hypatius wanted to surrender, and if Justinian had known, he might well have spared his life. But Theodora was infuriated by the uprising and urged the soldiers to show no mercy and kill everyone.

Hell hath no fury like a woman scorned.

542: Plague Strikes Constantinople. A deadly four-month plague epidemic devastated the Byzantine capital of Constantinople in the spring and summer of 542. At the height of the outbreak, some ten thousand people died each day of the disease, which was characterized by sudden fever and mysterious swellings on the thighs or the armpits, followed by coma, delirium, and death.

The historian Procopius wrote that those in delirium often "suspected that men were coming upon them to destroy them, and they would . . . rush off in flight, crying at the tops of their voices." In any event, the disease—probably the Black Plague—proved deadly. Burial grounds in the city filled quickly, and eventually city officials tore the roofs off towers of a nearby fort and filled the towers to the top with corpses.

By the time the plague began to abate in August, half the people in Constantinople had died. The other half had to live with the stench.

The plague killed about three hundred thousand people out of a total population of half a million, and was the cause of Constantinople's decline.

746–749: Plague Ravages Constantinople. Yet another plague, possibly carried to Constantinople by slave traders, devastated the population. The disease was further spread to what is now Italy and Greece, and is believed to have killed some two hundred thousand people. At least this plague wasn't blamed on the troops coming home.

817: Rome Burns in Great Fire. Fire broke out in the crowded central section of Rome and burned for six days, consuming the closely packed wooden structures. A second fire began soon after the first and burned for three more days. Only four of the city's fourteen sections were undamaged.

We can't blame Nero for this one.

930: Muslim Rebels Sack Holy City of Mecca. Karmathians, a Muslim reformist sect rebelling against the ruling orthodox caliphs, stormed Mecca and massacred some thirty thousand people. The rebels also stole the Muslims' sacred black stone, an important Islamic relic, which, according to legend, was given to Adam after his fall.

With the development of yet another religion, Islam, we have even greater potential for infighting among the faithful. By the way, when the stone was returned twenty years later, it was found to be broken.

1040: Fifty Thousand Die in Persian Earthquake. The Persian city of Tabriz (in modern Iran) was hit by a massive earthquake. Estimates of the dead were put at fifty thousand or more.

This was one of five big earthquakes that destroyed Tabriz over the centuries. The founding fathers didn't know they were building in an earthquake zone.

1084: Normans Sack Rome. Pope Gregory VII, hoping to break a siege of Rome by Holy Roman Emperor Henry IV, called upon the Norman Robert Guiscard for aid. The Norman army of thirty-six thousand men, mainly Muslims recruited by the Normans, successfully broke the siege, but then proceeded to sack the city. The marauders set fires, massacred thousands, and took thousands more as slaves.

The sacking of Rome has always been a favorite sport throughout history.

1106: A Very Bad Year for Venice. The year 1106 turned out to be disastrous for Venice. In January, heavy rains, high tides, and strong winds conspired to create terrible flooding within the city. The nearby town of Malamocco was washed completely away. Houses, churches, even the land itself, was washed into the sea by the high water and heavy, wind-driven waves. Seven hundred years later, the ruins of the lost town would still be seen underwater at low tide.

Within days of the flood, however, a fire broke out in Venice that spread through six parishes before it was finally put out. Then, on April 6, an even greater fire devastated the city. The blaze spread across the Grand Canal, consuming at least twenty-four churches and much of the city before dying out. Wooden houses lay in ruins, but the stone and marble Basilica of San

Marco and the Doges Palace survived, and thereafter use of wood for building was actively discouraged in Venice.

Smart thinking on the part of the city planners.

1169: Mount Etna Erupts. "Hell visited earth" as the Sicilian volcano Mount Etna erupted for the first time in centuries. Part of the volcano cone blew out explosively during the eruption. The accompanying earthquake and tidal waves killed over fifteen thousand people.

Old Mother Nature at work once more.

1170: The Murder of Thomas à Becket. A long-standing feud between King Henry II of England and Archbishop Thomas à Becket concerning Henry's authority over the Catholic church in England had finally gone too far. On December 29, four of the king's knights, fully armed with swords and axes, arrived at Canterbury Cathedral. Claiming to be acting under the king's orders, the knights cursed the archbishop and demanded he leave the kingdom. Becket refused, saying, "I trust in the King of Heaven." The knights left, but later returned and demanded entrance to the cathedral, where monks had sheltered the archbishop. Refusing to hide from his fate, Becket ordered the doors opened.

The knights entered with swords drawn, demanding, "Where is Thomas Becket, traitor to the king?"

"I am ready to die for my Lord," the archbishop answered unwaveringly, "that in my blood the church may obtain liberty and peace." (*St. Thomas of Canterbury,* edited by W. H. Hutton.)

The knights fell upon Becket with their swords, knocking him down and cracking open his skull. The martyred archbishop fell, his blood and brains spilling over the floor of the cathedral he was so determined to protect.

Henry II, as a penance (and maybe to assuage a guilty conscience), walked barefoot into Canterbury Cathedral and underwent a flogging at Becket's tomb.

Thomas did not die in vain, however. He was canonized, and thus began the famous pilgrimages which helped the town prosper and would later bring fame to Geoffrey Chaucer.

1175–1218: Genghis Khan, the Bloody Terror. After succeeding his father as chieftan at age thirteen, Genghis Khan led a savage Mongol army on an epic journey of conquest and destruction. His armies sacked and pillaged their way across Asia, creating an empire that stretched from the Pacific to the Black Sea.

The Mongols were little disturbed by the wholesale slaughter they used to gain their objectives. In six bloodthirsty months, Genghis Khan suppressed a rebellion in Herat, Afghanistan, by killing a reported 1.6 million people. When Genghis conquered Bokhara in 1218, 160,000 of Shah Mohammad's troops were killed.

"I will carry slaughter and cause devastation to my enemy . . . so my name will live," Genghis once said. His very existence terrified his subjects and no doubt discouraged attempts at rebellion. In fact, when he finally died, his armies put to death anyone who encountered his funeral procession.

Now, here's a guy who makes Mithridates, Caligula, and Nero seem like amateurs. Unfortunately, he is not the last.

1191: Massacre at Acre. One of the many bloody, and far from holy, incidents of the Crusades occurred during the Third Crusade, following the conquest of the Palestinian city of Acre by English King Richard I. The terms of surrender called for the vanquished Muslims to turn over the much-venerated Catholic relic known as the True Cross of the Crucifixion, as well as one hundred thousand dinars and sixteen hundred English prisoners. In exchange, Richard promised to release three thousand Muslim soldiers taken prisoner during battle.

When the Muslims refused to make full payment until their prisoners were released, Richard angrily ordered that the three thousand Muslim prisoners be brought to him. On the afternoon of August 20 the Christians marched the prisoners, bound with ropes, onto a plain that was in full view of the Muslim army only recently driven out of Acre. Richard gave the order, and the Crusaders slaughtered the defenseless prisoners with swords and lances.

Another barbarity committed in the name of God. Richard did have his perverse side.

1200–1202: Egyptian Famine. A greenish tint and a foul smell in the Nile River two months before its annual flooding in the summer of 1200 proved to be a bitter omen for Egyptians. The discoloration was caused by a less than normal rainfall at the Nile source, and that in turn meant the annual summer flooding of the lower Nile in Egypt was much less than usual. For Egyptian farmers, who depended heavily on the floods to replenish topsoil and to provide much-needed water, this resulted in parched fields and ruined crops.

As the year 1200 wore on, famine set in and hunger began to drive people to more and more desperate measures. They started eating dogs, then carrion, and then each other. Some even ate dung. As the death toll mounted—one inheritance was passed on to forty heirs in one month—people found themselves with an excruciating choice: Die of starvation, or kill.

Young children were murdered, roasted, and eaten—some by marauders who kidnapped them, and others by their own parents. Though an offense punishable by death in Egypt, cannibalism soon became the main food source. Eyewitnesses described caldrons with childrens' heads floating in them.

In Cairo people died by the hundreds each day. In Misr corpses were too numerous to bury, and were merely thrown outside the walls of the town. Only the vultures did not go hungry.

The Nile failed to rise again in 1201, but by this time much of Egypt was depopulated. To put the finishing touch on this series of natural disasters, an earthquake struck in May 1202.

1204: The Sack of Constantinople. Urged on by the Venetians, who had supplied them with ships, the French armies of the Fourth Crusade diverted from their intended goal—defeat of the Muslims in the Holy Land. Instead they succumbed to avarice, making a deal to restore a deposed Byzantine emperor in exchange for the riches of Constantinople.

The crusaders took Constantinople, capital of the Byzantine Empire, without resistance in July 1203 and restored the deposed emperor. When the people of Constantinople realized, however, that their emperor had agreed they would submit to the pope (they practiced Eastern Orthodoxy) and give the crusaders their riches, they rebelled and reimprisoned him.

In March 1204 the crusaders again attacked Constantinople, this time with a vengeance, setting fire to the city and leaving more than one-quarter of it in ashes. They ransacked the church of Saint Sophia, ripping jewels and gold from the altar, and looted sacred relics to sell in Europe. Thousands of fine art masterpieces were stolen by the Venetians. Even the plays of Sophocles and Euripides, up until then complete, were mutilated and ruined.

The crusaders created their own government, the so-called Latin Empire of Constantinople, which they ruled.

Once again, under the guise of Christianity, the crusaders act like barbarians.

1209–1229: Christian Against Christian: Albigensian Crusade. After more than a century of Crusades against Muslims in the Holy Land, the church in 1208 preached its first Crusade against fellow Christians, the heretical Albigensians in southern France. The Albigensian, or Cathar, movement had spread throughout France's Languedoc region and had even gained the support of noblemen there. But the movement aroused opposition of the church by denouncing church corruption, advocating a strict asceticism, denying the reality of the body, and rejecting the Old Testament, baptism, priesthood, and sacraments of the Roman church.

A long struggle to wipe out the heresy by peaceful means came to an end with the assassination of a papal legate in Toulouse, after he had excommunicated the feudal lord Count Raymond VI for sympathizing with the Albigensians. Pope Innocent III, blaming Raymond for the murder, called for a full-scale Crusade against the sect. For the most part, noblemen from the north answered the call, turning the Crusade into what amounted to an invasion of southern France by noblemen from the North.

In June 1209 an army of mercenaries led by northern French barons massed for their campaign to slaughter the heretics. Meanwhile, Raymond declared his penitence and joined the Crusade himself. At Béziers the crusaders slashed their way through the streets, slaughtering everyone in their path. A crusader who asked how he should separate the heretics from the faithful Catholics was told, "Kill them all; the Lord will know well who are His." Catholics and Cathars alike tried to take refuge in churches, but the undaunted crusaders went in and massacred them anyway. They butchered everyone—even women, babies, and priests—and killed seven thousand people in one church alone. Altogether at least twenty thousand people died in the massacre at Béziers.

Year after year the bloody campaign of terror against the Albigensians continued. In Bram the crusaders chopped off the noses of one hundred soldiers and gouged out their eyes. They left one soldier with an eye so that he could guide the mutilated Albigensians on to the next castle as a warning not to resist. The castle immediately surrendered.

The atrocities only got worse as the crusaders ravaged town after town. Crusaders ripped out the tongues and eyes of the defeated, dragged them with horses, or hacked them to pieces with swords. In Lavaur in 1211 the crusaders tried to hang eighty knights from one rope. When the rope broke, they slit the throats of their victims instead. Meanwhile, crusaders also tried to force the heretics to recant their beliefs and pledge allegiance to the church of Rome. Hundreds refused, preferring to burn themselves to death in massive bonfires.

In 1226 French King Louis IX led a massive new army into southern France to wipe out the last vestiges of the heresy, and in 1229 the long Crusade finally ended with the almost total defeat of the Albigensians.

Thou shalt not kill. Thou shalt not steal. Thou shalt not covet thy neighbor's house. . . .

1212: Fire Burns London. Flames that started in the church of Saint Mary Southwark spread unchecked through London, destroying much of the city. A great crowd of people was trapped on the (at this time) wooden London Bridge when fire broke out at both ends. By the time the fire was extinguished, some three thousand people had been killed.

This was the second fire to destroy London.

1212: Children's Crusade. Seized with religious fervor born of the Crusades, thousands of children in Germany and France set out to conquer the Holy Land and retrieve the Sepulcher of Christ. Two separate groups of children attempted to mount Crusades, but like the true Crusades the children tried to emulate, both expeditions ended in disaster.

In Germany during the spring of 1212, a ten-year-old boy named Nicholas began urging the children in his native Cologne to join him in a Crusade to Jerusalem. His enthusiasm for the cause was contagious. Soon thousands of children between the ages of six and eighteen had disregarded their parents' pleas and left home to follow Nicholas to Italy, where they intended to board a ship bound for the Holy Land. Their numbers grew steadily as children from every town they passed through became caught up in the quest.

Nicholas's band eventually numbered twenty thousand, though many of the smaller and weaker children were unable to make it over the Alps, collapsing along the way from exhaustion and starvation. Most reached Lombardy, where they split up into several groups, though it is not known whether this was by design or by accident. The largest group of more than seven thousand arrived in Genoa on August 25, but these children were forced to abandon their Crusade because no ships were willing to take them to the Holy Land. Several of the children made their way to Rome to ask Pope Innocent III to release them from their crusading oaths, but the rest of the group simply scattered across Italy, exhausted, humiliated, and penniless.

While Nicholas was leading his band of crusaders over the Alps, a similar movement was taking place in France. In June of that year, a French shepherd boy named Stephen claimed to have seen a vision of Christ, who handed him a letter to deliver to the king of France. Stephen set off on his errand with zeal, and soon tens of thousands of enthusiastic children joined him. It was not long before the horde of children decided to carry Christ's mission to the Holy Land. Stephen's band of thirty thousand eventually reached Marseilles, where it is popularly believed that two disreputable merchants, Hugh Ferreus and William Porcus, offered them free passage to Syria.

One medieval source reports that the children set off for the Holy Land in seven ships, but that a storm off the Isle of Saint Peter dashed two of the ships against the rocks, where they sank with all aboard. The remaining five ships are said to have docked at Bougie, in modern Algeria, and Alexandria, Egypt, where the merchants sold the children into slavery. The caliph-al-Nasir supposedly bought four hundred of them himself, and other children went to Saracen princes or slave merchants. It was reported that eighteen of the children were martyred by Saracens who attempted to make them renounce Christianity. As long as eighteen years after the disastrous crusade, Mascemuch of Alexandria supposedly still owned seven hundred of the crusaders, who were by that time full-grown men.

1268: Earthquake in Asia Minor. Some sixty thousand were killed by a violent earthquake that shook a wide area of Asia Minor.

The cradle of civilization is rocked.

1277: Floods Devastate Holland. Holland's susceptibility to severe flooding was well-known early in its history, and by the thirteenth century it became apparent that dikes were necessary to protect the low-lying towns from the sea. In 1277 a terrible storm flooded the country surrounding the Zuider Zee, submerging the towns and enabling enemy troops to capture the flooded cities by boat.

In 1421 another serious flood decimated the area when dikes near the city of Dort burst without warning. The resulting deluge swept away seventy-two villages, claimed more than one hundred thousand lives, and caused the city of Dordrecht to be permanently separated from the mainland.

In 1530 and 1570 two more devastating floods raged through Holland as the dikes again burst without warning. In both cases the raging waters were driven by high winds, claiming four hundred thousand lives in 1530 and another fifty thousand in 1570.

What would you expect from a country where two-fifths of the land is below sea level, and most of the rest of it is only three hundred feet above?

1281: The "Divine Wind" Saves Japan. The great Mongol conqueror Kublai Khan already ruled a vast empire that included all of China and stretched eastward across much of Asia. Even this had not sated Kublai Khan's desire for conquest, however; Korea, Burma, and from 1271, Japan all became victims of his dreams for greater glory. Both Korea and Burma fell before the invading Mongol hordes, but Japan proved a more difficult problem.

By 1281 the people of Japan fully expected yet another attempt at invasion by the determined Mongol leader. Still, the appearance in Japanese waters of nine hundred Mongol warships carrying some forty thousand warriors was a formidable sight. And this was only the advance group of a much larger force.

The Mongols successfully occupied a number of islands off the Japanese coast, but fighting ended abruptly when a deadly epidemic broke out aboard the Mongol ships. Soon some three thousand of the men had died and nearly all their supplies were gone. Help came in June, though, when the armada's main contingent arrived from China. This gigantic fleet, consisting of three thousand five hundred warships and smaller craft carrying more than one hundred thousand men, sailed into a large, protected harbor, apparently near modern-day Sasebo in southern Japan. Now the real battles for control of Japan got under way.

The Japanese had no big warships and could not fight the Mongols at sea. But because this invasion was expected, they had built high stone walls along the coasts to prevent enemy landings. All able-bodied men had been assembled and trained to fight. As the Mongols attacked these fortifications, the Japanese fought bravely from their stone ramparts, successfully repelling the Mongols.

Meanwhile, the Japanese also found a way to carry the battle out to the Mongol fleet. Using small craft, they attacked Mongol ships under the cover of darkness. Sailing their "mosquito fleet" undetected among the mighty Mongol warships, they boarded enemy vessels, battled against the Mongol troops aboard, and set the ships afire. Mongols were soon forced to lash warships together so that reserve troops could be quickly transferred to any ship that came under attack. While these harrying tactics reduced or damaged a number of Mongol warships, the Mongols were so numerous that it hardly mattered. The brutal fighting and bloodshed went on for some fifty-two days and threatened to continue until the Mongols made good their conquest.

Then, on August 14, a strange mist reportedly rose from the sea, to the wonderment of the Mongol invaders. Ominous rain clouds crowded the sky, and a strong shoreward wind came up. Soon a powerful storm struck full force, while Mongol captains all desperately sailed toward the mouth of the harbor against a strongly flowing tide. Arriving at the narrow opening all at once, the vessels rammed into one another by the hundreds, causing enormous destruction and total panic. According to Korean accounts, "The bodies of men and broken timbers of the vessels were heaped together in a solid mass so that a person could walk across from one point of land to another. . . ."

For two days the deadly typhoon ravaged the harbor. When at last the terrible winds subsided, Kublai Khan's armada was in ruins, and Japan was saved. The Japanese credited the fortuitous typhoon to intervention by the gods, thus giving rise to what later came to be known as the "kamikaze" (divine wind).

The typhoon started what became one of the greatest military disasters of all time. Of the thousands of warships and smaller craft assembled in the Japanese harbor, only about two hundred were still seaworthy, and they returned to the continent. According to a Chinese historian, this left some one hundred thousand survivors of the brutal storm abandoned along the Japanese coast with little hope of escape.

A large contingent is said to have taken refuge on a small island, where the soldiers began to cut down trees to build new ships to carry them home. Within a few days, however, the Japanese arrived on the island and slaughtered almost all, taking some twenty thousand prisoners. Later, most of the prisoners were massacred as well. Some reports say that only three of the prisoners were spared and returned to China, in order to inform Kublai Khan of the fate of his men.

The term "kamikaze," the divine wind, will be heard again later when the Japanese go to battle.

1282: Sicilian Vespers Massacre. Charles of Anjou, brother of the king of France, seized the crown of Sicily in 1266 and thereafter subjected the Sicilian people to cruel and tyrannical treatment at the hands of his French bureaucrats and soldiers. The Sicilians submitted to the oppression for nearly twenty years until finally, on March 30, 1282, a relatively minor incident in Palermo provoked them beyond endurance. They fought back with a bloody vengeance.

It was Easter Monday, and a large crowd of Sicilians had gathered at the Church of Santo Spirito in Palermo for a festival. Earlier that Easter weekend, French troops had appalled the pious Sicilians by storming the church and arresting several men suspected of not paying their taxes, manacling them as they knelt in prayer and forcibly dragging them off to prison. Despite this outrage, the festivities were continued, and as the crowd gathered at the church on Monday, the incident appeared to have been forgotten.

Shortly before vespers, however, two hundred Frenchmen suddenly arrived on the scene to mar the festivities. They had been ordered by the local justiciary to investigate the festival and make sure the Sicilians were unarmed and obedient.

The Sicilians submitted to being frisked for weapons by the swaggering Frenchmen while silently burning with resentment. During the search, a Frenchman named Drouet impudently accosted a young bride and thrust his hand into her blouse. The horrified young woman swooned into her husband's arms as he, outraged beyond reason, cried "Death to the French!" Immediately a young man burst from the crowd, snatched Drouet's sword from its scabbard, and slew him on the spot.

The crowd of Sicilians, filled with outrage borne of twenty years of oppression, was galvanized into action. Wielding sticks, rocks, and knives, the furious crowd fell upon the fully armed Frenchmen, overwhelming them in a short, vengeful battle. The churchyard ran red with blood, and though Sicilian casualties were high, they succeeded in killing all two hundred of the Frenchmen.

Their murderous fury unabated, the bloodthirsty multitude roamed through Palermo, seeking out Frenchmen and killing them without hesitation. Attempting to eradicate all traces of French blood, the frenzied mob slaughtered Sicilian women who had married Frenchmen, first butchering their children before their eyes, and even ripped out the wombs of women they believed had been made pregnant by Frenchmen. Persons of doubtful origin had knives held to their throats while they said the word *ciciri,* which the French had difficulty pronouncing. Those who pronounced it incorrectly were summarily slain. The bloodthirsty mob then began to spread throughout the countryside, butchering all Frenchmen they encountered. They even rushed into monasteries and slaughtered French monks.

More than two thousand were killed that first day, as the rebellion spread throughout Sicily. The uprising lasted for weeks, and when it was all over, thousands of French and Sicilians had been slain. After a period of war and unrest, Sicily eventually came under Spanish control.

This was just one skirmish in the continuing battle among nobles of many countries to feed their egos and grab the crown of Sicily.

1321: Massacre of Jews in France. In the years leading up to their banishment from France in 1394, French Jews were sporadically subjected to persecution at the hands of the government and outright massacre by mobs of Frenchmen. The massacre of 1321, in which large numbers of French Jews were killed, was instigated by a rumor that Jews had poisoned the wells in Paris.

When the marauders come back from the Crusades, they start picking on the little guys at home.

1347–1351: Black Death. Mariners returning to Europe in 1346 brought back tales of a deadly plague that left thousands of corpses piled up in cities throughout China and India. The next year the news came in a more ghastly form, as trading ships sailed into European ports with virtually all their crew dead or dying of the plague. Tradesmen infected with the bubonic plague in the Crimea spread the disease to Sicily, and from there to North Africa and to southern Italy. Within months all of Europe was consumed by the plague, which soon came to be known as the "Black Death."

Spread by fleas on rats, the plague caused black swellings the size of eggs on the armpit or groin. Fevers, headaches, vomiting, and dark spots on the skin followed. In some cases victims' blood became poisoned even before swellings, known as "buboes," could develop. These victims spat blood and died within three days. Victims who developed the buboes seldom survived longer than five days.

As the plague spread from country to country, it devastated whole populations. By 1348 millions were dying in England, France, Germany, and Austria. The stench of decaying bodies filled the air in cities, and entire familes sickened and died. Half the population of Florence perished within six months. Fifty thousand bodies were buried in one mass grave in London. In Vienna twelve hundred people died each day. As the space available for burial was taken up, the pope had to consecrate the Rhone River at Avignon so that bodies could be thrown into it.

Church bells tolled night and day for funerals. The government of Florence tried to prevent widespread despair by prohibiting ringing of bells for funerals and banning the publication of the numbers of dead.

All efforts to understand the causes of the plague or to stop its spread failed miserably. Penitents who believed the plague was a punishment delivered by God wandered in long processions from city to city, beating each other with whips to atone for the world's sins. But these flagellants only spread the plague farther.

Pope Clement VI called for a mass pilgrimage to Rome in 1350, but the journey of penitents just helped to spread the infection throughout Europe.

Soon the idea that dogs spread the infection became current in Europe, and people slaughtered them in great numbers. Right about the fleas; wrong about the carrier. The result was far from what had been intended, however. Killing the dogs eliminated the main predator of the rats whose fleas spread the plague.

In another wild misbelief that spread with the plague across Europe, Christians began to blame Jews for causing the plague, and in many cities massacred them. In Basel Jews were burned alive in wooden buildings; in Speyer they were put into wine casks and rolled into the river.

In Crimea a Tartar army afflicted by the plague used it to their advantage in battle. They catapulted corpses of plague victims over the walls of cities they put under siege. When the Scots invaded England, their troops became infected with plague and brought it back to Scotland, where it spread with deadly speed.

In the wake of the mass death, the need for lawyers mushroomed, because there were tens of thousands of estates to be settled. Prices plunged throughout Europe as the millions of deaths destroyed demand for goods. Meanwhile survivors went on wild spending sprees. Many threw themselves into revelry and debauchery, believing that pleasure and happiness helped prevent the infection. As Boccaccio put it, "Amid this general lamentation and woe, the influence and authority of every law, human and divine, vanished."

When the plague finally abated in 1351, an estimated twenty-five million people had died in Europe. About one third of the world's population had succumbed. No one was spared, not royalty or nobles, church officials or whole friaries, artisans or patrons of the arts, or Petrarch's Laura.

It was the most devastating disaster ever visited on the Western world, and consequently changed European society for the better and for worse.

1347: Saint Vitus' Dance Epidemic. In the fourteenth century a bizarre disease appeared in Europe, in which people would begin a twitching, ungainly dance that soon led to uncontrollable leaping, furious screaming, and foaming at the mouth. This obsessive, paroxysmic dance would last for hours, or for a day or more, until the victims fell exhausted to the ground.

Victims often gathered at the chapels of Saint Vitus, who was believed to have curative powers, and thus the name Saint Vitus' Dance was given to the disease. Modern researchers found the disease to be an unusual side effect of rheumatic fever, and today call it Sydenham's chorea.

Needless to say, the disease aroused strange fears in medieval times. Victims recounted visions of horrible demons, or rivers of human blood, or sometimes beatific scenes. Townspeople would gather to watch the spectacle, gazing with a mixture of horror and fascination. Some believed the disease was spread by sympathy, and held that unwitting onlookers often found themselves possessed by the dancing mania.

Saint Vitus' Dance was first seen in Germany in 1347, and spread to France and the Netherlands, then to Scotland. In Italy it was called "tarantism," after the tarantula whose bite was believed to cause it. It was treated with music, which helped soothe the victims, but elsewhere, treatments were often harsh. Victims were beaten, jumped on, dunked under cold water, and squeezed with huge tourniquets. Prayers, masses, and exorcisms were held. The disease abated in the seventeenth century, after ranging throughout central Europe. Today chorea is seen mostly as a childhood disease.

1358: Jacquerie Revolt in France. In France the epithet "Jacques Bonhomme" was an insulting name used by the nobility to refer to the peasant class, the jacquerie. Resentment against the aristocracy and the hardships of the Hundred Years War produced disastrous results in northern France when noblemen tried to impose a new tax on the jacquerie.

Suddenly in May the jacquerie rose in a bloody revolt. Armed with wooden staves and knives, mobs of peasants wantonly attacked noblemen and their families, vowing to exterminate the entire aristocracy. Rebels committed horrible atrocities; a knight was tied to a stake and forced to watch as his wife and daughter were raped repeatedly, then cruelly tortured and killed. Another knight was tied to a spit and roasted before the eyes of his wife and children, who were then offered the flesh to eat.

Many of the noblemen fled to safety with their families, while rampaging peasants looted and burned castles and towns left behind. It was not long before the nobility responded with equally brutal atrocities. Rebel peasants were slaughtered and hung from trees, and lured into parleys with noblemen only to be captured and decapitated. In the town of Meaux, raiding peasants were trapped in the marketplace and slaughtered en masse by horsemen with lances, who then flung the bodies into the River Maine. It is said that seven thousand peasants died in that clash alone. The revolt ended in June, less than a month after it began.

Not only the peasants are revolting, it seems.

1381: Wat Tyler's Bloody Rebellion. Local uprisings against an unpopular poll tax, coupled with restrictive wage laws and other grievances, finally kindled a two-month rebellion by peasants in early May that threatened to overthrow the English kingdom. A ragtag "army" of sixty thousand to one hundred thousand peasants gathered under the loose leadership of Wat Tyler, Jack Straw, and John Ball, and marched on London.

Refused an audience with the king, some thirty thousand of the angry peasants entered London, where they helped themselves to food and drink, then began a riot. Thirty-two of them died drunk in the Duke of Lancaster's wine cellar when the house burned down on top of them. Hordes of other angry, drunken peasants dragged foreigners into the street, and robbed and beheaded them. Another mocking, drunken mob paraded through the streets with the heads of the Archbishop of Canterbury and four others. In a frenzied moment elsewhere, the arms and legs were cut off a nobleman, his body then literally torn to pieces.

Wat Tyler was treacherously killed while negotiating with the king, and not long after, authorities gained the initiative. They were more methodic, but no less brutal than the rebels, executing some fifteen hundred peasants without trial to finally break the revolt.

More goodwill toward men.

1402: The Rise of the Black Slave Trade. In 1402 Juan de Bethencourt became the first European to settle in the Canary Islands, located off the coast of northwest Africa. Bethencourt brought with him good intentions and the fruits of European culture; he worked for several years to build churches and introduce Christianity to the natives. But at the same time, he made slaves of several of the islanders for his own personal use.

The Europeans' rediscovery of the Canary Islands, ironically known to the ancients as the "Fortunate Islands," heralded the beginning of the black slave trade, and what became a centuries-long tragedy. Slavery was not a new idea, and had been widely practiced in ancient times. It had largely been eliminated in Europe, thanks to the influence of the church. Now, however, Europeans established a modern form of slavery, in which millions of African blacks were enslaved and condemned to lives of misery and death.

Between 1418 and 1434, Portugal's Prince Henry commissioned many voyages of discovery along Africa's coast, in order to discover new lands and bring back information about coastal Africa. During one expedition to the Canary Islands, a number of natives were seized and brought to Portugal as slaves. And in 1442 Henry directed that several captured Moors be exchanged in their country for black slaves to be transported to Portugal. So it began. Soon a flourishing trade in black slaves developed, first between Africa and Europe, and then between Africa and colonies in the Americas.

Most of the slaves were taken from a narrow band of West Africa between Senegal and southern Angola. By 1700 the demand for slaves to work the plantations of South, Central, and North America was enormous, and slave traders carried gold, cloth, and rum to barter with African chiefs who willingly rounded up and traded away their own countrymen. The captured men and women were chained together and forced to walk as far as nine hundred miles to the coast. One trader wrote of the slaves' despair at having to leave their countries: "They often leap'd out of the canoes, boat and ship into the sea, and kept under water till they were drowned, to avoid being taken. . . ."

The voyages of slave ships across the Atlantic were, quite literally, deadly. Hundreds of slaves were forced to lie together in wretchedly confined spaces in the lower decks of the ships, with such poor sanitation that their quarters quickly became overwhelmingly foul-smelling. Disease was a constant problem, sometimes even striking the ship's crew, as well as their shackled cargo.

Though these conditions were bad enough, storms during the voyage often proved fatal for many of the slaves. With the hatches battened down for days on end, the misery of those confined below was more than they could survive. There were dangers during calm weather, too. When slave ships were becalmed, the voyage took longer, making food and water scarce. One slave ship captain cited a water shortage as sufficient reason for throwing fifty-four ailing slaves overboard during their long voyage.

Although the slave trade was finally outlawed by the British in 1807, huge profits were still to be made, and trafficking in black slaves continued for years afterward. When slave traders sighted an antislavery patrol, they cruelly drowned their entire human cargo to avoid being caught.

By the time the slave trade finally ended in the late nineteenth century, some twenty million Africans had been forcibly taken from their homelands and sold into slavery. Possibly as many as half of them died en route, overcome by the misery and hardships they encountered.

A prime example of man's inhumanity to man.

1415: Trial and Execution of John Huss. Despite misgivings, the Bohemian religious reformer John Huss decided to appear before the Council of Constance to defend himself against accusations of heresy. He traveled there of his own free will, with guarantees of free passage from the Holy Roman Emperor Wenceslaus. But once he arrived, the pope and cardinals refused to honor the emperor's guarantee. They made Huss a prisoner, and many months passed before he was given a hearing.

John Huss appeared before the council three times over the next months, finally being sentenced on June 6 to burn at the stake for heresy. On July 6 his prison clothing was removed and he was dressed in priestly garments, in order that they might be stripped from him as the charges of heresy were read aloud before the council. Next, his accusers placed the sacred church vessels in his hands, again so that they could be taken from him as a gesture of his sins. His head was shaved, and a tall cap placed upon him; it read "Heresiarch."

Later that day, when his executioners had bound him to the stake and were about to light the fire, they noticed that he was facing east. Deciding that he should not have the honor of facing the direction of the sunrise, he was unfastened, turned, and bound again. Now the fire was lit; flames soon licked at his feet and then engulfed his body in a miserable scorching death.

That, so his persecutors thought, ended the heresy of John Huss. Huss had been influenced by the English religious reformer John Wyclif, and brought these teachings, which anticipated the Protestant Reformation, to Bohemia (in modern Czechoslovakia). Huss saw corruption at every level of religious life and wanted to expose it. He spoke openly of the greed and ambition of monks, cardinals, and even the pope, describing "their covetousness, their luxury, their sloth. . . ." Not surprisingly, religious leaders soon turned against him and began to call his preachings heretical.

When Huss became rector of the university at Prague, his teachings were heard by thousands. That helped to bring the schismatic pope John XXIII into an open campaign against him. The pope excommunicated Huss from the church and declared that no one should offer him protection. Only by appearing before the Council of Constance was Huss to be allowed to defend himself and achieve his freedom once again. And so Huss was forced to travel to the council and appear before his accusers, where he was treacherously imprisoned.

During the first two hearings, his accusers repeatedly urged Huss to recant his statements. Repeatedly Huss refused to submit to the council, insisting that no teaching of his had been contrary to God's holy word. He never did recant.

Nor did the problem of John Huss end with his cruel execution. Instead, Huss's teachings mingled with a nascent movement toward Bohemian nationalism that in 1619 erupted into the bloody Hussite Wars, which lasted until 1634.

Never tangle with the hierarchy.

1417: Massacre of the Armagnacs. The Armagnacs and the Burgundians, two factions of French noblemen, had been fighting for control of the French throne since 1411, when in 1417 a popular uprising in Paris resulted in the imprisonment of all the Armagnacs in the city. The mob was not satisfied with mere incarceration, however, and later broke into the prison to slaughter the noblemen.

More brotherly love.

1431: Joan of Arc Burns at the Stake. It was Tuesday, February 21, when a young French farm girl named Joan of Arc was led into the chapel of a castle in Rouen to face some thirty-five

English judges. Though Joan trembled with fear, she still believed her faith would protect her from harm. The trial eventually lasted more than three months while the court considered more than seventy accusations against the nineteen-year-old girl. But her chief crime was that she had rallied French troops during the Hundred Years War, appearing at a time when all of France was in danger of falling to the invading English. Now that they were losing the war, the English wanted her dead.

Joan was only thirteen when she first heard heavenly voices instructing her to help the French cause. Eventually she led French troops to victory at Orleans, at Patay, and on many other battlefields. Finally captured during battle on May 24, 1430, she was taken to Rouen, then held by the English, to be tried for heresy and witchcraft.

The court convened forty times before finally reaching a verdict. Most of the meetings were in the chapel, but some were held in the prison, where Joan was either chained to a beam or locked in an iron cage. During the lengthy trial, Joan steadfastly defended herself by repeating she had been directed by God. The judges badgered and insulted her, calling her deceitful and dishonest. They claimed she was possessed by the devil, and refused to let her appeal to the pope.

Finally Joan was promised that, if she withdrew her testimony, she would be turned over to the church. If not, she would be burned at the stake. Terrified and in poor health, Joan signed the paper put before her, only to recant when she learned that the court had no intention of letting her live. Her execution was already being planned.

At nine o'clock in the morning on May 30, Joan was placed on a cart and led through the streets of Rouen to the fish market. There, a huge stake of plaster and wood had been erected that "struck terror by its height alone." As she was tied to the stake, Joan asked the watching crowd to pray for her. Then the executioner set fire to the kindling piled below her.

The flames first licked at her feet, then grew higher, as the terrified girl called to God, the angels, and the saints to protect her. Finally the fire overcame her; her head fell back, then forward, and she was dead.

The terrible murder failed to end the tide of French victories, and throughout intermittent fighting during the ensuing decades,

English-held territory on the European continent was reduced.

Joan of Arc was declared a saint by the Roman Catholic Church in 1920.

Nowadays she would probably be declared a schizophrenic.

1453: Fall of Constantinople. In the early hours of May 29, Byzantine Emperor Constantine XI left his family and friends in the imperial palace, knowing he would never return to them alive. Four days earlier, the attacking Turkish army under Mahomet II had finally blasted a hole in the great walls surrounding Constantinople, and now threatened to capture the great capital city of the Byzantine Empire.

Since the relentless Turkish attack began in early April, some six thousand Byzantine soldiers and three thousand other supporters had been holding out against a combined Turkish force of some seventy thousand men. But the Turks had also brought a huge cannon, the world's largest of that time, with a 2½-foot bore. The monstrous weapon had been constructed for the sole purpose of destroying the city's walls.

For two hours just after dawn on May 29, Emperor Constantine and his men held their positions in the breach, knocking back wave after wave of attacking Turks. Finally a fierce charge slashed through the line of defenders and killed the emperor. Hordes of Turkish troops swarmed behind them, trampling over the slain emperor's body.

The rampaging Turks at first killed every citizen they met, then took as slaves thousands who had sought refuge in the Hagia Sophia. They also plundered the city of its vast wealth. Constantinople had fallen, ending forever the centuries-old Byzantine Empire, the last remnant of the vast Roman Empire.

And to the victors belong the spoils.

1456: Earthquake Destroys Naples. Some thirty-five thousand people died when a massive earthquake hit Naples, Italy, on December 5. The quake left the city almost completely in ruins.

Whence the saying "See Naples and die."

1459: The Many Horrors of Vlad Dracula, "the Impaler." On April 2 Vlad II Dracula, prince of Wallachia (in modern Romania), entered the small town of Brasov and ordered his men to begin the systematic impalement of the townspeople. Tyrant and madman that he was, he needed no reason for his actions—some insult, real or imagined, could always be claimed. Thus, by the end of the day thousands of Saxon burghers dangled from the wooden stakes that had been driven through them. The stakes were then set upright in the ground in concentric circles on a hill near the town. Dracula capped this incredible atrocity by eating his dinner amid the gruesome scene, while his servants dismembered the bodies of the dead before his eyes.

This behavior was by no means unusual for Vlad Dracula, the historical inspiration for Bram Stoker's fictional vampire Dracula. Indeed, his reign as prince of Wallachia from 1456 to 1462 was studded with such bloody escapades. For example, shortly after becoming prince, he invited all of the beggars in the country to a feast at his castle in Tirgoviste, Wallachia. After the unsuspecting guests had finished drinking toasts to their benefactor and gorging themselves with delicacies, Dracula ordered the doors barred and the castle set on fire. By the next morning, nothing but ashes remained of the citizens whom Dracula considered an unnecessary burden to society. Dracula variously had his many victims boiled alive, skinned, hacked to pieces, disembowled, and tortured on the rack and the wheel. In the case of two Genoese ambassadors who refused to take their hats off in his presence, Dracula had their hats nailed to their heads.

Dracula's favorite method of punishment, however, was impalement. The stakes were generally rounded at the ends and oiled, so that his victims would not die too quickly. Quite often the victims were forced onto the stake in an upright position. For variation, many were impaled through the navel, the heart, or, in rare instances, upside down through the skull.

In 1462 Dracula heard that a contingent of Turkish envoys was coming to meet with him—ostensibly to negotiate a peace, but in reality to draw him into an ambush. Dracula turned the tables, trapping the envoys and two thousand soldiers who came with them, and taking the prisoners to Tirgoviste. There, on the outskirts of the city, they were impaled and left to rot, along with an incredible eighteen thousand others Dracula decided to kill in the orgy of mass impalement. When the Turkish Sultan Mehemet arrived before Tirgoviste six months later, he was greeted by the stench and skeletons of the twenty thousand corpses still impaled on stakes outside the city. This sight was said to have horrified him so much that he personally decided to quit the campaign.

Dracula is estimated to have impaled, tortured, and killed between fifty thousand and one hundred thousand victims before being deposed and imprisoned in 1462. Though the exact circumstances are not known, it is believed Dracula was decapitated in battle against the Turks shortly after being released from prison in 1474.

1478: Cruel Tortures of the Spanish Inquisition. A papal bull handed down in 1478 formally created the Inquisition in Spain, thereby condemning thousands over the years to imprisonment, torture, and death. While the Inquisition in other European countries tended to focus on cases of heresy, Spanish inquisitors directed most of their energies toward persecuting Jews, Muslims, suspected sympathizers, and certain types of criminals. The Spaniards also quickly gained a reputation for the harsh measures they used.

Fifteenth-century Spain, though ruled by Catholic monarchs, had large populations of Jews and Muslims, and Spanish Jews had risen to high positions in finance, medicine, commerce, and local government. Their prestige and wealth, as well as the fact that many Spanish citizens were in debt to Jewish bankers, led to widespread jealousy, giving Spanish Catholics further reason to attack those who adhered to the Jewish religion. In fact, before the Inquisition was established, Spanish clergymen appealed to Catholic King Ferdinand, promising him that confiscations of Jewish property and wealth would be worth a great deal. He quickly obtained the 1478 papal bull, allowing the appointment of "inquisitors" to deal with the evil influence of Jews and "conversos," Jews converted to Catholicism.

The first man appointed to the post of grand inquisitor was the infamous Tomás de Torquemada, a fanatical anti-Semite who was himself from a converso family. Appointed in 1483, he orchestrated a campaign of hatred against all Jews, and in 1492 finally convinced King Ferdinand and Queen Isabella to expel from Spain all Jews who refused to be baptized in a Christian ceremony. Further, he instigated nationwide searches, imprisonment, and the ruthless methods of torture now synonymous with the Spanish Inquisition.

Suspected heretics were taken into custody without warning and urged to confess their crimes. Those who did not were taken to the torture chamber, where they were persuaded to confess by brutal means. While occasionally an inquisitor became inventive and ordered such tortures as slowly roasting a victim's lard-coated feet over an open fire, most were content with three basic types of torture: the *garrucha, garotte,* and *toca*. With the *garrucha,* the victim was bound hands behind his back and was slowly raised off the floor by a rope attached to his bound wrists. Torturers then lowered him in a series of jerks that often wrenched his arms out of their sockets. The *garotte,* also known as the rack, consisted of a ladderlike structure with sharpened rungs. Inquisitors wrapped rope around the victim's arms and legs, and then gradually tightened the ropes, causing them to slowly tear through the skin and muscle down to the bone. The *toca,* or water torture, was more complex. A victim was bound to the rack, which was tilted slightly so that his head—held tightly in place by an iron band—was lower than his feet. Then inquisitors forced a cloth strip down his throat, clamped his nose shut, and poured a steady stream of water down the cloth. As the victim gagged and gasped for air, the cords binding him to the rack were slowly and inexorably tightened to cut through the flesh. Inquisitors never told the victim what his crime was, but would only repeat the phrase "Tell the truth" throughout the ordeal.

Torture, however, was considered only a means to confession, and once a confession had been extracted, there were many forms of punishment, including confiscation of property, imprisonment, whipping, and the wearing in public of the *sanbenito,* a penitential garment. The most extreme punishment, burning at the stake, was reserved only for those considered to be unrepentant or relapsed heretics.

During the first eighteen years of the Spanish Inquisition, an estimated eight thousand eight hundred people died by burning, and some ninety thousand were tortured and imprisoned. Although the Inquisition in Spain was not formally abolished until 1834, the "Holy Office" had lost almost all power by the beginning of the eighteenth century. Thereafter, its chief activity was the destruction of prohibited books.

Later in history there would be another "Torquemada" who was equally anti-Semitic and heinously sadistic. His victims will run into the millions.

1485: Outbreak of English Sweating Sickness. Sweating sickness first appeared in England in 1485 and spread rapidly among the populace. Apparently healthy individuals were struck down and died of the disease overnight. Largely confined to England, sweating sickness killed thousands in epidemics that occurred in 1485, 1506, 1517, 1528, and 1551.

It seemed to be more severe among the rich than the poor. One contemporary physician attributed it to filth and dirt.

1490s: Syphilis Epidemic Begins. The origin of a sudden virulent epidemic of syphilis which broke out in Europe in the 1490s is unknown. The disease first appeared in Italy, and by 1495 was reported in France, Germany, Switzerland, Holland, and Greece. By 1497 it had appeared in England and Scotland, and two years later was reported in Hungary and Russia.

As usual, foreigners were blamed for spreading the disease, especially those who were disliked. The Russians blamed the Poles; the English and Turks called it the French disease; the French termed it the Italian illness, and they, in turn, referred to it as the Spanish disease. The Spanish called it the sickness of Hispaniola, declaring it had come from what is now Haiti and was brought back by Columbus's crew. Medical historians now think that syphilis had been in Europe for years and that what Columbus's crew brought back was a new strain to which Europeans were not immune.

In any case, syphilis did not discriminate; people from all walks of life and all classes were infected. Doctors were mystified by the horrible disease, marked by pustules, skin eruptions, leg ulcers, and finally madness. Treatments were unusual and extreme: boiled vulture broth with sarsaparilla, or serpent's blood. One army doctor claimed to have amputated the genitalia of five thousand infected soldiers. The disease raged on for much of the next century until immunity began to develop and the severity of the epidemic abated.

1502: Hurricane Destroys Spanish Treasure Fleet. A fleet of thirty Spanish ships left the port and colony of Santo Domingo (in modern Dominican Republic) in early July, despite the warnings of Christopher Columbus, who was in the port and saw signs of a hurricane brewing.

The ships, loaded down with precious cargoes of gold and other valuables, were only a day and a half out to sea when they sailed straight into a fierce hurricane. The small, heavily loaded wooden caravels were no match for the furious winds and pounding waves. Some sank on the high seas, while others were blown far off course and battered on the reefs and coast of Santo Domingo. All but four ships sank or were wrecked, and five hundred of the officers and crew members were killed. Among the treasures spilled into the sea was a gold nugget reputed to be the size of a dinner plate.

Red sky at night, sailor's delight; red sky in the morning, sailor take warning.

1514: Hungarian Peasants Revolt. On April 16 Cardinal Thomas Bakócz published a papal bull calling for a Hungarian crusade against the Turks. While the noblemen had little desire to risk their lives fighting the Turks, the Hungarian serfs leaped at the chance to escape their bonds of servitude. By the tens of thousands they tossed aside their farming tools and joyously took up the cross.

The man appointed to lead the peasant army was György Dózsa, a Transylvanian nobleman. Dózsa sympathized with the men who followed him and was pleased to help them rise to glory from the oppression of serfdom. But the other Hungarian lords soon began to protest vehemently. Since their king had already concluded a peace with the Turks, they saw no reason for the pope to encourage the serfs to abandon their duties in the fields. Already the crops were suffering from the mass exodus of the workers, and the situation was bound to get worse, they claimed.

As was their habit, the lords soon resorted to force while trying to keep the peasants on the farm, capturing, beating, and threatening to harm the families of those who attempted to leave. They also complained loudly to the king and the cardinal, who eventually bowed to their wishes. On May 23 the crusade was suspended and the serfs ordered to return to their masters.

The peasant army, however, refused to disband. They had joined the crusade to escape their dismal lives as chattel of the wealthy, and now shifted their violent intentions from the Turkish infidels to their Christian masters. Dózsa, as their leader, called for a full-scale revolution, and drew up a program that called for the elimination of nobility and royalty.

Stirred by the vision of a new egalitarian regime, the peasants, one hundred thousand strong, swarmed across the countryside, burning crops and mansions, and slaughtering their masters. The rebels slit the throats of women and children as well, and even churchmen suffered their wrath.

The lords retaliated by calling upon János Zápolya—like Dózsa, a Transylvanian nobleman—to lead an army against the rebels. The disorganized peasants stood little chance against the crack militia led by Zápolya, and by October the peasant army was crushed.

The victorious Hungarian lords proved merciless in exacting their gruesome revenge on the captured Dózsa. Noting that he had planned to set himself up as king, they forced him to sit on an iron throne that had been heated white-hot and made him hold a scorching hot scepter. Then, as he slowly roasted to death, they placed a burning hot iron crown on his head and compelled his starving followers to cut off and eat pieces of his roasting flesh.

More than seventy thousand peasants and nobles were killed in the bloody revolt and its aftermath.

1520: "Sad Night" at Tenochtitlán. When Cortés arrived at the spectacular Aztec capital of Tenochtitlán (in what is modern Mexico) in November of 1519, he was greeted by the Aztec ruler Montezuma, who for a time believed Cortés to be a serpent god arriving to reclaim his throne. The Aztecs soon discovered the Spaniard's true purposes were conquest and confiscation of the gold and jewels in the opulent city.

The Aztecs finally rose up against the six hundred to seven hundred Spaniards after Cortés's men slaughtered hundreds of unarmed Aztec noblemen in the streets of Tenochtitlán. After days of bloody clashes, the Aztecs had the Spanish bottled up in the palace stronghold. On the morning of June 30, the Aztecs attacked again, bringing the Spanish force near defeat. What followed was the *Noche Triste* or "Sad Night" massacre, during which the desperate Spanish fought their way out of Tenochtitlán, at a cost of hundreds of Spanish lives.

Escape from the city was no easy matter. Not only were the Spanish surrounded by hordes of enraged Aztecs, the city of Tenochtitlán was itself an island in a large lake. A causeway led from the city to the lake shore, but the Aztecs had destroyed the bridges.

That night the Spaniards, carrying a horde of gold and jewels, succeeded in slipping past the Aztecs and then fought their way to the causeway. They crossed the first gap using a portable bridge they had constructed while plotting their escape, but once across, they discovered their bridge was stuck in place. When they came to the next gap in the causeway, with no bridge to help them cross, the mass slaughter began.

The soldiers were weighted down by their heavy armor and by the treasure of gold and jewels they refused to leave behind, and so became easy targets for the Aztecs. Aztec warriors moved swiftly through the darkness in lightweight canoes, attacking the Spanish on the causeway from all sides. As hundreds of Spanish soldiers were killed, many of them fell forward off the edge of the causeway into Lake Texcoco and quickly sank to the bottom. Soon the pile of bodies, treasure, horses, armor, and wagons grew so numerous that surviving soldiers raced across the pile to the next section of the causeway. Once they reached the next gap, the massacre began again, continuing until bodies and equipment again piled high enough to bridge the gap.

Cortés lost about half his men in the fighting, but eventually succeeded in escaping from the Aztec Empire.

But not for long. Later, Cortés came back with a vengeance.

Ca. 1520: Human Sacrifice Among the Aztecs. The Aztec civilization that the Spanish discovered in South America was surprisingly advanced, except for one particularly nasty religious ritual that called for human sacrifice. The practice no doubt shocked the Spanish. (But then again, this was during the Inquisition, so they couldn't have been too shocked.) The Spanish made the Aztecs stop the practice, which was one good point in their favor during their otherwise cruel conquest of the New World.

While the actual number who died over the centuries as part of this grisly ritual is not known, the Aztecs usually chose victims for sacrifice among enemy soldiers taken as captives during war. But the ritual killing was a sacred rite, not considered punishment or humiliation. The Aztecs believed their victims traveled to the gods bearing messages from the Aztec nation.

That was little comfort to the victims, however, as they were pinned down against a sacrificial stone by their hands, feet, and heads. A priest then sliced open the victim's chest, pulled out his heart, and raised it up in an offering to the gods. Arms and legs were then served at banquets, and wild animals got the rest. Fresh kill is always tastiest.

Various occasions apparently called for human sacrifice, including special festival days, celestial events, and the dedications of temples. According to chronicles, when Aztec King Ahuitzotl dedicated a new temple in the capital of Tenochtitlán, he blessed the event by offering the sacrifice of an incredible eighty thousand people to the gods. The gods must have been overjoyed.

1521: Disease and Spanish Reconquest of Tenochtitlán. Soon after driving out the Spanish conqueror Hernando Cortés in 1520, the Aztecs were attacked by an even deadlier enemy—smallpox. As it happened, one of the Spaniards killed during the fighting at the Aztec capital of Tenochtitlán carried the fatal virus. Aztecs who came into contact with the infected body acquired the smallpox, apparently unknown in the New World until then, and the disease spread rapidly throughout the capital.

Within two weeks the first Indians had died of the epidemic they came to call "the great leprosy." Those stricken became feverish, and their skin was soon covered with raw pustules. They quickly became so weak, they could neither walk nor stand, and an agonizing death followed soon after. Of those who survived, large numbers were left blinded and scarred.

The deadly epidemic spread from the city to outlying areas, and many who did not die of the disease starved to death. With so many people desperately ill, there was no one left to care for the very young or the elderly. "It became so great a pestilence among them throughout the land that in most provinces more than half the population died. . . . They died in heaps, like bedbugs. . . ." (*Historian's History of the World*, Henry Williams.) Between two and fifteen million Aztecs eventually died of the disease, possibly half of the entire population.

But while the Aztecs weakened and died, Cortés was strengthening his army and preparing for another assault on the island capital of Tenochtitlán. Like most Europeans, he and his soldiers were immune to the disease, probably because of the childhood exposure, and so they had nothing to fear from the raging epidemic. Having been granted reinforcements, Cortés now assembled a mighty army equipped with cannons, guns, and even thirteen brigantines, which they carried overland to use in attacking Tenochtitlán. No doubt Cortés remembered well his desperate battle on the causeway at Tenochtitlán in 1520, when he had to fight his way across it to escape from the island city to the shore of Lake Texcoco surrounding it.

After subduing the villages around Lake Texcoco in 1521, Cortés's forces began the deadly siege of the Aztec capital. The disease-ridden Aztecs fought heroically; bloody battles that cost thousands of lives and nearly destroyed the city went on for three months. But on August 13 the starving, diseased residents of Tenochtitlán could hold out no longer, and the city fell. Between one hundred thousand and two hundred thousand Aztecs had lost their lives to the Spanish.

The triumphant Spaniards ordered the city evacuated. The defeated Aztecs formed "a mournful train, husbands and wives, parents and children, the sick and the wounded, leaning on one another for support as they feebly tottered along. . . . Their wasted forms and famine-stricken faces told the whole history of the siege. . . ." Once the city was clear, the Spaniards plundered its gold, silver, and jewels. Not content with plundering the city alone, they razed it entirely, destroying the Aztec capital and effectively ending the existence of the once great empire.

And as the jubilant Spanish forces moved on in search of new treasure to plunder, they carried smallpox and other diseases to the native populations they conquered. Some 250,000 died after an outbreak of typhus in Cuba in 1545, and millions died in Brazil following an outbreak of smallpox in 1560.

All hail the conquering heroes.

1524–1525: Peasants' War in Germany. The young woman knelt before the mob of rebellious peasants and begged them to spare her husband's life. The two-year-old child she held in her arms squirmed and began to cry as the peasants angrily pushed her aside. Meanwhile, a young rebel danced merrily before her, laughing and playing the death march on his fife.

The woman's husband, Count Louis of Helfenstein, and his men were forced to stand against a wall while the peasants, armed with spears, rushed at them in an angry mob. All were killed, including Helfenstein's wife and baby. His wife's body was tossed on a nearby dung cart.

The peasants' revolt in Germany continued for nearly a year. The religious Reformation did not necessarily inspire the revolt, but it had a strong influence. Leaders like Martin Luther had, through their teachings, encouraged the peasants to think about religious liberty, to refuse those who forced their beliefs on others, and to realize their own importance as individuals. Erasmus remarked to Luther, when they witnessed atrocities in the bloody revolt, "We are now reaping the fruits that you have sown."

The peasants of Germany had long resented the inequities of the class system: their lives of hard work and low pay, and the taxes levied upon their meager incomes. They were ready for revolt when a group of villagers in the Black Forest rose up against an abbot on July 19, 1524, because he refused to let them select their preacher. Before long, people in neighboring towns joined their ranks, and by January 1525, dozens of German provinces and towns were in open rebellion.

The peasants soon issued a list of twelve demands. These included the liberty to choose their own preachers, the abolition of tithes and slavery, and the right to hunt and fish where they pleased. Martin Luther's first reaction was to urge the princes to be merciful. Some of their demands, he insisted, were reasonable and should be granted. He warned the peasants, however, that their conduct was outrageous, that they were acting like heathens, and that "the duty of a Christian is to be patient, not to fight. . . ."

But the rebellion had developed a momentum of its own. The peasants began to wander through the countryside, waving a tricolor flag, black, red, and white, as a signal to revolt. Soon they became more violent as well, plundering castles and killing all who resisted.

The Imperial Army was brought in to quell the revolt. They marched to the town where the Count of Helfenstein and his family had died, and burned it to the ground. In battle after battle the professional soldiers easily defeated the poorly trained peasants. Though their ranks grew weaker, the peasants still refused to surrender. Both sides committed bloody atrocities; when the army discovered the young man who had played the fife before the unfortunate woman and child, they chained him to a post, built a fire, and watched him burn.

Finally, on May 15, the army surrounded the peasants. Unarmed, the rebels had drawn their wagons in a crude circle for protection. Many were ready to give up. Still, their leaders urged them to resist, insisting that "the arm of the Lord" blessed their cause. Just then, it is said, a rainbow appeared in the sky, which many saw as a sign of divine protection.

When the peasants still refused to surrender, the army attacked in force. The peasants ran for their lives, but there was no escaping. Some five thousand of them were killed in the bloodbath.

Martin Luther's Protestant Reformation movement brought war as well as profound social and theological questioning.

1527: The Sack of Rome. One more time. This occasion began with the Duke of Bourbon, a Frenchman who was very upset with his king, Francis I. The duke negotiated with the Holy Roman emperor and Henry VIII of England to divide up France. The king discovered the conspiracy and was duly upset, but he failed to capture the escaping duke. After a few skirmishes, King Francis was captured, but released when he promised the duke he could return to France and keep his possessions. But the king reneged. So the emperor made the duke the governor of Milan, but he didn't give him any money to support his army. Lacking resources, there was only one thing to do, of course, and that was sack Rome. On May 6 the duke led an unruly army of Spanish and German mercenaries into Rome. There the soldiers began a long, continuous orgy of violence and destruction in the city rich with long-accumulated treasures and Renaissance artworks. They attacked the unarmed clergy, nobility, merchants, and other Roman citizens with rapacious greed.

Citizens were tortured to make them pay ransoms or reveal the whereabouts of hidden valuables. Gangs of drunken soldiers dragged women out of their homes, or nuns out of their convents, and raped them. As all semblance of order dissolved, soldiers roamed the city, murdering, torturing, and looting at will. Incredibly, the lawless violence and chaos continued unabated for over nine months until the army finally withdrew.

1528: Hurricane Wrecks Spanish Explorers' Ships. Spanish explorers returning from one of the first expeditions to Florida sailed into a powerful hurricane on September 28. All the ships of the flotilla were wrecked, and only twenty of the four hundred Spaniards aboard the ships survived.

You would think they would have listened to a weather report.

1531: Violent Quake Hits Lisbon. On January 26 a great earthquake shook the Portuguese capital of Lisbon, demolishing some fifteen hundred houses and killing about thirty thousand people.

A minor jolt compared to what's to come.

1545: Sinking of the *Mary Rose*. English King Henry VIII's flagship *Mary Rose* foundered in Portsmouth harbor on July 19. The 120-foot warship took seventy-three men to the bottom with her. She was successfully raised from the sea by archaeologists in 1982.

Ooops!

1546: Massacre of the Waldenses. A Protestant sect connected with the Calvinists, the Waldenses in France resided chiefly in Provence. Ongoing troubles between French Catholics and Protestants turned to butchery in 1546, when French King Francis I ordered the massacre of the Waldenses. Attacking some twenty-two towns and villages at night, the Catholics slaughtered thousands of Waldenses, and burned and looted their homes.

Instead of the Christians against everybody else, we now have the Christians against the Christians.

1556: Great China Quake Kills Over 830,000. Silt blown by the winds from the Gobi Desert piled up century after century into high banks of soft clay in the northern Chinese province of Shensi (now Shaanxi). Eventually Chinese peasants began to dig out caves in the soft clay, and by the sixteenth century millions of them had taken up residence in the huge clay banks.

Disaster struck on January 23, 1556, however, when a powerful earthquake rolled through Shensi, Honan, and Shansi (now Shanxi) provinces in northern China. Though few details are known, the violent shaking collapsed the high banks of soft clay and buried alive hundreds of thousands of Chinese peasants in their makeshift cave dwellings. While the death toll of 830,000 is a rough estimate, this disaster is believed to be among the worst in history.

1559: Five Spanish Ships Sink in Storm. A fleet of thirteen Spanish ships anchored off what is today Tampa, Florida, was ravaged by a storm on September 19. Five ships and six hundred people were lost.

And they probably thought this was the calm coast of Florida.

1562: Massacre at Vassy, France. Friction between French Catholics and Huguenots (Protestants) demanding religious freedom had reached dangerous proportions before the government issued the edict of January, which granted Huguenots religious freedom. French Catholics were incensed, and among those who rushed toward Paris to convince the government of the terrible danger of Protestantism was a nobleman, the Duke of Guise.

Along the way, the duke and his followers passed through the small French town of Vassy one Sunday in March. Encountering a group of Huguenots conducting religious services in a barn, the Catholics began to taunt the worshipers. Suddenly a stone hit the duke in the face, which apparently provoked the duke's soldiers into charging the Huguenots with swords drawn. More than sixty villagers were killed, and all the rest were wounded.

The duke, it was said, rode calmly on, taking no notice of the atrocity against the Protestants. Word of the massacre traveled quickly throughout the French countryside, though, stirring Huguenots to open revolt. The resulting conflict in France lasted for thirty-six years, and became known as the Wars of Religion.

Love thy neighbor.

1570: Massacre at Novgorod. The Russian Czar Ivan the Terrible (definitely a type A personality) arrived in the city of Novgorod on January 2, leading a restless army that had already slaughtered citizens in towns and villages all along its path. He had come to murder the people of the city, apparently because he believed they opposed him.

On arriving, his soldiers first built high wooden walls around the city, so that no one could escape, and sealed churches and monasteries to prevent anyone seeking sanctuary. Leading citizens and merchants were locked inside their homes while soldiers arrested city officials and clergymen. Then, before beginning the massacre, Ivan decided he needed money to pay his army. He announced that each priest and monk would pay a fine of twenty rubles. Those who could not pay were stripped and flogged to death in the town squares.

Then, on January 9, Ivan ordered the killing of the general population to begin. Each day the army was ordered to round up a thousand citizens, who were then brutally tortured and killed in front of Ivan and his young son. Parents watched their children being bludgeoned to death, while elsewhere women were slowly burned to death over fires. Holes were carved in the frozen ice of the river at Novgorod, and hundreds were killed by being pushed into the frigid water. Ivan was just living up to his name.

These and other atrocities lasted for five weeks, during which time an estimated sixty thousand people were put to death. Finally, on February 12, the czar assembled what remained of the citizens of Novgorod and, announcing they were pardoned, blamed the city's archbishop for bringing on the massacre and told them to "forget your wrongs!"

Easy for him to say.

1572: Massacre of Saint Bartholomew. The Eve of Saint Bartholomew in Paris should have been a day of celebration. Noblemen and royalty had gathered to celebrate the wedding of King Henry of Navarre to the sister of French King Charles IX. The union represented an alliance between two opposing forces in France: the Catholics and the Huguenots (French Protestants). Strife between these religious groups had already caused two wars, and France's stability was again at stake.

Charles IX was a weak, ineffective king. His mother, Catherine de Medici, had ruled France during his minority and still had great influence over the young ruler. It was she who planned the assassination of Huguenot leader Gaspard de Coligny, and when the attempt failed, she persuaded her son the Huguenots would rise up against him.

Thus the conspiracy began. Late on the night of Saint Bartholomew's Eve, when most of Paris was asleep, Charles's royalist supporters locked city gates, chained boats to the docks to prevent their use for escape, and set guards at city crossroads. All royalists wore white crosses on their hats to distinguish themselves, and they marked houses where Huguenots lived with other crosses.

Then, at exactly 2:00 A.M. on August 24, the bells of the city began to ring, a signal for the killing to begin. Royalist murderers, well plied with drink and roused to a frenzy by charges of heresy against their victims, took up their arms. At first, targeted Huguenot victims were located and put to death. These included Coligny and other well-known Huguenot leaders in Paris.

Even the first killings were barbaric. Lords and their families, including wives, small children, and bewildered servants, were rounded up and struck brutally with clubs and swords, then hacked to death. Huguenot guards were shot down or stabbed and left to die in the streets. Some victims were tossed, still alive, from windows to be crushed on the streets below. The corpse of Coligny was beheaded, then dismembered and hanged for public display. Royalists screamed, "Kill them . . . kill them!" as they struck down their victims in this orgy of death.

As the day progressed, the violence changed in nature. The killers turned into a wild mob, joined by beggars and thieves. The first victims had been selected for slaughter, but now the killing was done wildly, randomly, often to get the victims' possessions. Anyone with wealth became a likely target. One writer observed, "If a person had money, or a well-paid office, or dangerous enemies, or even hungry heirs, then he was deemed a Huguenot."

The Seine became thick with floating bodies, some still alive. Corpses were dumped off bridges and thrown from roofs. One murderer tossed young children, screaming, into the waters. Others shot at those who struggled to stay afloat.

By midday, Paris officials pleaded with Charles to stop the violence. Finally the king issued orders to end the carnage, but he was largely ignored. Days passed before the killing finally stopped. By then, tens of thousands of people had died. And the violence had spread to other provinces where still more Protestants were imprisoned and brutally murdered.

Charles was learning to be a king, but he still needed a few lessons in mob control.

1574: Victory by Flood in Holland. The people of the Netherlands at this time were in revolt against their Spanish overlords, and in 1574 they resisted valiantly as Spanish armies laid siege to the city of Leiden. Citizens of the fortified city were determined to hold out to the last man as Spanish troops settled in lowland areas.

Outnumbered, the Dutch could not break the invasion, and

with supplies cut off by the Spanish, famine soon became a serious problem. Hundreds died of hunger, while people began eating anything that might possibly sustain life: grass, leather, roots, and offal.

In these dire straits, the Dutch could do little more than hope. But they knew how susceptible their kingdom was to flooding, and the fierce storm that struck the area on October 1 and 2 was probably looked upon as a godsend. Indeed, the sea did come to their rescue, breaking through dikes several miles from the encamped Spanish army. Some twenty thousand unsuspecting Spaniards drowned as a result. The siege was broken.

1587: Lost Colony of Roanoke Island. In one of the earliest British attempts to establish a permanent settlement in America, one hundred colonists landed on Roanoke Island (in modern North Carolina) in 1587. The governor, John White, sailed back to England for supplies that year, but his return to Roanoke was delayed until 1590. When he finally arrived, he found no trace of the colonists, save the word "Croatoan" carved on a tree. Virginia Dare, White's granddaughter and the first English child born in the American colonies, was among those missing. The colonists' disappearance remains a mystery today.

The colonists might have been a little wary of being left on the island. After all, the fifteen men who had been left there the previous year were nowhere to be found.

1588: The Disastrous Voyage of the Invincible Armada. Spanish King Philip II, an ardent Roman Catholic, was determined to end the Protestantism that flourished in England under Queen Elizabeth, as well as to repay the English for interfering in his war in the Netherlands. Besides, he was mad at Sir Francis Drake for attacking Spanish colonies in America. To this end he chose to attack England with a two-pronged invasion: a massive land army from the Netherlands was to be ferried across the English Channel from Calais, France, and a great Spanish fleet, carrying about nineteen thousand more soldiers, was to sail to Calais to support the invasion.

Philip's "invincible" Spanish Armada contained no less than 130 warships and other vessels carrying some thirty thousand sailors, soldiers, and galley slaves. The big Spanish galleons, armed with powerful short-range cannons, were a formidable threat to the English navy, but the mighty ships were also slow and hard to maneuver in battle.

Legend has it that the English naval officers Sir Francis Drake, Sir Martin Frobisher, and Sir John Hawkins were playing a game of bowls when an officer arrived to inform them that the Armada had been sighted in the English Channel on July 29. Drake answered calmly, "We have time enough to finish the game." And so they did, before assembling the English fleet of 197 faster, more maneuverable ships armed with long-range cannons. It would be the 130 Spanish ships against the 197 British.

The English warships skirmished with the mighty Armada on July 31, August 2, and August 4, and avoided defeat by staying out of range of the heavy Spanish guns and by taking advantage of their own maneuverability and longer-range cannons. Their experienced skippers were "nimble antagonists, who continued to tease, maltreat, and elude" the Spanish. But the tactics failed to break up the Armada's defensive formation. The English guns were too far away to seriously damage the big galleons.

Meanwhile, the Spanish found problems of their own making. When the Armada's commander, the Duke of Medina-Sidonia, anchored his great fleet off Calais on August 6, he discovered the army from the Netherlands was not yet ready for the invasion. Unfortunately for them, at midnight on August 7 the English struck, sending eight fire ships sailing directly into the anchored Armada. The Spanish captains desperately tried to grapple and tow the burning ships away from the main fleet, but could not reach them all. In the ensuing panic, Spanish ships let go their anchors and sailed hastily for open water. To add insult to injury, they ran out of ammunition.

The great fleet was suddenly in desperate straits, literally. First the English fleet blocked a westward retreat through the English Channel toward Spain—the only way back was to sail northward around the British Isles before turning south to Spain. Worse yet, the Spanish ships lost their advantage of defensive formation when they fled the fire ships. The next day the faster English warships attacked the scattered Spanish ships and cut many of them to pieces. Then the English ran out of ammunition.

While the bulk of the Spanish ships managed to escape, thanks to a change in the wind, the disaster was just beginning for the Spanish. As they sailed northward, they soon realized that most of their food was gone, and their summer clothing was not adequate for the increasing cold of the North Sea. Preparing for a long and difficult voyage around the British Isles, they reduced rations and threw soldiers' horses overboard so that they would not have to feed them.

Storms descended upon the crippled fleet and continued to batter the ships for two long weeks. Many froze to death on board the ill-fated ships, while others fell overboard to their deaths in the icy waters of the North Sea. Huge waves drove the damaged vessels onto the rocky coasts of Scotland and Ireland, dashing them against the cliffs. Corpses washed up on the British shores by the hundreds.

By the time the doomed Armada reached Spain, only seventy-six ships remained, and more than half the men originally on board had died. The English lost fewer than one hundred men in battle, but not a single ship. A form of food poisoning, however, killed about three thousand.

The Armada's disastrous defeat marked Spain's decline as a major European power, helped the Protestant Reformation to survive, and started the English on the way to naval supremacy.

It was also the first gun battle between fleets propelled only by sails: the English with their speed, maneuverability, and long-range light shot against the Spanish heavy cannons. A new type of naval warfare had developed. What fun.

1589: Assassination of Henry III. French King Henry III, embroiled in the French Wars of Religion, had recently enraged Catholics by allying himself with the Protestants. During an audience with the king on August 1, a fanatical monk, Jacques Clement, stabbed Henry in the stomach. Henry pulled out the knife, cutting the assassin's face with it before guards arrived and killed the monk. Henry died the next day of his wounds, and the Protestant Henry of Navarre became Henry IV, the first of the Bourbon kings.

After a nine-year struggle to secure his kingdom, Henry, obviously an advocate of the "if you can't beat 'em, join 'em" philosophy, converted to Catholicism and brought prosperity and order to France.

1591: Eruption of Philippine Volcano Taal. Located south of modern-day Manila, the volcano Taal erupted with a rush of poisonous gases. Thousands of people in the surrounding area suffocated.

Mother Nature burps again.

1591: Storms Destroy Twenty-nine Spanish Ships. A fleet of seventy-five ships sailing from Havana to Spain was hit by a series of storms during the Atlantic crossing. Twenty-nine ships were lost, most of them off Florida, and about five hundred people lost their lives.

1600: Storms Wreck Spanish Convoy. The *Flota de Nueva Espana,* a sixty-ship convoy bound from Cadiz to Veracruz, Mexico, was hit in September by two separate storms that sank seventeen ships. Some one thousand people were drowned.

More deaths in the dash to settle the New World.

1601–1604: Half Million Russians Die in Famine. A shortage of rye sent the price of bread skyrocketing in Russia, and by 1601 the poor were starving to death by the tens of thousands. For a time cannibalism was commonplace, and despite relief efforts by the Russian government, over five hundred thousand people starved to death.

Did anyone suggest they eat cake?

1604–1611: Bloodthirsty Beauty Secret. Countess Elizabeth Bathori of Transylvania, the widow of a Hungarian count, somehow became obsessed by the notion that her beauty was fading. Legend has it that one day in 1604 the countess was giving a servant girl what she considered a well-deserved beating, when the unfortunate girl's blood splashed into her face. When Elizabeth washed the blood from her cheeks, she concluded that it had increased her beauty. (And you thought mud packs were bizarre.)

Having decided it was necessary to bathe in virgin's blood every morning, the countess sent her servants out daily to search the countryside for likely victims. Soon she found that the blood of peasant girls was not enough; she needed the blood of aristocratic young women. So she opened a finishing school for girls, thus collecting a large number of suitable victims right on her premises.

In 1611 four corpses were accidentally discovered near the

countess's castle. At last her dreadful secret was revealed. Authorities later estimated that some 650 young girls died for her vanity. They burned Elizabeth's servants alive, but could not execute the countess because she was of noble birth. Instead they bricked her up in an apartment within her castle. She lived there for four more years until her death.

And you said you didn't believe in vampires.

1608: Disastrous Fire at Jamestown. On January 7, less than a year after the British settlement at Jamestown was founded (in modern Virginia), a fire destroyed most of the one hundred colonists' food, clothing, and shelter. Sixty-two colonists subsequently died of starvation and exposure.

No one ever said it would be easy.

1622: Spanish Ship Disaster Kills Thousands. A large convoy of ships sailing from Havana, Cuba, to Spain was struck by a vicious hurricane on September 6, not long after leaving Havana. Crews struggled to control their ships in the raging sea while trying to return to Havana, but nine of the vessels disappeared off the Florida Keys, and several others apparently were lost on the high seas.

The surviving ships limped back to Havana. All of them had lost their masts, and many had jettisoned their cannon and part of their cargo to stay afloat. While the exact number of people lost in the disastrous storm is not known, estimates of the dead run into the thousands. Three of the ships that disappeared carried treasure in the form of silver bullion and coins.

Greed conquers all.

1626: Seventy Thousand Die in Naples Earthquake. Naples, Italy, and some thirty villages in the surrounding countryside lay in ruins on July 30, after a deadly earthquake that killed tens of thousands struck the region.

A little rumble every couple of centuries keeps the Neapolitans on their toes.

1628: The Short Voyage of the *Vasa*. The sixty-gun *Vasa*, the newly constructed flagship of the Swedish navy, sank on her maiden voyage, killing fifty of the four-hundred-man crew. Incredibly, the ship went under even before clearing Stockholm Harbor, after water poured in through gunports left open on the *Vasa*'s port side.

So they made a little mistake.

1629: Wreck of the *Batavia*. After being shipwrecked on an island off Australia, 316 passengers aboard the Dutch merchant ship *Batavia* found their troubles had just begun. Before rescuers arrived, some one hundred of the survivors were murdered by mutineers who had been stranded on the island.

This was just for fun and pleasure. They didn't eat anyone.

1631: Eruption of Mount Vesuvius. Some four thousand people were killed after Mount Vesuvius, south of Rome, erupted on December 16. The volcano spewed huge amounts of ash, while seven fast-moving lava streams poured down from its mouth, destroying six towns in their path.

Mighty Vesuvius strikes again.

1638: Indonesian Volcano Explodes. Located on the island of Timor in modern-day Indonesia, the 10,500-foot volcano peak blew itself apart in a cataclysmic eruption, killing hundreds of people in the area.

1638: Shimabara Rebellion. In the early seventeenth century, Japan's feudal government actively opposed the spread of Christianity. To test for Christians, they forced those they suspected to tread upon bronze plaques bearing images of Christ or other Christian figures. If the suspects refused, they were presumed to be Christians and were subjected to horrible tortures until they recanted their faith. Those who refused to recant were beheaded.

Peasants of the Shimabara Peninsula finally revolted against this harsh treatment in the spring of 1638, and some twenty thousand peasants seized an abandoned castle. Local noblemen mobilized an army of one hundred thousand men to attack the rebels.

For weeks the drastically outnumbered peasants held out in the bloody fighting, killing some ten thousand of their enemy. But when government troops finally captured the castle, they massacred the surviving defenders. It is said that only about one hundred of the twenty thousand or more rebels escaped alive. The rebellion increased Japan's hostility toward Christianity, and led to the exclusion of all foreigners from Japan in 1639.

Yet another bunch of revolting downtrodden peasants.

1642: Three Hundred Thousand Die in China Flood. Rebels battling the Ming Dynasty rulers deliberately broke river dikes at the city of Kaifeng in China's Honan province in 1642, flooding the city and the surrounding plains. Hundreds of thousands died as a result.

That hardly seems like fair play.

1645: Explosion Rocks Boston. Almost one-third of the Massachusetts Bay colony of Boston was destroyed following an explosion of gunpowder being stored there. Three people were killed.

1656: Collision of Spanish Galleons Kills 644. The galleon *Nuestra Señora de las Maravillas* sank after colliding with a second galleon while maneuvering at night off the Bahamas. Of the seven hundred passengers aboard, only fifty-six were rescued. The ship was carrying inestimable treasure when it sank.

1657: Tokyo Fire. Thousands of highly inflammable wooden structures and a year of drought created ideal conditions for a massive fire in Tokyo, capital of Japan's ruling shoguns. Legend has it that the fire started when a priest attempted to burn a kimono cursed with bad luck. Whatever its cause, the small fire that began in February was whipped into a massive wall of flames by gale-force winds.

Flames swept from house to house and across Tokyo's narrow streets, raging south and east for two days, while consuming houses, temples, palaces, and shops. Then a sudden wind shift drove the flames back toward the center of the city and the shogun's castle. Thousands of people perished in the flames, either trapped by the advancing fires or trampled by stampeding crowds.

After three days the flames died out, but smoke still darkened the ruined city. Snow began to fall, and homeless survivors then faced cold and famine, which would kill many of them. Overall, some one hundred thousand people perished in the calamity.

The priest was right. That kimono was bad luck.

1665: Great Plague of London. In 1664 London was a bustling city of some five hundred thousand citizens. But by September of 1665, one could walk down deserted streets at midday and see house after house boarded up, marked by red crosses and the prayer "Lord have Mercy on us." Such was the devastation wrought by an outbreak of bubonic plague that began almost unnoticed in outlying communities near the city in December 1664.

With the approach of warm spring weather, increasing numbers of people suddenly began to feel feverish and nauseous, and then discovered the hard, swollen, purplish spots on their bodies that characterized the Black Death. Carried by fleas on rats, the disease spread rapidly through overcrowded slums along narrow streets, where residents drank foul water and lived without proper sanitation facilities.

By royal order, houses suspected of being infected by the plague were locked and the occupants were virtually held prisoner within. Some of these unfortunate souls resorted to desperate measures to escape, and the watchman posted outside the door of a locked house was sometimes attacked with a sword or pistol.

At night one could hear the sound of a handbell, and a man shouting, "Bring out your dead," as the "dead carts" roamed the city, gathering corpses. The bodies were dumped into huge pits outside the city, and one contained over eleven hundred bodies before it was covered over.

Wealthier citizens, including the king himself, fled to the countryside, but poorer citizens leaving the city were attacked by villagers fearing the contagion. By the time the plague abated the following winter, about one hundred thousand people had died.

The good news is that, though this was the worst plague, it was also the last.

1666: West Indies Hurricane. A powerful hurricane lashed the islands of Guadeloupe, Martinique, and Saint Christopher with high winds and heavy rains on August 4. Thousands were killed, including some two thousand soldiers who were aboard a fleet of ships lost during the storm.

1666: The Great Fire of London. The king's baker, Thomas Farynor, put out fires in the ovens at 10:00 P.M. before leaving his bakery shop to go to bed, or so he swore later. Awakened by smoke in his quarters above the bakery about 2:00 A.M. on Sunday, September 2, Farynor and his family narrowly escaped the fire by crawling out a garret window. Farynor's assistant, who was terrified of heights, remained behind and became the fire's first victim.

Farynor's shop was located on Pudding Lane, between London Bridge and the Tower of London. A long summer drought had left the city vulnerable to fire, and now it spread across the lane to Star Inn, where straw and fodder for horses quickly ignited.

Next, the Lord Mayor Sir Thomas Bludworth was awakened at 3:00 A.M. and brought to the scene of the fire. Annoyed at having his sleep interrupted, the mayor reportedly groused, "Pish! A woman might piss it out." He returned to bed, but the fire continued burning. Saint Margaret's Church across from the Star Inn soon caught fire. From there flames spread to the Thames Street wharves, where hemp, ropes, oil, and pitch fueled the flames.

London awoke Sunday morning to find the fire already burning uncontrollably. Flames rising through the belfry of the church of Saint Magnus the Martyr helped spread panic as Londoners suddenly realized this was no ordinary fire. Terrified citizens began a mad scramble to save their possessions, some hauling them from one house to another as the fire relentlessly pursued them. Meanwhile, boatmen, in true entrepreneurial spirit, charged enormous amounts to carry furniture, gold, and goods across the Thames River to safety.

Samuel Pepys, who recorded the fire in his diary, climbed the Tower of London on Sunday morning. He described the fire growing, "in corners and upon steeples and between churches and houses, as far as we could see up the hill of the city, in a most horrid malicious bloody flame . . . one entire arch of fire from this to the other side of the bridge, and in a bow up the hill. . . . It made me weep to see it."

In the street, Pepys met the lord mayor, who now atoned for his underestimation of the fire. To the king's messenger, the mayor cried, "Lord, what can I do? I am spent. . . . I have been pulling down houses. But the fire overtakes us faster than we can do it."

The fire roared on, day after day, even as such desperate

measures as blowing up the houses in its path continued. King Charles II joined the struggle to fight the blaze, his coat covered with soot and smoke. On Tuesday thirty-four churches collapsed in flames. Among them was the magnificent Saint Paul's Cathedral, with its six-acre lead-covered roof.

"How horridly the sky looks," Pepys wrote, "all on fire in the night. It was enough to put us out of our wits."

Not until Thursday, September 6, was the blaze brought under control. By then thirteen thousand houses and eighty-seven churches had been destroyed. The Custom House, Royal Exchange, forty-four company halls, several prisons, and four bridges had fallen. The city that had lost more than fifty thousand to the plague a year before now stood in utter ruins, and more than one hundred thousand people were homeless. Yet, miraculously, only eight people died in the five-day fire.

1669: Eruption of Mount Etna. The notorious Sicilian volcano Mount Etna (from the Greek word meaning "to burn") rumbled ominously during the early months of 1669. Perhaps the Sicilians living in the area should have heeded the warnings being issued by Europe's largest and most active volcano. They included twenty-two minor eruptions of rocks and gases in only the first two months of the year. And on March 8, when a strong earthquake also jolted the region, the volcano's "horrible roarings . . . exceedingly terrified the inhabitants."

It was late in the evening on March 11 when Mount Etna suddenly erupted three times with a horrible fury, beginning the volcano's most destructive eruption up to that time. Enormous boulders weighing three hundred pounds and more were hurled high into the air and came crashing down miles away from the volcano, flattening dwellings and killing people and livestock. The air filled quickly with burning smoke, ash, and cinder, suffocating some inhabitants and burning the eyes of sailors at sea ten miles away. The sparks and cinders became a "fiery deluge" that covered and incinerated an area six miles square. The mountain's thundering roar could be heard fifty miles away, and the Sicilian town of Nicolosi and several smaller villages were completely destroyed.

Suddenly Mount Etna split open with a fissure almost ten miles long. Huge holes appeared, spewing flames, smoke, sulfurous gas, and a deadly flow of lava, which threatened to engulf nearby towns. Even Catania, a port city about eighteen miles from the volcano, was not safe. Realizing the danger of the lava flow, a resident of the city rounded up fifty volunteers and raced to intercept it. The fiery river of molten rock was by this time moving directly toward Catania, and the men desperately hoped to rechannel it.

Covering themselves with wet cowhides for protection, they dug frantically, trying to creat new paths for the lava to follow. But their efforts aroused residents in the nearby town of Paterno, who feared the new channel might direct the deadly lava straight toward their town. So they attacked the men from Catania, finally forcing them to give up their digging. A friendly, helpful gesture.

The molten rock flowed relentlessly toward Catania, finally coming up against high stone walls that had been hurriedly built to protect the town. But it was no use; the lava river climbed effortlessly up over the walls and poured into the city. Catania was flooded with molten rock that destroyed nearly every building in the city and killed more than fifteen thousand inhabitants. Only a small portion of the city's castle survived the devastating lava flood. In all, some twenty thousand people lost their lives during the eruption.

There have been about 140 eruptions of Etna since recorded history, but this was the worst. And it may happen again.

1671: Buccaneer Sir Henry Morgan Sacks Panama. Buccaneers, bands of adventurers who roamed on the high seas during the seventeenth century, laid claim to many destructive exploits, but for sheer audacity, none can compare with the pillaging and burning of Panama, then one of Spain's chief cities in the New World. The Welsh buccaneer Sir Henry Morgan launched this ambitious venture in 1670 with thirty-six ships and some two thousand men. His chief aim, of course, was the horde of gold and silver he expected to plunder from the opulent Spanish city.

Morgan's army of buccaneers first captured Fort Saint Laurent, then set off for the city by marching overland across the Isthmus of Panama. The Spaniards withdrew before the oncoming buccaneers, burning their houses and taking with them everything edible. For ten days Morgan's men lived on a diet of leaves and grass, plus the meat of the few horses and cows they managed to find. On January 27 the starving and exhausted buccaneers finally reached the city of Panama.

There the larger Spanish army of twenty-four hundred foot soldiers and four hundred horsemen attacked Morgan's position after driving twenty-four hundred wild bulls ahead of them. The buccaneers were saved from being overrun and trampled by a swampy marsh, which slowed the bulls and Spanish cavalry enough to allow the buccaneers' sharpshooters to cut the Spanish down. Six hundred Spaniards died before they withdrew, leaving an unknown number of wounded, who were hacked to death or shot by the buccaneers.

Morgan then led his men into the city, bent on gaining its riches. However, most of Panama's residents had by now fled to a nearby island, taking most of the valuables with them. Thus, for all his efforts, Morgan gained little of the gold and silver he had sought. Instead he found only more mundane items—a fortune in iron, flour, wine, and spices stored in the city's warehouses and shops. Wanting none of these, the enraged Morgan ordered the city burned. Over the next few weeks, Morgan's men looted the city and burned Panama to the ground.

It is said that Morgan deserted his army of buccaneers soon after leaving Panama, taking most of the valuable booty with him.

The escapades of Henry Morgan and his ilk made excellent scenarios for Hollywood's swashbuckler films.

1672: Black Plague at Naples. A devastating outbreak of the Black Plague hit Naples, Italy, killing some four hundred thousand people before it ran its course.

Those fleas were merciless.

1678: French Fleet Sinks in the Caribbean. On the night of May 3, a French fleet sent to capture the Dutch colony of Curaçao was wrecked on a reef off Aves Island, near contemporary Venezuela. Of the twenty French ships, only two escaped the catastrophe, which claimed the lives of over twelve hundred men.

A slight navigation error here.

1685: The Bloody Assizes. The crime of high treason excited the anger of Judge Lord George Jeffreys, appointed to try those involved in the Duke of Monmouth's abortive rebellion against England's King James II. Jeffreys took particular delight in cursing and abusing the prisoners, tormenting them with detailed descriptions of the tortures he was about to impose upon them. Some were beheaded, but Jeffreys's favorite sentence was to have the prisoner hanged, then taken down while still living and disemboweled with a sword.

Throughout the county of Somersetshire, crossroads, village greens, marketplaces, and even churches were decorated with Judge Jeffreys's grisly work, as human heads or the quartered remnants of bodies were mounted on poles. One nobleman who protested such cruelty was silenced when a corpse was suspended by chains on his estate. Some 320 of Monmouth's followers were executed, and hundreds of other prisoners were punished by public floggings or whippings. Later, James II fled the country, and Jeffreys spent his last days in the Tower of London.

Our Bill of Rights wisely forbids cruel or unusual punishment.

1687: Tragic Blast Destroys Parthenon. Although the rich colors had long since worn away, in 1687 many of the marble statues of the renowned Greek sculptor Phidias still adorned the pediment of the Parthenon. This ancient temple to Athena that crowned the city of Athens had remained largely intact for well over a thousand years, but in one instant, the ancient monument to reason and order was blasted to ruins.

Turkish armies, at the time in control of Athens, at first had used the Parthenon as a mosque, then later converted it into a gunpowder magazine. In 1687 a Venetian army laid siege to Athens, and during the fighting an explosive shell landed squarely on top of the Parthenon. Munitions stored there went up in a terrific explosion that tore the elegant stone structure to pieces—columns buckled, pediments crashed down, and statues were hurled to the ground. Heartbroken, the Venetian general Francisco Morosini later attempted to salvage the temple, but there was little hope of ever restoring it to its previous glory.

Modern-day pollution will later break down the rest of it.

1690: Schenectady Massacre. During King William's War, sporadic fighting erupted between French and English colonies in North America. But in February 1690 a raiding party of 110 French colonials and Iroquois Indians attacked the unsuspecting village of Schenectady, New York, and massacred sixty residents, including seventeen children. Many others were captured and taken to Canada.

The old joke is that the name Schenectady comes from the Indian word meaning "skin neck today."

1692: Glencoe Massacre. When William III became king of England, he required the Highland chieftains, under penalty of death, to take an oath of submission to him and his rule by January 1, 1692. The chieftain of the Macdonalds of Glencoe, however, was delayed by a blizzard, and did not take the oath until January 5. The king was informed of the missed deadline, and he ordered the Macdonald clan eliminated.

On February 1 the king's loyal Captain Campbell of Glenlyon and 120 of his men arrived at clan Macdonald, where they were hospitably entertained for twelve days. At 5:00 A.M. on February 13, however, Campbell ordered his men to slaughter everyone under seventy years of age. During the vicious early morning bloodbath, most of the Macdonalds managed to escape into the wilderness, where they were forced to remain in hiding for many months. Of the 150 adult men in the clan, 38 were slain.

Definitely not a nice way to treat your hosts.

1692: Salem Witchcraft Trials. When the four young children of a wealthy family in Salem, Massachusetts, began exhibiting strange symptoms, their parents became concerned. The children had been barking like dogs, purring like cats, and on occasion acting as though they had been struck blind or dumb. Not long before the strange behavior began, the oldest child, a girl of thirteen, had been soundly scolded by an elderly Irish servant named Goody Glover.

Called in by the children's parents, a doctor proclaimed the children had been bewitched by Goody Glover, who was promptly arrested and brought up on charges of being a witch. The poor woman gave what were considered insensible answers to questions in court, and when it was revealed she was a Roman Catholic, the woman was found guilty of witchcraft and executed. Needless to say, the children's odd behavior stopped abruptly after the incident.

But the strange fear of witchcraft spread throughout the Massachusetts colony. Encouraged by ministers who claimed that witchcraft went hand in hand with atheism and the devil, the colonists accused and tried dozens of alleged witches. Soon the jails were full, and a special witch court had been established in Salem for the speedy trial and punishment of witches. If they protested their innocence, it was considered proof of guilt. If, confessing to avoid punishment, the accused contradicted herself, guilt was still certain: The "devil" was speaking. Young children were frequent witnesses, occasionally children of the accused woman herself.

Arrests and trials of witches continued for several years until 1696, when the Massachusetts legislature adopted a resolution against them.

1692: Jamaica Hit by Tidal Wave. An earthquake rocked Port Royal, Jamaica, on June 7 and then sent a giant tidal wave crashing into the town. Port Royal was demolished, and in a matter of minutes some three thousand people were killed.

1693: A Year of Destruction in Italy. Earthquakes and volcanic eruptions are not uncommon in the history of Italy, but this year proved particularly violent. Some ninety-three thousand people died in a Naples earthquake, while another sixty thousand were lost in a second quake that shook Catania. The volcano Mount Etna also erupted violently in 1693, killing another eighteen thousand people on the island of Sicily.

A double whammy from old Mother Nature.

1694: Hurricane Founders British Ships. Anchored in Carlisle Bay at Barbados, twenty-six British ships were sunk by a violent hurricane that struck on September 27. Some three thousand people aboard the merchant ships were drowned.

1695: HMS *Winchester* Sinks. The British man-of-war, armed with sixty guns, hit a reef and sank off Key Largo, Florida, in September. Four hundred people died in the wreck.

1703–1704: Tokyo Earthquake. On December 30 a massive earthquake struck the Japanese city of Tokyo, crumbling buildings and opening great fissures in the ground. Some thirty-seven thousand people were killed by the disaster.

At the same time that the quake shook Tokyo and the surrounding area, a series of monstrous tidal waves swept the coastline, carrying entire villages and all their inhabitants out to sea. In the mountains of the Hakone district, the quake opened hundreds of fissures in the peaks, causing boiling water to spout freakishly over nearby villages and farms.

A week after the quake, while the Japanese hastily buried their dead, calamity struck again: Fire broke out in nearby Koishikawa just as hurricane-force winds hit the area. Winds soon created a deadly inferno that destroyed what little of this city remained following the disastrous earthquake. More than a thousand people died in the fire alone.

1711: Black Plague in Holy Roman Empire. Black Plague, the scourge of Europe in the Middle Ages, struck again in 1711, this time in the Holy Roman Empire. Some five hundred thousand people died in this outbreak of the plague.

And just when they thought it was safe to go back out on the streets.

1715: One Thousand Die in Wreck of Spanish Ships. A convoy of twelve ships laden with gold and silver, as well as cocoa and other merchandise from Spain's New World colonies, sailed into a fierce hurricane off the Florida coast on July 30. Bound for Spain from Havana, Cuba, the ships were relentlessly battered by the towering waves and raging winds. Officers and crew alike fought valiantly to keep their ships afloat, but to no avail. Eleven of the twelve ships sank or were totally wrecked in the storm-tossed waters, and some one thousand passengers, officers, and crewmen were killed.

Miraculously, almost fifteen hundred survivors managed to reach the shores of Florida by swimming or hanging on to floating pieces of wreckage. Some time passed before rescuers from Saint Augustine and Havana reached them all, however, and a number who survived the storm died of exposure, thirst, and hunger.

And another trove of gold and silver was laid to rest in the briny.

1719: Killer Snowstorm in Sweden. A large caravan of travelers in Sweden was heading for Trondheim, Norway, when it was caught in a severe snowstorm. Some seven thousand people in the caravan died.

1720: The South Sea Bubble. Faced with the problem of an overwhelming national debt, the British government devised a scheme to transfer thirty-one million pounds of the debt to the thriving South Sea Company, which claimed to have a monopoly on British trade with Spanish America. Interest in the South Sea Company surged as a mania for quick profits developed, driving share prices from one hundred pounds to over one thousand pounds within months.

To accommodate the crowds clamoring for the stock, banks set up tables in the streets of London. Predictably, numerous fraudulent companies also sprang up to take advantage of the rage for investment, selling shares in such unlikely schemes as extracting oil from radishes. Also, it was later found that at least three government ministers took bribes and engaged in South Sea stock speculations.

Prosecution of the frauds led to a general distrust of stock companies and a stampede to sell, causing South Sea Company share prices to plunge to 135 pounds. Thousands of people lost their life savings in the financial panic, and suicide rates soared. Meanwhile, the British economy was also shattered by the collapse of the stock. One member of Parliament voiced the feelings of many when he suggested that the directors of the company be sewn into a sack and tossed into the Thames.

Perhaps a suitable punishment for those involved in modern-day stock frauds and bank scandals?

1722: Ergotism Outbreak in Russia. Some twenty thousand Russians died horrible deaths after eating bread made from rye infected by a deadly fungus. The fungus caused a severe nervous disorder in victims called ergotism, which resulted in delusions, convulsions, burning pain, and finally death.

These symptoms were not blamed on witches, at least.

1727: Earthquake Hits Persia. A massive earthquake demolished the Persian city of Tabriz, in modern Iran, killing over seventy-five thousand people.

It had been seven hundred years since the last one. Not a bad average.

1729: Constantinople Fire. More than seven thousand people died and twelve thousand buildings were decimated in a great fire at Constantinople, capital of the Ottoman Empire. Fire struck again in 1750, destroying twenty thousand buildings; in 1756, burning fifteen thousand buildings; and in 1782, leveling ten thousand buildings.

Not enough firemen; or too many arsonists.

1731: Deadly Earthquake Rocks Beijing. On November 30 Peking (now Beijing), China, was struck by a massive earthquake that demolished much of the city and killed about one hundred thousand people.

1732: Five Hundred Drown as Ship Sinks Off Mexico. As a small fleet of Spanish ships carrying a cargo of mercury arrived off the coast at Veracruz, Mexico, the galleon *Nuestra Señora de la Concepcion* unexpectedly foundered and sank, killing hundreds.

Mercury is a highly toxic metallic element. No estimates regarding the number of dead fish are given.

1735–1740: Diphtheria Outbreak Hits New England. Primarily striking children, the diphtheria epidemic that began in 1735 raged throughout New England for five years. In some towns the deadly disease killed 80 percent of the children under ten years of age.

1737: Cyclone and Earthquake Demolish Calcutta. October was a terrible month for the sprawling, overcrowded city of Calcutta, India. Located on the Bay of Bengal, the city was struck by a cyclone on October 7 that sent a forty-foot tidal wave crashing ashore. Some three hundred thousand people died in that disaster, and just days later, on October 11, another three hundred thousand were killed when an earthquake rocked the ruined city.

These disasters must have, however, alleviated some of the overcrowding.

1738: Massacre at Delhi. In 1738 Nadir, the shah of Persia, invaded India and defeated a huge Indian army before the great city of Delhi—the battle lasted just four hours and resulted in the deaths of some twenty thousand Indian soldiers.

Accepting the surrender of Indian Emperor Muhammad Shah, Nadir and his soldiers triumphantly entered the city of Delhi. They allowed Muhammad to return to his throne, but claimed territories in western India and took the royal treasure as part of the terms of surrender. Then Nadir imposed an enormous ransom on the people of Delhi.

The angered citizens rose up against the Persians, who responded by slaughtering them by the tens of thousands. The terrible massacre ended only when Muhammad begged for an end to the killing. An eyewitness reported that some 150,000 people were slain in the uprising, although this figure is believed to be greatly exaggerated.

Render unto Caesar . . .

1751: Stockholm Burns. Beginning at noon on July 31, a series of suspicious fires broke out in Stockholm, Sweden, and though each was brought under control over the next few days, a total of one thousand buildings were burned. Authorities arrested several suspected arsonists.

1752: Three Successive Fires Ravage Moscow. Citizens of Moscow scarcely had time to recover from a fire on May 23 before another disastrous fire broke out on June 3. This fire, whipped up by a strong southwesterly wind, raged throughout the day and into the night, until the conflagration cut a swath of destruction five to six miles long.

Apparently set by arsonists, who were seen lighting combustible matter in several places and were subsequently caught, the fires of June 3 destroyed thousands of homes and businesses and numerous churches and monasteries before subsiding on June 4. Then still another fire started on June 6, this one ravaging the center of Moscow.

After this third fire subsided, the luckless inhabitants of Moscow lived amid the rubble of eighteen thousand burned-out buildings. Though no one ever knew how many people had been killed, fully one-third of the city had been consumed by the fires.

1754: Earthquake Demolishes Cairo. Thousands of people were buried in the ruins of Cairo, Egypt, following a deadly earthquake in September. About forty thousand people were killed, and half the houses in the city were demolished.

1755: Lisbon Earthquake. A massive earthquake struck the bustling port city of Lisbon, Portugal, on November 1 with such force that its shocks were felt across Europe and North Africa. The quake, and subsequent seismic waves and fires, killed between fifty thousand and one hundred thousand people and left Lisbon in ruins.

The first shock hit about nine-thirty on the morning of All Saints' Day. Within two minutes, thousands of buildings collapsed, a fifteen-foot-wide fissure opened in the middle of the city, and thousands of people were crushed to death. The great cathedrals of Lisbon collapsed onto hundreds of worshipers gathered for All Saints' Day prayer.

Lisbon, a city of 275,000 people, was transformed into a scene of horror. Survivors reported seeing buildings swaying "like corn in the wind." The grinding of stone against stone as buildings collapsed created, as one survivor put it, "the most dreadful crunching, jumbling noise ears ever heard." Clouds of dust kicked up by falling debris darkened the city. The streets were filled with people caught by flying debris, either crushed to death beneath massive stones or screaming for a priest to hear their last confession.

Repercussions of the quake were felt far from Lisbon. Fifty-foot waves slammed into Cornwall, England, and reached the Gulf of Finland. Ironically, Mount Vesuvius in Italy suddenly *stopped* erupting. The quake even shook the West Indies. Some ten thousand people were killed in Fez and Meknes, Morocco.

In Lisbon, those who survived the first three shocks between nine-thirty and ten o'clock thronged the streets. Of the thousands who took refuge by the city's marble docks, hundreds were washed away by a fifty-foot seismic wave of seawater.

By ten-thirty, fire joined the destructive forces of earth and water as massive flames erupted in the center of Lisbon. Probably kindled by debris falling into kitchen fires, the flames spread wildly. "Every element seemed to conspire to our destruction," one survivor said. The buildings still standing were quickly burned. Lisbon's culture went up in flames, too, as the opera house, convents, and palaces succumbed. The flames consumed two hundred paintings by such masters as Titian, Rubens, and Correggio, along with eighteen thousand priceless rare books and numerous maps used by Portuguese explorers over the centuries.

Soon chaos reigned in the city. Convicts freed by the collapse of the prison roamed the streets, looting and committing other crimes. Officials responded by setting up gallows in a ring around the city to hang looters. Priests, in their wisdom, wandered the streets looking for heretics to burn, believing the disaster represented God's punishment of Lisbon for its sins.

By the time the last fires burned out, some seventeen thousand of the twenty thousand buildings in Lisbon had been destroyed. Asked by the king of Portugal what could be done to help the beleaguered city, Secretary of State Marquis de Pombal replied succinctly, "Sir, we must bury the dead and feed the living."

If God was punishing Lisbon for its sins, it must have been a wicked, wicked city.

1755: Severe Earthquake Rocks Boston. The worst earthquake ever experienced in the history of Boston, Massachusetts, occurred in the early morning on November 18. The ground heaved with a long, wavelike motion, fissures opened, and walls and chimneys collapsed, but no one was killed.

And you thought earthquakes in America only hit California.

1756: Black Hole of Calcutta. This little incident struck back at the forces of imperialism. Following the capture of British-held Calcutta by native rebels on June 20, some sixty-four British prisoners were locked up for the night in a small prison cell, measuring just eighteen feet by fifteen feet, with only two small windows for air.

The crowding and oppressive heat proved more than the men could stand, and they soon began to suffer from lack of air, as well as dehydration. One by one they began to drop, and by morning all but twenty-one had suffocated to death in the cramped prison cell.

The incident gained widespread attention at a time when British colonial rule was expanding in India. Originally the number of men crowded into the cell had been put at 146, but that figure was later found to be exaggerated.

1769–1770: Indian Famine Kills Millions. An eighteen-month drought in Hindustan, India, created a terrible famine in the province. Millions of people starved to death.

1769: Lightning Ignites Powder Magazine. Huge quantities of gunpowder were being stored at the church of Saint Nazaire, in the northern Italian city of Brescia, when on August 18 a bolt of lightning set fire to the church. Soon after, the powder magazine exploded, killing some three thousand people and demolishing all the buildings in the surrounding area.

1770: French Ship Sinks, Killing Seven Hundred. The *L'Oriflamme,* a French merchant ship carrying over seven hundred passengers and crew, sank during a storm off Valparaiso (in modern Chile). Only a handful survived.

1772: Java Volcano Blows its Top. Papandayan, an eighty-seven-hundred-foot volcano in Java, erupted with a great explosion on August 11 and 12, blowing away about four thousand feet of the top of its volcano cone. Over forty villages and towns were destroyed, and some three thousand people were killed.

1776: Caribbean Hurricane Ravages Shipping Trade. Some six thousand people aboard a convoy of French and Dutch merchant ships were drowned on September 6 when a deadly hurricane sank one hundred of the ships off Point Bay, Martinique.

Now the French and Dutch are joining the Spanish.

1778: Wyoming Valley Massacre. During the American Revolution, some of the Tories—American colonials who remained loyal to the British king—joined forces with Indian tribes to raid frontier towns in New York and Pennsylvania. One of the most brutal raids took place on July 3 in the Wyoming Valley in Pennsylvania. There some eight hundred Tories and Indians massacred more than two hundred unsuspecting Americans, a bloody act the Tories later blamed on the Indians.

Enough of this petty bickering.

1780: The Gordon Riots. When the British Parliament passed the Catholic Relief Act, abolishing previous anti-Catholic legislation, it had little idea that this would lead to anti-Catholic rioting against both Catholics and Parliament itself. However, on Friday, June 2, Lord George Gordon, an obscure member of Parliament who had been against passing the Catholic Relief Act, marched toward Parliament at the head of a mob of several thousand Protestant demonstrators. Gordon planned only to deliver to Parliament the grievances of his newly formed Protestant

Society, but once there, the twenty-nine-year-old Gordon couldn't control the mob's behavior.

As the lords approached Parliament, their coach windows were broken and some coaches were overturned and destroyed. Lords were cut by the flying glass, and many were punched and kicked as they tried to escape. When the crowd ripped the wheels from the Bishop of Lincoln's coach, he fled to a nearby house, changed clothes, and then clambered over roofs to safety.

From that point on, the violence grew worse. Over the weekend several Catholic churches were burned. Then, on Tuesday, June 6, a mob turned on Newgate Prison. A witness described the rioters as laughing defiantly amid the smoke and flames, smashing their way through the roof of the burning prison to let the prisoners out. Meanwhile another mob attacked Lord Mansfield's house, and refused to withdraw even when several of them fell dying after being shot by guards.

On Wednesday, June 7, thirty-six separate fires could be seen burning from one vantage point alone, while the streets echoed with the shouts of rioters and the gunshots of soldiers. Many were wounded or killed by gunfire, while others died in the flames of the buildings the rioters set afire. Some of the more bizarre deaths occurred when liquor from a demolished distillery flowed into the street. Rioters scooped it up in pailfuls and drank, only to be poisoned by the nonrectified alcohol.

By the time Lord Gordon was arrested on Thursday, June 8, over four hundred people had died in the riots. Gordon was tried for high treason, but was rightly acquitted on the grounds that his intentions had not been treasonable.

Just another occasion of religious prejudice getting out of hand.

1780: The Great West Indies Hurricane. A killer hurricane swept through the West Indies on October 10–12, flattening Barbados and Martinique and sinking almost every ship in its path.

Residents on Barbados reported seeing a red and fiery sunset before the storm. That night torrents of rain came, and in the morning the full force of the storm finally hit. Furious winds knocked over everything on Barbados—buildings and trees. Some six thousand people died when their homes collapsed on them or when they were hit by wind-borne debris. The roar of the wind was so loud, terrified inhabitants cowering in their cellars could not even hear their houses crashing down above them.

Meanwhile, the story of destruction was much the same in Martinique, where some nine thousand people died. A forty-ship French convoy also sank near Martinique, taking the lives of four thousand soldiers who were aboard. In all, twenty thousand to thirty thousand people died in what came to be called "The Great Hurricane of 1780."

This was way before we started giving hurricanes cute names.

1781–1782: Influenza Epidemic. A worldwide epidemic of influenza apparently began in the autumn in China, and during the following months spread to India, Europe, and North America. At the height of the epidemic in Russia, some thirty thousand were stricken daily, and in Rome, two-thirds of the population came down with the disease. No figures are available for the number of deaths caused by the epidemic.

1782: Gale Wrecks Barbados. A powerful storm packing high winds ravaged the Caribbean island of Barbados, killing thousands on the island itself and sinking many ships off its coast.

This is the second hurricane in two years to wipe them out.

1783: Earthquake Hits Italy. For eight years Italy experienced a series of major earthquakes, but the worst one shook southern Italy on February 4 and 5. This earthquake leveled the city of Calabria and more than 180 towns in the area around it.

Huge fissures opened up in the earth, some of them 225 feet deep and 150 feet wide. Many people and livestock were swallowed up by these great chasms, from which powerful geysers of boiling water soon began spewing. Incredibly, the water lifted out some of those trapped in the fissures, a few of them still alive. Though badly burned, some of these lucky souls actually survived the quake.

Elsewhere, rivers and streams dammed up by debris created a wave of mud seventy yards wide and fifteen feet deep that flooded the town of Scilla. Fires broke out in the ruined cities and towns, and aftershocks plagued the area.

The earthquake killed some thirty thousand outright, while

twenty thousand to thirty thousand others died as a result of the aftershocks and the famine that followed.

This is the same part of the Mediterranean that's been crumbling and quaking since the dawn of history.

1783: Iceland Volcanic Eruptions. In late May an eerie, bluish haze appeared over the Icelandic volcano Mount Skaptar, and a series of tremors that began on June 1 sent many families into tents for fear their stone houses would collapse. Then on the morning of June 8, the Lakagigar fissure, a fifteen-mile-long rip in the earth's crust, tore open, and for two months spewed forth lava at a prodigious rate.

One river in Iceland disappeared entirely as a new river of liquid rock, steaming with poisonous gases, eventually filled and overflowed the six-hundred-foot-deep riverbed, creating a fifteen-mile-wide delta in the coastal lowlands. On July 29 a second eruption replaced yet another river.

Overall, some three cubic miles of lava obliterated rivers, villages, and farms over a two-hundred-square-mile area—the largest lava flow in recorded history. Floods from melted glaciers and displaced rivers only worsened the damage. Some nine thousand people were killed and twenty villages were destroyed by the lava flows.

Ash obliterated the summer sun, and a similar noxious blue cloud spread over Iceland, eventually reaching as far as North Africa. Livestock began to sicken, the hides rotting from their bodies. Soon humans developed boils and deformities on their bodies; their hair began to fall out, their eyes stung, and their gums swelled.

In the infamous "Haze Famine" that followed, trees, grasses, crops, and wildlife withered and died, while fish disappeared from the poisoned coastal waters. As starvation set in, horses were seen eating each other, and people resorted to chewing on rope or the raw hides of animals for nourishment.

Now even the horses are practicing cannibalism.

1784: First Hailstorm Deaths in the United States. A terrible hailstorm accompanied a thunderstorm at Winnsborough, South Carolina, on May 8. Hailstones measuring up to nine inches in circumference fell, killing several blacks. They became the first recorded fatalities from a hailstorm in the United States.

1787: Slave Ship Founders. A sudden gust of wind on May 17 overturned the British slave ship *Sisters,* killing all but three of the five hundred slaves aboard. Only two crewmen survived the sinking, which occurred on the voyage from Africa to Cuba.

1789: Cyclone Hits India. A cyclone ravaged Coringa in early December, driving three huge storm waves into the city in a single day. When the waters receded, only piles of sand and mud remained, and just one house. Over twenty thousand people were killed.

1790–1792: Skull Famine in India. Severe drought brought on a terrible famine in Bombay and other parts of India. Cannibalism became widespread, and the fact that there were so many unburied dead gave rise to the name "skull famine." No figures are available for the total number of deaths.

1792: Russian Persecutions of the Jews. The Russians were by no means the first people in Europe to persecute the Jews—the English banished them in 1290, and by the end of the fifteenth century, Spain, Portugal, and France had followed suit. But in 1792 the Russian empress Catherine the Great instituted a somewhat different form of persecution of the Jews. She created the "pale"—a zone in which Jews were required to live and from which they were forbidden to leave.

The millions of Jews in the pale had few rights: They could not own property or engage in farming, and were severely restricted in the types of work they could do for pay. As a result, unemployment was rampant, and many Jews were forced to live in abject poverty. By the 1860s the government began making exceptions for Jews who were merchants, artisans, or who had other qualifications, allowing them to live anywhere in Russia.

Soon after Czar Alexander II was assassinated in 1881, however, the pogroms against Jews began. Jews were accused of being involved, even though the assassin himself was not a Jew. Mobs of angry Russians attacked Jews in over two hundred cities and towns, and destroyed their property. Sporadic incidents of attacks on Jews continued over the years until 1903–6, when pogroms again became frequent and widespread.

Any excuse to pick on the Jews. Sometimes no reason.

1792: Plague Sweeps Through Egypt. Some eight hundred thousand Egyptians died as a terrible plague ravaged the country this year.

Fortunately, it didn't spread elsewhere.

1792: Assassination of Gustavus III of Sweden. On the evening of March 16, 1792, King Gustavus III, wearing a cloak and mask, moved among the dancers attending a masquerade ball at the Grand Opera House in Stockholm. Earlier that evening, an anonymous note had been slipped to him, detailing an assassination plot by dissatisfied nobles that was to take place in that very ballroom, and imploring him not to attend.

Undaunted, he stepped into the brilliant glow of the chandeliers, admiring the stage scenery and the costumes of the dancing masqueraders; yet he surely must have wondered which of them might be planning to attack him at any moment.

Suddenly five men in dark cloaks and masks surrounded him. One of them produced a pistol wrapped in raw wool to silence it, and fired. Panic broke out as the king, bleeding but still alive, was carried off by friends, and doors and exits were sealed. The ringleader, Count Ankarstrom, escaped but was arrested the next day. Gustavus III died on March 29.

This was the case of a great and wise king being done in by a bunch of jealous aristocrats.

1792: British Battleship Capsizes. While in for repairs at Spithead in southern England on August 29, the famed 108-gun warship *Royal George* unexpectedly capsized while thirteen hundred sailors, workers, and others were aboard. About nine hundred people died in the tragedy, causing great embarrassment to the English naval establishment.

1792: The September Massacres. The massacres that took place in the city of Paris from September 2 to 6 were among the bloodiest episodes of the French Revolution, serving as a cruel prelude to the Reign of Terror of 1793. Roving mobs, seeking revenge on anyone connected with the recently overthrown aristocracy, stormed the jails where many noblemen, royal attendants, and clergy were imprisoned. What happened to the Princess de Lamballe was typical: she was dragged from prison by her hair, hanged, and then disemboweled. Her mutilated body was dragged through the streets and put on display for two days.

At one prison, clergy were led outside two at a time. Their throats were cut and their bodies exhibited to torment the next victims being led out. Citizens paraded the streets carrying the heads and bodies of victims on pikes, a kind of spiked pole used as a weapon during the period. Mangled bodies lay piled against houses as men, women, and children were decapitated, hanged, run through with pikes, and even roasted alive. Before this sordid orgy came to a close, some twelve hundred prisoners perished, along with a number of their tormentors, who were killed while fighting over their victim's valuables.

Unreasonable acts in the Age of Reason.

1793: Deadly Explosion of Japanese Volcano. The volcano Unsen dominated a small island off the coast of Japan until April 1, when the volcano exploded and the remnants of the island sank beneath the sea. About fifty-three thousand people on the island were killed.

It wasn't just the Greek Islands that had their ups and downs.

1793–1794: Reign of Terror. After four years of revolt against the monarchy, the republican government of France was itself dangerously close to falling victim to the social upheaval that had brought it into being. Radical elements threatened to tear apart the faction-ridden government from within, while revolts by monarchists and invasions by foreign armies tried to reinstate the recently deposed king.

The execution of King Louis XVI on January 21, 1793, presaged the beginning of a new and disastrous phase in the revolution—the bloody Reign of Terror. Perhaps the change arose because attacks on France by foreign armies created widespread fear among the masses. Already such fears had helped spark the barbarous September Massacre in 1792, when mobs took helpless royalists from their prison cells and cold-bloodedly slaughtered them. Or perhaps the change came about because the violent passions unleashed by the revolution had finally gone beyond all reasonable control.

Whatever the reason, popular hatred and fear gave new power to radical elements in the revolutionary government. Then, in early April 1793, the Committee of Public Safety was established to try all enemies of the revolution—a loose category of people encompassing priests, aristocrats, immigrants, royalists, and former government officials.

A leading radical, Maximillien Robespierre, took over leadership of the committee in July, and thereafter the bloody Reign of Terror began in earnest. On September 5 the revolutionary government officially adopted the slogan "Let us institute terror as the order of the day." Soon the committee was empowered to try any persons suspected of opposing the revolution and to convict them without right of appeal. A Law of Suspects passed on September 17 widened the powers of the committee even further, granting such a vague definition of "suspects" that virtually anyone could be arrested.

And they were. In Paris the prisons soon overflowed with thousands of "suspects." Priests, nuns, immigrants, and aristocrats were rounded up and locked into the crowded, disease-ridden prisons. Then, to make room for more suspects, convents, churches, and hotels were confiscated and converted to prisons.

Those convicted by the tribunal were sent directly to the guillotine, set up in the center of Paris at the Place de la Revolution. A French adaptation of devices used elsewhere, the guillotine had been introduced by the revolutionary government in 1792 as a more humane means of executing criminals. Now, however, it was to become an instrument of mass extermination. Month after month the committee fed the guillotine. Suspects, convicted on even the slightest pretext, were marched to the guillotine's raised platform, where they were forced to put their necks into the machine's blood-spattered wooden yoke. The condemned suffered a last moment of terror before the whole platform rumbled at the downward slide of the guillotine's heavy steel blade.

Carts waited beside the guillotine to carry away the heads and decapitated torsos of the executed. Meanwhile, crowds of peasants and workers gathered to sing, dance, and drink while they watched the slaughter of the priests and aristocrats.

Outside of Paris, the Terror went on without the benefit of the guillotine, and in Nantes, Jean-Baptiste Carrier persecuted suspects with a ferocious zeal. Between December 1793 and January

1794, he ordered the drowning of at least two thousand. The suspects—pregnant women and children among them—were crowded into the hulls of ships that were then deliberately capsized in the Loire River, drowning everyone aboard. Guards chopped off the arms of those who tried to escape, or held the condemned underwater with boat hooks. Corpses littered the riverbanks. Soon the water became too contaminated to drink, and disease spread throughout the city, killing the tormentors as well as the tormented. Meanwhile, untold numbers died in the squalid prisons. To his credit, however, Robespierre recalled the perpetrators of these indiscriminate atrocities.

While it might seem impossible to make the Terror any harsher, a new law passed on June 10, 1794, did just that. Suspects no longer had a right to a trial, and convictions were allowed without any evidence of guilt being presented. Virtually everyone brought before a tribunal was sentenced to die.

The new system had the desired effect: There were more executions within six weeks than in all of the previous year. Executioners announced the names of prisoners about to be executed, laughing while adding the gibe "These are they who have gained prizes in the lottery of Saint Guillotine." In Paris, sixty people were guillotined per day, and residents near the Place de la Revolution in Paris had to abandon their homes because of the unbearable stench of blood. "Things go well," one official wrote. "See, the heads fall like slates."

Finally, though, the tables turned and a secret opposition to Robespierre began to develop. After using the machinery of the Terror to eliminate his opponents on the right and left in the revolutionary government, Robespierre himself was arrested and executed on July 28, 1794. No doubt to the relief of thousands. That brought a halt to the orgy of hate, but not before some seventeen thousand people had been executed. Many others among the estimated three hundred thousand to five hundred thousand people imprisoned that year died of disease and abuse in prisons.

And so the name of Robespierre goes down in history beside Caligula, Genghis Khan, and Ivan the Terrible.

1793–1804: Yellow Fever Wars. In 1793 British troops invaded the French colony of Saint Domingue (now Haiti) to quell a slave rebellion. Initially victorious against the rebels, they soon met an invisible and deadly enemy—yellow fever.

By June 1794, British soldiers were suddenly succumbing to symptoms of headache, dizziness, burning fever, and vomiting of blood. As the disease attacked the liver, bile turned the skin and eyeballs the ghastly yellow hue that gives the fever its name. Within a week, a general hemorrhage often left the victim dead.

The British gave up their war by October 1798, after some 12,700 soldiers died, mostly from yellow fever. Then, in 1802, Napoleon decided to reconquer the colony, and the whole process repeated itself. By the time the French gave up in late 1803, twenty-four thousand soldiers in the thirty-three-thousand-man French army in Saint Domingue had died, and seven thousand more men who had been sent home as invalids were likely to die. At least the wars were shortened.

Not until 1900 was the cause of yellow fever linked to mosquitoes, thereby making control of the disease possible.

1793: Yellow Fever Epidemic in Philadelphia. Fear of the terrible yellow fever epidemic caused many people in Philadelphia, Pennsylvania, to flee the city in the autumn of 1793. Thousands died before the epidemic abated later in the year.

Those mosquitoes had traveled north.

1794: Ecuadoran Volcano Erupts. About forty thousand people were killed during an eruption of the volcano Tunquraohua and a simultaneous earthquake, which combined to destroy the city of Riobemba.

1795: Copenhagen Fire. Fire broke out in the dockyards of Copenhagen, Denmark, on June 6, and high winds soon spread the flames into the most heavily populated section of the city. For forty-eight hours the disastrous fire raged, consuming the town hall, thousands of shops and homes, and three hundred gin distilleries.

Denmark's Prince Royal worked all night in the streets, directing the desperate effort to stop the blaze, but fire fighters did not finally control the blaze until they tore down all houses in its path.

When the fire was finally out, more than a third of the city lay in ashes. Over thirteen hundred buildings had been destroyed, and eighteen thousand homeless people now camped in tents in the streets. The government distributed free bread and beer to those left without a home.

Well, the gin was all gone.

1796: The White Lotus Rebellion. Faced with official persecution by the Ch'ing Dynasty, the White Lotus Society, an illegal religious sect with followers throughout China, began an open revolt in February. As the revolt spread through central China, rebels were joined by various desperate groups, including bandits practicing martial arts, smugglers, mercenaries, and peasants who were forced into fighting. Seeking to extinguish the rebellion and eliminate the rebel leaders, government troops laid waste to villages and fields, torturing and killing citizens indiscriminately.

The revolt continued for almost ten years, with rebels waging guerrilla warfare from mountain strongholds. The government countered by creating local fortresses big enough to house the peasants and store grain, thus cutting off supplies and additional recruits from the rebels. Government armies were also reinforced by local militias, and by 1805 some one hundred thousand rebels had been annihilated. Though it ultimately failed, the White Lotus Rebellion marked an important step in the decline of the Ch'ing Dynasty.

1797: Ecuadoran Earthquake. On February 4 a tremendous earthquake collapsed buildings, released avalanches, and started volcanoes erupting in a disaster that devastated five provinces. The city of Quito, Ecuador, was demolished, while whole mountains and rivers were also moved in the affected area.

Citizens of the village of Cuero may have had time to look up and see the mountainside rolling down upon them before the entire village was buried without a trace. Even as a mountain tumbled down upon the village of Masdro, the ground split open, and the houses, churches, and streets disappeared into the fissure. Only two people there survived.

Meanwhile, a flood of lava erupted from the volcano Ygulaga, sweeping away more than five villages in its searing path. The area was later described as a lake of smoldering lava.

Estimates of the dead were put at forty thousand or more.

1798: New England Blizzard. High winds and driving snow lasting from November 17 to 21 buried houses in New England under great snowdrifts. Hundreds of people died.

1799–1800: Yellow Fever Ravages Spain and North Africa. A yellow fever plague that began in April 1799 spread relentlessly across Spain and northern Africa. Moving from city to city, the epidemic lasted about two to three weeks in each place.

Everywhere it struck, at least a third of the population perished, and ironically, the strong and healthy tended to succumb first, with the weak and elderly following. During any given outbreak, the death rate surged exponentially each day, and in Fez, Morocco, up to fifteen hundred people died each day at the height of the epidemic.

Survivors had the grim job of shoveling hundreds of corpses at a time into mass graves. Whole villages were virtually wiped out; in one, only four people survived out of six hundred. One observer described the North African villages as "uninhabited ruins."

Meanwhile, so many wealthy landowners died that whole farms were left without owners. Laborers and servants suddenly found themselves in possession of land, horses, and livestock; they became known as "the inheritors."

By the time the epidemic ended in 1800, some eighty thousand Spaniards and countless thousands of North Africans had died.

1800: British Warship Sinks After Catching Fire. The frigate *Queen Charlotte* was engulfed in flames on March 17 soon after some hay stored on the deck caught fire. The seven-hundred-man crew was unable to extinguish the fire, which soon spread to the rigging and burned through the decks. Nearly all of the crew drowned when the frigate finally sank.

1805: Earthquake in Naples and Calabria. The evening of July 26 was unusually cool in Naples, Italy. Then large waves suddenly appeared on the sea. People walking in the surf and on the beach felt the odd sensation of the ground falling away beneath their feet, while fish rose to the water's surface and splashed wildly. All at once the first of several mighty tremors struck the city, ringing church bells and stopping the town clocks at precisely 9:57 P.M.

Anxious residents noticed an enormous column of smoke rising above the nearby volcano Mount Vesuvius and could hear two weak explosions within the crater. Several more shocks jolted Naples, Calabria, and surrounding towns that night, knocking down or damaging thousands of buildings. In Naples, where four thousand homes and buildings were demolished, frightened survivors spent the night on the streets or in open fields. Many inland towns and villages were completely destroyed, their inhabitants crushed beneath their collapsing homes. Some twenty-six thousand people lost their lives.

1807: Luxembourg Powder Magazine Explodes. During a storm on June 26, a lightning bolt struck a gunpowder magazine in the fortress at Luxembourg, touching off a tremendous explosion. The blast wrecked part of the city of Luxembourg and killed 230 people.

What a boon to humankind the invention of gunpowder was.

1810: Wreck of British Frigate Kills Four Hundred Ninety. The frigate *Minotaur* ran aground off Texel, Holland, in high seas on December 22 and sank in shallow water. Only 110 of the crew of 590 survived.

1811: Massacre of the Mamelukes. Mamelukes (from the Arabic word for "owned") were white male slaves who served in special units in the Ottoman Empire. Over the centuries they gained control of both the military and the government in Muslim-held Egypt. Seeking to break that control, the viceroy of Egypt, Muhammad Ali Pasha, tricked the Mamelukes into assembling at the Citadel in Cairo, and there massacred nearly five hundred of them on March 1. Others not present were hunted down and beheaded.

That's one way to get rid of the competition.

1811: Tornado Wrecks Charleston. A deadly tornado, one of the worst ever in the United States, struck Charleston, South Carolina, shortly after noon on September 10 and razed much of the city. Though the number of dead was not recorded, one estimate put the death toll at more than five hundred.

Charleston seems to have been located in the wrong place.

1811: Two Thousand British Sailors Die in Storms. A flotilla of British warships returning to England from duty in the Baltic was battered by a series of storms. Both the *Saint George* and *Defence* sank off the English coast, taking some two thousand men to the bottom with them. Strangely, parts of the ships' broken hulls came back up to the surface some time later, with the bodies of hundreds of dead sailors strewn on the decks.

They didn't lie full fathom five in this tempest.

1811–1812: New Madrid Earthquakes. A group of French settlers dancing at a lively party were probably the only people still awake in New Madrid, Missouri, late on the night of December 15. Flat-bottomed barges on their way downriver to New Orleans were moored as usual for the night, tied to trees on islands or along the banks of the Mississippi River. Suddenly the whole area was rocked by a massive earthquake, the strongest in the United States up to that time.

One observer recalled an enormous noise, like loud thunder, followed instantly by the deafening squawks of thousands of geese and other wild birds that, terrorized by the chaos, landed in large numbers on the boats moored along the river. Some birds even landed on the heads and shoulders of the frightened people on board the boats. Bright flashes of light illuminated the darkened sky, and residents raced out of their homes in fear as their houses collapsed, trees swayed and trembled, and the ground sank under them.

Fissures began to open in the ground, causing huge trees to break and fall, and swallowing dwellings and people alike. Enormous chunks of the riverbank tumbled into the Mississippi. In one area an entire graveyard slid down into it. The river churned and boiled with the violently shaking earth, while waves lashed the shore, sinking many of the boats moored there.

A young boy who watched the terrifying turmoil recalled that the land itself seemed to be moving in huge waves. The ninety-square-mile Reelfoot Lake in northwest Tennessee was created in a matter of minutes that night. The bottom of a swamp simply dropped, and water from a nearby creek rushed in to fill it. Elsewhere, earth, water, mud, rocks, and chunks of dirt blew straight up into the air with amazing force.

Although several towns near New Madrid were completely leveled by the earthquake, there were surprisingly few casualties, partly because so many people in the area lived in log cabins, which withstood a lot of shaking. (Architects take heed.) But the calamity was hardly over. Some people said that throughout that fateful winter, the land hardly ever seemed to be at rest. For almost two months the region was repeatedly shaken by shocks and quakes. One resident counted 1,874 shocks between December 16, 1811, and February 7, 1812, when the deadliest one of all occurred.

This time the town of New Madrid was completely destroyed. The massive commotion of the earth shook the Mississippi's riverbed so violently that two new waterfalls were created where none had been before. For hundreds of miles the river flowed backward for a time. Presumably part of the riverbed had been lifted high enough to send the water running northward, instead of to the south.

The devastating earthquakes that plagued New Madrid were felt over an area of 1.5 million square miles, nearly half the area of the continental United States. In Washington, D.C., windows and chandeliers rattled ominously, while in Charleston, South Carolina, the quake rang church bells.

1812: Earthquake Destroys Caracas, Venezuela. Many citizens in Caracas were in church on March 26, Holy Thursday. Without warning, a massive earthquake struck the city, its tremors collapsing three churches onto the penitent masses and killing everyone inside. Fifteen-foot-thick columns supported one of the churches, yet they could not withstand the quake. Scores of troops were killed when a giant fissure opened up and swallowed their barracks.

Within minutes, 90 percent of Caracas lay in ruins, and thousands of people were trapped and screaming for help from within the city's homes, churches, and other buildings. Rescuers freed some two thousand trapped survivors, but fifteen thousand people were killed in the city and surrounding area. In the quake's aftermath, famine and disease killed another five thousand people.

1812: Moscow Burns. From the hills outside Moscow on September 12, the French emperor Napoleon gazed with satisfaction on the beautiful and ornate city below him. Napoleon believed the conquest of Moscow would bring about the surrender of Russia, making it his greatest victory yet.

But disturbing reports began to reach the emperor: Sentries brought news that the entire city of 250,000 appeared to be almost completely deserted. "Moscow deserted! A most unlikely event!" Napoleon declared. Two days later the French troops entered the evacuated city, and Napoleon set up headquarters inside the massive palace of the Kremlin.

That did nothing to stop the disturbing reports, however. Fires were breaking out all over the deserted city. At first Napoleon blamed them on accidents or on looting by his own troops. But the fires broke out anew every time the French put them out. Soon the truth became apparent: The Russians had released prisoners and ordered them to burn the city. Count Rostopchin, governor of Moscow, posted a notice to Napoleon on his palace: "I set fire to my house, that it may not be polluted by your presence."

Napoleon, staring at the spreading flames from his vantage point at the Kremlin, could not believe the Russians would burn their greatest city. "What a people!" he exclaimed. "The barbarians! Such terrible tactics have no precedent in the history of the civilization! A demon inspires these people!"

Soon the fires were burning in every part of the city. They spread from house to house, filling the air with black smoke. Canopies of fire covered whole streets as gale-force winds whipped the flames still higher. One French witness said the city looked like "a volcano with many craters."

Surrounded by flames in the Kremlin, Napoleon still clung to hope of victory. Late in the night, by the light from the blazing city, he wrote a letter to Czar Alexander demanding Russia's surrender. But soon the Kremlin itself was burning. Napoleon watched the fire through windows that were too hot to touch.

Finally the flames forced Napoleon to give up his prize and flee with his guard through the burning streets. Count Philippe de Seguar described Napoleon's evacuation: "Only one way was open—a narrow winding street already afire from one end to the other, which seemed more like an entrance to that hell than an escape from it. But the emperor without hesitation rushed into this dangerous passage, and forced his way ahead in the roar and crackling of flames, the crash of floors and ceilings, and the fall of burning beams and red-hot sheets of iron roofing. . . . We were walking on the floor of fire, under a sky of fire, between walls of fire."

"The fires went on for six days and nights," one witness wrote, "so that it was impossible to tell night from day." While Napoleon waited outside the city, many of his soldiers risked the flames to loot the burning city. Many died when buildings collapsed on top of them. Meanwhile, Napoleon ordered the execution of anyone suspected of starting the fires. One officer described how "at every step, one trod on dead and scorched people, and the corpses of incendiaries hung from many half-burnt trees."

Rain fell on September 18, gradually extinguishing the blaze. By that time nine-tenths of the once great city had been destroyed. Only about twenty-three hundred houses still stood, and half of its two thousand churches were burned to the ground.

Staring at the ruined city on September 18, Napoleon muttered, "This presages great misfortunes for us." A month later the first snows began, and Napoleon, denied both winter quarters and a major source of supplies for his great army, began his disastrous retreat from Russia. And it wasn't to the strains of Tchaikovsky's 1812 Overture.

What price glory?

1814: Sleeping Philippine Volcano Suddenly Erupts. For thirteen years the volcano Mayon on Luzon, the Philippines, had remained silent, so that villagers had dared cultivate the fertile slopes of the once active volcano. All that changed suddenly at 8:00 A.M. on February 1, when the volcano exploded in eruption, blasting forth a thick column of burning lava, flying stones, sand, and ash.

The twenty thousand villagers in the area fled for their lives while the volcano bombarded them with hot stones and lava. Raining down for two hours, the stones piled thirty feet deep in places and crushed or seriously injured many of the fleeing villagers. People ran with tables, chairs, boards, even tea trays, held over their heads for protection. Those who took shelter in buildings were crushed or burned out as flaming cinders ignited houses and churches.

Screams were obliterated in the volcano's deafening roar, and soon a dense cloud of soot and smoke plunged the area into darkness. When the sky finally cleared at 2:00 P.M., five villages had been completely destroyed, and the ground was littered with the bodies of some twelve hundred people who had been killed.

1814: Washington, D.C., Burns. When the War of 1812 broke out between the United States and Britain, the American capital of Washington, D.C., was still a small town of some eight thousand people. The White House, the two wings of the Capitol (but not the rotunda), and some other public buildings had been constructed by this time, but the town was largely unprotected by military fortifications.

Thus, when a raiding party of some forty-five hundred British soldiers approached the city on August 24, a hastily organized militia put up only token resistance and promptly fled. Soon after, most of the residents of Washington evacuated the city with like speed, as officials set fire to stores of munitions, a frigate, and other warships at the navy yard.

The British marched unopposed into Washington that evening, and after an outraged Washingtonian shot the horse out from under the British commander, the soldiers set fire to the unfinished Capitol building by firing artillery at it. At the deserted White House, soldiers found a sumptuous banquet that President Madison had prepared to celebrate an American victory. After eating their fill, the British set fire to the building. The Treasury and State Department buildings, a barracks, storehouses, archives, and other public buildings were also burned.

The British raiders did not go completely unmolested, however. A hundred or so British soldiers were killed or wounded in an accidental explosion while setting fire to an arsenal, and several more were killed when a sudden storm collapsed buildings on them on August 25. That, and the approach of a regrouped American force, gave the British sufficient cause to leave, which they did by cover of darkness late that evening.

This is the famous incident in which Dolley Madison didn't get to eat her ice cream but did save the presidents' portraits from being torched.

1815: Indonesian Volcano Explodes. Until April 15, 1815, the Indonesian volcano Tambora had been thought to be extinct, and soldiers at British forts in Indonesia mistook the volcano's first deep rumblings for distant cannon fire. Soon, however, it became clear Tambora had come to life. Great volumes of ash spewed out of the thirteen-thousand-foot peak and plunged the area into utter darkness for days.

Then, on April 11, the volcano exploded and spewed out some thirty-six cubic miles of ejecta—the largest volume in history. The blast also created a tremendous whirlwind that sucked up people, livestock, and houses. Meanwhile, a tidal wave slammed into coastal areas, adding to the destruction.

When the cataclysmic eruption was finally over, Tambora had blown away four thousand feet of its cone, and some twelve thousand people living around the volcano had been killed. Ash from the volcano wiped out crops in the surrounding area, causing a famine. An estimated eighty-two thousand people later died of starvation and disease. This eruption is believed to have caused the infamous "year without a summer" of 1816, when unusually cold weather brought famine to North America and Europe.

Never, never trust a sleeping volcano. Or an extinct one.

1816: Year Without a Summer. On the morning of June 6, snow began falling in the northeastern United States. The snowfall amounted to twenty inches in some places, with flakes as large as two inches across. The blizzard and killing frost that persisted for five days ruined crops, forcing farmers to plow fields under and replant. But in July, and again in August, and yet again in September, the snow and frost returned.

No one could understand what one diarist called "the most gloomy and extraordinary weather ever seen" in which snowfalls colored red, blue, and brown had fallen, and the sky was obscured by a dusty haze. The only thing certain was that crops had failed miserably, and hunger and famine loomed ahead. By winter, people grubbed for wild onions, and ate pigeons and groundhogs to survive.

Meanwhile, all across Europe the cold weather devastated crops. In the Loire Valley of France, rioting mobs, furious at the excessively high price of grain, attacked grain carts on the way to market. In East Anglia, England, citizens brandishing sticks and iron spikes and carrying banners that read "Bread or Blood" looted and vandalized their way through several towns. In Dundee, Scotland, a grain dealer's home was looted and burned by a frenzied mob. By the spring of 1817, people in Switzerland were reduced to catching stray cats for food. Sickness and fever accompanied the starvation, and in Ireland an estimated fifty thousand people eventually died as a result of a typhus epidemic precipitated by the harsh famine.

It was not until 1920 that the unusual weather was linked to the 1815 eruption of Mount Tambora, a volcano on the other side of the world in Java. Scientists concluded that the volcano blasted up into the stratosphere huge quantities of fine dust particles, which remained suspended there for years and reduced the amount of warming sunlight able to reach the earth's surface. The opposite of the greenhouse effect.

We are forever at the mercy of untamed nature.

1819: Earthquake in Italy Kills Twenty Thousand. The cities of Genoa and Palermo, Italy, were demolished by a massive quake in late August. Thousands of people were buried in the rubble of collapsed buildings.

1820: Manila Massacre. A mob of native Filipinos, which at one point reached ten thousand to fifteen thousand in number, went on a bloody rampage in Manila from March 9 to 11. Apparently incited to riot by the Spanish, the Filipinos attacked and brutally murdered about 125 foreigners before the mob was dispersed.

1822: Aleppo Earthquake. A violent earthquake, lasting for ten or twelve seconds, struck the Syrian cities of Aleppo and Antioch and their surrounding areas at 9:30 P.M. on August 10. Many houses and large buildings collapsed, crushing or trapping the terrified occupants.

The deadly tremors devastated a third of the villages and cities in Syria. In all, some twenty thousand people died, and an equal number were injured. Survivors were further terrified by continuing aftershocks that occurred for the next two months. By then, countless thousands of villagers and farmers faced the grim prospect of winter's onset without homes or sufficient shelter.

1822: Deadly Cyclone in India. In June about fifty thousand people living near the mouth of the Ganges River were killed when a powerful cyclone struck the region.

1822: Eruption of Galung Gung. Some four thousand people were killed and one hundred villages were destroyed in Java when the volcano Galung Gung erupted twice, first with a torrent of boiling mud on October 8, and then with a massive explosion on October 12 which blew away the top of the volcano.

On the Pacific Ocean floor there are approximately ten thousand volcanoes about three thousand feet high. Most are extinct. There are about five hundred active volcanoes in the world. About 5 percent erupt in any given year. The Pacific is still a hotbed of activity.

1824: Barrackpore Mutiny. The Indian soldiers of the British Forty-seventh Regiment of Native Infantry recognized two different imperatives: those of the caste system that had dominated life in India for many centuries, and those of the British army. In addition, the soldiers had a number of grievances against the British, not the least of which was that the British were offering camp followers more pay than the soldiers themselves.

Matters came to a head on November 1, when the British commander ordered Indians in the regiment to carry their own supplies for a long march because pack animals were not available. But caste system taboos forbade the soldiers to do so, and when the British colonel arrived at the assembly area, he found only a few soldiers present.

Defying orders, the soldiers had stayed behind, with knapsacks off and their muskets loaded. They chased away the colonel and the officers of the regiment, and later that day, more Indian soldiers joined the mutiny. Meanwhile, the British brought in artillery and reinforcements.

Next morning at dawn, the British opened fire with the cannons. About a hundred of the mutineers were killed, and of the many prisoners taken, twelve who were deemed to be the leaders were hanged. The rest were sentenced to fourteen years at hard labor. The army erased the regiment's name from the army list, but the Indians' resentment was not to be dispensed with so easily. In fact, the brief revolt proved to be a harbinger of the bloody Sepoy Mutiny of 1857–58.

The British government did reprimand the military authorities for their rigidity. The Indians would get their revenge later.

1824: Cairo Fire. In the early afternoon of March 21, a relatively harmless fire began at a military barracks located in the old fortified Citadel at Cairo, Egypt, but the flames soon spread to a nearby arsenal where munitions were stored. The first explosion of gunpowder chests an hour or two later leveled surrounding buildings in the Citadel and helped spread the fire farther. Residents of the area fled in panic through the city's narrow streets. Later that day two other explosions shook Cairo, but it was not until the next day that the fire seriously threatened the main powder magazine, which contained enough powder to blow up the entire city. Troops battling the blaze thus narrowly averted a major disaster when they succeeded in keeping the flames from the magazine. Nevertheless, the fire destroyed most all the buildings in the old Citadel and killed some four thousand horses, mules, and camels.

1824: Ten Thousand Drown in Saint Petersburg, Russia. A furious gale on November 19 caused the Neva River to spill over its banks, flooding the Russian city of Saint Petersburg with amazing speed. While the storm continued to rage, rapidly rising waters overtook people in the city's low-lying areas before they could escape.

In just a few hours, Saint Petersburg was inundated by floodwaters one story high. Struggling to survive, the hapless citizens watched their homes, livestock, and businesses float away. A whole regiment of soldiers was lost when their barracks were completely covered by the rising waters.

Although the waters receded just eight hours after the flood began, some ten thousand people had lost their lives, and property losses were enormous. Perhaps the worst news, however, was that nearly all stores of food for the coming winter had been destroyed. Saint Petersburg's agony had just begun.

1825: New Brunswick Fire. In early October a fire of unknown origins began deep in the vast woods of the Canadian province of New Brunswick. A long season of drought had baked the forests as dry as tinder, and the fire spread relentlessly. Heat and smoke from the advancing flames eventually reached the town of Fredericton, but no one even guessed the extent of the blaze then. Finally heavy winds swept through the area on October 7, carrying torrents of burning cinders and driving flames into the towns of Fredericton and Newcastle.

Houses were instantly incinerated, killing many people in their beds. Those fortunate enough to have time to escape fled onto the Saint John River in boats, canoes, and log rafts. There they were pelted by windblown cinders, and some boats burned on the river. Meanwhile, the night sky was lit with the reflection of fires extending for miles into the distance.

Before the fire finally burned out, the smoke burned the eyes and lungs of people as far away as Montreal and even Baltimore. Some 160 people died in the flames, and four million acres of forest were destroyed.

1826–1837: Cholera Epidemics Ravage Europe. A painter of pottery had the dubious distinction of becoming the first person in Britain known to have contracted cholera. He suffered with vomiting, chills, fever, and diarrhea. His face was covered with cold sweat, and his lips were blue, while his voice and pulse became so weak as to be almost imperceptible. Amazingly, he recovered, but a few days later another worker in the same area collapsed with identical symptons and died.

Doctors called the quickly spreading malady "summer diarrhea." Actually, it was just the beginning in Britain of what became a devastating cholera epidemic throughout Europe. Millions in Britain and other European nations eventually died of the disease.

Cholera had been an ever-present threat in India since the fifth century. But until the early nineteenth century, this intestinal scourge had largely been confined there. The increase of trade and contacts with other countries slowly began to spread it in epidemic outbreaks, first in Asia, then in Europe and the rest of the world. Some nine hundred thousand Europeans died of it in 1831 alone. Renewed, worldwide cholera epidemics in 1840–42, 1863–75, and 1893–94 killed millions more.

Cholera recurs annually in India.

1826: Massacre of the Janissaries. The Janissaries, members of the Turkish sultan's five-centuries-old elite guard, had become a dangerous and unruly force in the empire of the Ottoman Turks. Resisting the sultan's attempts to introduce Western army formations and drilling, the Janissaries finally broke into open revolt. On June 10 some twenty thousand gathered at the Atmeidan, a square in Constantinople, and soon after, began looting and rioting.

Sultan Mahmud II, alarmed at the ruthless power wielded by the Janissaries, had been looking for an occasion to get rid of them. The time had come. The sultan surrounded the Atmeidan with sixty thousand loyal soldiers and began firing grapeshot into the encircled hordes of rebels. Many of the Janissaries fled to a nearby barracks, but the sultan's relentless forces set fire to it while also peppering the burning building with grapeshot. In following days, other Janissaries who had escaped were hunted down and beheaded. In the capital alone, well over twenty thousand of them were killed.

1829: Broken Dike Floods Danzig (Gdansk), Poland. The Vistula River, clogged by vast chunks of snow and ice, ripped apart dikes near Danzig (Gdansk) on April 9. Floodwaters poured into the low-lying city and surrounding pastureland. Within hours houses were flooded to their roofs as waters rose five feet above the top of the dike.

A great wave of water broke through the dike and rushed through the poorest section of Danzig, crushing everything in its path and carrying away entire houses. Hundreds of survivors in Danzig managed to climb to roofs or onto church steeples, where they clung desperately for days, without food, waiting for rescue boats to arrive. As waters began subsiding by the fourteenth, a heavy snowstorm hampered rescue efforts.

About four thousand houses were flooded, and ten thousand cattle drowned. Some twelve hundred people died in the floods.

1830: The July Revolution in France. On the morning of Monday, July 26, the Parisian newspaper *Moniteur* announced in print that the French king, Charles X, had made some major changes in the country's government. Contrary to the constitution, he had suspended the liberty of the press, dissolved a newly elected government chamber, and restructured the French election system, giving greatest power to his own ministers.

It took a while for the news to spread through the city, but soon anxious groups of people began to collect on Paris streets. Some began to throw stones through windows of government offices. By afternoon, the editors of newspapers and journals issued a public statement: "Legal government is interrupted, and that of force has commenced. In the situation in which we are placed, obedience ceases to be a duty. . . ."

The next day, police began to seize and smash the journalists' presses. Violence broke out, and the streets of Paris were quickly filled with angry and unruly mobs. Some thirty thousand printing workers and factory laborers who had been dismissed from work swelled the unmanageable crowds. French soldiers took to the streets and tried to keep order, but were enormously outnumbered by the defiant French citizens. By July 29 the soldiers had fled from Paris, and the city was left entirely in the control of its triumphant citizens.

Some two thousand people were wounded in the insurrection, and another one thousand lost their lives. King Charles was forced to flee the country, and when he abdicated, Louis Philippe was proclaimed the new king of France.

Charles obviously didn't know the term *constitutional monarchy*.

1831: Hurricane Devastates Barbados. A hurricane lashed the island of Barbados on August 10 and 11, killing about fifteen hundred people and causing more than $7.5 million in damages.

1832: Bad Axe Massacre. Hundreds of Sac and Fox Indians, evicted from ancestral lands in Illinois by white settlers, were massacred by army soldiers and other whites on the banks of the Bad Axe River, close to the point at which it empties into the Mississippi River, some twenty miles south of La Crosse, Wisconsin. Led by Chief Black Hawk, the Indians were trying to escape across the Mississippi when whites began shooting them, killing even women and children. The state of Wisconsin formally apologized for the massacre in 1990.

Too little and too late.

1833: Fifty Thousand Die in Calcutta Cyclone. A deadly cyclone consumed Calcutta and the surrounding area in May, wiping out three hundred villages and killing tens of thousands of people.

1833: Two Passengers Die in Train Wreck. In what is the earliest recorded train wreck involving the deaths of passengers, a Camden & Amboy train derailed and crashed at twenty miles per hour near Hightstown, New Jersey, on November 8. Two people were killed, and twenty-four others were injured, including Cornelius Vanderbilt, who suffered a broken leg. Vanderbilt subsequently refused to ride a train for the next thirty years because of the incident, then relented and organized the New York Central Railroad. Former U.S. President John Quincy Adams was also on the wrecked train, but escaped unhurt.

A new mode of transportation; a new method of killing ourselves.

1834: Fire in British Parliament. At 6:30 P.M. on October 16 a fire broke out near the entrance to the Houses of Parliament in London, and within a half hour the two houses were engulfed in flames. Among the irreplaceable items lost in the blaze was the original warrant for the execution of King Charles I.

1835: Darwin Witnesses Chilean Earthquake. On February 20 the naturalist Charles Darwin, ashore while his ship HMS *Beagle* was anchored off the Chilean coast, lay down to rest in an apple orchard. Suddenly the ground beneath him began to shake. Staggering to his feet, he could barely stand up, and later described the feeling that "the world, the very emblem of all that is solid, had moved beneath our feet like a crust over a fluid."

Even so, Darwin had yet to realize the awesome destructive power of the earthquake. Later he saw that the port of Talcahuano looked "as if a thousand great ships had been wrecked." Battered ships and their cargoes, roofs of houses, and other debris lay piled on the shore, and the town itself had been wrecked by the earthquake and tidal waves.

The inland town of Concepcion was flattened within six seconds by the quake, as the ground buckled and tossed like a wild sea, and entire blocks of houses collapsed. Overall, some five thousand persons died in the calamity. Darwin, though horrified by the carnage, nevertheless used the experience of the earthquake to speculate on a theory of the origin of continents.

Never let an opportunity pass.

1836: The Fall of the Alamo. In 1835 American settlers living in what later became the state of Texas rebelled against the

Mexican government, then in control of the territory. Organizing a provisional government, the rebels named Sam Houston as leader of their small army and began their fight for independence against the far superior Mexican army, led by General Antonio Santa Anna.

The Alamo, a Franciscan mission at San Antonio, Texas, soon became a symbol of the Americans' determination to win their independence. Manned by a small force that included renowned frontiersmen Jim Bowie and Davy Crockett, the Alamo was surrounded by Santa Anna's four-thousand-man army on February 23. Major William Travis, in command at the Alamo, appealed to Sam Houston for reinforcements, but only a handful of volunteers managed to slip through Mexican lines. On March 3, before the actual fighting for the Alamo began, Major Travis informed his tiny force of just over 180 men that there would be no reinforcements, and offered them a chance to leave. Only one man took him up on the offer.

The Mexicans began their attack at night on March 5. Twice the Alamo defenders bravely turned back charges by the overwhelming Mexican force. But on March 6 the Mexicans successfully stormed the Alamo's northern wall, and within a few hours, had killed all but five of the Alamo's defenders.

Santa Anna had paid a terrible price for the victory, however. He lost over fifteen hundred men and squandered ten days time in defeating the Alamo. Perhaps that was why he let his soldiers slaughter the last five Americans, and why he allowed the bodies of the dead to be mutilated and burned.

The heroic stand of the doomed rebels was not destined to be forgotten, however. Confronting a larger Mexican force at the Battle of San Jacinto in April 1836, Sam Houston rallied his troops with the now famous cry "Remember the Alamo!" The Americans' victory in that battle secured the independence of Texas.

The fate of the one man who left the Alamo is not known.

1836: Theater Fire Kills Seven Hundred in Russia. The Lehman Theater in Saint Petersburg caught fire during a performance on December 30. Hundreds of theatergoers were trapped in the blazing building.

1837: Mississippi Steamboat Collision. On October 31 the side-wheel steamer *Monmouth* collided with the *Tremont* on the Mississippi River near Profit Island. Three hundred people were killed in the accident.

Fulton's invention gave us a new method of navigation, both romantic and, at least here, dangerous.

1840: Natchez Tornado. About 2:00 P.M. on May 7, a fierce wind came up from the southwest as a dark cloud approached the riverfront town of Natchez, Mississippi. Another cloud formation moved from the opposite direction, and the collision of the two fronts at Natchez apparently unleashed both a tornado and torrential rains, which amounted to nine inches before the storm ended. Tornado winds ripped through Natchez, peeling off roofs and crushing whole buildings. The air became a whirling mass of shingles, bricks, timbers, and even heavy ox carts, scattering debris from wrecked buildings everywhere. Meanwhile, out on the Mississippi River, the tornado tore away the superstructure of one steamboat and capsized another, with great loss of life. The Natchez ferry and sixty other flatboats were also sunk. In all, the tornado killed 317 people at Natchez, many of them by drowning in the Mississippi.

1841: Erie Steamboat Fire. The steamboat *Erie* left Buffalo, New York, for Chicago on August 9 with a fresh coat of paint and varnish on the outside. But inside in its boiler room a disaster was waiting to happen: Containers of inflammable turpentine had been stowed there, close to the hot boilers. When the turpentine finally exploded, the ship's fresh paint and varnish caught fire immediately, spreading the flames in all directions like traces of gunpowder. The ship's 250-plus passengers desperately tried to escape as the fire engulfed the steamboat. Well over a hundred immigrant passengers crowding the ship's steerage section were probably trapped there and burned alive. Lifeboats were swamped as other, now hysterical passengers on deck overloaded them. Some of these people were drawn into the still-turning paddle wheels. Others jumped straight into the choppy waters and survived by clinging to pieces of floating debris until help arrived. By then, however, the disaster had killed some 242 people.

1841: Hurricane Wipes Out Saint Jo, Florida. A hurricane annihilated Saint Jo (near modern Apalachicola) in September, leveling all the buildings and killing four thousand people.

Saint Jo is no longer on the map.

1842: Train Crash Near Versailles, France. On May 8 a train filled with dignitaries who had attended the king's fete at Versailles was returning to Paris when an axle broke on the locomotive. The engine and the passenger carriages overturned, and the wooden passenger cars quickly caught fire. Over fifty people were killed in the wreck, many of them burned alive in the carriages.

1842: Tornado Again Ravages Natchez. For the second time in two years, Natchez, Mississippi, was hit by a deadly tornado. The twister killed some five hundred people when it landed on June 16, but property damage was much less than the disaster of 1840.

1845–1848: Irish Potato Famine. Nearly half of Ireland's eight million people were small tenant farmers who depended on the potato crop for their food. A one-acre plot of potatoes was enough to feed a family of four; grain and other crops had to be exported to pay the rent on the farm. But in 1845 a strange new blight caused the potatoes to rot in the ground. Four years of terrible famine had begun.

Millions went hungry as the blight devastated the 1845 crop. In 1846 hopes for a good harvest that would save the people suddenly ended when the plants blackened and withered to the ground overnight. The smell of rotting potatoes spread despair throughout Ireland. Women sobbed in the fields as they realized another year of hunger lay before them.

With the spring harvest completely destroyed, the poor farmers were left with nothing to eat. Millions wasted away from hunger and disease. To make matters worse, the winter of 1846–47 turned out to be brutally cold. Gaunt, starving women wandered through the streets, begging for food. Families with nothing else to eat gnawed on weeds. Landlords evicted thousands of starving families who could not afford to pay their rent.

In Skibbereen, one witness described looking into a hovel

where "six famished and ghastly skeletons, to all appearances dead, were huddled in a corner on some filthy straw, their sole covering what seems a ragged horsecloth, their wretched legs hanging about, naked above the knees. I approached in horror, and found by a low moaning they were alive."

The nation was so ravaged by hunger, disease, and cold that only about one-eighth of the usual crop was sown in 1847. The harvest of 1848 again was disastrous. Weakened by starvation, the people succumbed to epidemics of cholera and typhus. One witness described Ireland as "one mass of famine, disease, and death." Emaciated women wandered through the streets, carrying corpses of children in their arms, begging for the money to buy a coffin.

Help from the British government was slow in coming, and what arrived was not nearly enough. Rather than subsidize food supplies for the starving, the government enacted a scheme to put the hungry to work building roads and canals. But the pay was too little; food prices were generally high because of bad harvests throughout Europe. Meanwhile, exports of grain continued throughout the crisis; the peasants needed the sales of grain to pay their rents.

Scattered rebellions broke out across Ireland. Some looted corn storage bins or broke into bakeries. A few of the starving got themselves arrested so that they could be fed in jail. All who could afford passage left Ireland for Canada or the United States, but the squalid conditions aboard emigrant ships killed thousands en route. Altogether a million and a half people fled Ireland during the famine.

By the time the potato harvest recovered in 1849, Ireland had lost more than a quarter of its population to emigration or death. An estimated one and a half million people had died from starvation, exposure following eviction, or disease caused by the famine.

Another example of man's inhumanity to man in the face of profound tragedy.

1845: Quebec Fire. On May 28 a ferocious wind spread a fire from a tannery throughout much of the lower section of Quebec, Canada. About fifteen hundred buildings were destroyed, and some lives were lost, though no figures are available.

1845: Chinese Theater Burns. About 1,670 people were killed when a theater in Canton, China, caught fire in May.

1845: Fire Ravages New York City. On July 14 a terrible fire that began at 3:00 A.M. in New York City lit the early morning sky. Originating on New Street, it spread to a building filled with a large amount of saltpeter, used in making gunpowder. People throughout the entire city then heard the tremendous roar of the exploding saltpeter, while the blast set fire to buildings up to one hundred feet away.

Fires now raged through the city streets, sending up clouds of smoke, cinders, and sparks. Fire fighters doggedly fought the flames and finally managed to contain the blaze at about 1:00 P.M. In the ten hours since the fire had started, over one thousand buildings and property worth ten million dollars had been destroyed, and an unknown number of persons killed. New York, however, was to have little respite: Five months later, on December 16, yet another major fire struck the city.

It got people thinking about the need for a real good fire department.

1846: Donner Party. On October 28 ninety pioneers bound for California found themselves trapped by heavy snow near Truckee Lake (now Donner Lake) in the Sierra Nevada Mountains. As food supplies dwindled, the party was forced to slaughter their cattle, horses, and even their dogs, for food.

On December 16 a party of seventeen set out from the camp to cross the mountains and find help. After several had died of starvation and the others resorted to cannibalism, the seven survivors staggered into an Indian camp in mid-January and reported the plight of the others at Truckee Lake.

Meanwhile, the pioneers back at Truckee Lake were reduced to eating boiled rawhide. The bodies of the dead littered the camp, because the survivors were too weak to bury them. At least one man resorted to eating the frozen bodies.

Only forty-eight members of the original Donner party finally reached the safety of Sutter's Fort in California. Forty-two had starved to death.

This way across the mountains is now called the Donner Pass. Don't take it in winter.

1847: Japanese Earthquake. A massive earthquake struck the Japanese city of Nagano, located in the northern part of the island of Honshu. About thirty-four thousand people lost their lives.

Mother Nature altering the Pacific again.

1848: French February Revolution. For days there had been a tense standoff in the streets of Paris between angry crowds demanding government reforms and soldiers loyal to the government of King Louis Philippe. Then, at 9:00 P.M. on February 23, a mysterious explosion occurred outside the Foreign Office.

The soldiers, thinking they had been attacked, opened fire on the crowd, and a number of demonstrators were killed or injured, while still others were trampled in the mad rush to flee the gunfire. When the shooting stopped, demonstrators loaded the dead into a cart and paraded about the city, calling for vengeance. That night, street barricades went up throughout the city as the angry demonstration became an open revolt.

The next morning the army was given orders to shoot rebels, but later that day the Tuileries palace came under rebel gunfire, and the king decided to surrender. As he delivered his abdication in the Palais Royale, the mob broke in, and after clambering about in a wild rampage, finally drove the royal family and ministers away. Both the Tuileries and the Palais Royale were sacked the next day, while in the provinces outside Paris, mobs stripped and burned chateaus, demolished bridges and railway stations, and tore up rails from the tracks.

Following the king's abdication, the short-lived French Second Republic was instituted. Unrest during the early months culminated in a workers' revolt and bloody street rioting during May 1848, before the government finally established order.

These French do love their revolutions.

1848: Incredible Tale of the Omega. The British emigrant ship *Omega,* with 345 passengers and crew aboard, lost her masts in a severe storm in the Atlantic in February. In danger of foundering, the *Omega* transferred nearly all her passengers and crew to three passing vessels. One of those vessels subsequently sank in heavy seas, taking 115 people to their deaths. A shortage of water resulted in the deaths of seventy other "rescued" passengers. The *Omega,* meanwhile, returned safely to port.

The captain no doubt remembered the phrase "Don't give up the ship."

1848: Great Fire in Constantinople. Flames spread rapidly through a fruit bazaar in Constantinople, the capital of the Ottoman Empire, and eventually destroyed about twenty-five hundred shops. Some two hundred people died in the blaze.

1849: Steamboats Burn in Saint Louis Fire. Fire swept through the downtown district of Saint Louis, Missouri, on May 17, destroying fifteen city blocks, the city docks along the Mississippi, and twenty-seven steamboats moored there.

1850–1864: Taiping Rebellion Kills Millions. After reading Protestant tracts distributed by missionaries, Hung Hsiu-ch'uan claimed to have a vision in which God revealed to him that he was the younger brother of Jesus Christ and was destined to save the world. After several years of preaching, Hung began to put his vision into action.

In 1847 his followers formed the God Worshipers Society, a religious and military movement. Hung taught a religion made up of a peculiar blend of Old Testament Christianity and Confucianism, calling for a joint ownership of property, equality between men and women, redistribution of land and wealth, and a strict morality that forbade gambling, alcohol, tobacco, opium, and all forms of luxury.

Within three years Hung's movement had attracted some thirty thousand devoted followers, among them peasants, miners, unemployed boatmen, bandits, and others disaffected with the Ch'ing regime. In 1850 Hung declared the founding of a new dynasty of Great Peace (T'ai P'ing) and called himself the Heavenly King of the Heavenly Kingdom. The bloody Taiping Rebellion had begun.

In July 1850 the rebels began taking control in Kwangsi province. Village after village fell to the rebellion, and by the beginning of 1853, rebels had conquered the provincial capital of Hupeh. With each success, Hung's armies grew, soon swelling to more than a million fanatically devoted soldiers. In March 1853 the triumphant rebels sailed down the Yangtze River aboard a massive armada to Nanking, the second largest city of the empire, conquering the city and renaming it "The Capital of Heaven."

Suddenly it appeared the Ch'ing Dynasty itself might collapse. If Hung had attacked Beijing and Shanghai immediately, that might well have happened. Instead, he remained in Nanking to celebrate victory. Not long thereafter, a small expeditionary force was defeated before reaching Beijing.

For three more years the Taiping Rebellion raged throughout China. Six hundred walled cities fell to the rebels, and sixteen of China's eighteen provinces suffered invasions. Hung's troops looted their conquests with abandon, destroying temples, pagodas, and countless religious treasures.

The rebels ultimately managed to alienate Confucians, thus undercutting their attempts to win sympathy throughout China. Hung also failed to set up an orderly system of government within the provinces he had conquered. Meanwhile, internal dissent within the movement was also getting out of hand. Hung's chief supporter, Yang Hsiu-ch'ing, began claiming to have visions in which God spoke directly to him. In 1856 Hung finally had Yang assassinated by Wei Ch'ang-hui, a king serving him in the north. But Wei slaughtered thousands of Yang's supporters as well as Yang, and Hung was forced to order Wei's assassination.

Then came a disastrous defeat in 1860 when the rebels tried to conquer Shanghai, and by July 1864 their armies were driven to surrender at Nanking. Hung, faced with defeat, committed suicide, and nearly one hundred thousand of his troops did so as well in a bloody end to the rebellion. In all, the fourteen-year revolt claimed a total of about twenty million lives throughout China. The rebellion severely weakened the Ch'ing Dynasty, and Chinese Communists today look to the rebellion as a forerunner of their own.

All this carnage in the name of Great Peace. A case of too many people having visions. Maybe they were really delusions of grandeur.

1850: Coastal Steamboat Sinks. The Irish steamer *Royal Adelaide* foundered in heavy seas off the coast at Margate, England, on March 29, drowning some two hundred passengers and crew.

1851–1855: Tuberculosis Epidemic in Britain. About 250,000 people died in Britain during a five-year outbreak of tuberculosis.

1851: Fire in the Congressional Library. It was a quiet Christmas Eve until a watchman in Washington, D.C., noticed smoke coming from the windows of the Congressional Library in the Capitol building. Help was summoned, and a group of men went to investigate. Upon entering, they found a small fire on the opposite side of the room.

Up to that point, it could have easily been extinguished, but by opening the door, the men let in a draft of fresh air that sent flames shooting up the shelves of books and across the balconies that lined the upper story of the huge room. Firemen arrived, but the weather was so cold that their hoses were frozen, and had to be thawed out.

Meanwhile, flames raced through the library, consuming irreplaceable books, archives, and artworks. An original portrait of Columbus, Stuart's portraits of the first five presidents, statues of Washington, Jefferson, and Lafayette, were all destroyed before the blaze could be controlled. All thirty-five thousand of the valuable books in the main library were completely destroyed, but one particularly important piece of paper—the original Declaration of Independence—was saved.

1851: San Francisco Fire. Most residents of San Francisco were at home at 11:00 P.M. on May 3 when a small fire broke out in a paint shop in Portsmouth Square. In minutes fire enveloped the front of the building. Nearby structures, like most others in the city, were built of wood, all tinder-dry, and to make matters worse, a breeze sprang up.

Firemen responded quickly, but the wind-borne blaze spread out of control, and soon entire neighborhoods exploded into flames. Tens of thousands of terrified residents raced from their homes, sometimes only just ahead of the advancing fire.

The fire continued for two days, stopping only when it reached the harbor. Even there, dock workers frantically chopped away burning wharves and piers to protect ships at their moorings. When the fire finally burned itself out, it had claimed thirty lives and done more than $3.5 million in damages.

It won't be the last catastrophe to hit San Francisco.

1852: *Birkenhead* Sinks Off Cape Town. On February 26 the *Birkenhead,* a British frigate powered by steam-driven paddle wheels, ran aground and sank at Danger Point, near Cape Town (in modern South Africa). Four hundred fifty-five of the 630 soldiers and crewmen aboard the ship perished.

Evidently the captain's charts were not altogether accurate.

1852: Fire Hits Montreal. A blaze broke out in a poor section of Montreal, Canada, on July 9 and quickly spread through the city. Before the blaze was extinguished, about eleven hundred buildings were destroyed and some fifteen thousand people were left homeless. No deaths were reported.

1853: Norwalk River Bridge Railroad Accident. A New York and New Haven Line express train failed to heed a warning signal and sped onto an open drawbridge on May 6, sending the locomotive and four cars tumbling into the Norwalk River near South Norwalk, Connecticut. Forty-six passengers were injured in what was the worst U.S. railroad accident of that time.

It sure surprised the engineer.

1854: City of Glasgow Disappears at Sea. The steamship *City of Glasgow* departed from Liverpool on March 1, bound for Philadelphia with 373 people aboard. The steamer and all aboard disappeared without a trace sometime during the Atlantic crossing.

1854: Charge of the Light Brigade. During the siege of Sebastopol in the Crimean War, an overzealous British captain apparently misinterpreted his orders on purpose. As a result, the British Light Brigade, consisting at that point of 607 horsemen armed only with swords, were ordered on October 25 to attack a far superior Russian force made up of six divisions of cavalry, six battalions of infantry, and thirty cannon.

Without hesitation, the Light Brigade ranged themselves in two lines and began to advance, quickening their pace as they drew closer to the enemy. The Russians opened up with thirty cannons when the British were still twelve hundred yards away. The furious volleys failed to stop the Light Brigade; the cavalrymen only closed their ranks as comrades fell wounded and dead.

At last reaching the line of artillery, the cavalrymen hacked down the gunners where they stood or drove them away, then charged through a column of Russian infantry and scattered them.

Meanwhile, Russian guns mounted on hills opened fire from above, and Russian lancers attacked from the flank. Their sabers flashing furiously, the British attempted to cut their way through the enemy forces, and were about to succeed when the Russians began firing grapeshot and canisters into the melee, killing both their own men and the British cavalry.

Of the 607 members of the Light Brigade, only 198 made it back to their own lines, just twenty-five minutes after the calamitous charge began. The battle was later celebrated in Tennyson's "Charge of the Light Brigade," thus bringing immortality to the gallant men who followed an arrogant captain's orders.

1855: Clipper Ship Sinks in Ice Field. The *Guiding Star,* a clipper ship carrying 480 passengers and crew on an Atlantic crossing, sailed into a massive ice field on January 9 and disappeared.

These icebergs will prove to be very hazardous to the health of transatlantic passengers.

1856: Deadly Gunpowder Magazine Explosion. On April 3 a lightning bolt struck the Church of Saint John on the island of Rhodes. The church, used by the occupying Ottoman army to store huge quantities of gunpowder, blew up in a tremendous explosion that killed about four thousand people.

We've heard this gunpowder story before.

1857: Earthquake and Fire Ravage Tokyo. On March 21 a violent earthquake shook the Japanese city of Tokyo and the surrounding region. The quake itself killed thousands, but that was only the beginning of the destruction that struck the sprawling metropolis.

Fires broke out soon after the earthquake and began spreading among the highly flammable paper and wood homes in which most Japanese lived. Sixty-mile-per-hour winds suddenly began whipping the fires into fast-moving walls of flame. Fire killed nearly all the 107,000 people who died in this disaster.

1857: The Sepoy Mutiny. One hundred years after the British established their supremacy in India, dissatisfaction with colonial rule had become widespread, especially among the British army's native troops, known as sepoys. Offended by the British army's introduction of cow and pig fat to grease rifle cartridges, Bengali soldiers at the British garrison at Meerut finally rebelled on May 10 and seized Delhi. The mutiny spread quickly, soon involving some eighty thousand native soldiers and the general populace as well.

Many British officers and their families were slaughtered by the rebels. In one case, more than two hundred British women and children were assembled in a house and brutally hacked to death. The bodies were dismembered and mutilated before being tossed into a well.

The British moved to send in reinforcements, but travel from England was slow. Soldiers on route to China were detoured to India. Others were sent from England in ships, on the long voyage around the Cape of Good Hope. Thus it was not until 1858 that the British succeeded in putting down the rebellion. Soon after, the British government took direct control of government in India, ending rule by the British East India Company.

The revolt was the result of a clash of social and religious systems—the British instituting reforms in their own rigid way, and the Hindus, particularly the higher castes, resisting. They, of course, had the most to lose.

1857: The Tragic Fate of the *Central America*. A furious hurricane wracked the side-wheel steamer *Central America* one day after it left Havana, Cuba, for New York City on September 8. The ship's 474 passengers included many miners returning from the California gold fields by way of Panama. There were some three tons of gold bars and coins aboard worth up to a billion dollars today.

Serious troubles began when the ship started filling with water from a leak in the hull and from waves crashing over the decks. Passengers and crew bailed all night, but it was not enough. The ship's engine eventually failed, and she drifted helplessly for four days while the storm raged.

Finally, on September 12, women and children were put aboard lifeboats for transfer to a nearby ship. Just as the last lifeboat left, an enormous wave crashed over the ship, sending it spinning down to the bottom about 160 miles off the South Carolina coast. Lightning flashes revealed scores of survivors struggling for their lives in the dark, violent sea, but only 153 of the 575 passengers and crew aboard the ship were saved.

The hoard of gold aboard the *Central America* attracted the attention of treasure hunters, naturally, but the sunken wreck under a mile and a half of water was not located until 1987, whereupon ownership of salvage rights became tangled in legal claims of insurance companies, salvage groups, and others. It was not until 1990 that a federal judge awarded the gold to the salvage group that had discovered the sunken treasure.

1857: Russian Warship Sinks in Storm. The eighty-four-gun Russian warship *Leffort* sank in a storm in the Gulf of Finland on September 23, taking 826 crewmen and passengers to the bottom.

1858: Fire Wrecks London Docks. Apparently caused by the spontaneous combustion of material stored in warehouses, a great fire broke out in the London docks on June 29. Flames spread to a number of adjoining warehouses, one of which exploded after saltpeter inside it ignited. Some two million dollars in damages was reported.

1858: Fire Aboard Passenger Liner. The *Austria,* a Hamburg-America liner making a North Atlantic crossing to Halifax, caught fire and sank on September 13, with a loss of 471 lives.

1859: *Royal Charter* Sinks. The merchant ship *Royal Charter* ran aground and broke apart in heavy seas off Liverpool on October 25. Four hundred fifty-nine passengers and crew died.

And the bell tolled again at Lloyds of London, the big maritime insurers.

1860: Lake Michigan Steamer Sinks. *Lady Elgin,* a side-wheel steamer chartered by Chicago Democrats for an outing on Lake Michigan, sank on September 7 after colliding with a schooner. Of the more than four hundred passengers and crew aboard, 287 perished in the accident.

The rest became Republicans.

1862: Typhoon Kills Thousands in China. A powerful typhoon raged through Canton and Whampoa (now Whangpoo) on July 27, virtually annihilating both Chinese cities. Towering winds and driving rains engorged the Pearl River, which flows through both cities, to more than twelve feet above its highest normal level.

Thousands of boat-dwellers drowned as the storm tore their boats to pieces, while the thousands of frail houses crowding the shore in coastal areas proved equally inadequate shelter from the forces of wind and water. By the end of the storm, not a single house still stood in the entire city of Whampoa. Meanwhile, corpses were everywhere in the flooded river; the government finally offered a bounty of one dollar per body, which led to some fifteen thousand corpses being retrieved from the river. That was only a fraction of the death toll, however, which ultimately reached forty thousand people.

1862: Battle of Antietam. On September 17, in the fields near Antietam Creek and just north of the small Maryland town of Sharpsburg, forty thousand Confederate soldiers under General Robert E. Lee faced a Union force with more than twice as many men. The shots fired early that morning marked the beginning of what was to become the bloodiest day in the Civil War.

The battle began at dawn, when Union artillery loosed a withering barrage of shell and canister on General Stonewall Jackson's Confederate infantry, which was positioned on one side of a cornfield. Union soldiers then tried to charge through the rows of corn, but Confederate riflemen mowed them down with rifle fire. At 7:00 A.M., Jackson received reinforcements and succeeded in driving Union forces back.

The point of attack now shifted to the southeast, where Confederate troops were positioned along a sunken road. After almost four hours of bitter fighting, Union soldiers overran the sunken road, which was so littered with the dead and dying that it was christened "Bloody Lane."

Meanwhile, farther east, Union General Ambrose Burnside's troops were incurring heavy losses trying to cross a bridge defended by Georgia sharpshooters. At 1:00 P.M. the Federals successfully stormed the bridge, threatening to cut off Lee's line of retreat until Confederate reinforcements arrived to help drive Burnside back.

Fighting ceased as night fell—neither side claimed a victory—and the following day, Lee withdrew his battered troops across the Potomac. The number of killed and wounded totaled 12,410 for the North and 10,700 for the South—more casualties than any other single day of fighting in the Civil War.

America's Civil War is known as the first "modern" war in history. There were nearly one million casualties on the battlefields. Welcome to the industrial age.

1863: New York City Draft Riots. The first federal draft law was passed on March 3, 1863, to furnish raw recruits for Union armies then fighting the Civil War. The law immediately aroused bitter resentment among many in the North, especially in New York, where the law threatened to affect mostly indigent Irish laborers crammed into barely habitable tenements. Even New York State governor Horace Seymour furiously opposed the measure.

Two provisions of the new law particularly outraged opponents of the draft: the sale of draft exemptions for three hundred dollars, and the exclusion of blacks. The exemption meant that those with money could buy their way out of serving in the army, unfairly shifting the burden on the poor, such as New York City's Irish laborers. Whether President Abraham Lincoln even had the right to conscript men was also a subject of heated debate.

Despite the opposition, the law was passed—the Union desperately needed men as the war with the South dragged on and casualties mounted. The first draft lottery was held on Saturday, July 11, and on Sunday the newspapers published the names of the first 1,236 draftees. New York City's Irish neighborhoods simmered with resentment, aggravated by the midsummer heat.

On Monday, July 13, the resentment turned to outright anger as knots of draft opponents armed themselves with clubs, crowbars, and brickbats, and began collecting at the draft office at 677 Third Avenue. At 10 A.M. a mob of five hundred protestors surrounding the office starting throwing bricks and stones, and then broke into the building. Rioters seized and destroyed lottery records while terrified employees escaped out the rear. Whipped into a frenzy, rioters set the building on fire, which in turn set the whole block ablaze.

By noon the mob had swollen to fifty thousand rioters who fanned out along Third Avenue, looting and burning everything in the area. Police could do little to control the mob. Superintendent John A. Kennedy rushed to the draft office and tried to subdue the crowd, but after being brutally assaulted, he was carried off to the hospital.

Blacks, exempt from the draft, became a target of the rioters. Seven were seized and lynched by roving mobs; another ten or twelve were beaten to death or thrown into the river. Then thousands of rioters attacked and burned the Colored Children's Orphan's Asylum, though the two hundred children and their guardians managed to escape.

Martial law was soon imposed, and the shooting of the rioters began. Soon hundreds of bodies of slain rioters lay in the streets of New York City's midtown district.

At nightfall scattered gangs of rioters still preyed on the city. Though not nearly as widespread as on Monday, rioting continued until July 16, when Union regiments arrived from Gettysburg to help police. Before order was restored, a staggering total of twelve hundred men, women, and children had been killed.

Another senseless riot by an angry mob in the heat of summer.

1863: Deadly Church Fire in Santiago, Chile. On December 8—the Feast of the Immaculate Conception—a very special service was planned in the Jesuit Church of La Compania, Chile. A visiting papal representative from Rome apparently compared Santiago's fine seventeenth-century church unfavorably with some in Rome, and the local priest now promised "I will give him . . . such an illumination as this world has never seen." He certainly did.

The interior of the church was decorated with many yards of draped muslin, pasteboard, and paper. More than twenty thousand colored oil lamps hung from the ceiling, so many that church servants had to begin lighting them in the middle of the afternoon to be ready for the evening service.

On this tragic evening the church was packed with some three thousand worshipers. A spark from one of the lamps set off a blaze near the altar which spread instantly to the decorations, and from there to the roof. Priests quickly escaped through the sacristy door, which they shut behind themselves.

Worshipers meanwhile raced toward the main door, their only exit now, and in the panic, many tripped and fell. Others fell over them, and soon a "living barricade" of victims piled on one another blocked the doors, trapping others inside. Some twenty-five hundred people, mostly women, died in the tragedy.

1864: Fort Pillow Massacre. On April 12, during the U.S. Civil War, Confederate forces led by General Nathan Forrest forced the surrender of Fort Pillow, near Memphis, Tennessee. As it happened, the Union garrison there was mostly made up of black soldiers. Confederates had been angered by the use of blacks as soldiers, and had no clear policy on whether to treat captured blacks as prisoners of war or as rebellious slaves.

Following the fort's surrender, Confederates began a cold-blooded massacre of the six hundred Union troops at Fort Pillow, about four hundred of whom were black. Confederate troops fired point-blank into groups of soldiers with their arms raised, bayoneted them, and hacked them with sabers. Those who ran were chased down and killed like animals. Wounded soldiers in the hospital were shot to death and the hospital burned, and even women and children at the fort were methodically slaughtered. Bodies of blacks, living and dead, were heaped in piles and set afire. Meanwhile, two black soldiers who had been buried alive managed to dig their way out and escape.

More than three hundred people, mostly blacks, died in the massacre, sparking an outrage in the North. Confederates later agreed to treat captured blacks as prisoners of war. The general was personally exonerated, however. He later became grand wizard of the Ku Klux Klan.

1864: Sand Creek Massacre. Some twelve hundred Colorado militiamen attacked a Cheyenne Indian camp in Colorado, despite the fact the Indians were then negotiating for peace. Some four hundred Indians were slaughtered in the unprovoked attack on November 29.

Another Indian massacre for which the United States military was so famous.

1864: Calcutta Cyclone. Nearly three hundred vessels were moored in the busy port of Calcutta, India, on October 5, and visitors thronged into the city for the opening day of a religious festival. Though the weather was stormy, there was no real indication of the disaster that was about to strike—a powerful cyclone just hours away was heading straight for the city.

The storm hit so quickly, there was no chance to evacuate to safety farther inland. Suddenly furious winds ripped trees out of the ground, smashed native Indian huts, and tore roofs off the houses of British colonials. Crowded passenger trains tumbled from the tracks, and in the harbor, ships tore loose from their moorings and were wrecked in the heavy seas.

At 3:00 P.M. a thirty-foot-high tidal wave struck, crushing some two hundred ships in the harbor before rolling into Calcutta, where it flooded most of the city and killed some fifty thousand people. Another thirty thousand people died after the storm, as disease spread through the ruined city.

Another washout in India.

1865: General Lyon Burns at Sea. The one-year-old *General Lyon,* a propeller-driven steamship, caught fire and sank on March 25, taking some four hundred passengers and crew to the bottom off Cape Hatteras, North Carolina, an area once called the "graveyard of the Atlantic."

1865: Assassination of President Abraham Lincoln. On the evening of April 14, while attending a play at Ford's Theater in Washington, D.C., President Abraham Lincoln was fatally shot by John Wilkes Booth, a twenty-six-year-old actor who had been serving as a Confederate secret service agent.

Only five days earlier, the bloody four-year Civil War had finally come to an end with Robert E. Lee's surrender at Appomattox. The mood in Washington, D.C., was jubilant, though Lincoln's joy must have been mixed with some anxiety. During the war there had been rumors the Confederate government planned to kidnap him, but since the Confederate surrender rendered that pointless, hostility to Lincoln now manifested itself in the form of death threats. On the night of Lincoln's assassination, eighty letters threatening his life lay on his desk.

What Lincoln could not know, however, was that the vehemently pro-Southern John Wilkes Booth had already made two unsuccessful attempts to kidnap him, and now swore to avenge the crippled South by assassinating him and others in his cabinet.

On the morning of April 14, after seeing a notice in the newspaper that President and Mrs. Lincoln would be attending the play that evening, Booth began preparing his treacherous plot. At 6:00 P.M., after luring the stagehands to a tavern, Booth entered the deserted theater and made his way to the presidential box. He prepared a board to jam the door of the foyer outside the box, and drilled a peephole in the box door to enable him to watch the president's movements.

Luck was with Booth that evening. After Lincoln was seated, an unreliable bodyguard left his post outside the presidential box, so that it was unguarded when Booth arrived shortly before 10:00 P.M. Booth slipped into the foyer and jammed the door shut with the board he had placed there earlier. Then, watching the president through the peephole, Booth waited for a specific scene in which he knew there was only one actor on stage.

The moment came: Booth pushed open the box door, fired one shot into the back of the president's head at point-blank range, and leaped to the stage fourteen feet below. Although he broke his leg upon landing, he turned toward the audience brandishing a dagger and proclaimed, *"Sic semper tyrannis"* (Thus ever to tyrants). He then limped off the stage, made his way to the back door, and escaped on a horse that an accomplice had ready.

The theater audience watched all this with great confusion, and not until Mrs. Lincoln screamed, "He has killed the president!" did anyone realize what had just happened. Lincoln's comatose body was carried to a house across the street, where he died at 7:22 the following morning.

Authorities chased Booth for days, and finally cornered and fatally shot him in a burning barn near Bowling Green, Virginia, on April 26. Booth's accomplices, who not only helped him escape but also attempted the unsuccessful assassination of Secretary of State Seward that same evening, were all caught and hanged.

In the months and years following Lincoln's tragic death, speculations about various sinister conspiracies abounded. It is certainly true that a number of factions had reasons for wanting Lincoln dead. While many in the South at that time may have wanted revenge, it has never been proven that Booth was acting at the behest of the Confederate government. It has also been suggested that Lincoln's enemies in the Federal government, who resented his conciliatory attitude toward the defeated South, knew of the assassination plot and did nothing to stop it. Since Booth revealed nothing to interrogators before his death, the truth about such speculations will probably never be known.

There will be much speculation in the same vein after the assassination of another president.

1865: Fiery Explosion of the *Sultana*. Though there were about one hundred regular passengers and eighty crewmen already aboard the steamboat *Sultana* for a trip up the Mississippi River on April 24, a horde of 2,134 Union soldiers were allowed to board at Vicksburg. Though that dangerously overcrowded the steamboat, which had a capacity of just 376, the soldiers had just been released from Confederate prisons and were anxious to get home.

As the side-wheel steamer left Vicksburg on her way to Cairo, Illinois, the soldiers stretched out side by side on their blankets to fill nearly every free inch of space in the steamboat all the way down to the boiler deck. The trip upriver was delayed briefly on April 26 while a leak in one of the steamboat's four boilers was repaired at Memphis. Though that was no cause for alarm, the dangerous overcrowding certainly was. That night the captain, J. C. Mason, remarked to one of his lieutenants that "I'd give all the interest I have in this boat if we were safely landed in Cairo."

Mason never got the chance. At 2:00 A.M. on April 27, about eight miles north of Memphis, a boiler exploded and ripped through the steamboat with the force of a bomb. The blast hurled several hundred men into the chilly waters of the Mississippi, along with boiler debris and pieces of the deck. One man who had been asleep suddenly woke up to find himself in the water.

The *Sultana*'s twin smokestacks collapsed, crushing men beneath them. An upper deck fell at one end and spilled men and cots directly into the burning remains of the boiler. Fire leaped up from the boiler, quickly spreading along the decks and cabins until the steamboat was engulfed in flames. Panicked soldiers jumped overboard by the hundreds or were pushed into the water by those shoving desperately from behind.

Many drowned soon after they jumped in, because the water was so crowded with people struggling wildly to stay afloat. In that melee even hardy swimmers were pulled down. The lifeboats, meanwhile, were either ruined by the fire or inaccessible because of it. Only one made it into the water, and that one went in upside down.

Several boats left from Memphis to pick up survivors after the explosion, and a former Confederate soldier with a sturdy canoe single-handedly rescued fifteen Union soldiers from the water. Many of those who survived, however, simply drifted until they reached shore, some as far away as Memphis.

Officially the terrible explosion killed 1,547 people, making it one of the worst ship disasters of all time. There is uncertainty about how many soldiers actually were aboard, however, and some estimates put the death toll substantially higher.

At first the repaired boiler was blamed for the explosion, but it was later found that another of the boilers had blown up. A much smaller explosion on the *Sultana*'s sister ship the following year seemed to show that the tubular design of the boilers was at fault—they were originally built for use on the less muddy upper Mississippi.

1866–1870: Famine and Fever in Northern India. A four-year drought spread famine from the Bengal region across much of northern India, during which some 1.5 million people died. A fever epidemic that caused the deaths of some 250,000 people broke out in the Northwest after the famine.

Pandora's Box never seems to close over India.

1866: Disappearance of the *Monarch of the Seas*. The great waves of European immigrants who arrived in the United States during the nineteenth and early twentieth centuries were just beginning to build when the American ship *Monarch of the Seas* departed Liverpool, England, on March 19 with nearly seven hundred passengers aboard. The ship carried mostly English, Irish, and Scottish emigrants bound for New York, along with some sixteen hundred tons of freight. But the hopeful passengers were not destined to make it to the New World. The two-thousand-ton ship disappeared without a trace, presumably sunk somewhere in the mid-Atlantic. No one knows what happened to the 738 passengers and crew, none of whom were ever rescued or seen again.

And once again the bell tolls.

1866: Firecracker Burns Portland. During Fourth of July celebrations at Portland, Maine, a carelessly thrown firecracker set fire to a boatbuilder's shop. A strong wind quickly spread the flames through the business district, ultimately destroying some fifteen hundred buildings. No deaths were reported.

1866: Twenty-five Hundred Homes Burn in Quebec Fire. Strong winds buffeted the city of Quebec, Canada, all night

October 15. But the winds themselves were harmless until, at 4:00 A.M., fire broke out in the home of a grocer. Driven by the unrelenting winds, the blaze quickly spread from one wooden house to another. By the time fire fighters had set up their hoses almost an hour later, at least ten houses and numerous shacks had already gone up in flames. The fire spread out of control through city streets lined with wooden houses, and later that day three separate fires could be seen raging within the city. By the time the fire burned itself out at 5:00 P.M., twenty-five hundred houses had been destroyed and eighteen thousand people left homeless.

1868: South American Earthquake. Much of South America was rocked by an earthquake on August 13, with Peru and Ecuador being especially hard hit. Some twenty thousand people were killed in the quake.

1870: Constantinople Fire. Beginning on Sunday, June 5, when many people were away on holiday trips, a terrible blaze destroyed a square mile of the ancient city of Constantinople (now in Turkey), razing some three thousand buildings in the city's Armenian and Christian districts.

Entire families found themselves cut off from escape by the fast-moving fire, while helpless bystanders who were safely beyond the wall of flames watched them perish. Elsewhere in the city, some Muslims surrendered to fate, locking themselves in their houses to await death. Still others, panic-struck, created wild scenes of confusion in the city's streets as many of Constantinople's finest buildings were consumed by the blaze.

When the disaster was over, it was found that fire, smoke, and collapsing buildings had killed an estimated nine hundred people.

1870: Ironclad Warship Sinks. A British ironclad turret ship, the *Captain*, foundered and sank during a storm in the Bay of Biscay on September 6. Most of the ship's crew were among the 483 dead.

1871: Bloody Week. Immediately after France's humiliating defeat in the Franco-Prussian War, an assembly of revolutionary workers gathered in Paris to resist the newly formed government of the Third Republic. With the sympathy of most of the French National Guard, the Commune seized control in Paris in March.

Bloody Week, the suppression of the Commune, lasted from May 21 to 28.

On May 21 seventy thousand French government troops poured into Paris to retake the city from the rebels. Historian Gabriel Hanotaux described the following week: "From this point on there was war in the streets, but a war without method, without guidance, without a chief, a war without discipline, the struggle of despair."

The street fighting was indeed a war. Commune leaders torched building after building, and even set fire to the Tuileries palace. Flames soon engulfed the historic palace, consuming the lavish furnishings it contained and causing the roof to cave in. Meanwhile, strong winds spread fires throughout the city. Thick black smoke filled the air, along with the incessant roar of gunfire in all central quarters of the city.

By May 24 the fury of the struggle increased. The Commune set fire to the ancient municipal building Hotel de Ville. Mass executions began as the Commune rounded up and slaughtered its enemies in the streets—priests, archbishops, and police agents among them. Meanwhile, government troops set up tribunals to try, convict, and execute captured rebels.

By the night of May 25, Hanotaux wrote, "The center of Paris was one immense furnace. . . . The Seine, whose waters were already dyed with blood, rolled through Paris like a bed of fire." Now, when men fell dead on the Commune's street barricades, women and children took their places at the guns as "a strange frenzy excited these brave but feeble beings," Hanotaux wrote.

On May 26 the all-but-defeated Commune led its last prisoners on a death march through the streets. Forty-eight priests and policemen were slaughtered at once in the Rue Haxo. Finally the rebellion collapsed on May 28, and government troops roamed the streets announcing, "The army of France has come to save you. Paris is delivered. . . . Today the conflict is over, order is reestablished."

Delivered, but devastated nonetheless. Some seventeen thousand people were killed in the fighting and mass executions before the revolt was put down. And as one witness put it, " 'Paris the beautiful' is Paris the ghastly, Paris the battered, Paris the burning, Paris the blood-splattered, now."

Each French republic has its Paris riots.

1871: Great Chicago Fire. This, the most destructive fire in American history, ravaged 3⅓ square miles of Chicago in just twenty-seven hours on October 8 and 9, killing over 250 people. More than ninety thousand people were left homeless, and estimates of damages reached two hundred million dollars.

Chicago, at this time a booming city of about 335,000, had suffered an unusual autumn drought and heat wave with temperatures over one hundred degrees. Closely packed wooden houses, barns, and shanties of the poorer west side were tinder-dry and ripe for a major fire.

Then, around 9:00 P.M. on October 8, a small blaze broke out in a barn belonging to Patrick and Catherine O'Leary, of 137 DeKoven Street. Legend has it that Mrs. O'Leary's cow kicked over a lantern while she was milking. The O'Leary's probably were asleep at the time, though, and the mystery of the fire's origin has never been completely solved.

Fire soon spread throughout the west side neighborhood's maze of shanties, barns, pigsties, and chicken coops. Chicago's meager fire department did not even arrive on the scene until an hour later, but that was not the worst of it. A hot, dry wind now blew out of the west and soon intensified, with speeds recorded at sixty miles per hour. By midnight seven square blocks had been leveled. Flames leaped upward thirty to forty feet, while hot winds drove the fire eastward through lumberyards, mills, and wooden cottages.

Chicago's fire department tried desperately to halt the advancing flames, but as the *Chicago Tribune* reported, "The whole air was filled with glowing cinders, looking like an illuminated snowstorm." Whichever way the wind blew, the fire spread.

Not even the Chicago River, which separates Chicago's western district from the south side, could contain the blaze. Shortly after midnight, firebrands blew across the river to ignite roofs on the far shore. First to go was the squalid waterfront section known as Conley's Patch. Fire raced through it, consuming saloons, brothels, gambling halls, and cheap hotels. Whole buildings were devoured by flames in minutes while drunks and prostitutes clambered noisily into the street. One bartender was seen madly toasting the fire just before a burning ceiling collapsed on top of him.

Heroic efforts to stop the wild blaze all failed. Officials even tried to establish a fire block by dynamiting buildings, but fierce winds moved the fire unpredictably. Now tens of thousands of refugees filled the streets as the rapidly advancing wall of flames herded them toward Lake Michigan. Meanwhile, a jeweler stood outside his burning shop, handing out gems and jewelry to passing refugees rather than giving them up to the fire. One by one, theaters, hotels, banks—even city hall—burst into flames.

Chicago's near complete destruction was assured on October 9. At noon a burning board, carried by the raging wind, sailed across the Chicago River's eastern fork into the city's affluent northern district. The board landed on the city's only water-pumping station. When the station went up in flames, water for the city's fire fighters was cut off, and the blaze raged unchecked. Fires jumped from one mansion to the next through the north side, and in the end consumed all but two homes in the entire district.

Thousands of refugees, driven to the shore of Lake Michigan, waded into the lake and stayed for hours, their faces burning in the searing heat while their bodies went numb in the bitter cold water.

By 3:00 A.M. on October 10, the murderous wind abated and the fire soon died out. When it was over, at least 17,500 buildings had been destroyed. Ironically, though, the O'Leary's house was not one of them. It remained standing beside the charred wreckage of their barn.

1871: Fire Ravages Peshtigo. Months of drought had baked dry the woods and grasslands surrounding Peshtigo and other nearby towns in eastern Wisconsin. On the evening of October 8, hot, dry, gale-force winds arrived—winds that hundreds of miles to the east caused the Great Chicago Fire that same evening. When the wind hit, small fires already burning in the woodlands were suddenly whipped up into great walls of flames racing toward Peshtigo.

Most of the two thousand residents had no warning. The sun had just set, and families were settling down in their homes to spend a pleasant Sunday evening together. Only a few lumbermen and mill workers outside in the gusting winds saw the angry red glow on the horizon and realized that danger was approaching. No one, however, was prepared for the firestorm that followed.

Peshtigo, as it happened, was surrounded by swamps that, during the long, hot days of recent months, had been producing significant amounts of swamp gas—containing explosive methane gas. Well before the advancing fires actually reached Peshtigo, the searing heat touched off the swamp gas in a huge explosion. The fiery blast sent scorching hot jets of air rolling through town, blowing roofs off buildings and lifting whole houses into the air.

The blast of searing air was so hot that anything combustible, from horse carts to whole buildings, burst into flames, and dozens of people died simply from breathing the superheated air. Meanwhile, the winds continued to blow full force, picking up cinders and chunks of burning debris, and creating a veritable hurricane of fire. A great gust of wind lifted one whole house off its foundation and high into the air, where it exploded and showered burning debris on the people below.

Hundreds of frantic townspeople who survived the initial blast raced to the nearby Peshtigo River and submerged themselves in its swiftly moving waters. Others crowded onto the bridge, hoping that the conflagration would not cross the river, but the high winds swept the fire over the water, setting the other bank on fire. Then the bridge ignited in a massive burst of flames and suddenly collapsed, dumping hundreds of townspeople, horses, and carts into the swirling river.

In the center of town, volunteer firemen attempted to battle the blaze engulfing them, but the fire hose burned to ashes almost immediately. Elsewhere, desperate men lowered wives and children into wells on top of goods hastily stashed there by merchants. Instead of finding sanctuary, however, the hapless refugees suffered a horrifying fate: The goods ignited and burned them all alive.

The intense heat of the flames reduced everything to cinders. About fifty victims sought shelter in a brick building, thinking that its sturdy walls would protect them from the flames. The next day, however, nothing was left but white ashes and two watches. Similarly, seven men were seen digging a ditch when the conflagration hit, but all that remained afterward were their charred shovel blades.

By the time the awful inferno had burned itself out, Peshtigo had been totally destroyed, and 1,152 of its citizens had been killed, as well as some 350 people in nearby towns. The fire burned over four million acres of forests and grasslands before dying out.

1872: Spectacular Mount Vesuvius Eruption. Because of Vesuvius's long history of eruptions, those who lived around the volcano knew all too well how deadly it could be. They were prepared to flee at a moment's notice when it erupted again on April 24, but visitors who came to watch the spectacle ignored the warnings of officials to stay clear.

Over the following few days, Vesuvius put on an awesome display, erupting with ear-shattering roars, belching smoke, spewing two great rivers of lava, and hurling red-hot rocks, some as big as forty-five feet in diameter, high into the air. Lava flows, sixteen feet deep in places, destroyed two villages, though all the inhabitants escaped in time. But the spectacle apparently so mesmerized sightseers that over two dozen were incinerated when lava flows unexpectedly surrounded them.

Is this what they call a tourist trap?

1872: Boston Fire. A blaze that began in a building in the downtown district of Boston, Massachusetts, on November 9 spread quickly from building to building until the entire downtown district was engulfed in flames. Firemen managed to halt the advancing wall of flames the next day by blowing up several blocks of buildings, but not before 930 buildings—virtually the entire downtown district—had been razed. Twelve people were killed.

A quick way to urban renewal.

1873: The *Atlantic* Sinks Off Nova Scotia. The British steamship *Atlantic,* en route to New York, approached Halifax, Nova Scotia, in heavy seas on the night of April 1. The stop at Halifax was unscheduled, but the captain estimated their coal supply to be dangerously low because of storms during the voyage, and ordered the change in course. Then, at 2:00 A.M., while a thousand people slept in cabins belowdecks, the *Atlantic* ran aground on Meagher's Rock at the entrance to Halifax harbor.

As the vessel hit the rock, huge waves broke over her decks, carrying away the lifeboats on the port side. Crew members rushed to launch the remaining boats. One was made ready, and several passengers climbed into it, only to have another monstrous wave sweep them into the sea and crush the hull of the boat.

The *Atlantic* then keeled over onto her port side and sank, drowning all those still belowdecks and many who stood on deck as well. Parts of the masts remained above water, and some people survived by climbing into the rigging. One crewman swam to the nearby rock carrying a lifeline, by which many then managed to swim to safety. Others who tried to reach the rock drowned; some were unable to hold on to the rope because of the numbing cold water, while others fell back into the deadly surf as they tried to climb up the slippery, seaweed-covered rock.

In all, some 550 people died in the disaster, including all of the women and children on board.

1874: Fire Aboard Ship Kills 468. The immigrant ship *Cospatrick* caught fire and sank off Auckland, New Zealand, on November 17. All but five of those aboard died by fire or drowning.

1875: Garonne River Flood. About one thousand people were killed in France on June 22 when the Garonne River overflowed, demolishing Verdun, Toulouse, and a number of villages.

1876: Turkish Massacre in Bulgaria. When the Bulgarians rebelled against their Turkish overlords, the Turks responded in 1876 with a bloody repression that came to be called the Bulgarian Horrors. The Bulgarian town of Batak suffered one of the most infamous attacks at the hands of a group of ill-disciplined Turkish irregulars, known as the Bashi-Bazouks.

For the most part there were only women and children in Batak when the Bashi-Bazouks were sent into the town. Nevertheless, the Turks embarked on a bloodthirsty rampage. They split open the skulls of children with their sabers or decapitated them outright. Heads littered the streets, and infants were spitted on bayonets and carried about the town. The Turks even ripped open the bellies of pregnant women to stab the fetuses.

Villagers who sought shelter in their houses were trapped as the Turks broke down the doors and killed everyone inside. Then the rampaging soldiers set fire to the houses.

Bodies and parts of bodies were thrown in random heaps—

within the walls of a churchyard measuring fifty by seventy-five yards, some three thousand bodies were piled four feet deep. But most of the fifteen thousand victims were left where they fell, to rot or be devoured by dogs.

Reports of the terrible repression in Bulgaria reached European newspapers, and the outrage helped bring about creation of an autonomous Bulgarian state in 1878.

Do unto others.

1876–1878: Famine Strikes India Again. First the monsoon failed to bring seasonal rains in southern India, causing a drought that ruined crops there in 1876; then in 1877 it failed in the north and brought so much rain to the south that flooding again ruined the crops there. In the resulting famine, some five million people died.

1876–1879: Famine Kills Millions in China. By 1876 three years of severe drought had already taken their toll in the provinces of China. Crops had failed, the price of food had soared, and people were starving to death. Villagers were reduced to eating thistles, weeds, and even bits of wood to stay alive. Women and children were sold into slavery and prostitution for meager sums.

Many villages were completely wiped out by starvation. Others were emptied as people fled to other areas in search of food. In winter some famine victims who had lost their homes sought shelter in enormous, crowded underground pits, and many of them died there. Others burned their houses for warmth during the long winter months and then had no shelter at all.

Thievery, mob violence, suicide, and cannibalism became commonplace, as hundreds of thousands of people tried desperately to stay alive. The government punished such lawbreakers with mass beheadings or the terrible "sorrow cage," a wooden structure in which criminals were abandoned to slowly die of starvation.

By August of 1879, shortly before the prolonged drought finally ended, some thirteen million Chinese had perished as a result of hunger, disease, and predation.

1876: Hundred-Foot Tsunamis Wreck Japanese Coast. A subsea earthquake spawned huge tidal waves on June 15 that crashed ashore along a three-hundred-mile section of coastline in northeast Japan. About twenty-eight thousand people were killed, and over six thousand buildings were wrecked.

1876: Battle of the Little Bighorn. Warriors from a number of Indian tribes, including the Sioux, Cheyenne, and Hunkpapa, defied the U.S. government's orders to report to reservations in 1876, and instead chose to follow the lead of the medicine man Sitting Bull. Soon three thousand Sioux warriors were camped in tepees sprawled along the Little Bighorn Valley.

The job of subduing Sitting Bull's forces fell to Brigadier General Alfred Terry, who formed what was called the Yellowstone Expedition to seek out the Indian encampment. While en route, Terry's forces, with General George Custer serving under him, linked up with additional troops under Colonel John Gibbon. Terry then split the force into two columns, giving Custer command of the Seventh Cavalry.

Terry ordered Custer to march no more than thirty miles a day in a "wide sweep" toward the Indian camp, in order to arrive at the Little Bighorn no sooner than June 26. Terry then rode with Gibbon's troops, who had to march more slowly because of the gatling gun division among them. On June 26 both units were to attack the Indians simultaneously in a two-pronged attack.

Instead of following orders, Custer pushed his men to ride as many as seventy-eight miles in one day, and arrived within striking distance of Sitting Bull on the afternoon of June 25. Though his soldiers and their horses needed rest, and his Indian scouts warned him the enemy's greater numbers made victory impossible, Custer immediately violated orders and mobilized to attack.

Dividing his seven-hundred-man cavalry, Custer took five companies of men and rode toward the most populated part of the Indian camp. Apparently Custer assumed the Indians would flee, and planned to cut them off. To start the Indians running, Custer sent Captain Marcus Reno and the other seven companies to attack one end of the Indian village.

Reno's men attacked first and soon found themselves outnumbered and outgunned—the cavalrymen had only single-shot carbines, while many Indians had repeat-action Winchesters. Reno was forced into a gradual retreat, and though he lost about one hundred men, his column fared much better than Custer's did.

Hearing Reno's men begin their attack, Custer then led his

charge into the other end of the encampment. He, too, found himself outnumbered and outgunned. The Indians, apparently about fifteen hundred to two thousand strong, fought Custer ferociously, buoyed by their superior numbers and by a recent vision of Sitting Bull's that showed them vanquishing many white soldiers. Warriors plentiful "as the leaves on the trees" rushed at Custer's position and surrounded him.

The bloodbath lasted between thirty and fifty-five minutes. Custer was apparently killed by Indian gunfire, and soldiers who tried to retreat were cut to pieces. Over 250 soldiers died in the massacre, though six soldiers lived long enough to be marched to the Indian camp and killed there. Of Custer's whole column, only a horse called Comanche survived the massacre.

Who said the best offense is a good defense? It sure wasn't George Armstrong Custer.

1876: Bengal Cyclone Wipes Out One Hundred Thousand. Just before midnight on October 31, a tremendous cyclone struck the coastal area around the mouth of the Megna River in Bengal, India. Thousands of residents on the mainland were shaken from their sleep or immediately drowned by twenty-foot waves crashing over their houses, while offshore islands were being wiped out entirely.

Within thirty minutes floodwaters rose as high as forty feet in the coastal city of Backergunge. Terrified residents climbed onto the roofs of their houses, only to find the roofs themselves being torn away. Drifting helplessly in the raging floodwaters, many clung desperately to pieces of wreckage to keep from drowning. Others survived by climbing into the palm and coconut trees that dotted the area.

While a horrific total of some one hundred thousand people died during the storm, the disaster was far from over. In the storm's aftermath, fully one hundred thousand more died of diseases that spread rapidly among the survivors who had been left without pure water and food and without proper health and sanitation facilities.

1876: Brooklyn, New York, Theater Fire. Shrieks of "Fire!" echoed through the hall as actors at the Brooklyn Theater on the evening of December 5 kept their composure, pleading with the nine hundred theatergoers present to leave calmly. But the audience watched with growing alarm as flames consumed the theater curtain. Lacking water or fire-fighting equipment, stagehands vainly tried beating out the fire, apparently started when a lamp ignited a backstage curtain. Though the flames spread rapidly, those members of the audience in the orchestra section made a fairly orderly exit. However, hundreds in the upper galleries panicked, rushing madly for exists and crushing those who blocked the way. Some husbands whose wives had fainted carried the women to safety over their heads to prevent their being trampled. Despite such heroic rescue efforts, the fire killed 295 people.

1876: Ohio Train Wreck. Slowed by a terrible blizzard on the night of December 29, the West-coast-bound eleven-car *Pacific Express,* carrying 150 passengers, crept out onto an iron bridge just outside Ashtabula, Ohio. About 8:00 P.M., with the train on the bridge, there came a sudden, heart-stopping crack as the entire 160-foot span collapsed. Passengers barely had time to realize the horror of what was happening before the train plunged seventy-five feet to the frozen Ashtabula Creek below. Minutes after the fall, overturned heating stoves set fire to the wrecked passenger cars, even as icy creek water bubbled in from underneath. Terrified passengers lucky enough to survive the fall, the fire, and the freezing water still had to face the blinding snowstorm, and before the night was over, ninety-two people had died.

1878: Yellow Fever Epidemic in Memphis, Tennessee. Already on the decline after the Civil War, Memphis, Tennessee, suffered another devastating setback when a yellow fever epidemic broke out in mid-August. Little was known about the disease then—except that it was deadly and spread rapidly. By early September some twenty-five thousand people had fled the city out of fear of contracting the disease, thereby turning Memphis into a virtual ghost town and helping to spread the disease throughout the South. Of the remaining twenty thousand who stayed in Memphis, some seventeen thousand did contract the fever, and five thousand of them died of it. Doctors, priests, and others who remained risked their own lives to care for the sick and dying. One local madam sent away her "girls" and cared for patients in her bordello before succumbing to the fever herself.

Citizen militias meanwhile attempted to stem the rising tide of robberies and public disorder. The epidemic finally ended in October, soon after the fall's first cold snap hit the South, but by this time some fourteen thousand people had already perished from yellow fever in Memphis, New Orleans, and other parts of the South.

1878: Sinking of Excursion Steamer. The *Princess Alice* sank bow first in a matter of minutes after being hit amidships by the collier *Bywell Castle* near Woolwich, England, on September 3. Six hundred forty-five people, many of them women and children, died.

1879: Tay Bridge Collapse. Extending for some two miles across Scotland's Tay River Estuary, the Tay Bridge had been hailed as an engineering marvel because of its great length. Though work had begun in 1871, the bridge was not opened until 1878 because of various problems, including construction accidents that killed twenty workmen. Nevertheless, when Queen Victoria traveled across the bridge in 1878, she was so impressed by its beauty and size that she knighted construction engineer Thomas Bouch for his design.

The afternoon of December 28, 1879, some eighteen months after the Tay Bridge opened, turned dark and stormy. By evening, heavy rains fell, and gale-force winds gusting to seventy-five miles per hour churned the waters of the Tay Estuary. Although it was a Sunday, the Sabbath, one train had been allowed to make the round trip from Dundee to Burntisland in Scotland, by way of the Tay Bridge. Finally, just after 7:00 P.M., the seven-car train approached the Tay Bridge on its return leg to Dundee. Eighty people, including passengers and the train crew, were aboard.

Visibility was poor because of the rain, but a railway signalman watched the train creep across the bridge at three miles per hour, with only its red taillights piercing the darkness. Just as the lights disappeared between upper girders of the center span, there was "a fearful blast," with flashes of light. When the train lights did not reappear, the alarmed signalman tried to telegraph Dundee, but the line was dead.

Meanwhile, on the Dundee side of the bridge, railway workers became worried some minutes later when the train failed to appear. With telegraph lines dead, there was no choice but to send someone to find out what had happened. Battered by howling winds and rain, a locomotive foreman bravely crawled onto the exposed single-track bridge on his hands and knees. Inching his way into stormy darkness, he ventured far out onto the bridge before halting abruptly. Suddenly there was nothing ahead of him except rails dangling down toward the water ninety feet below. The bridge was gone.

Perhaps the combined stress of gale-force wind and the weight of the train caused the center span to collapse, or possibly the span had already begun to give way in the high winds. Whatever happened that fateful evening, the whole seven-car train and tons of twisted iron girders crashed downward some ninety feet to the dark, storm-tossed Tay Estuary. All eighty people, including women and children passengers and the entire train crew, were killed.

Passengers inside the train never had a chance. Those who might have survived the terrible fall were drowned as the train sank beneath the waves in waters forty-five feet deep. Even if victims had had time to try saving themselves before passenger cars sank, their efforts would have been in vain. In accordance with rules on British railroads, doors on passenger cars were locked.

Following the disaster, a Court of Inquiry investigation determined that bridge designer Thomas Bouch had failed to consider the effect of strong winds on the structure. Further, materials used in its construction were found to be of poor quality. These mistakes were not repeated in construction of a second Tay Bridge (1887), which still remains in use today.

Thomas must have slept through physics class.

1881: Assassination of Czar Alexander II. Two members of a radical populist movement called Land and Liberty ambushed Russian Czar Alexander II as he returned by carriage from a parade in Saint Petersburg on March 13. The assassins stood on either side of the street, armed with glass bombs filled with nitroglycerin. As the czar passed, one assassin hurled his bomb underneath the carriage; it blasted off the back of the vehicle but left the czar unharmed. As the shaken czar left the carriage, the second assassin hurled his bomb directly at the czar's feet. The explosion mangled both of the czar's legs and tore out one of his eyes. He died less than two hours later. The assassination led to a period of severe repression under Czar Alexander III.

We now call these bombs Molotov cocktails.

1881: French Opera House Fire. Gas lamps accidentally ignited scenery onstage shortly before a performance at Nice's municipal opera house on March 23, starting a fire that completely destroyed the building. Among the seventy dead were a number trampled to death by panic-stricken theatergoers fleeing the fire.

A modern innovation; a familiar disaster.

1881: President James Garfield Assassinated. At the Baltimore and Potomac Railway Station in Washington, D.C., it seemed an ordinary Saturday morning on July 2. The few passengers in the waiting room might, perhaps, have looked up and noticed the president of the United States strolling by with one of his cabinet officers shortly after 9:00 A.M., but the president's departure for a summer vacation with family and friends was otherwise unheralded.

Suddenly a small, sallow-looking man with thin whiskers and a slouch hat rushed up behind Garfield, and from five feet away shot the unsuspecting president twice. Garfield fell to the floor, blood spurting from wounds in his arm and his back, but still very much alive. The assassin, gun in hand, walked out the door and was promptly arrested by police. Newspapers later described the killer, Charles Giteau, as a "half-crazed, pettifogging lawyer," disgruntled at being turned down for an office in the Garfield administration.

The nation, still remembering the assassination of Lincoln sixteen years before, was overtaken by grief as the mortally wounded president struggled to live. Crowds thronged to the White House and gathered in the streets of New York, waiting for bulletins on his condition. Garfield finally succumbed to his wounds late in the evening of September 19. That night church bells throughout the nation tolled to mark his passing.

1881: South Atlantic Coast Gale. A hurricane lashed coastal areas from Florida to the Carolinas on August 27, flooding lowlands, knocking down buildings, and killing some seven hundred people. In Charleston, South Carolina, winds of nearly fifty miles per hour and high seas combined to level buildings on the mainland and on nearby islands. Only the lighthouse remained standing on Sullivan's Island. Meanwhile, many ships still at sea when the gale struck were wrecked along the coast or sank in deep water. Two days after the storm, the sole survivor of the foundered collier *Mary G. Fisher* was picked up at sea. Rescuers found him naked and delirious, still clinging to the piece of his ship's cabin that had kept him afloat throughout the fierce storm.

1881: Vienna Ring Theater Fire. Flames turned Vienna's ornate opera house, the Ring Theater, into a death trap just before an evening performance on December 8. Some 850 people died, making this the worst theater fire of all time.

Theatergoers, in a festive mood during the Feast of the Immaculate Conception, flocked to the Ring Theater in downtown Vienna, Austria, to see a 7:00 P.M. performance of Offenbach's opera *Les Contes de Hoffman,* which had opened to rave reviews the night before. By 6:50 inexpensive seats in the four upper-level balconies had filled to capacity with between one thousand and two thousand people, though the ground-level orchestra seating remained largely empty, because the wealthier patrons usually arrived late. About that time a lamplighter backstage accidentally grazed overhanging canvas scenery with his torch, and the highly flammable painted canvas burst into flames.

Screams of fire backstage were muffled by the heavy stage curtain, and the audience out front continued milling about the theater, oblivious to the danger. Those who noticed an unusual light behind the curtain mistook it for a theatrical light used in the elaborate production.

Performers and the stage crew backstage panicked as they ran from the spreading flames. No one thought to lower the iron curtain designed to keep a stage fire from spreading into the auditorium, to pull the fire alarm, or to open the five waterspouts above the stage.

Moments later, a horrified audience watched the stage curtain billow outward and burst into a sheet of flame. Up in the crowded balconies, people stampeded toward the narrow, winding staircases leading to ground level. But just as the mad rush began, someone backstage turned off the gaslights to prevent an explosion, leaving the theater in total darkness. Hundreds of people shoved desperately to get at the stairs as smoke filled the hallways and flames spread through the theater.

Dozens of people, including many children, were trampled to death in the panic. Many other victims succumbed to the smoke, while some jumped or fell from the upper balconies. One woman who jumped crashed on top of two other people, and all three died.

Fire fighters knocked down walls to free some of those trapped in the narrow hallways. When the flames became too intense, they held out cloths to catch others who jumped from the upper galleries and windows, thus saving 112 lives.

Meanwhile, many of the wealthy theatergoers who were fashionably late arrived to find flames shooting from the theater's roof. Dressed in evening clothes, they stood helplessly outside with hordes of other spectators, listening to the screams and prayers of hundreds dying inside.

After the fire was extinguished four hours later, 850 people were dead and hundreds more injured, many disfigured for life. For all of them the Ring Theater, a showcase for comic opera, had instead played out the grimmest of tragedies.

Someone should have been in charge of backstage fire drills.

1882: Storm Devastates Bombay. An estimated one hundred thousand people were killed during a fierce storm on June 5 when a great tidal wave crashed ashore and inundated the coastal area.

1883: Polish Circus Burns as Firemen Fall Through Ice. Some six hundred people crowded into a makeshift wooden structure to see the traveling Circus Ferroni at Berditschoft, Poland, on January 13. Then a series of accidents and blunders turned the performance into a catastrophe in which 430 died.

The fire, possibly started by a carelessly discarded cigarette, began in the rear of the building. A circus worker allowed a draft to fan the small blaze when he opened a door to get water to put out the fire. Next, as the fire spread out of control, a clown tried to alert the spectators, but they thought his warning was part of his comic circus act. When other circus workers appeared to confirm the warning, the audience suddenly broke into panic, and many victims were trampled to death in the mad rush to escape, even before the fire threatened them. Meanwhile, the local fire brigade was hopelessly delayed. Fireman tried to cross a frozen river on the way to the fire, but the ice broke beneath them!

Water tricks must not have been in their repertoire.

1883: Krakatoa Erupts. A volcanic island between the main Indonesian islands of Java and Sumatra, Krakatoa unleashed the most violent eruption in modern times on August 26 and 27.

The volcano, inactive since 1680, first rumbled to life again in May 1883. Finally, on Sunday, August 26, Krakatoa began erupting with such force that its explosive blasts shook houses one hundred miles away. A dark cloud of ash seventeen miles high filled the air around Krakatoa and became so thick, it blocked out the sunlight. Hot stones and ash fell in an avalanche that destroyed buildings and bridges, and made roads impassable up to one hundred miles away.

As if that were not enough, Krakatoa stirred fifteen other volcanoes on Java into violent eruption that day. The sea, sixty degrees hotter than normal, was blanketed by a floating layer of pumice that eventually became ten feet thick. Meanwhile, the air was thick with sulfurous volcanic gases. Blasts from repeated explosive eruptions charged the air with lightning bolts and whipped up destructive tornadoes and water spouts to further impede those trying to find safety.

But there was no safe place for many miles around Krakatoa. While hot ash and rocks showered down from above, the earth trembled, fissures opened, and buildings collapsed. Sometime that Sunday night, a fifty-square-mile tract of coastal land sank beneath the sea, as did a chain of small islands off Java. While Krakatoa continued to be the most violent, still other volcanoes began erupting on Java and Sumatra. The island of Merak—just three miles from Krakatoa—sank into the sea, only to be replaced later by fourteen new volcanic islands.

The devastating finale to Krakatoa's orgy of destruction came the following Monday, August 27, in four cataclysmic explosions at 5:30 A.M., 6:44 A.M., 10:02 A.M., and 10:52 A.M., possibly caused by the sudden mixing of large volumes of searing hot lava and cold seawater inside the volcano. The third and strongest of the explosions was heard over twenty-nine hundred miles away.

After blasting forth huge quantities of lava and ash, Krakatoa's great volcanic cone apparently collapsed in upon itself. Thus, fully two-thirds of this island, once twenty-five miles long and seventeen miles wide, sank beneath the sea.

So much volcanic ash and debris now filled the air that the region was plunged into total darkness for two and one-half days. The atmospheric shock wave circled the globe several times in each direction—registering clearly on barometers as it passed—and spawned still more destructive tornadoes on Java and Sumatra.

Worst of all, the upheavals created huge tidal waves—tsunamis—between 50 and about 120 feet high. Propelled outward from Krakatoa, they swept over coastal towns of Java and Sumatra, causing most of the over thirty-six thousand deaths attributed to the Krakatoa eruption. The waves ultimately traveled for thousands of miles, reaching as far as South America and Africa's Cape Horn.

Krakatoa hurled some five cubic miles of debris into the upper atmosphere, and traces of it remained there for over two years. The resulting distortion of sunlight produced brilliant and sometimes strange sunsets and sky glows. The sun appeared blue in South America, and for months set green in Honolulu. Brilliant red sky glows after sunset were at times mistaken for distant fires. Volcanic dust blocking out sunlight was even blamed for a one-degree-Fahrenheit drop in average temperatures throughout the northern hemisphere during the nineteenth century.

To say this blast changed the face of Indonesia would be an understatement.

1883: The Steamship *Daphne* Capsizes. Hundreds of workers were still aboard the five-hundred-ton steamship *Daphne* as she was launched into the Clyde River near Glasgow, Scotland, on July 3. For some reason, however, the ship slid down the ways too quickly, causing the unfinished ship to begin rocking sharply from side to side after it hit the water.

Apparently panicked by the possibility of the ship capsizing, the workers aboard *Daphne* began running back and forth as the ship rocked, and within three minutes the ship did capsize. Many of those on the deck were hurled bruised and bloodied into the water, where strong river currents drowned them in large numbers. The bodies of those working belowdecks were found later, piled one on top of another at doorways with tools still in their hands. The accident killed 195 of the 200 workmen on board.

Maybe she was whacked too hard with the bottle of champagne.

1884: Cyclone Rips Through Southeastern U.S. A cyclone gathered force in the Gulf of Mexico on February 19 and drove inland, cutting a path of destruction across the southern United States. At Columbus, Georgia, the storm split, with one storm system tearing northwestward across Georgia and the Carolinas, and a second devastating Georgia.

Furious winds that swept across the southern states collapsed houses and devastated entire communities. Egg-size hailstones and driving rains followed in the wakes of the cyclones. In Georgia, winds carried a piano half a mile, while in South Carolina, the storm hurled a man three hundred yards through the air before crushing him to death. One victim was found with a timber driven through his abdomen. By the time the storm blew out to sea in the Atlantic, some eight hundred people had been killed.

And you thought the cyclone scene at the beginning of *The Wizard of Oz* was the product of someone's vivid imagination.

1885: Battle of Khartoum. The garrison town of Khartoum in the Sudan was surrounded in mid-1884 by a strong force of Sudanese rebels led by Muhammad Ahmed, who claimed to be the Mahdi, a divine leader in the Muslim faith. Defended by a small force of Egyptians under the leadership of British colonial administrator Charles Gordon, the garrison miraculously held out for months while the British government stubbornly refused to send troops to relieve Khartoum. When finally a small force was sent, it arrived two days too late. The rebels had taken Khartoum on January 26 and executed Gordon. Forces led by Herbert Kitchener (later lord) eventually reconquered the Sudan.

The British government's hesitation caused the death of one of the truly brave people in history.

1886: Earthquake Shakes Eastern United States. On the morning of August 31, an earthquake shook much of the eastern

United States, from Charleston, South Carolina, to Boston in the East, and from Milwaukee to New Orleans in the West. Charleston was hit hard, with 110 deaths.

People in Charleston are beginning to get nervous.

1887: Deadly Earthquake Shakes Riviera. In the early morning of February 23, all-night revelers in Nice, France, were just heading home from a pre-Lenten carnival ball. Their ornate costumes were weirdly inappropriate for what happened next. Suddenly walls cracked and church bells clanged as the earth rumbled with the first shock of a quake at 6:00 A.M. Crowds of frightened people prayed in the streets, while others formed long lines at church confessional booths until a second shock sent them scurrying back into the streets for safety.

Throughout the French and Italian Riviera, buildings crumbled, burying hundreds in the falling ruins. Whole villages built on the picturesque mountainsides were lost in great avalanches that slid down into the valleys below. Some three hundred persons were killed together in one Italian town when their church collapsed upon them. In other towns and villages, people were swallowed by the fissures opening up in the ground.

Tremors continued throughout that deadly February day, and thousands of people slept in the cold streets that night, fearing new shocks. Over two thousand people died in the quake.

Did the long lines at the confessionals signify a pervasive Catholic guilt or a recklessly irreverent way of life, or both?

1887: Paris Opera Fire. The opera *Mignon* had just started at the aging wood and brick Paris Opera Comique on May 25 when a gas jet set fire to the scenery on stage. The audience of several hundred theatergoers watched in horror as the entire stage immediately burst into flames. One actor pleaded with the audience to remain seated until fire exits were opened, thus allowing most people on the lower level to escape. But those on the upper levels scrambled to get out, becoming hopelessly entangled in panicked masses at the narrow stairways. One woman coolly made her way around the outside of the building on a narrow cornice, ignoring the flames bursting above her, until she reached a fire escape. Others, trapped on the roof and pleading to be rescued, were instantly incinerated when the roof, its supports burned away, suddenly collapsed. In all, some two hundred people died in the fire, most of them in the upper galleries.

Gaslight was a great boon to culture.

1887: Chatsworth Railway Disaster. An excursion train, packed with some nine hundred passengers, was behind schedule when it left Peoria, Illinois, en route to Niagara Falls on August 10. Then, just after passing through Chatsworth, Illinois, the engineer saw a fire on the tracks ahead and to his horror realized that the wooden trestle bridge over a small, six-foot-deep gully was burning. The seventeen-car train was traveling too fast to stop in time; so the engineer decided to try crossing the burning structure at full speed.

The first engine made it across, though the cars behind it were not so lucky. Six day coaches, three baggage cars, a tender, and two other passenger cars all dropped into the gulley with the collapsing bridge, the cars crashing into one another on impact. Burning debris, railroad cars, and bodies of the dead and injured passengers were strewn about the crash site. A survivor recalled, "The groans of men and screams of women united to make an appalling sound, and above all could be heard agonizing cries of little children who lay pinned alongside their dead parents."

In a matter of moments, 82 people were killed and some 270 were critically injured. But the death toll probably would have been much higher if the six coaches at the rear of the train had not stopped just before reaching the fallen bridge.

Well, the engineer was partly right.

1887: Exeter Theatre Fire. A full house of some fourteen hundred theatergoers packed the Theatre Royal in Exeter, England, for the performance of *Romany Rye* on September 5. At about 10:30 P.M. a gas lamp set fire to one of the fly curtains backstage. As thick smoke and flames spread through the auditorium, most people seated on the lower level managed to escape in orderly fashion. Panic swept over those in the gallery, however, and people rushed wildly for the stairs, trampling those who fell. One man, a soldier named Scattergood, made it down the gallery stairway only to turn back up into the crush to rescue some children crying for help. The children got out, but Scattergood was later found burned to death. The fire, which illuminated the whole city, killed some two hundred.

Always sit in the orchestra seats.

1887: Flooding in China. The Yellow River (Huang Ho) in Hunan Province changed its course for the ninth time in twenty-five hundred years, breaking through dikes on September 28, 1887, and flooding thousands of square miles.

Although there were signs that the Yellow River was going to change it course again—its mouth was silting up as it had in the past—millions of residents living in the surrounding Hunan plain hoped it would not happen in their lifetimes. Several populous cities and some three thousand villages lay near the Yellow River, and none of them were on high ground.

On September 28 the river was swollen by snow melting in the mountains far upstream. The waters pounded against a dike holding it in its course near Ching-Chow, until suddenly, in an area southwest of the city, part of the dike gave way. The torrent of water burst through the opening, tearing a hole in the dike twelve hundred yards long. A great wall of water twenty miles wide and ten feet deep swept across the plain at about twenty miles per hour, uprooting trees, tearing buildings off their foundations, and washing away entire villages.

Frantic inhabitants, running for high ground, were swept away by the faster-moving flood. Hundreds of thousands sought safety in treetops, clutching desperately to the branches. In the heavily populated cities, hundreds of thousands drowned when they became trapped in buildings or the force of the flood waters dashed them into walls and drowned them.

When the torrent finally abated, not a village or city remained. Instead, a huge lake ten to thirty feet deep covered an area of ten thousand square miles. Rescue crews paddled about in boats, taking in victims hanging on to floating debris and plucking others from treetops. What was once the riverbed was now the only dry land for thousands of miles.

The devastation did not end when the waters receded, however; almost all the livestock had drowned, and the crops were ruined. Many people lucky enough to survive the flood died of starvation in the months following. Some 1.5 million people lost their lives in the flood, and more than 3 million were left homeless.

Millions of Chinese have lost their lives in floods and famines over the centuries. Yet millions continue to struggle. A dauntless people.

1887: Four Hundred Die in Fire Aboard Steamship. The British steamship *Wah Yeung* was engulfed in flames and burned to the waterline while in the Canton River outside Hong Kong on November 15. Those not killed by the fire drowned trying to escape the burning wreck.

1888–1891: Jack the Ripper Terrorizes Whitechapel. Her body was found in a dimly lit spot directly beneath a railroad archway in Whitechapel, England. The location, well chosen by her killer, was midway between two bright lamps. This was a popular place for prostitutes to wait for customers in the late hours of the evening, and police had trouble keeping the area clear. On the night of the murder in 1891, however, no witnesses were found who could give information about the crime.

The victim, who went by the name of "Carrotty Nell" because of her bright red hair, was well-known to police as one of the women who frequently loitered in the area late at night. A young police officer, on night duty for the first time, found her lying in the shadows and, supposing her asleep, turned on his flashlight.

Instead of a sleeping harlot, he confronted an appalling sight. Nell's throat had been cut all the way through her neck to her spinal column. Blood gushed from the terrible gash, and as the young officer stared in horror, the victim opened her eyes. Just then, he heard the footsteps of someone running nearby. Uncertain whether to remain with the dying woman or pursue the fleeing suspect, he blew his whistle for assistance. By the time help arrived, the murderer was long gone. The victim, whose real name was Frances Coles, died almost immediately afterward.

A friend of the dead woman reported they had been together just after midnight and met a young sailor. He accosted them both and behaved violently; she warned Frances not to go anywhere with him. "The next thing I heard was this morning . . . when someone told me a woman had been murdered near Leman Street. I said at once, 'I believe that's Frances.' "

Carrotty Nell was the ninth and last victim of a vicious murderer who had been stalking and killing women in a square-mile area of Whitechapel since 1888. Called "Jack the Ripper" by the press and public, the murderer had evaded capture despite the strenuous investigations of police and considerable public panic in the area. The police at one point went so far as to photograph the eyes of one victim on the theory that the murderer's image might be recorded on the retinas. Nice try. The theory was later discredited.

All of the Ripper's victims were women of low social class, women who walked the streets. Most died of savage throat wounds, although many were also victims of mutilation, leading police to opine that the murderer had a considerable knowledge of human anatomy. Perhaps a medical student practicing his craft? All were killed at night, close to dwellings where people slept; yet no witnesses were ever found. In all but one case, not even a sound was heard. That case, one of the first, was the worst of all. Two neighbors heard a woman scream, "Murder!" during the early morning hours but paid no attention because such noises were common where they lived. Nice neighborhood.

The victim turned out to be Mary Jane Kelly. Despite the officers patrolling Whitechapel, the killer had lured her into a miserable lodging house. There she had been so terribly mutilated that her body could not be identified for several days. Both legs and ears had been sliced from her body, and the floor of the room was slick with blood and flesh.

When the murders stopped, one official explanation was that the killer had been admitted to a mental hospital. Or perhaps that medical student passed his exams with flying colors? The murders were never solved officially, although there have been a few unofficial suspects throughout the years.

The case of Jack the Ripper remains one of the most famous unsolved murders in the annals of English crime, and speculation about his identity is rife even today. The case also provided the subject matter for many books and dramatic productions, and a reason for not going out alone at night.

1888: East Coast Blizzard. New York City was enjoying the warmest day of the new year on March 10, in the midst of its mildest winter in seventeen years. Temperatures hovered in the fifties. The next day, despite the development of a furious storm off the coast of Delaware, New York's forecast for March 12 predicted only "clearing and colder, preceded by light snow."

The forecast proved deadly wrong; a storm described as a "white tornado" moved rapidly up the Atlantic coast in the middle of the night. Waking up on March 12, New York City residents were stunned by the sight of nearly two feet of snow on the ground and a howling blizzard with forty-five-mile-per-hour winds. The temperature was a frigid fifteen degrees. One observer said, "The air looked as though people were throwing buckets full of flour from all the rooftops."

The storm crippled the eastern seaboard from Washington to Boston. Furious winds raised mountainous waves that dashed the coast; boats foundered and were driven aground.

By midmorning March 12, winds had increased to eighty-five miles per hour in New York. Roofs and church steeples collapsed, windows were smashed, and telephone poles toppled. The city ground to a halt as trains and horse carriages became stranded; even snowplows pulled by twenty horses could not make their way through massive snowdrifts. Some fifteen thousand people were stranded on elevated trains stuck between stations. In true New York fashion, some would-be "rescuers" with ladders charged each stranded passenger a hefty two-dollar fee before letting them down to the ground.

Overflowing hotels put up stranded guests on cots in their halls and bathrooms. Among them was Mark Twain, who wrote to his wife: "Crusoeing on a desert hotel." A young Theodore Roosevelt briskly walked three miles through the blizzard for a business appointment. When the man he was to meet failed to show up, the irritated Roosevelt wrote him, "I presume the blizzard kept you at home," and then walked back through the blizzard.

By the night of March 12, roads and rail lines were blocked, telephone and telegraph lines were down, and New York City found itself virtually cut off from the outside world. Meanwhile, people froze to death in the streets as snowdrifts piled as high as fifteen feet. With food and coal for heat already becoming scarce, fears of serious shortages mounted.

The furious, snowy winds literally picked up small children, flung them through the air, and dropped them onto enormous banks of snow. One man wearing snowshoes claimed to have walked over snow so deep, he was up to treetops. Another claimed to have nearly suffocated when huge icicles formed on his mustache, blocking his mouth and nose. Huge chunks of ice lodged in the East River, forming a bridge from Manhattan to

Brooklyn. Crowds walked across the ice rather than wait for the ferry—until the ice floe broke loose and many people had to be rescued.

The blizzard finally ended on March 13, but the process of digging out the city took days. The bodies of people frozen to death remained buried under massive snowdrifts for days in some cases. Ultimately the blizzard probably killed as many as eight hundred people, two hundred of them in New York City alone.

Our weather forecasts are more accurate now. Usually.

1888: Hailstorm Kills 250. Hailstones as big as baseballs bombarded the Moradabad district of India near Delhi on April 30, demolishing the roofs of houses, knocking down trees, and killing those unfortunate enough to be without shelter.

1889: Johnstown, Pennsylvania, Flood. Situated at the bottom of a gorge and at the junction of two rivers, Johnstown was a frequent victim of flooding. The thirty thousand residents of the small Pennsylvania city and surrounding floodplain had become used to this inconvenience, however, and when floodwaters rose, they simply retreated to the upper stories of their homes.

Few people thought about another hazard confronting Johnstown—Conemaugh Lake perched at the top of the gorge some sixteen miles from the city. Covering 450 acres and reaching depths of seventy feet, the man-made lake had originally been built as a reservoir, but was purchased in 1852 by a group of wealthy Pittsburgh industrialists for use as a private fishing lake. They removed the discharge pipes of the dam so that the lake would remain full, and partially blocked the spillways to prevent fish from escaping. The practical effect of these alterations was to remove all means of relieving pressure on the dam, and thereby set the stage for its eventual collapse.

On May 31 a heavy rainstorm inundated the floodplain, the water rising up to ten feet in parts of Johnstown. Residents once again moved upstairs in their homes to wait out the flood, as they had done so many times before. Meanwhile, Lake Conemaugh was rising six inches an hour.

At 3:10 P.M. the dam finally broke, spewing twenty million tons of water down the gorge and into the valley below. The entire lake emptied in less than forty-five minutes, and after leveling the small towns in its path, the torrent of water reached Johnstown. A train engineer a few miles from town blew his train whistle as a warning, and many residents were able to make it to the hills in time. Most, however, were not so lucky. The raging water crashed through the town at almost forty miles per hour, carrying with it houses, farm animals, train cars, and machinery from the now-flattened Cambria Iron Works.

One survivor remembers seeing "an advancing rotary wave of black water, forty feet high" and "huge tree trunks lolling in the air as they turned endwise and disappeared." Thousands clung desperately to the roofs of their homes, which had been lifted off their foundations and carried along by the churning deluge. A stone bridge on the far side of town blocked much of the floating debris, creating a thirty-acre island of wreckage in which hundreds of victims were trapped. Other people flocked to this island as a safe haven from the raging floodwater, only to face a greater horror when the wreckage caught fire at 6:00 P.M. Over two hundred victims perished in the flames.

When the floodwaters finally receded the next day, over twenty-two hundred people were dead, and more than ninety-nine entire families were wiped out. Among the more fortunate of the survivors, though, was a five-month-old baby. The infant was found unharmed in Pittsburgh after floating seventy-five miles downstream on the floor of a house.

There was no official word on the loss of fish in Conemaugh Lake.

1889–1890: Worldwide Influenza Epidemic. The "Asiatic" influenza epidemic began in May 1889 in Russia, struck North America the following December, and spread throughout the world, reaching Australia by March 1890. Though no figures for the number of deaths are available, in Germany alone an estimated 1 percent of the population died.

1891: Rescue of British Harpooner. While at sea in February, a harpooner aboard a British whaling boat accidentally fell overboard and was swallowed up by none other than the whale he had been hunting. One might suppose that such accidents happened from time to time in a dangerous profession like whaling, but what happened next was almost beyond belief.

Some two hours later, the whaler's shipmates hauled aboard a whale they had just killed. As usual, work began immediately on cutting up the huge carcass—until one sailor noticed something odd about the whale's stomach. When they cut it open, out fell the missing harpooner, still very much alive.

The strain of having been so close to death in those strange circumstances left the man temporarily insane, but he recovered after two weeks. He told his shipmates that the heat and humidity in the whale's stomach had been especially unbearable, though he had been able to breathe well enough.

For the record, the harpooner's name was not Jonah.

1891: Swiss Railroad Bridge Collapse Kills 120. A newly constructed bridge over the Birs River near Basel, Switzerland, collapsed when a train made up of two locomotives and twelve passenger cars moved out onto it. The two locomotives and three passenger cars dropped to the river below, killing or severely injuring all those aboard.

The Swiss have long been known for the exactitude of their engineering projects.

1891: Caribbean Hurricane. A powerful hurricane battered the island of Martinique on August 18, and in just four hours killed about seven hundred people and caused over ten million dollars in damages.

1891: Earthquake Shakes Up Central Japan. On October 28 one of the most powerful earthquake shocks ever recorded hit heavily populated central Japan, instantly shifting the ground by up to forty feet along a sixty-mile fault line. About two hundred thousand houses and ten thousand bridges were knocked down, and seventy-three hundred people were killed.

1892: Oil City, Pennsylvania, Catches Fire. Heavy rains the previous month had already caused flooding at Oil City when on June 4 a thunderstorm broke over the city. Suddenly there was a loud explosion, and flaming oil, apparently loosed from a ruptured storage tank, began flowing on the rushing floodwaters straight into the town of Oil City, and nearby Titusville as well. Fire killed 130 people and destroyed both towns.

1892: Lizzie Borden Ax Murders. On the morning of August 4 in their home in Fall River, Massachusetts, Abby Borden was hacked to death with nineteen blows from an ax, and her husband was likewise killed by eleven blows to the head. Though daughter Lizzie was the prime suspect in the brutal murders, she was acquitted after one of the most sensational trials in U.S. history. She lived quietly in Fall River until her death in 1927.

Lizzie's story spawned a lot of literature—and one ballet.

1893: Hurricane Kills One Thousand in the South. An Atlantic hurricane with winds of one hundred miles per hour, torrential rains, and heavy seas roared into Georgia and South Carolina on August 28, leaving coastal areas from Savannah to Charleston in ruins. The storm raged from the afternoon to midnight, smashing houses, ripping up trees, destroying boats, and flooding coastal islands.

One witness described Charleston as looking as if it had "passed through a great siege of shot and shell and a subsequent deluge." Ancient trees lay toppled, tangled with wreckage of houses. Parris Island, South Carolina, was swamped under fifteen feet of water, and a tidal wave at Port Royal, South Carolina, wiped out the entire town. The storm killed an estimated one thousand people.

1893: Killer Hurricane Hits Gulf of Mexico. The second major hurricane to hit southern states this year struck the coasts of Louisiana, Mississippi, and Alabama on October 1. Packing 120-mile-per-hour winds, the storm destroyed everything in its path.

The Louisiana islands of Grand Isle and Cheniere were flooded by massive waves. Houses crumbled as winds tore off roofs and flood waves carried away the walls. Survivors swam from one standing house to another, but each building seemed to collapse as soon as they reached it. In New Orleans and Biloxi, Mississippi, winds slammed boats onto shore and knocked down factories and other structures. In Alabama fifteen hundred downed trees covered one fifteen-mile section of road, while in the city of Mobile, crowds waded through water up to their armpits and rode in boats down main avenues. Amid all this destruction, an estimated two thousand people were killed.

1893–1894: Deadly Cholera Epidemic. Another in a series of outbreaks of cholera in the nineteenth century, this epidemic spread worldwide and killed millions in a two-year period.

It was during this epidemic that the composer Tchaikovsky died.

1894: Forest Fire Incinerates Hinckley, Minnesota. Four months of drought left the forests of eastern Minnesota ripe for catastrophe, and by the end of August small fires were already burning in woodlands near Hinckley, Minnesota. The final ingredient, high winds of up to eighty miles per hour, suddenly sprang up on September 2, whipping the fires into a massive wall of flame that raced toward Hinckley, a quiet town of twelve hundred people.

With barely any warning, the fire suddenly appeared, consuming the lumber mill and other buildings on the outskirts. By noontime a priest was running from door to door, screaming, "Run for your lives! Run to the gravel pit, run to the river! Save yourselves!" Meanwhile, enormous tongues of flames driven by the winds were already invading the town.

Almost five hundred terrified residents of Hinckley clambered aboard a train before it roared out of the station, which was already in flames. Paint dripped from the train's side in the intense heat generated by the fire. The bridge over the Kettle River was completely engulfed in flames when the train reached it, but with the furnace of wind-driven fire behind them, the engineer had no real choice but to take the train across. Two minutes after the train cleared the bridge, the weakened structure collapsed into the river.

Another train, the Duluth Limited, ground to a stop outside of Hinckley as massive flames suddenly flared up on all sides. About one hundred terrified refugees ran toward the train, scrambling aboard as the engineer started backing it up.

"The wild panic was horrible," one passenger said. "Every fear-crazed person was for himself, and they did not care how they got out of the swirling, rushing avalanche of flame." Refugees who could not climb on board in time collapsed in the flames.

The intensity of the heat smashed windows in all the cars, and the baggage car went up in flames. The engineer struggled to stay at his controls in heat so intense, his clothes caught fire. When the train finally stopped at Skunk Lake some six miles outside of Hinckley, the engineer fell dead. But thanks to his efforts, three hundred people found safety in the lake until the fire burned down.

For those left behind in Hinckley, there was little hope of escape. Just as the first train pulled out, powerful winds blew a torrent of flames over the town. Buildings were consumed so quickly by flames, they seemed to be melting. Some people who tried to escape on horseback headed straight into the fire that spread everywhere at once. Shallow streams around Hinckley became death traps as hundreds of people tried to take refuge in them. But because there was too little water, these people were simply roasted alive. In the end, a gravel pit filled with stagnant water proved to be the town's only place of refuge. One hundred people waded into the pit—along with horses, cows, and dogs instinctively drawn there—while the fire raged all around them.

Within hours, nothing stood in Hinckley except the charred walls of the schoolhouse and the railroad roundhouse. Meanwhile, the entire valley between the Kettle River and Cross Lake was destroyed. The towns of Mission Creek, Pokegama, and over a dozen others met the same fate as Hinckley. In all, some 600 people were killed, 413 of them in Hinckley alone.

Hell has less fury.

1895: Spanish Warship Founders. *Reina Regente,* a Spanish cruiser returning from Tangiers, foundered and sank in a storm near the Strait of Gibraltar on March 13. All 402 officers and crew aboard went down with the ship.

1896–97: Famine Hits India Again. Some five million people in India died of famine and disease in 1896 and 1897, following a severe drought. The deadly combination of drought and famine killed another 1.25 million during 1899 and 1900.

Another round of cruel population control.

1896: Cripple Creek Conflagration. Cripple Creek, Colorado, was a gold rush town of ten thousand rough-and-ready miners, gamblers, saloonkeepers, and their "hostesses." During a fight at the dance hall on April 25, an overturned kerosene lamp started a fire that eventually burned down almost all the buildings in town. Days later, a grease fire in one of the remaining hotels spread to a nearby storehouse containing a half ton of dynamite. The tremendous explosion that resulted demolished the last of the buildings still standing in Cripple Creek.

And you wonder why they called it the Wild West.

1896: Deadly Twister Devastates Saint Louis. Bolts of lightning began to light up the sky west of Saint Louis, Missouri, an hour before the tornado struck on May 27. By 6 P.M. the lightning seemed continuous. A torrential downpour began as the wind rose to terrifying speeds.

For twenty minutes the tornado tore through a six-mile section of the city. According to one report, winds reached an incredible, if not impossible, 560 miles per hour. Whatever the wind speed, the destruction wrought by the storm was indisputable.

High winds peeled off roofs and tore houses apart, blew streetcars off their tracks, and filled the air with shingles, signs, bricks, glass, and tons of other debris. Straws of wheat were driven a half inch into a tree by the powerful winds, and a wooden two-by-four was driven through a piece of iron five-eighths of an inch thick.

Amid all this havoc, a man saw a baby spiraling down out of the sky and actually managed to catch it in his arms, only to find the infant was already dead. The baby was one of 306 people killed in the storm. Another 2,500 were injured.

It doesn't just happen in Kansas, Toto.

1896: Japanese Tidal Wave. The evening of June 15 seemed no different from any other on the northeast coast of Japan, but offshore a submarine earthquake created a huge tidal wave that, by the time it reached Japan, was eighty feet high and some three hundred miles wide.

People along the Japanese coast went to bed early as usual, and so many never knew what hit them when the monster wave crashed into their villages. Rampaging through streets and houses and into the fields beyond, the wave wiped out whole families in an instant. Its rapidly receding waters swept entire coastal towns into the ocean.

Only a handful of the six thousand citizens of Kumaishi survived the sudden deluge, and the story was much the same up and down the northeast coast. In all, some twenty-eight thousand people perished in the disaster, and thousands of homes vanished.

1897: Tragic Fire at Paris Charity Bazaar. Hundreds of Paris aristocrats and the charitably minded wealthy thronged the Rue Jean Goujon in Paris on May 4, browsing the closely packed stalls built to represent Old Paris shops. Suddenly a flash fire broke out and swept the entire bazaar in just minutes, killing some two hundred of the Paris elite and severely injuring many others.

1898: Sinking of the *Maine*. When growing opposition to Spanish colonial rule in Cuba led to riots in Havana, the United States sent the battleship *Maine* to protect American citizens and property there. At 9:45 P.M. on February 15 the warship lay at anchor in Havana Harbor, with most of the 360 navymen aboard belowdecks.

Suddenly an explosion in a magazine located below the crew's quarters jolted the big ship. Then a horrendous blast, apparently touched off by the first explosion, lifted the entire ship out of the water and rained fragments of iron and brass for three hundred yards around.

Hundreds of sailors were trapped as water surged into the torn hull. Sailors jammed one escape ladder, clawing each other in a frantic effort to escape, but most of the men below had little time to find a way out. Meanwhile, crewmen on deck desperately tried to throw overboard explosives from the remaining magazines, but fires set off new explosions that quickly sank the battleship.

The actual cause of the explosion, which killed 264 United States sailors, was never discovered, but rumors that Spain was somehow involved were whipped up by sensationalistic stories in popular newspapers of the day. They championed the cry "Remember the *Maine,* to hell with Spain!" and called for armed intervention by the United States. Just a few weeks later, they had their wish with the outbreak of the Spanish-American War.

It was a lovely little war from which Theodore Roosevelt gained fame and glory, and the United States emerged as a world power.

1898: Collison at Sea Kills 571. On July 4 the French liner *Bourgogne* collided with a British ship, *Cromartyshire,* in a fogbank off Nova Scotia. The French liner sank quickly, and only a few of the six hundred people aboard got away safely before she went under. The *Cromartyshire* picked up survivors and returned safely to port.

1898: Blizzard Hits Coastal Northeastern U.S. A howling blizzard along the northeastern coast from New York to Maine on November 26 and 27 dumped heavy snows throughout the area and ravaged coastal shipping. Driving snow, sixty-mile-per-hour winds, and heavy seas caused over one hundred shipwrecks, with Boston Harbor and the Massachusetts coast being the hardest hit.

New York City was paralyzed by a snowfall that measured over eight inches, and heavy snows blanketed other cities farther north along the coast. Meanwhile, the gale-force winds and blinding snow littered the shores of Massachusetts with demolished ships.

Some sailors froze to death in the ships' riggings before the vessels were wrecked on the shore, and ice covering the ships was so thick that rescuers could not even read the vessels' names. More than one hundred ships washed ashore, dozens of them completely destroyed. Deaths caused by the storm reached 455.

1899: New York's Windsor Hotel Burns. Guests and visitors at New York's luxurious Windsor Hotel watched the Saint Patrick's Day Parade on Fifth Avenue from the windows of their rooms on the afternoon of March 17. One of them, standing at a second-floor window at 3:00 P.M., casually lit a cigar and tossed the lighted match out the open window. Just then a gust of wind stirred the lace curtains, and the match set them on fire. The curtains exploded into flames, which quickly spread up to the drapery above and then to the walls.

As the fire spread with devastating speed, a hotel waiter rushed onto the sidewalk screaming, "Fire! Fire!" Unfortunately, the parade music drowned out his voice, and crowds on the street did not realize the Windsor was on fire until smoke and flames began pouring out the the hotel windows.

Terrified hotel guests tried climbing down safety ropes anchored to their windows, but many fell to their deaths because they could not hold on to the coarse rope. Fourteen others panicked, leaping from windows to their deaths. The hotel was completely gutted within an hour after the fire began, and in all, ninety-two people were killed and scores were injured in the tragic hotel inferno.

If you're old enough to smoke, you're old enough to know how to put out a match.

1900–1907: Sleeping Sickness Epidemic. During the nineteenth century, the region around Lake Victoria in Uganda had become thickly populated, thanks to the fertile soil and ample rainfall that made farming a dependable livelihood. But beginning in 1900, hundreds of people in this otherwise prosperous area began to fall sick and die of the dread local disease *lumbe,* what European doctors knew as African sleeping sickness or trypanosomiasis, a viral disease of the brain.

Death came in stages of increased suffering: The victims first suffered headaches, listlessness, insomnia, and feelings of oppression. The second stage brought severe daytime drowsiness and signs of mental disintegration. Finally, in the third stage, agonizing pain, coma, and then death overtook the victim. There was no cure. Native doctors and missionaries could only try to ease the suffering of the thousands, and then the tens of thousands, struck down by the disease, by setting up primitive hospitals and camps in an effort to try to isolate victims from other villagers.

The disease had always existed in Africa but had been confined to relatively small, isolated areas. European colonization during the nineteenth century, however, was changing the way of life in Africa. Vast areas of the continent were now being opened to trade and development, and people moved about more freely. Presumably Africans infected with sleeping sickness traveled to new areas, thereby helping spread the disease. And the insect that carried the disease, a species of the tsetse fly, was moving, too.

As it happened, this relative of the common housefly also flourished in the fertile soils of the Lake Victoria region. Once infected by the microscopic parasite that actually caused sleeping sickness, the flies passed the parasite into the blood of any creature they bit. The parasite then moved through the bloodstream to the victim's central nervous system, where it caused the characteristic symptoms and slow, agonizing death associated with sleeping sickness.

The British, who had made Uganda a protectorate in 1894, acted to stem the disease's progress once it had reached epidemic proportions in 1900. Commissions of scientists and doctors began to study the disease to try to find the cause and how the disease spread. The first breakthrough came when a British army doctor found a direct correlation between areas where the disease was prevalent and where tsetse flies were found in large numbers.

Then the parasite itself was isolated, first in African livestock and then in laboratory monkeys.

Knowing the cause of the epidemic and the means by which it was transmitted was little help to the Ugandans, who were dying by the thousands. Finally the British commissioner in Uganda appealed to the local tribal chiefs to help move the entire surviving population out of fly-infested areas. By 1907, after seven years of suffering and death, the drastic measure of relocation had halted the dreadful epidemic. But by then some two hundred thousand Africans had already died.

1900: Utah Coal Mine Explodes. An accidental explosion of blasting powder in a coal mine at Schofield, Utah, on May 1 killed 201 miners and wrecked two mine shafts. Poison gases that filled the mines after the explosion smothered many of the miners.

Coal mining is the pits.

1900: Boxer Rebellion. Deep resentment over the growing influence of Western culture in Chinese life erupted into a short-lived revolt by the Chinese secret society of I-Ho-Chuan ("Righteous and Harmonious Fists"). Called "Boxers" by foreigners because of the calisthenics society members performed to supposedly make themselves impervious to bullets, they were especially resentful of Christian missionaries, and by May 1900 began attacking them in rural areas around Peking (now Beijing).

In June European powers organized a twenty-one-hundred-man force to protect foreigners at Peking, but the empress dowager, a true xenophobic, who had previously made a show of denouncing the Boxers, used imperial troops to turn back the European troops before they could reach the city. At this point tens of thousands of Boxers rampaged throughout Peking, attacking Christian missionaries and foreigners, killing Chinese suspected of being Christians, and burning homes and churches. The situation worsened on June 18, when the empress dowager ordered the killing of all foreigners. The Boxers immediately murdered the German foreign minister and besieged the Westerners and Chinese Christians who had taken refuge in churches and embassies.

An eighteen-thousand-man European relief force finally reached Peking on August 14 and put down the revolt, freeing the Westerners and Chinese Christians and forcing the empress dowager to flee. In later negotiations, China was forced to pay heavy reparations and make even more commercial concessions to the foreign governments.

And the Boxers discovered only Superman can stop a speeding bullet.

1900: Italian King Umberto I Assassinated. A gun-toting anarchist shot Italian King Umberto I three times at Monza, Italy, on the evening of July 30. The king died shortly afterward of his wounds. The assassin, Angelo Bresci, was captured at the scene and later committed suicide in his prison cell while awaiting execution.

The monarchy wouldn't live much longer in Italy, either.

1900: Galveston Hurricane. Before this devastating storm, Galveston was a bustling town of thirty-eight thousand, widely known as a wealthy seaside community and one of the nation's busiest centers for exporting grain. Experts also knew of its vulnerability to a serious hurricane—the city was located off the Texas coast on a six-square-mile sandbar, which rose just five to nine feet above sea level. However, local residents had no fears: Bridges connected Galveston with the mainland some two miles away, and in the past, major hurricanes had always veered away from the city. Thus, experts who had called for a sea wall to protect the city were easily ignored, and few people evacuated to the mainland as this latest hurricane approached.

Unlike past storms, though, the hurricane kept heading straight for Galveston, and by 4:00 A.M. on Saturday, May 8, thirty-mile-per-hour winds whipped up the surrounding sea and lashed the city with driving rains. Throughout the early morning, rain and wind became increasingly violent. The side of Galveston facing the mainland began flooding by 10:00 A.M. Then winds shifted and water rose up the seaward side. Meanwhile, houses began collapsing before the raging wind, which intensified by the hour. Ultimately, winds reached an estimated 120 miles per hour, but the exact speed will never be known—the local wind speed gauge was itself blown away after showing an eighty-four-miles-per-hour reading.

By early afternoon, several feet of water washed over Galveston's lower streets, and panicked citizens—at last recognizing disaster was upon them—fled to higher ground. Others, not so lucky, were crushed along with their homes when a twenty-foot-high tidal wave crashed ashore, smashing houses and trees into a pile of jumbled rubble twelve hundred feet farther inland.

Flooding claimed half the city by 3:00 P.M., and by then all four bridges connecting Galveston with the mainland were down. People now had no choice but to remain in their collapsing houses or to brave the waist-high water and roaring winds that hurled debris with deadly force. Some of those who ventured out found safety amid huge piles of debris and in buildings that withstood the storm. Others met with death, like those who drowned or were decapitated by wind-borne roof slates.

At the Ursuline Convent, which remained standing throughout the terrible storm, sisters managed to save over one thousand people floating helplessly amid the flooded streets. They did so by pulling the struggling victims from the fast-moving water with poles and ropes.

Meanwhile, almost all one hundred children and fifteen sisters at the Catholic Orphanage Asylum were killed after that building collapsed. As the building crumbled, each nun tied eight of the helpless babies to her waist and waded out into the storm-tossed floodwaters. Their bodies were found later, with the dead infants still lashed to them.

Finally, about midnight, the storm ended and floodwaters receded quickly. By this time the hurricane had killed some six thousand people and destroyed nearly every building in Galveston, but the disaster was still not over. Even as stunned survivors surveyed the wreckage the following day, hordes of looters descended upon the city by boat. The looters spared nothing, and some were even caught with pockets full of rings—still on fingers they had hurriedly detached from corpses. Over 250 looters were shot and killed by soldiers and the local militia before order was restored. And once again looters, like vultures, had descended on the victims for one brief moment of triumph.

Rebuilding began soon afterward, and in a few years a new city had replaced the old, this time with a protective sea wall. That's for sure!

1901: President McKinley Assassinated. On Friday, September 6, U.S. President William McKinley held a public reception in the Temple of Music at the Pan-American Exhibition in Buffalo, New York. The president stood on a raised dais waiting for the end of a musical performance, after which he was to greet the hundreds of onlookers gathered at the hall.

Just after 4:00 P.M., a plainly dressed man stepped forward toward the president; his hand, observers recalled, was bandaged or wrapped in some way. As McKinley smiled and extended his hand in greeting, the man pointed a gun at him and shot twice. Immediately two Secret Service men and a bystander caught the assassin, Leon Czolgosz, a self-proclaimed anarchist from Cleveland, Ohio.

After the shots, the president turned pale and sat down in his chair, insisting, "I am not badly hurt, I assure you." But he was rushed to the hospital, where surgeons succeeded in removing only one bullet. The president survived for a week before finally dying of his wounds at 2:15 A.M. on September 14. Czolgosz was convicted and electrocuted later in 1901.

Over the years the United States had enacted immigration laws against admitting polygamists, paupers, tubercular persons, and various criminal types, among others. To this list were added anarchists.

1902: Steamer Sinking Drowns 739. The British steamer *Camorta* foundered and sank in heavy seas off Rangoon, Burma, on May 6. Only a few of the more than seven hundred people aboard survived the accident.

1902: Mount Pelée's Deadly Eruption. An enormous volcanic explosion ripped away the side of the Caribbean volcano Mount Pelée on May 8, sending a giant gaseous fireball rolling down the mountainside onto the town of Saint Pierre, Martinique. Over thirty thousand people were incinerated in less than three minutes.

Warnings of the impending disaster began weeks beforehand. Mount Pelée rumbled ominously, and ash and debris began falling on this picturesque Caribbean seaport town while sulfur fumes fouled the air. Eventually birds fell dead, killed by poisonous gases, and horses suffocated in the streets. At night the mountain peak glowed red in the darkness, while boiling mud avalanches killed workers in the fields and destroyed a nearby sugar mill, and a mountain lake hissed and boiled from the heat of magma below it. Meanwhile, hordes of insects and snakes driven by the heat moved down the mountain into Saint Pierre.

Despite all this, the city was not evacuated. An important election was approaching, and the governor needed the townspeople's votes. Urging the newspaper editor and religious leaders to assure the people there was no cause for alarm, he finally ordered troops to block all roads leading from the city, just hours before disaster struck.

At 7:50 on the morning of May 8, four tremendous explosions ripped the crater of Mount Pelée. Huge flames rose from the crater itself, and a powerful gas explosion literally blew out the side of the mountain, sending an enormous fireball down the mountainside, like a "monstrous blowtorch." The superheated gases, white-hot bits of rock, and dust rained down on the thirty thousand people in Saint Pierre, flattening everything for ten square miles around. A survivor from a ship anchored in the harbor described the phenomenon as "a solid wall of flame . . . a hurricane of fire. . . . The town vanished before our eyes."

The cloud, called a *nuée ardent,* had internal temperatures of over 1,300 degrees Fahrenheit and traveled at speeds approaching one hundred miles per hour. An unusual phenomenon sometimes associated with volcanic eruptions, it resulted from a blockage in the volcano's cone during the eruption. Fiery gases trapped inside the volcano exploded and blew a hole in the side of the mountain, releasing a huge ball of gases and debris.

Many victims in Saint Pierre died of breathing the hot gases, their lungs destroyed instantly; others actually boiled to death. Many victims were discovered with their clothing intact and unburned because the superheated cloud passed too quickly to ignite the cloth. But the fiery gases nevertheless swelled and blistered their bodies, the terrible heat turning their bodily fluids to steam and exploding their brains.

There were just two survivors in Saint Pierre. A shoemaker, frightened by the volcano's advance warnings, had locked himself in a stone basement days before the catastrophe. He later became a tour guide, leading curious tourists through the ruins of the town that had been his home. The other survivor, a convicted murderer, was locked in a cell when the fiery cloud hit. Blinded and badly burned, he survived for four days before being discovered, still trapped in his cell. Later, after his sentence had been commuted, he became a missionary.

Needless to say, the governor lost his captive votes.

1902: Guatemalan Volcano. In late October the coffee crop, one of the largest in Guatemala's history, stood ready to be harvested in the coastal mountains. But the sudden eruption of the volcano Santa Maria on October 25 wiped out the crop, burying it under seven feet of volcanic sand and ash.

The coffee crop was far from the only loss in this massive eruption, however. The twelve-thousand-foot volcano ejected huge quantities of hot rocks, poisonous gases, and ash, threatening the cities of Quetzaltenango, San Felipe, and Mazatenango, and various mountain villages. Six inches of volcanic matter covered Quetzaltenango, and earthquakes toppled buildings throughout the region. The cloud of ash over Santa Maria rose eighteen miles above the raging volcano, which eventually blew out one side of its cone. Some six thousand people throughout the region were killed in the disaster.

1903–1908: Plague Sweeps Over India. A persistent epidemic of plague lasting for years afflicted India, and at its height killed forty thousand people per week in places in the north. About four million people died before the epidemic abated in 1908.

1903: Iroquois Theater Fire. Chicago's Iroquois Theater was just five weeks old on December 28 and had been hailed as "a palace of marble and plate glass, plush and mahogany and gilding." The 1,602-seat theater was also supposed to be "absolutely fireproof," which might explain the lack of even basic fire-fighting equipment and the fact that all but three exits were locked when the fire broke out.

On December 28 some two thousand patrons packed the posh theater—well beyond its rated capacity—for the matinee of *Mr. Bluebeard*. At 3:20 P.M., with the show in progress, sparks thrown off by an electric arc lamp started a fire backstage. For a crucial minute the small flame burning some canvas scenery could have been quenched easily, but the new theater's sprinkler system remained unfinished. Stagehands slapped futilely at the burning scenery about twelve feet above the stage, and six tubes of powder extinguisher, the theater's only fire extinguishers, did nothing.

Within a minute the fire was out of control, spreading to other scenery and along oiled ropes. One performer fainted while bravely trying to continue singing. The audience was calm when the show's star, Eddie Foy, cried out for someone to lower the asbestos curtain. But the Iroquois's much-vaunted fireproof curtain, like its other fire precautions, did not exist.

A confused stagehand lowered instead a flammable painted backdrop, which stuck halfway down and concentrated the blaze in the stage area. A sudden draft of wind from the rear entrance then blew a huge ball of fire directly into the audience. Panic-stricken, the crowd broke into a "mad, animal-like stampede" as the rest of the scenery burst into flames.

Drapes, carpeting, and the theater's other luxury appointments caught fire in seconds. Hundreds of people fled the theater's balcony and gallery, which emptied into just one corridor. Desperate multitudes soon clogged the passage, and those who fell, including many children, were crushed to death.

Victims fortunate enough to reach exits found most of them locked. Piles of bodies of burned and suffocated victims eventually built up at the doors to a height of six feet. Meanwhile other panic-stricken hordes turned the theater's grand marble staircase into a deadly chute, in which struggling victims suffocated in piles twenty bodies deep.

A young elevator boy, Robert Smith, courageously took his elevator up several times to rescue unconscious performers from upper-level dressing rooms. On his final trip, the control box caught fire, so that he had to thrust his hand through the flames to reach the switch.

In all, the fire claimed 602 victims, mostly women and children. The Chicago coroner's jury later placed responsibility for the tragedy on seven men, including the theater's president, two stage crewmen, and various city officials. None was ever convicted, but the fire resulted in a much stricter fire code for public buildings in Chicago.

So much for "absolutely fireproof."

1904: Fire Destroys Baltimore. At 10:48 A.M. on February 7 a small fire broke out in a six-story dry goods warehouse in downtown Baltimore, Maryland. Though the Baltimore Fire Department responded quickly to the alarm, a hurricane-force wind rapidly spread the flames to neighboring buildings in the heart of the downtown area.

The intense heat of the fire drove back the fire fighters, and the fire soon raged out of control, engulfing the wood-frame buildings in the downtown business district as tens of thousands of Baltimore's citizens watched. The mayor even ordered buildings in the path of the fire dynamited in an unsuccessful effort to check the fire's spread. Other cities responded by sending fire equipment, but lack of standardization of the equipment left many of the engines idle, while the fire blazed completely out of control.

The fire raged for two days, consuming some twenty-five hundred buildings in a 140-acre area of downtown Baltimore, until finally the wind stopped blowing and the fire died out. Despite the tremendous property loss—at eighty-five million dollars, the second worst for a U.S. fire—only one person, a fireman, was killed during the disaster.

The fire destroyed Baltimore's charm, but it did gain wide streets, pavement, and sewers.

1904: *General Slocum* Burns. The 250-foot paddle-wheel steamer *General Slocum* left New York City's Third Street pier about 9:00 A.M. on June 15 for a day long excursion around the city's waterways. Most of the fifteen hundred passengers on board were women and children belonging to a German immigrant church in the Bronx.

After about an hour, as the vessel steamed by Manhattan's 130th Street, passengers spotted flames shooting from an open paint locker in the forward part of the ship. Some observers claimed that combustible materials in the paint locker had ignited; others maintained a kitchen fire caused the blaze.

In any event, the *General Slocum*'s dry wooden frame burned easily, and fresh paint on the ship's sides spread the fire rapidly. Soon frantic passengers, many of whom could not speak English, were screaming for help. They rushed to the open decks, and then crowded toward the stern to escape the fire.

What could have been a relatively minor emergency quickly escalated into a disaster. For one thing, the ship was in very poor condition. Fire hoses were rotten and so full of holes, they were useless. Someone had filled life preservers with sawdust and inserted metal rods in them to bring them up to mandatory legal weight—passengers who took them sank like stones when they hit the water. Lifeboats were lashed in place with wire. Worse yet, the crew knew little or nothing about dealing with emergencies. Instead of attempting to confine the fire, they opened hatches and doorways, allowing the flames to spread to the upper decks.

But that was not all. For some reason, the steamer's captain, William Van Schaick, did not turn the *Slocum* toward the Manhattan shore, then only three hundred yards away. Instead he headed upriver into a strong northeast breeze toward North Brother Island. The wind sent huge flames shooting backward to the stern, where many frightened passengers huddled.

On reaching the island, Van Schaick crashed the ship bow first onto the rocky shoals, leaving the stern jutting out in over thirty feet of water. That trapped the frantic, screaming women and children at the stern, because few could swim and there was no way to get by the fire in the forward section. Many victims burned to death, while others jumped and drowned in the harbor. The vessel's paddle wheels kept churning, sucking in and injuring many of those who chose to jump. A mass of floating dead bodies quickly accumulated by the burning steamer and became so tightly packed that some survivors actually walked across it to the shore. Finally the *Slocum*'s upper decks collapsed, hurling those who remained there into the fires below.

Meanwhile, as soon as the *Slocum* grounded, captain Van Schaick and two pilots stepped off the bow section of the steamer without suffering so much as a scratch. Most other crewmen also rushed to save themselves, ignoring the cries of the desperate passengers. A few valiant crewmen, joined by others from nearby tugs, pulled as many as they could to safety, but the fate of 1,021 of the 1,500 passengers had already been sealed.

The *General Slocum* fire became the worst harbor disaster in American history. Captain Van Schaick, then sixty-one years old, was eventually convicted of manslaughter and sentenced to ten years in Sing Sing. President Theodore Roosevelt pardoned him in 1908 due to his advanced age.

The owners of this wreck got away with murder.

1905: Massacre of Russian Demonstrators. Dissatisfaction with the czarist regime and increasing demands for a representative assembly finally culminated in a massive demonstration against the czar in Saint Petersburg on January 22. Unarmed men, women, and children singing hymns and carrying crosses marched through the streets toward the Winter Palace, intending to petition their czar to redress the grievances.

The czar was not in the city, however, but his security chief was. Waiting outside the palace grounds for the demonstrators were government troops armed with whips, rifles, and swords. Troops at first attacked the demonstrators with whips, trying to disperse them, but the crowd refused to back down. The guards then resorted to rifles and swords to prevent the people from approaching the palace, and for several hours they fired into the gathering, with deadly effect.

As demonstrators fell dead or bleeding in the streets, others fought back by tearing up paving stones and hurling them at the officers; one general was beaten and trampled to death. Soon people armed themselves with knives and carpentry tools and erected barricades. Before the close of Bloody Sunday, as the massacre is now known, well over one hundred people had died, and hundreds more had been wounded.

A mere Sunday tussle. Just wait awhile.

1906: Discovery of Typhoid Mary. While investigating a series of typhoid outbreaks in New York, a sanitary engineer for the Department of Health found that in twenty of the cases he investigated, all of the households had just engaged a new cook—a woman named Mary Mallon. Tests verified that she was a carrier of the disease, and that each time she used the toilet, typhoid bacilli remained on her hands—and were later transferred to the food she prepared.

"Typhoid Mary" was detained at New York's Riverside Hospital until 1910, when she promised to give up cooking. Upon her release, she again worked as a cook, however, changing jobs frequently and using aliases, and at nearly every place she worked, typhoid broke out soon after her arrival. She was caught and returned to Riverside Hospital in 1915, where she remained until her death in 1938.

Typhoid Mary Mallon was responsible for at least fifty-three cases of typhoid, three of them fatal.

No one ever complained about her cooking, though.

1906: Courrières Mine Explodes. The coal mines in the Pas de Calais region of Northern France were the most productive in the country, yielding highly combustible coal used in smelting and gas manufacture. The network of tunnels in the mine complex was extensive, covering several miles and having outlets at Courrières, Lens, Verdun, and other small villages throughout the countryside.

At 7:00 A.M. on March 10, shortly after 1,795 men had descended into the subterranean tunnels to begin the day's work, a huge explosion at the mouth of the Courrières tunnel blew the roof off the mine office and flung mining cars and cages through the air. Flames shot out of the tunnel entrance, killing or stunning many of the men and horses that happened to be nearby. Meanwhile, the blast also ripped through the tunnels, causing many sections to collapse and trapping well over a thousand men underground.

Rescuers immediately began to dig their way through the collapsed entrances to reach the miners before noxious gases overcame them or the air supply was exhausted. Those rescued from the mouth of the Courrières tunnel were horribly burned from the explosion, but the rest of the miners, scattered throughout the honeycomb of underground tunnels, were faced with the horrifying fate of asphyxiation.

At one of the entrances, frantic rescuers were able to reach an elevator cage. But they soon discovered that the shaft below was blocked and that the cage could not descend more than some 450 feet—over 150 feet short of the tunnel below. At other entrances, some of the miners lucky enough to escape safely made heroic efforts to save their comrades. One courageous man went back into a partially cleared tunnel fourteen times to rescue his coworkers one by one, only to succumb to asphyxiation on the fifteenth attempt.

Gendarmes were sent in by the government to control the thousands of family members massed at the mine's entrances. Many of these grieving souls were driven into a frenzy by rumors that men below had been heard tapping on pipes, a sure sign some of them were still alive. However, the mine engineer grimly predicted that it would take eight days to clear the debris from the central tunnels, and that the men trapped there would surely die of ashpyxiation or starvation before they could be reached. That did nothing to stop a man identified only as Sylvestre, who made a mad dash through the line of guards and rushed into the mine to save his brother. He did not leave the tunnel alive.

The engineer's prediction unfortunately proved true, and by the time all the tunnels had been cleared, only 735 of the original 1,795 miners had been taken out alive. The other 1,060 miners, plus a number of would-be rescuers, had asphyxiated in the tunnels hundreds of feet below ground. The cause of the explosion was never precisely determined.

1906: Great San Francisco Earthquake and Fire. Though most people in San Francisco were asleep at 5:13 A.M. on April 18, police sergeant Cook, then patrolling Washington Street, literally saw the quake coming. Hearing a deep rumble, he looked down the street just in time to see it undulating. "It was as if the waves of the ocean were coming towards me, billowing as they came." Before he even had time to think of what was happening, the jolt threw him to the ground.

The destructive tremor, measuring 8.3 on the Richter scale, thundered on through the city, throwing buildings off their foundations, buckling pavement, and twisting steel streetcar tracks. Hundreds of people were buried by falling rubble while still in their beds.

Throughout the San Francisco area the massive force of the quake ripped, twisted, and scarred the landscape. Earth waves up to three feet high toppled redwood trees like toothpicks and threw massive boulders across fields. Great fissures opened and closed—one on a dairy farm near San Francisco swallowed an unfortunate cow whole, leaving only its tail twitching above ground.

In less than two minutes, the earthquake was over. The screams of hundreds of victims trapped in the rubble pierced the morning air. Meanwhile, thousands of more fortunate survivors emerged from their damaged homes and milled about in a daze, looking at the wreckage around them.

The rich hastily abandoned their valuables and got out as best they could. Perhaps the most famous man of his time, the venerable tenor Enrico Caruso, nearly went mad with terror in his hotel room after the quake. Not knowing what to do, Caruso's conductor ordered him to sing, which not only brought Caruso back to his senses but also gave heart to refugees passing by the hotel. The young actor John Barrymore, not yet famous, calmly walked out of his hotel after the quake and, finding a bottle of brandy, proceeded to get drunk for the next two days.

The denizens of the notorious Barbary Coast section of San Francisco were far less innocent, however, and took the opportunity to begin a spree of looting and other crimes. Undaunted prostitutes even set up shop in makeshift tents by the end of the first day.

The situation could have been much worse immediately after the quake that morning. Though the violent shaking had collapsed buildings in large numbers, many others had sustained only minimal damage. What San Franciscans could not know then was that the quake had only begun the destruction of their picturesque city. Fires soon did the rest.

Several blazes broke out in heavily damaged areas soon after the quake subsided, and then a breeze from the bay began sweeping the flames from building to building. Fire engines responded quickly, but firemen soon discovered the quake had broken water mains. Desperate fire fighters pumped sewage through their hoses in an attempt to douse the fires. When that failed to stop the advancing flames, they resorted to dynamiting sections of the city. Meanwhile, the fires raged on, consuming thousands of buildings and destroying property at a rate of one million dollars every ten minutes.

Hundreds of soldiers, ordered to shoot suspected looters on sight, patrolled the ravaged streets after martial law was declared. They witnessed horrifying scenes of misery as the fire advanced relentlessly through the once beautiful city. Hapless victims, partially crushed under fallen buildings, begged the soldiers to shoot them before the flames burned them alive. Then, too, there was the danger of live wires twitching on the ground, liable to electrocute the unwary in an instant.

Thousands of people abandoned everything they owned and joined the growing tide of refugees thronging the streets, desperately seeking a way to escape the disaster. Many managed to get out, while others watched fire ravage the city for three days from relatively safe vantage points, such as Union Square and Russian Hill.

At the end of the three-day horror, some 700 people had been killed, several thousand more injured, and more than 225,000 left homeless. Over twenty-eight thousand buildings were lost in the 4.7-square-mile area of San Francisco destroyed by the quake and fire.

As in the days of antiquity, another great city was destroyed, but evidently not all its sinners.

1906: Quebec Bridge Collapses. At 5:47 in the afternoon of August 29, ninety-two workmen were getting ready to finish their jobs for the day. They worked atop a bridge being constructed across the Saint Lawrence River between Quebec and Montreal, a project that had been plagued with problems and delays during the two years since it began. The workmen looked up to watch a locomotive pulling three cars filled with iron onto the south side of the structure.

Suddenly an anchor pier on the south side gave way, and eight hundred feet of enormous, uncompleted superstructure crashed into the river below, along with the ill-fated workmen, the locomotive, and untold tons of steel. Eight of the men were quickly rescued by boats sent to the scene. Others were trapped within the twisted wreckage and carried to their deaths beneath the surface of the water. A few were still caught beneath the heavy rubble at the shoreline of the river and screamed to the rescue workers for help.

Unfortunately, it was dark, and the tide was coming in. The rescue workers could hear the trapped workers but could do little to free them, and as the tide rose, most of the victims were drowned. In all, some seventy people died as a result of the tragic bridge collapse.

1907: Night of Death Aboard a "Joy Line" Steamer. Below-zero temperatures and a fifty-miles-per-hour gale greeted passengers aboard the Joy Line ship *Larchmont* on February 11 as the side-wheel steamer left Providence, Rhode Island, for New York. But that was just the prelude to disaster. At 11:00 P.M. the schooner *Harry Knowlton,* blown off course that stormy night, rammed into the *Larchmont*, punching a huge gash in the ill-fated steamer's port side.

While the *Knowlton* barely managed to make it to port, the *Larchmont* sank in just fifteen minutes, off Block Island. Most passengers either drowned in their cabins or were scalded to death by escaping steam when the ship's main steam line was ruptured. Of those who made it to the deck, most were in their nightclothes, hardly adequate protection against the below-zero temperature and freezing winds.

The few who managed to escape on life rafts were tortured by cold winds and heavy seas. They were soon covered with ice, freezing their hands and feet. One man slit his throat to end his agony. Later that night, one life raft washed up on Block Island with all seven people on board frozen to death. Only one lifeboat with nine people, including the captain, survived the tragedy when they were picked up the following day. In all, 332 passengers and crew died as a result of the sad "Joy Line" disaster.

Once again, however, the captain made it to safety.

1907: West Virginia Mine Disaster. A massive explosion ripped through two adjoining coal mines of the Consolidated Coal Company at Monongha, in the worst ever U.S. mining disaster up to the present day. About 10:00 A.M. on December 6, the coupling broke on a string of mining cars loaded with coal. The runaway cars apparently crashed into an electrical line in a mine tunnel, and the resulting electrical fire ignited coal dust, which is highly explosive. The blast was instaneous and widespread. Three hundred sixty-two of the men inside the mine were killed, their bodies mangled and burned by the fiery explosion, and then entombed by the subsequent cave-ins. Only four men managed to escape alive, and it took rescuers over three weeks to recover bodies of all the dead.

Electricity, a boon to civilization, a boom to coal miners.

1907: 239 Miners Killed in Explosion. The Darr coal mine at Jacob's Creek, Pennsylvania, was rocked by an apparent gas explosion on the morning of December 19. Only one of the 240 miners in the shaft escaped alive.

1908: Tragic Fire at Ohio Elementary School. An overheated furnace set fire to the Lake View school at Collingwood,

Ohio, on March 4. The fire spread rapidly, killing 171 of the 360 children in the classrooms, and 9 teachers.

1908: Strange Blast in Siberia. On June 30, in the largely uninhabited Tunguska forest of central Siberia, there was a sudden blast of such explosive force that some twenty-five square miles of forest were instantly flattened. The sound of the explosion was deafening, and the shock wave rocked the whole area. Because the region is so remote and sparsely inhabited, mainly by reindeer herders, the mysterious blast went almost unnoticed by the outside world.

Local newspapers did record the eerie event, one reporter recalling that "a heavenly body of a fiery appearance cut across the sky. . . ." Travelers on the Trans-Siberia Railroad also claimed that something looking like a giant meteor streaked through the sky. But no meteorite was ever found, nor was there a crater in the ground to show where a meteorite had struck. Because there was no obvious cause for the mighty blast, it became a source of mystery and fear for people of the area.

The evening of the frightful blast was the first of about two months of "bright nights" throughout the northern hemisphere, with the night sky so light that people claimed they could read without lamps and take photographs out of doors. The sky was reportedly "a delicate salmon pink," yet no one connected this odd phenomenon with the June 30 blast.

Many people believed that these were unusually strong displays of the aurora borealis, although in many ways the evening lights seemed unlike anything they had ever seen before. A meterologist in 1930 concluded that the horrific blast had scattered millions of tons of atmospheric dust, which then reflected light from the sun, thus lighting up the skies with a pinkish color.

And yet the cause of the blast itself has never been definitively explained. Some people claim that an alien spaceship traveled close to Earth, and a nuclear explosion on board cause the fireball. Others say that a miniature black hole struck the earth at Tunguska and, passing through the planet, set off shock waves powerful enough to devastate an entire forest.

It is more likely, however, that a comet, meteor, or asteroid heading directly toward the earth exploded in midair just above the area of destruction in Siberia, causing the Tunguska blast. In fact, one scientist observed that in the area at the very center of the devastation, trees were stripped of their branches and killed, but left standing. An explosion occurring in midair just above them would account for this phenomenon. Scientists do agree on one fact, though: Whatever caused the mysterious blast was from outer space. Microscopic particles of the heavy metal iridium and other materials left by the explosion are definitely extraterrestrial.

I rather like the spaceship theory.

1908: Messina Earthquake. The historic city of Messina on the island of Sicily collapsed into ruins during severe quakes on December 28. The earthquake also claimed Reggio di Calabria, a town opposite Messina on the Italian mainland, as well as many villages surrounding both places. At least 160,000 people died, and some estimates put the death toll as high as 250,000.

The first two- to three-second quake, a warning really, woke the people of Messina and surrounding areas at 5:25 A.M. Next came longer shocks ranging from ten to forty seconds each and measuring 7.5 in magnitude. Stone buildings crumbled and fell to the ground, killing tens of thousands outright and leaving thousands more trapped in the rubble. Vast craters as deep as eighty feet opened in the ground, swallowing hundreds of people and animals at a time. Water mains burst and reservoirs broke open, flooding the cities. Gas mains erupted into flames.

In the port city of Messina, thousands of victims were thrown from their beds. They stumbled into the darkened streets while all around them buildings crumbled, the ground cracked, massive fires erupted, and the trapped and injured cried pathetically for help. Then hurricanelike winds and rains besieged the ruined city.

A giant sea wave forty to fifty feet high crashed onto the shores at both Messina and Reggio at the frightening speed of five hundred miles an hour. Sweeping inland for blocks, the wave obliterated everything in its path and killed thousands more. After it passed, one man rushed to his child's bedroom only to find several fish in the bed where his child had been.

One survivor described the scene in Messina as "terrifying, beyond words; Dante's *Inferno* gives but a faint idea of what happened." In the channel, lighthouses vanished into the raging sea. Five thousand survivors in Messina wandered through the darkness, furious rains, and fires that quickly consumed half the city. Meanwhile, arms and legs of trapped victims, some alive and some dead, protruded from the rubble.

Some of the lucky ones who survived worked desperately to save victims still trapped in the debris. Others, overwhelmed by the tragedy, wandered aimlessly. Meanwhile, about 750 convicts escaped after the Messina prison collapsed and now roamed the streets, looting and preying on stunned survivors.

The first outside relief arrived the morning of December 29, when three Russian battleships reached Messina. Some six hundred sailors started digging out the thousands trapped beneath the rubble and restoring order to the ruined city, where crazed survivors fought with knives over the few scraps of food they could find. A British fleet joined the effort by 1:00 P.M. that day. Even Italy's King Victor Emmanuel and the queen journeyed to Messina to help dig out survivors. The king witnessed the pathetic sight of an old man, maddened by the terror, dancing with a dead child in his arms and singing merrily about how there had been no earthquake.

In the surrounding villages, mass pyres to burn the dead and avoid pestilence were, ironically, the only signs of life to alert rescuers to the presence of survivors. At least 25,000 died in Reggio di Calabria, and tens of thousands more perished in surrounding areas. In Messina alone, though, over 80,000 of its 147,000 residents died—so many that the ruined city became known as *La Citta Morta,* the city of the dead.

1908: Fatal Air Crash in Maryland. A plane being flown by none other than the famous inventor Orville Wright developed mechanical problems and crashed on September 17 during a demonstration flight at Fort Meyer, Maryland. Orville escaped with injuries, but his passenger, Lieutenant T. E. Selfridge, was killed, making this accident one of the earliest fatal air crashes involving the new heavier-than-air craft.

With the invention of the airplane we can go farther faster, and crash harder. One thing Orville forgot was the seat belt.

1909: Explosion and Fire at Illinois Coal Mine. Two hundred fifty-nine miners were killed following an explosion and fire at a coal mine in Cherry, Illinois, on November 13.

1910–1913: Last Major Outbreak of Black Plague. Though small outbreaks persist, the world's last serious epidemic of Black Plague struck China and India in 1910. Millions perished before the epidemic abated.

1910: Washington Train Wreck. In late February, passengers and crew on board two trains at Wellington, Washington, were stranded by a severe blizzard. Avalanches and the relentless storm halted the trains on a narrow ledge, part of the way up a steep mountainside. For a week terrified men, women, and children watched helplessly as increasingly frequent snowslides roared by—as close as one hundred yards from the trains—and fell four hundred feet to the canyon below. Two parties of men left the trains on February 27 and 28, braving the threat of avalanches to summon help from Scenic Hot Springs, nine miles west of Wellington and fifteen hundred feet farther down the mountain.

At 1:45 A.M. on March 2, however, a snow pack broke loose two thousand feet above the trains, and the resulting avalanche swept them into the canyon below. One hundred eighteen people died in this disaster.

1910: *Los Angeles Times* Fire. The typesetters and pressmen in the *Los Angeles Times* building on First and Broadway were busy preparing the morning edition of the newspaper at 1:00 A.M. on October 1 when a horrendous explosion shook the city.

In the composing room the floor burst upward, smashed several workers into the ceiling, and blew apart the machinery. A second blast followed as flames shot upward through the three-story building, engulfing the entire structure.

Workers ran to windows of the upper stories as the blaze raged behind them. On the ground below, firemen stretched out their nets as some workers made the leap to safety, while others who waited too long were overtaken by the fire and fell backward into the inferno. The city editor, stunned by the blast, missed the net and hit the pavement. By daybreak only two walls of the building remained standing, and twenty-one out of one hundred workers had perished.

Later in the day on October 2, a suspicious-looking suitcase was found at the home of the publisher of the *Times*. Police carried it to a safe location in an adjacent park only seconds before it exploded.

At the time, Los Angeles was the symbolic center of the antiunion forces in the United States, with the *Times* in the forefront of the movement. The newspaper blamed the explosion on a bomb planted by the unions and called it the "Crime of the Century." The labor unions claimed the explosion had been caused by a gas leak, and that the suitcase had been planted by antiunion sympathizers. There was much evidence that the unions were, indeed, correct in their assumptions, but they could not still the voice of the *Times* and its powerful political allies.

The alleged perpetrators were finally brought to trial and defended by Clarence Darrow. During the trial, for some unknown reason, they changed their plea to guilty, though they were widely believed to be innocent.

The event, the trial, and the aftermath seemed to have been mired in the mud of politics and deceit.

1910: Forest Fire in Montana and Idaho. Some two million acres of forests were burned and eighty-five people were killed in an August forest fire that spread over parts of western Montana and into Idaho.

1910: British Coal Mine Disaster. A total of 344 miners were killed by an explosion at the Number 3 Bank Pit Colliery in Hulton, England, on December 21.

1911: Triangle Shirtwaist Company Fire. Just ten minutes before quitting time on March 25, the six hundred employees of New York's Triangle Shirtwaist Company were startled by the ringing of a fire alarm. The employees—mostly sixteen- to twenty-three-year-old immigrant girls—panicked as flames broke out in a pile of oil-soaked rags on the eighth floor and spread rapidly to piles of cotton cloth and hanging shirtwaists, the fitted shirts for women manufactured by the company.

Screaming employees on the eighth floor rushed between the closely spaced sewing machines to the narrow exit and raced for stairways and the elevator. Workers on the ninth and tenth floors saw flames shooting from the windows below, and soon the fire spread to those floors. There was only one narrow fire escape, and many were trapped on the upper floors. A number of girls burned to death while waiting in vain for the elevator. Others forced open the elevator doors when it stopped running, and thirty women leaped into the shaft to escape the fire, their broken bodies piling up at the bottom.

Other employees rushed to the windows. Crowds on the street watched in horror as girls, their hair and clothes on fire, threw themselves out of the windows, and crashed through sidewalk covers into the basement below. The dress of one falling girl caught on a wire, leaving her hanging in midair until the flames ate through her dress and she plunged the rest of the way to the ground. Fire nets were useless as girls toppled into them four and five at a time. A thirteen-year-old girl hung by her fingertips from a tenth-floor window until flames reached her and she fell to her death.

Thirty minutes after the fire began in the supposedly fireproof building, 145 employees, mostly young girls, were dead.

Fireproof building maybe. But what about the material inside?

1911: China Devastated by Flood. The Yangtze River (now Ch'ang Jiang) spilled over its banks in early September, causing widespread destruction in a rich farming area where over two million people lived. Flood waters inundated the region, creating a thirty-five-mile-wide lake covering parts of five provinces in China.

Some one hundred thousand people were drowned outright by the flooding. But many more fell victim in the weeks that followed as famine and pestilence spread throughout the region, where both crops and food stocks had been destroyed. Over five hundred thousand fled the area, and some one hundred thousand of those who survived the flood died of starvation. Meanwhile, gangs of starving men began robbing and killing for food and valuables.

Another attempt by Mother Nature to wipe out the population of China.

1912: Unsinkable *Titanic* Lost. Could it be anything more than coincidence? Writer Morgan Robertson published a novel in 1898 about a mammoth new ocean liner that was eight hundred feet long and presumed to be unsinkable. In the book, the liner sank in the Atlantic while on her maiden voyage. Incredibly, the ship was named *Titan* and sank after hitting an iceberg during the month of April.

That was fourteen years before the White Star luxury liner

Titanic departed from Queenstown, Ireland, on April 9, 1912, beginning her maiden voyage to New York. She was considered the greatest ship afloat and completely unsinkable, thanks to the watertight compartments dividing up spaces inside her hull. The *Titanic* was huge; at 882 feet long, she was a "great fifteen-story floating palace," complete with elevators, wide staircases, restaurants, theaters, bars, Turkish baths, tennis courts, swimming pools, and gardens. There were 2,207 passengers and crew aboard for this maiden voyage, among them such wealthy men as John Jacob Astor, Benjamin Guggenheim, and Isidor Straus.

Even before she left Ireland, however, the elements were conspiring against the *Titanic.* The warmest winter in years had caused a record number of icebergs to break away from polar caps. Despite the fact that the *Titanic*'s captain had deliberately taken a course farther south to avoid icebergs, he nevertheless received regular reports of them from other ships along the way. Then, at 9:40 P.M. April 14, as the ship passed the Grand Banks of Newfoundland, a wire came in from a nearby ship: "Much heavy pack ice and great numbers of large icebergs." But the *Titanic*'s wireless officer did not realize the ship was directly ahead of the *Titanic,* and because so many warnings had already been received, he delayed delivering the message to the bridge.

When lookouts up on deck suddenly spotted a forty- to fifty-foot-high iceberg looming dead ahead, it was too late to avoid a collision. Despite the helmsman's attempt to steer away from the giant iceberg, the *Titanic* hit it with a glancing blow that tore a three-hundred-foot gash below the waterline along the starboard side. Berthed higher up on the ship, first-class passengers saw the massive iceberg shining through their windows; those in second class had portals of their cabins broken by ice; and steerage passengers were thrown into a panic by the full force of the collision. The damage was done in a mere ten seconds, but it would take over two hours more for the great liner to sink to the bottom.

The first distress signals went out: "Require assistance immediately struck by iceberg." Later the ship sent out more desperate messages, including SOS, making the *Titanic* the first ship ever to use that distress call. Up on deck, the ship's horns boomed as excess steam vented from the now-stopped engines, while stewards calmly asked passengers to leave their compartments, politely adding, "Bring your life preservers, please."

Passengers and most of the seven hundred crewmen gathered on deck, and soon after crewmen began loading women and children onto the lifeboats. Already it was clear most of the men would have to remain on board: *Titanic* carried enough lifeboats for only 1,178 people. A few men disguised as women sneaked aboard the lifeboats, and in a notorious incident, the White Star Line director saved himself by jumping into the last lifeboat while it was being launched.

Meanwhile, on the ocean liner *Carpathia,* which was in the general vicinity, the captain was wakened with the news of the distress calls. *"Titanic?"* he said. "That's impossible. She's the greatest ship afloat." But the *Carpathia* fired up her boilers and headed straight toward the *Titanic,* speeding through the dark, ice-ridden water in a desperate bid to get to the stricken liner before she went under.

One ship, the *Californian,* was only five minutes away from the disaster scene, but its radio was turned off for the night. When the *Titanic* fired signal rockets, the captain thought the luxury liner was only throwing a party. He went back to sleep.

At 2:15 A.M., *Titanic* issued her last message: "Engine room filled up to boilers—SOS. SOS." Soon after, the boilers exploded and the ship lurched downward bow first, standing for several minutes with its stern almost perpendicular to the sea. From the lifeboats, survivors watched the masses of doomed passengers scurrying on the decks. Many jumped into the icy waters, while others, like Captain E. J. Smith, went down with the ship. Through it all, the band kept playing—first ragtime tunes, then solemn hymns.

Within an hour the *Carpathia* arrived and rescued hundreds from the lifeboats. But for 1,517 others, including such notable men as Astor, Guggenheim, and Straus, it was far too late. The *Titanic* lay undisturbed in her watery grave for over seventy years before being located in 1985 by scientists using remote control underwater camera equipment.

1912: Japanese Steamer Sinks. The steamer *Kichemaru* foundered and sank in heavy seas off the coast of Japan on September 28. Over one thousand people lost their lives.

1913: Welsh Mine Explosion and Fires. At 6:00 A.M. on October 14, a crew of 935 men and boys went to work as usual in the Lancaster and York mines at the Universal Colliery in Sengenhydd, just outside Cardiff, Wales. Two hours later a tremendous explosion ripped through the Lancaster mine with such violence that it literally shook the entire town. Part of the Lancaster mine caught fire, and searing flames forced workers to abandon rescue efforts for a time while they concentrated on containing the fire. Meanwhile, at the adjacent York mine, rescuers brought out almost five hundred trapped miners in groups of twenty. By that evening, a huge crowd of forty thousand onlookers had gathered to watch rescue operations, but there was little hope for those still in the burning Lancaster mine. Eventually 439 men, the bodies of some horribly mangled by the explosion, were found dead.

Man was not destined to dig holes in the earth and pull out its resources.

1913: New Mexico Mine Explosion. Most of the coal miners working in Mine No. 2 of the Stag Canyon Fuel Company at Dawson, New Mexico, were trapped one hundred feet or more below ground by a blast that occurred at 3:00 P.M. on October 22. Caused by a buildup of coal dust in the mine, the explosion sealed off all exits. Rescuers did free five trapped miners within the first few hours, but the mine filled with deadly gases after the explosion, making rescue efforts extremely hazardous. Miners from Pennsylvania, Kansas, Wyoming, and Colorado continued to arrive at the scene over the next two days to help in the rescue efforts, but to no avail. In all, 263 miners died as a result of the explosion or of asphyxiation.

1914: Steamer Sinks Off Brazil. Some 445 people died on March 5 when the Spanish steamer *Principe de Asturias* ran aground on rocks and sank off the coast of Brazil.

The captain wasn't watching where he was going.

1914: Ship Passengers Drown as They Sleep. With fog obscuring navigation in the Saint Lawrence River on May 29, the Canadian passenger liner *Empress of Ireland*, bound from Quebec to Liverpool, came to a stop to let the Norwegian collier *Storstad* pass by. The captains of both ships were aware of the presence of each other in the immediate vicinity, but the Norwegian ship only slowed; it did not stop.

Suddenly appearing out of a thick fogbank at 1:30 A.M., the Norwegian collier plowed into the *Empress of Ireland*'s port side, tearing open a hole that ran half the liner's length. While the *Storstad* was not seriously damaged, water poured into the liner's torn hull, sinking her with incredible speed.

There was no time to wake the 1,482 passengers, most of whom drowned in their bunks. One lucky couple, who had slept through the collision itself, woke in time to see the nightmarish sight of water flooding their cabin. Crawling on their hands and knees, they made it up to the deck, already sharply tilted, and escaped the doomed ship.

Miraculously, over 450 persons managed similarly harrowing escapes in the scant fifteen minutes it took for the *Empress of Ireland* to sink to the bottom. But for 1,024 other passengers and crewmen who went down with the liner, there had been too little time.

1914: The Spark That Ignited World War I. Archduke Francis Ferdinand, heir to the throne of Austria-Hungary, had been warned not to visit the province of Bosnia (in modern Yugoslavia) because of extreme unrest among Serbian nationalists seeking independence from Austria. The warning quickly proved accurate. Even as the archduke and his wife, the Duchess of Hohenberg, arrived in Bosnia's most important city, Sarajevo, on June 28, a Serbian nationalist threw a bomb into their car. The archduke, however, got the device out of the car before it exploded.

A major international incident seemed to have been averted, but later that day another Serbian nationalist, Gavrio Princip, emerged from a crowd and fired into the archduke's car. The first bullet hit the duchess in the abdomen. As she collapsed across her husband's lap, the archduke exclaimed, "Sophie, remain alive for our children." Then a second bullet tore into his jugular vein, and the archduke fell to the floor of the car.

Both the archduke and the duchess died of their wounds, but the ultimate tragedy had just begun. Outraged by the assassination, the Austrian government declared war on Serbia, which in turn led to declarations of war by major allies of both countries. History turned a bloody page and World War I had begun.

The assassination was as good an excuse as any. The allies had been spoiling for a fight.

1914: British Battleship Explodes. While taking on ammunition at Sheerness Harbor in England on November 26, the battleship HMS *Bulwark* suddenly exploded, killing 788 officers and crewmen.

1915–1919: French "Bluebeard" Murders Ten Women. Henri Desiré Landru, known as the French "Bluebeard," reportedly launched a series of grisly murders of lonely women in 1915 by placing advertisements for a wife in various French newspapers. After romancing each of the ten women over the next five years, Landru won their hearts and then lured them to his villa in the French countryside. In one case, he bought a two-way ticket for himself—and a one-way ticket for his fiancée, who was never seen again.

Prosecutors claimed that Landru murdered his fiancées and then dismembered their bodies and incinerated them in an oven at the villa. "The draft is excellent," Landru reportedly said. "It will burn anything." Landru, a furniture merchant, then sold the possessions of the fiancées he murdered.

Landru was convicted—and executed—for killing the ten women and the son of one of them, despite the fact that not a single body was ever recovered. The lack of bodies might have resulted in an acquittal had prosecutors not forced Landru to admit that he had killed one of his fiancées' three dogs by hanging it. From that point in the trial, public opinion turned sharply against Landru, and prosecutors thereafter made frequent allusions to Landru's cruel act.

Love me, love my dog.

1915: Deadly Mexican Train Wreck. After capturing Guadalajara, Mexico, from rebel forces, government soldiers eagerly awaited the arrival of their families and loved ones aboard a special train. The train left Colima for Guadalajara on January 18 with some nine hundred family members packed aboard twenty passenger cars. Although most passengers crammed themselves into the squalid cars, many could find room only on the roofs, while still others rode precariously on the rods underneath the cars. As the overcrowded train headed down a steep grade, the engineer lost control. The runaway train careened faster and faster down the long hill, causing the people riding outside the cars to lose their grip and fall away. Finally the entire train jumped the track and plunged into a deep ravine. Of all those aboard the train, only about three hundred survived the horrible wreck, and of these, only six were uninjured.

1915: First Use of Poison Gas by Germans. On April 24, during the second battle of Ypres in World War I, Germans fired artillery shells filled with chlorine gas at Allied positions on the French front. This marked the first use of poison gas in the war, which subsequently saw both sides using even more terrible gases, including mustard gas and phosgene. Vast numbers of soldiers on both sides were maimed and killed by these new weapons.

All's fair in love and war.

1915: Sinking of the *Lusitania*. As the British Cunard steamship *Lusitania* set out from New York to Liverpool on May 1, its 1,918 passengers and crew knew they faced the danger of attack by German submarines. Germany had declared a blockade of Britain on February 17, but recognizing America's continuing neutrality in World War I, the German government had recently run advertisements in New York newspapers warning Americans against crossing the Atlantic on British ships. Postcards for sale as passengers boarded the 762-foot-long ship sported the grim caption "Last voyage of the *Lusitania*." "From the day we sailed, we complacently spoke of the possibilities of the German menace," one passenger said, "but no one believed it."

Seven days later, the entire world believed it. On the afternoon of May 7, as the *Lusitania* approached the shores of Ireland, lookouts spotted the periscope of a German U-20 submarine within one thousand yards of the ship. A passenger playing quoits on the deck saw a white streak through the water and exclaimed, "There's a torpedo, coming straight at us." Passengers, at that moment relaxing or eating lunch, were startled when the big liner shuddered at the violent explosion as the torpedo slammed into its side. A second torpedo struck moments later.

Immediately the ship began to list sharply on the starboard side. Most passengers felt too stunned by the sudden impact even to panic. One survivor said, "There was not so much excitement as one would expect in such a catastrophe. It occurred so suddenly that we had not much time to realize what was happening."

The sharp list of the ship made it impossible to launch lifeboats from the port side. And damage to controls made it impossible to slow the ship, which barreled forward at a high speed, thus swamping boats as they were launched. The first boat put out, filled with children and only a few adult women, capsized immediately, throwing the children wildly into the sea. All of them died. Meanwhile, passengers in the first cabin were eating lunch when the torpedo struck. Most refused to join the scramble to get on boats, thinking there would be time for a rescue before the ship went down. Many did not even bother to put on a life belt.

As the *Lusitania* sank deeper and deeper, the sea filled with the bodies of desperate passengers and crew. Many leaped into the water with only a life belt to protect them. They clung to capsized boats or to scraps of debris. On deck, weeping crowds of women and children waited anxiously to board lifeboats.

Then, at 2:33 P.M., just twenty-one minutes after the first torpedo hit, the *Lusitania* disappeared bow first beneath the waves. A survivor described how "women and children . . . had clustered in lines on the port side, and as the ship made her plunge . . . this little army slid down toward the starboard side, dashing themselves against each other as they went until they were engulfed."

Nine hundred people went down with the ship, and many in boats drowned as well when the powerful suction of the sinking liner pulled them down. As the ship went under, survivors heard a final, "appalling" shriek rising in unison from the hundreds perishing at that moment.

Several hours later, rescue ships arrived to save those floating among the debris. Other rescue workers pulled the floating dead off the waters. One drowned woman still clung to the corpse of her baby. Altogether, 1,198 died, including 124 Americans. Despite German government claims that the *Lusitania* had been attacked because it was secretly carrying arms, American outrage over the sinking played a major role in bringing the United States into the war.

Germany did promise, however, that it wouldn't sink passenger ships anymore without a warning first. Damn sporting of them.

1915: Turks Massacre Armenians. Amid the fighting and unrest caused by World War I, Armenians in Turkish-held Armenia once again became the object of wanton slaughter. In one instance on May 12, bands of Kurdish horsemen rode into an Armenian village, sacked it, slaughtered over 250 people, and carried off the women. Armenians had suffered in sporadic massacres since 1894.

The Turks didn't believe in live and let live.

1915: Head-on Collision of Trains in Scotland. An error by a railroad signalman sent a troop train carrying five hundred soldiers crashing head-on into a local passenger train at Gretna Green, Scotland, on May 22. Adding to that, an express train then slammed into the wreckage and overturned. In all, 227 people were killed and another 246 were injured.

Boy, did they get their signals crossed.

1915: Deadly Floods in China. Flooding rivers, rising to as much as a whopping seventy-nine feet above their banks, sent millions of gallons of water surging into the Chinese provinces of Kwangtung (now Guangdong), Kwangsi, and Kiangsi (now Jiangxi) in mid-July. The raging floodwaters washed away entire villages and left the rooftops of many other villages as the only safe place, where thousands of people were stranded.

Because of flooding in the surrounding countryside, all transportation to the city of Canton (now Kuang-chou) was cut off, except by steamship. Water reached a depth of ten feet in parts of Canton, knocking out electric power and all communications. With fire-fighting equipment lost under floodwaters, a fire in the upper stories of buildings in Canton spread out of control, eventually destroying thousands of buildings.

When the waters finally subsided, it was estimated that more than one hundred thousand people had died in one of the worst floods of modern times.

1915: Explosion of British Warship. A total of 405 men were killed on December 30 when the British cruiser *Natal* blew up in Cromarty Harbor in Scotland.

1916: Ten Thousand Die in Netherlands Flood. With so much of their homeland below sea level, people in the Netherlands live with the constant threat of deadly floods. In January

1916 that threat once again became a reality as abnormally high tides battered, then broke through, the dikes that had kept the North Sea waters at bay.

Ten thousand people were killed in the disaster. Whole villages and farms were flooded, herds of livestock were swept away, and rich farmland was contaminated for years by the salt water. The situation was worse on coastal islands. By high tide on the night of January 13, the entire Isle of Marken was underwater, with only the roofs of houses still protruding above the floodwaters. When the flood tide finally retreated, it scored a new channel that divided the island in two.

1916: Battle of Verdun. Situated on the Meuse River in northeastern France, the fortress of Verdun and the miles of defensive works associated with it formed the keystone of Allied lines on the western front during World War I. The town of Verdun itself was surrounded by ramparts and an intimidating array of sixty forts, twenty of which were massive structures constructed of reinforced concrete.

German General Erich von Falkenhayn chose this seemingly impregnable fortress as the focal point for a fierce German offensive. His objective was not so much to gain ground as it was to batter the French army enough to force it into submission. To that end he massed over 1,220 heavy guns along an eight-mile front before Verdun, and at dawn on February 21, unleashed a furious artillery barrage on the fortress.

Thus began the Battle of Verdun, one of the longest and bloodiest battles in history. For months German and French infantrymen alike faced an almost constant hail of bullets and exploding artillery shells. Soldiers on both sides grimly endured the hardships of life in the muddy trenches, which was punctuated by the horror of poison gas attacks, bloody offensives that went nowhere, and the incessant shelling from distant batteries. The battlefield itself became an open graveyard as thousands of dead soldiers lay unburied for weeks, the fighting at times never stopping long enough for such considerations.

When the bitter attacks and counterattacks finally ceased in December, and the German offensive stopped, the lines were essentially unchanged, and more than one million French and German soldiers had been killed or wounded. The exact number of those killed in the ten-month battle has never been determined—even today the remains of unidentified infantrymen are still being discovered.

Thank you, General von Falkenhayn, for your contribution to history.

1916: Russian Munitions Factory Blows Up. A terrible explosion at the La Satannaya munitions factory on November 16 demolished the entire factory, killing about one thousand Russian workers.

1916: Ramming of Chinese Troop Ship. The Chinese cruiser *Hai-Yung* was maneuvering in a fogbank off the Chinese coast on August 29 when it rammed the steamer *Hsin-Yu* and nearly cut it in two. Some one thousand Chinese soldiers aboard the steamer were drowned.

1917–1934: Russian Revolution—the Terrible Toll. By the Fall of 1915, more than one million Russians had died in battle in World War I. But even that huge loss pales beside the estimated twenty million people who died of famine and influenza in Russia during the critical years of 1914–24. The nation, ravaged by war, disease, and increasingly severe economic hardship, was being driven toward a cataclysmic upheaval in 1917, one that would change the face of the nation for decades to come.

Continuing reverses in the war had severely weakened the czarist government by 1917, and serious food shortages that began in January of that year led to uprisings throughout the nation. By March, strikes, demonstrations, and mass mutinies among the armed forces had brought Russia to the brink of disaster. Finally, on March 15, Czar Nicholas II abdicated, ending the hated monarchy. A provisional government was set up, but the turmoil was far from over.

In April, Vladimir Lenin returned to Petrograd (modern St. Petersburg) and called for the overthrow of the provisional government, thus beginning the second stage of the Russian revolution. The Bolshevik party membership soon surged to two hundred thousand people as soldiers agitated for an end to the war, peasants demanded ownership of the land, workers called for control of their factories, and the nation demanded food. By July desertions depleted the army, and the streets filled with violent crowds of demonstrators. Everywhere peasants seized control of the land, and workers occupied factories. The Bolshevik slogan, "Peace, Land, and Bread," rang through the streets.

Finally the government of Russia itself fell to the Bolsheviks when they stormed the Winter Palace in Petrograd. Bolsheviks had already taken control of the news agency, the state bank, and mail and telegraph offices. On November 7 Bolshevik forces surrounded the palace where the provisional government was holding an emergency session. Two sailors climbed to the top of the palace and tossed three hand grenades inside. Meanwhile, the rebels blasted the palace with rifles, machine guns, and cannons. Then, at 2:00 A.M. November 8, a band of Bolshevik soldiers charged through the doors of the palace and declared everyone inside under arrest. Angry mobs milled about as officials of the provisional government were led out and taken to prison.

Now that the Bolsheviks had seized the government, they had to fight to keep control of the country. Already a new epidemic of typhus was breaking out. (It killed three million between 1917 and 1921.) To end Russia's disastrous involvement in World War I, the Bolsheviks hastily concluded a disadvantageous truce with the Germans and withdrew from the fighting. But in May 1918 a bloody civil war broke out between the Bolsheviks, known as the Reds, and anti-Communist forces, known as Whites.

Then, on July 16, 1918, the Bolsheviks executed the former czar along with his wife, son, and four daughters, shooting them one by one. "I saw that all the members of the czar's family were lying on the floor with many wounds in their bodies," wrote a witness. "The blood was running in streams. . . . The heir was still alive and moaned a little. Yurovsky went up and fired two or three more times at him. Then the heir was still."

Hatred between warring Reds and Whites rose to new levels following the brutal execution of the czar and attacks on Bolshevik leaders by Whites later in July. In August 1918 the Bolsheviks began what is known as the Red Terror, a campaign to exterminate their enemies. Both Reds and Whites then began indiscriminate executions in which more than one hundred thousand people eventually died. Another two million people were forced to flee the nation to escape Communist rule.

Between 1921 and 1922, as the civil war neared an end, a terrible new famine broke out, killing millions more (see separate entry, 1921–23). Even after the Bolsheviks won the civil war in

1922, the suffering was still not over. Millions more died following the outbreak of a malaria epidemic in 1923. Then massive famines in 1932–34, caused by forced collectivization of land and the peasants' destruction of livestock, killed another five million people.

As if all this death and misfortune were not enough, or perhaps because of it, Soviet dictator Joseph Stalin embarked in 1934 on a wide-ranging purge of his enemies, real and suspected, both in the Communist party and outside it. Mock trials, secret arrests, and secret executions continued into the late 1930s. It is estimated that millions of Soviet officials, their families, and others were either imprisoned, forced to leave the country, or executed during the purge.

1917: Exploding Munitions Plant Blasts Silvertown, England. On January 19 a small fire broke out in a World War I British ammunition factory in the town of Silvertown, Essex. As workers frantically tried to put the fire out, it became clear that the plant would explode, and the alarm was given.

As hundreds of workers fled, a massive explosion, similar to a volcanic eruption, shook the town and surrounding countryside, shooting flaming timber, red-hot iron, and other debris high into the air. A series of smaller subsidiary explosions then rocked the area, causing further death and destruction.

A flour mill next to the munitions plant was wrecked and caught fire, trapping a number of women working there. Many other factories and houses in the area around the munitions plant were destroyed by the blast or set afire by its flaming debris, and the shock wave from the explosion shattered plate-glass windows up to a mile away. More than three hundred died as a result of the destructive explosions, and hundreds more were injured.

One of the unpleasant side effects of war.

1917: Sinking of British Transport. On February 21 the British transport *Mendi,* carrying 806 black South African laborers from England to Le Havre, France, collided with the liner *Darro* in a thick fog off the Isle of Wight. Screams and cries for help pierced the mists, and although rescue efforts began almost immediately, the poor visibility made it difficult to even locate the sinking ship and those who jumped overboard. Despite heroic rescue efforts, the ship sank too quickly to save more than a portion of those aboard. Within twenty-four minutes the *Mendi* disappeared beneath the waves, taking 627 of the laborers and crewmen with her.

A need for the invention of radar is obvious.

1917: Munitions Ship Explodes at Archangel. The Russian naval station at Archangel was devastated by a terrible explosion on February 20 when a munitions ship blew up during unloading. Some fifteen hundred people were killed and about three thousand injured. The ship was blown completely apart.

Volatile stuff, munitions.

1917: Romanian Train Wreck Kills Five Hundred. A railroad train derailed and crashed near Chirurcha, Romania, on February 21. Wrecked cars caught fire, and panicked passengers fought each other while trying to escape the flames. Hundreds were killed by the crash, the subsequent fire, and explosions of ammunition aboard the wrecked train.

1917: Tornadoes Ravage Eight States. A rash of killer tornadoes on May 26 swept through Illinois, Indiana, Kansas, Kentucky, Missouri, Tennessee, Alabama, and Arkansas, leaving dozens of towns in ruins and thousands of victims homeless.

The deadly storm system apparently began over Mattoon, Illinois, as two giant, blue-black clouds collided. The collision spawned a massive tornado that destroyed five hundred houses in Mattoon and moved on to create a 293-mile-long swath of continuous destruction.

Meanwhile, other tornadoes touched down on May 25 and 26 in Illinois and the other affected states. They took erratic courses, leapfrogging from town to town, destroying buildings, stripping entire cotton crops from the ground, and wreaking havoc upon terrified residents. At least one Kentucky telephone operator, however, was found by rescuers still working at her post even after a tornado had ripped off the roof overhead and severely damaged most of the wires. The destructive storms claimed 249 lives and left more than 1,200 injured.

Killer clouds strike again.

1917: Bohemian Munitions Plant Blows Up. Some one thousand workers at the Boleweg, Bohemia (in modern Czechoslovakia), munitions factory were killed on June 23 when the plant suddenly exploded.

Preparing for war is just as dangerous as waging it.

1917: British Battleship Blows Up. The British battleship *Vanguard* blew up on July 9, apparently after ammunition in her magazines accidentally ignited. A total of 804 officers and men were killed.

Perhaps they kept their powder too dry.

1917: Nova Scotia Blast. Two ships, the *Mont Blanc* and the *Imo*, approached each other slowly in the narrows connecting Nova Scotia's Halifax Harbor with Bedford Basin on December 6. It was a clear, bright day with good visibility, but because of a misunderstanding of signals exchanged, the two vessels suddenly wound up on a collision course.

The *Mont Blanc*'s captain desperately maneuvered his ship to minimize the impact of a collision on his cargo, and for good reason. His ship was later described as "a floating bomb": In the two afterholds were 580 tons of TNT, the forward hold stored tons of volatile picric acid, and the decks were piled with tanks of benzine.

When the collision occurred, the *Imo*'s bow cut deep into the *Mont Blanc*. The explosive TNT was untouched, but twenty-five barrels of benzine broke open and spilled onto the acid in the forward hold. A huge fire erupted immediately. Crew members on the *Mont Blanc* vainly attempted to fight the fire and then tried unsuccessfully to sink the ship before it exploded. As the crewmen frantically abandoned the *Mont Blanc* and rowed toward land, hundreds of curious villagers gathered at the shoreline to watch the spectacle.

The explosion was seen and heard by ships fifty miles at sea. The *Mont Blanc* virtually disappeared as the tons of explosives ignited in the vessel's hold, but that was not all. The blast leveled two square miles of the north end of Halifax; the suburb of Richmond was totally obliterated, its old wooden buildings instantly demolished. The blast tossed people through the air or buried and crushed them beneath tons of debris. The *Imo*, which had been heading toward the opposite shore, was lifted from the water and deposited on dry land. Nearby freight cars were thrown as far as two miles away.

Casualties were heavy. Two-thirds of all crew members on ships in the harbor were killed. In nearby schools and orphanages, nearly all the children perished as the buildings tumbled down upon them. Flying debris and glass killed or blinded hundreds. More than three thousand buildings were either flattened or burned to the ground by the blast and subsequent fires.

Numerous acts of heroism were reported. A railroad signalman refused to leave his post since an incoming train was approaching and had to be warned; he burned to death there. A dock worker rescued dozens of people from burning debris despite having been partially blinded himself by the blast.

Plumes of black smoke that could be seen forty miles away towered over Halifax, but there was no way to put the fires out—there was no fire department left to battle the hundreds of fires burning in the blasted area. Instead the blazes were left to burn themselves out, while survivors searched for those still trapped in the debris.

Some sixteen hundred people were killed by the blast, and another eight thousand injured. In all, the blast and fires did more than thirty million dollars in damages.

War is hell.

1917: French Train Crash Kills Hundreds. The engineer of a World War I train carrying more than one thousand French soldiers from the Italian front on December 12 had declared the train unsafe. Two trains had been coupled, and most of the nineteen cars had only primitive air brakes. But the engineer's superiors threatened him with court-martial if he refused to take the train on the hazardous trip through the high passes of the French Alps.

As the train headed down a steep incline near Modane, France, sparks flew from the overworked brakes, finally igniting wooden floorboards on the passenger cars. Worse yet, the train proved impossible to control on the steep grade and quickly gathered speed until it was careening downward at ninety miles per hour. Meanwhile, winds whipped the flames through the crowded cars.

Finally the baggage car and eighteen passenger cars broke loose from the runaway train while rounding a curve and smashed into a wall near Modane, France, the engine miraculously remaining on the tracks. Fire quickly spread through the wrecked cars, burning the dead and injured. It was one of the worst train crashes in history, taking the lives of 543 soldiers.

Military arrogance + command − responsibility = disaster.

1918–1919: Influenza Epidemic. In the spring of 1918 a new, virulent type of flu appeared in the army training camps at Fort Riley and Camp Funston in Kansas. Over eleven hundred men suddenly became ill, and forty-six died in the first known cases of this flu strain. They were far from the last, and within a year, the new strain of Spanish flu would claim more than twenty-two million lives worldwide.

Though it is possible the flu epidemic broke out in several places simultaneously, American troops appear to have played a major part in the early stages of its spread. Soldiers in Kansas who had not yet been stricken by the disease were transported to the European front that spring and probably carried the virus with them. The disease swept through American forces stationed in France during the last months of World War I.

By the fall of 1918 every major army fighting in Europe had a significant number of their fighting forces bedridden with the disease. It continued to spread like wildfire throughout Europe as trains and ships helped transport the disease into previously uninfected areas. American President Woodrow Wilson, British Prime Minister David Lloyd George, and French Premier George Clemenceau were all ill with the flu while negotiating the Treaty of Versailles.

The United States reported only mild cases of the disease until the fall of 1918, when the epidemic reached its height. Then influenza complicated by pneumonia claimed lives on a scale never before seen in the United States, and local and state governments desperately tried to get the epidemic under control. Schools were closed in Boston and Washington, D.C., in an attempt to halt the contagion, and the New York Public Library even stopped circulating books.

In New York City the health commissioner urged people to kiss only through a handkerchief, and five hundred people were arrested for spitting. San Francisco made the wearing of face masks mandatory, though none of these measures slowed the progress of the epidemic. The flu outbreaks in army training camps were so serious that the government called off the October draft. During the last week in October, the killer virus claimed more than twenty-one thousand lives in the United States—then the highest seven-day death toll in U.S. history.

The hallmark of this disease, popularly called the Spanish flu, was its swiftness. In a South African mine, a lift operator was seized with a sweating paralysis so quickly that he lost control of the machine. Twenty-four miners plunged to their deaths at the bottom of the shaft. In Washington, D.C., a young woman called the authorities to report that two of her roommates were dead, another ill, and that she alone remained untouched by the disease. By the time the authorities reached the apartment a short while later, all four young women were dead.

Unchecked, the virus spread across the globe, even wiping out entire Eskimo settlements. More than 450,000 lives were lost to it in Russia, 375,000 in Italy, and 228,000 in Great Britain. In India, where poverty and overpopulation made the virus spread much more quickly, 5,000,000 died. More than 550,000 Americans died of the disease—more than ten times the American losses in battle during all of World War I.

1918: Brooklyn Train Wreck. On the evening of November 1, an inexperienced motorman running the crowded Brighton Beach commuter train took a curve too fast, causing the five wooden train cars to jump the track and crash into the barrier at the Malbone Street tunnel in Brooklyn, New York.

The first car smashed head-on into the barrier, slid sideways, and was immediately crushed as the following cars plowed through it. The other cars as well were smashed by the impact, and many of the passengers were killed or seriously injured by the jagged timbers. One man was found in his seat impaled by a steel beam which the impact had thrust through the floor of the car. Ninety-seven passengers died in this terrible crash.

The newest mode of transportation claims its victims.

1918: TNT Explosion Rips Pennsylvania Plant. Some two hundred people were killed on May 18 when a TNT explosion blew up the Aetna Chemical Company plant at Oakdale, Pennsylvania.

TNT was the preferred explosive for military use.

1918: Collision at Sea Kills 425. The American steamer *Otranto* collided in heavy seas with the transport *Kashimir* in the North Channel between the Scottish and Irish coasts on October 6. The *Otranto* sank following the accident, with a loss of 425 lives.

1918: Deadly Fires in Minnesota and Wisconsin. Savage fires driven by gale-force winds on October 12 whipped through forests in areas surrounding Duluth, Minnesota, and in northern Wisconsin, burning ten thousand square miles of timberland and destroying twenty-one towns.

The ravaging flames swept into the town of Cloquet, Minnesota, so rapidly that evacuees boarding an outbound train on October 12 found themselves in the middle of a blazing inferno. Flames licked at the cars and shattered the windows as the train raced from the station to escape the fire.

The intense heat and flames killed hundreds. Seventeen people baked to death in a storm cellar, and fourteen others drowned in a well where they had sought refuge. In all, eight hundred died during the conflagration, and twelve thousand were left homeless.

Minnesota, despite being called "the land of lakes," has more than its share of wildfires.

1918: Sinking of Steamship *Princess Sophia*. During a storm off the coast of Alaska on the night of October 24–25, the Canadian-Pacific steamship *Princess Sophia* struck a reef lying west of Juneau. Rescue boats responded to the distress calls from the stranded vessel, but by dawn on October 25 it appeared the grounded ship had sustained no damage and was in no immediate danger.

Rescuers decided evacuation was unnecessary, though they remained at the scene to wait for the water to rise and dislodge the ship. Not smart. That evening another terrible storm arose. As those on the rescue boats watched in horror, high winds and waves picked up the *Princess Sophia,* dashed her against the reef, and sent her to the bottom. All 398 persons aboard the ship perished.

The band was not playing.

1918: Munitions Train Explodes. In a busy railroad yard at Hamont, Belgium, during World War I, a bonfire set by children on November 21 spread out of control and set afire two German munitions trains waiting on a nearby track. The trains exploded in a massive burst of flame, destroying most of the surrounding town as well as three crowded German ambulance trains.

Hundreds of Belgians were crushed to death when the force of the explosion collapsed their houses, and burning debris flew through the air, setting fire to the devastated village. The explosion and subsequent fires killed more than 1,750 people, many of them German soldiers who had been plundering trains at the railroad yard.

Play with fire and get burned. Play with bombs and die.

1919: The Massacre of Amritsar. More than ten thousand Indian demonstrators crowded the square outside the British fort at Amritsar, India, on April 13. They had come to protest the British colonial government's reinstatement of repressive emergency powers, designed to deter and punish subversive activities during World War I. According to the fort commander, the Indian protesters were "offensive, and laughed and jeered at the British. . . ." Armed with axes lashed to long poles, the natives reportedly tried to gain entrance to the fort.

At this point, British troops fired on the crowd. The square had only one exit, and the demonstrators were massacred as they tried desperately to flee. More than 350 people were killed, and another 1,200 were seriously injured.

Following the shooting, the British declared martial law in India, and public floggings and other repressive measures were instituted to punish the Indian people and keep order. Defending the floggings, a British official declared that "only natives of good physique were chosen." Bloody decent of him. He was undoubtedly whipped as a schoolboy.

The massacre and its aftermath are believed to have contributed significantly to the success of Mahatma Gandhi's noncooperation movement, which began the following year.

1919: Volcanic Lake in Java Erupts. During the many years the volcano Keluit in Java had been dormant, the volcano's mouth filled with water to form a crater lake. When Keluit finally did erupt on May 20, a torrent of mud and water spewed down the mountainside, killing some fifty-five hundred people in the surrounding area.

1920: French Liner Sinks. The liner *Afrique* ran aground and sank on reefs off La Rochelle, France, on January 11. Five hundred fifty-three of the passengers and crew lost their lives.

Those treacherous reefs again.

1920: Earthquake Devastates Gansu, China. An earthquake measuring 8.6 on the Richter scale wreaked incredible devastation on the province of Gansu, in north central China, on December 16. A huge below-ground roar accompanied by harsh winds and dust storms signaled the beginning of the disaster. Throughout an area three hundred miles long and one hundred miles wide, the land seemed to "walk" as entire mountains collapsed into valleys, and hills rumbled over plains. Massive landslides wiped out virtually all life in some areas.

Whole villages were buried under heaps of rubble. Muslim leader "Ma the Benevolent" and three hundred disciples were buried by a landslide moments after they had declared a holy war.

Throughout ten large cities and numerous villages, people and livestock were crushed to death in their homes or buried in landslides, bringing the estimated death toll to some 180,000 people. Gansu province was hit again in 1927 by an earthquake that killed 100,000 people. Yet another devastating quake killed 70,000 more in December 1932.

Gansu is not high on the list of places to retire to.

1921–1923: Famine in the Soviet Union. Crop failures caused by drought and the turmoil caused by the harsh transition to communal farming and a communist economy imposed by the Bolshevik revolutionary government led to massive famine in the Volga River region of the Soviet Union. In some areas, farmers, their ranks exhausted by World War I and the revolution, cultivated only half the amount of land as before the war.

By July 1921, twenty-five million people faced possible starvation. Crowds of peasants left their farms and homes, walking eastward and crying for food. Elsewhere, peasants slaughtered livestock and horses to survive. Some subsisted on a mixture of dried leaves and grain husks. At least half a million children were orphaned by the famine, and during the harsh Russian winter, many destitute youngsters trekked through the snow in search of food. Many froze to death along the roads. Despite an international relief effort, millions died of hunger.

1921: Kronshtadt Rebellion. Sailors at the Russian fortress at Kronshtadt near Saint Petersburg had supported the Bolshevik takeover in Russia, but in March 1921 rebelled against the repressive regime under Lenin. They demanded economic reforms, release of political prisoners, and greater political and civil freedoms. Soviet troops attacked the rebels soon after the revolt began, killing or imprisoning all those who survived the assault.

So much for civil rights.

1921: Mayhem Aboard Sinking Chinese Steamer. On March 18 the steamer *Hong Koh* was carrying eleven hundred Chinese from Singapore to Amoy (now Xiamen). A scheduled stop at Swatow (now Shantou) was aborted due to low tide. The angry passengers bound for Swatow became unruly. Can you blame them? No sooner had the captain quelled this near riot with a show of firearms and a hot water hose than the ship struck rocks and foundered.

The already agitated passengers became panic-stricken. Blood spattered over the deck of the sinking ship as passengers, fighting over seats in the lifeboats, attacked each other with hatchets, knives, and axes. Hundreds perished when their overcrowded lifeboats sank or were dashed to pieces against the side of the ship. More than one thousand persons drowned or were hacked to death in this bloody calamity.

Mob mentality in its finest hour.

1921: Crash of the *R-38*. The British dirigible *R-38*, the largest airship built up to that time, broke in half and fell into the Humber River at Hull, England, on August 24, killing forty-four people. Five people aboard the craft survived the crash.

This brought the British airship industry to a temporary halt.

1921: German Dye Plant Explodes. At 7:30 A.M. on September 21, two massive explosions rocked the Badische synthetic nitrate plant in Oppau, Germany. The blasts, attributed to a faulty gas compressor, blew the entire factory high into the air, leaving a gaping hole in the ground 130 yards wide. Three trains bringing workers in for the morning shift were buried in the debris, which was drenched with ammonia used in manufacturing operations at the plant. The explosions were felt as far as fifty miles away and caused storefronts twelve miles away to collapse. They claimed 565 lives and injured more than 2,000 people.

1922: Heavy Snows Hit Eastern Seaboard. A great snowstorm lasting from January 27 to 29 blanketed the eastern seaboard from South Carolina to Massachusetts with heavy snows. Washington, D.C., was hit with twenty-eight inches, and snow in New York City caused the collapse of the Knickerbocker Cinema, killing 120 people in the audience.

1922: Swatow's Twin Typhoons. A pair of devastating typhoons struck the area surrounding Swatow (now Shantou), China, beginning at 10:00 P.M. on August 2. The storms began with thunder and driving rain, followed by winds of one hundred miles per hour. Then a massive tidal wave slammed into the shoreline, adding to the devastation.

Swatow and five other towns were almost completely destroyed by the furious wind and waves. The storms tore trees up by their roots, collapsed buildings, and flooded coastal areas with eight feet of water. Meanwhile, the relentless wind and waves wrecked numerous sampans, drowned their occupants, and drove the wrecks two hundred feet inland.

Afterward, the sea around Swatow was filled with wreckage and floating bodies of the drowned. The typhoon killed an estimated sixty thousand people.

1923: Great Kwanto Earthquake. As if to forewarn disaster, flocks of birds reportedly flew away from the area of Tokyo, Japan, early in the morning of September 1. Then, shortly before noon, a series of powerful earthquakes rocked the entire area around Tokyo and nearby Yokohama. The land, even whole mountains, pitched and rolled as if riding on giant waves of water. Seismologists at Tokyo Imperial University watched their instruments begin to tremble, then pitch and rock, and finally fall to the floor.

The quake caused some parts of the sea floor near the epicenter, about sixty miles offshore from Tokyo, to rise eight hundred feet; other parts fell as much as fifteen hundred feet. An American tourist recalled, "We saw the bottom coming up in places in the harbor." Roads buckled in the wild shaking, and buildings crumbled. One man barely escaped from his office building before a fissure opened up and swallowed it whole.

Violent upheavals also created deadly landslides. About two hundred schoolchildren aboard an excursion train were killed when a landslide buried the whole train. An entire forest on Mount Tanzawi surged down the mountainside, carrying a village along with it into the bay.

The quake also created a thirty-six-foot-high tsunami, and unleashed destructive tornadoes. But by far the greatest damage was caused by fire, which raged throughout both Tokyo and Yokohama for three days. Because the quake struck at noon, it overturned tens of thousands of charcoal braziers that had been lit to cook midday meals, and the burning coals quickly set fire to the traditional paper-and-wood houses. Typhoonlike winds did the rest, and soon thousands of fires were burning out of control.

As fire swept through Tokyo, over thirty-eight thousand residents sought shelter in an open waterfront area. The huddled mass of refugees suddenly became horrified victims when a fire tornado raced through the area. All but a few hundred were quickly burned to death in a solid mass of bodies. Meanwhile, sparks and burning debris falling from the air ignited hundreds of small ships anchored in the bay.

In Yokohama many tried to flee the flames by seeking refuge in the Yokohama Specie Bank, a structure that was reportedly fireproof. Many died trying to reach the building. Those who made it died in the bank's basement, overcome by heat and lack of air.

In one residential area, flames forced many residents to the edge of a one-hundred-foot cliff where, finally, they had to jump to save themselves. They fell onto the bodies of those dead or injured who had jumped before them. Many other frightened victims sought shelter on wooden bridges, which were then ignited when the people's belongings caught fire.

Thousands of Yokohama residents leaped into the bay to save themselves from the raging fires. There they clung to bits of floating debris or clambered aboard boats. They were safe until the Standard Oil facility and its oil reserves suddenly exploded, pouring over one hundred thousand tons of flaming oil into Yokohama Bay. At about the same time, a tornado roared down the Sumida River, destroying those few boats, loaded with survivors, which remained afloat.

One survivor described the fire in Yokohama: "Here and there a remnant of a building, a few shattered walls, stood up like rocks against the expanse of flame, unrecognizable. . . . It was as if the very earth were now burning."

Those fires were eventually put out, though the carnage continued. According to Japanese legend, the sun goddess caused major earthquakes out of dissatisfaction with the emperor, who was required to resign to appease her. Emperor Hirohito, however, sought to absolve himself by accusing Koreans living in Japan of offending the spirits. Thus some four thousand Koreans were eventually rounded up by the Black Dragon Society in Tokyo and publicly beheaded in the streets.

Altogether the incredible series of disasters that struck the Tokyo-Yokohama area destroyed about 60 percent of Tokyo and over 80 percent of Yokohama. Some 140,000 people were killed in these heavily populated areas, and another 200,000 were injured.

Very clever of the emperor.

1924: Babb's Switch Christmas Eve School Fire. This Christmas Eve some two hundred proud parents and their children packed into the little one-room schoolhouse in Babb's Switch, Oklahoma, for a special holiday show. Up on a stage, Santa Claus was passing out presents to children when he accidentally bumped the Christmas tree next to him. That overturned a lighted candle among the decorations, setting the tree on fire. The audience "rose as one" in panic and rushed toward the only exit. People jammed against the door, which opened inward, until finally by sheer weight of numbers, they broke through it.

Meanwhile, others still inside the schoolhouse tried desperately to get out by breaking windows, but heavy wire mesh mounted over the outside of the windows blocked their escape, while winter winds blew into the room, whipping up the flames. Hopelessly trapped, entire families huddled together before being consumed by fire. The teacher, Mrs. Florence Bill, died in a desperate attempt to save some of her pupils still trapped inside.

Ultimately the tragedy claimed thirty-six lives, many of them children who just moments before had been joyously celebrating the arrival of Christmas.

1925: Midwestern Tornado. At least 689 people were killed and over 2,000 more injured on March 18 when the deadliest tornado in U.S. history tore a three-hundred-mile path of destruction through Missouri, Illinois, and Indiana.

At 1:00 P.M. in the eastern Missouri town of Annapolis, the massive storm swiftly descended upon the Ohio River Valley, the tornado funnel smashing the town to ruins. In nearby Poplar Bluff, Missouri, a restaurant customer eating apple pie was suddenly amazed to see first the roof, then the walls of the restaurant torn away around him, while he was left miraculously uninjured. So began the deadly storm's five-hour rampage that devastated towns in three states.

The funnel lifted while the storm crossed the Mississippi River into southern Illinois, where it gathered even more force and diverged into several twisters. One tornado funnel struck ground again twenty-five miles east of the river. At 3:00 P.M. it destroyed Murphysboro and De Soto, Illinois, so quickly that some described it as happening "in the twinkling of an eye."

In De Soto one survivor described the storm as "a crash of thunder preceded by two blinding flashes of lightning, after which there was nothing left." A schoolhouse filled with children literally exploded because of the sudden change in air pressure when the tornado swept over it. So powerful were the winds that the helpless children were literally torn apart. Elsewhere in De Soto, hundreds of houses collapsed on anyone who happened to be inside.

After the storm had flattened these towns and moved on, rescuers wandered the ruins, trying to free survivors who screamed for help from beneath the sea of debris. In one case a rescuer spotted nothing more than the top of a baby's shoe protruding from the wreckage. Tugging at it, he extracted a baby girl who had been buried alive but somehow escaped injury.

In Parrish, Illinois, all but three of the town's five hundred residents were either killed or injured. In Griffen, nine people huddled around a lighted coal stove in a grocery store were roasted by the fire that ravaged the remains of the store after the tornado hit.

Twice more the tornado funnels lifted back into the cloud as the deadly storm moved onward. But they touched ground again, wreaking havoc first at Carmi, Illinois, near the Indiana border, and then at Princeton, Indiana.

At Princeton the storm again struck with sudden fury and left bizarre scenes of destruction in its wake. The body of an unfortunate woman was found sucked partway up the chimney of her house, while a barber's chair, torn from the town barber shop, wound up in a field two miles away. At the railroad yard, freight cars were thrown hundreds of feet through the air and smashed to the ground. Four people caught driving in a car outside Princeton were sucked out by the tremendous winds just before the car was flattened. All four lived to tell the story.

By 6:00 P.M. the vicious tornado reached the end of its three-hundred-mile path of destruction, finally dying out as it headed in the direction of Indianapolis. Property damages were estimated at five hundred million dollars. Though the official death count stood at 689, dozens of other people simply vanished and probably were among the storm's many victims.

1926: Florida Hurricane. This terrible storm hit shortly after midnight on September 17, battering Florida's east coast between Miami and Palm Beach with torrential rains and flag-ripping winds that lasted into the next day. Winds reaching 130 miles per hour shattered windows, tore off roofs, blew down wood-frame houses, and actually twisted large hotel buildings on their foundations. One distraught woman fled from four different collapsing houses before the storm abated. In Miami, hardest hit, hundreds of buildings were wrecked, and the dead and injured were reported strewn about the streets. Meanwhile, the booming development town of Hollywood was one of several leveled by the hurricane. Only the Masonic Temple remained standing there. Storm-tossed waters of Florida's Lake Okeechobee also burst through dikes and flooded a large area. Ultimately about 450 people died, thousands more were injured, and thousands of buildings were destroyed.

It won't be the last hurricane.

1926: Explosions Rip Apart Chinese Troop Ship. The fifteen hundred troops aboard the Chinese ship *Kuang Yuang* thought they would soon be fighting for the warlord of Eastern Central

China in a battle of China's ongoing civil war. But on October 16 that quickly changed when a fire touched off ammunition stowed aboard the ship.

Anchored at Kiukiang on the Yangtze River (now Chang Jiang), the ship erupted into horrendous fiery explosions, with missiles and shells exploding wildly in all directions. One explosion tore away the anchor, and the ship drifted out of control, launching missiles haphazardly on other nearby ships and on the city. Soldiers who survived the initial explosions and fires had no choice but to jump into the river, even though many of them could not swim. Some twelve hundred of the soldiers drowned or were burned to death before the ship lodged on a mudbank and burned down to its waterline. Exploding shells and missiles also caused many other deaths in the waterfront area, but the total number of casualties was never determined.

The Chinese invented fireworks.

1927: Panic Kills Children at Montreal Movie Theater. Hundreds of children crowded into the Laurier Palace movie theater in Montreal on January 9, eagerly anticipating the matinee performance of a comedy titled *Get 'Em Young*. Shortly after the movie began, a small fire broke out in the projection room, but was quickly brought under control. The incident would have ended there had not children seated in the gallery panicked.

Rushing to get out, a few youngsters apparently fell as they rushed down a stairway from the gallery. What followed was a deadly chain reaction. Other children toppled onto them, while the frightened crowd continued pushing forward. Within seconds the stairwell became a mass of tightly packed, screaming children hopelessly trapped—just five steps away from the exit.

When help arrived, the children were so tightly wedged in that twenty men working together could not separate the pile of bodies. Firemen finally resorted to chopping holes from underneath the stairs and through an outer wall. By then, most of the youngsters they freed had died in the crush. Only one of the seventy-eight victims was over sixteen years old.

1927: Mississippi Valley Floods. Heavy rains inundated the Mississippi Valley in late April, causing the Mississippi River to rise up to the flood stage. One by one levees began to break, flooding towns in the lowland areas and finally submerging seventy-five hundred square miles.

In Little Rock, Arkansas, raging waters made a bridge vibrate so much that the friction caused coal in railroad cars on the tracks above to ignite. Meanwhile, some sixty thousand people were left homeless by the flooding.

Authorities in New Orleans, fearing their city would also be flooded, dynamited a levee below their city. Though the delta below New Orleans was flooded, the move relieved pressure on levees protecting the city itself and prevented a major disaster there. Before Mississippi floodwaters receded, 313 people had died.

1927: Tornado Wrecks Saint Louis. At 1:00 P.M. on September 29, the air in Saint Louis suddenly became thick and stifling, while lightning bolts seemed to flash everywhere. A dark tornado cloud appeared as the storm arose with astonishing violence, and witnesses reported the air filled with mysterious "sheets of fire," possibly from static electricity.

Ripping into Saint Louis, the tornado packed eighty-mile-per-hour winds that smashed windows, uprooted trees and telephone poles, tore off roofs, tossed cars around as though they were children's toys, and lifted helpless bystanders into the air. The whirlwind carried a bizarre collection of flying bricks, tree limbs, glass, clothing, and garage doors as it demolished whole sections of the city.

Then, almost before shocked observers even knew what had happened, the tornado was over. The wealthy West End residential area of Saint Louis had been particularly hard hit; it lay in utter ruin, with many of its stately homes and tall elms reduced to a tangled mass of rubble. Survivors in the six-square-mile area of destruction dug desperately through tons of debris, seeking missing friends and family members. When the rescue work was completed, officials put the toll at eighty-five dead and thirteen hundred injured. Some eighteen hundred homes had been destroyed as well, all in just five minutes.

1927: Pittsburgh Gas Explosion. The world's largest tank of natural gas was located in Pittsburgh, Pennsylvania. It was seventy-five feet high—and it was supposed to have been empty when sixteen workers using blow torches set out to repair it about 9:00 A.M. on November 14. But the torches set off a gas explosion so powerful, it shook the city with the violence of an earthquake. The giant tank was lifted high into the air in a ball of fire, then ignited two nearby gas tanks with a thunderous roar. The explosion leveled houses and factories over a square-mile area and hurled huge chunks of the metal tank more than a mile. Many miles away, skyscrapers shook, and shattered glass rained down on terrified pedestrians. The blast even buckled the streets, cracking water mains and flooding parts of the city with waist-deep water. Miraculously, only twenty-eight people died from the explosion, and just five hundred were injured.

1928–1929: Famine in China. Famine brought on by prolonged drought held much of northwest China in its grip for two years and killed some three million people. Hardest hit was Shensi Province (now Shaanxi), where bodies lay in the streets and whole villages were depopulated.

1928: Saint Francis Dam Breaks. The sudden collapse of the Saint Francis Dam in San Francisquito Canyon, California, on March 13 released a massive wall of water that killed 350 people and caused more than fifteen million dollars in damages.

The 185-foot-high Saint Francis Dam, located north of Los Angeles, had been weakened by heavy rains and a buildup of silt behind it. But no one expected the complete collapse that occurred at about 1:00 A.M. Both the east and west sides of the dam gave way, leaving only the center portion of the dam standing.

In the Santa Clara River Valley below the dam, the only warning people had was a furious roar of onrushing water. Within moments after the break, billions of gallons from the five-mile-long reservoir began pouring into the valley. Suddenly a seventy-eight-foot-high wave was speeding down the course of the normally sluggish Santa Clara River. Spreading out across the river's sixty-mile-wide floodplain at a rate of five hundred thousand cubic feet per second, the flood raced relentlessly toward the Pacific Ocean seventy-five miles away.

Towns in its path were devastated by the onslaught of water in the dead of the night. Victims who awoke to the roar of approaching water struggled to throw on clothes and escape, but most never made it that far. A three-year-old girl was found dead wearing a coat thrown over her nightclothes and one untied shoe. Many had their clothes torn off their bodies by the raging waters.

Floodwaters demolished ranch houses and cottages, washing away even their foundations. An eighty-year-old man said his house "crumpled as though it were built of cards"; he was pulled wildly downstream, clinging to a piece of his roof, until one of his sons pulled him to safety on a plank.

The violent waters tore the bark off trees and scoured vegetation from the hills. All bridges in the flood's path were knocked out, and a power plant eight miles below the dam was completely destroyed. In the town of Santa Paula, the flood scooped up three hundred houses and deposited them in a single pile of debris.

Most of the flood's 350 victims were crushed to death by debris or boulders even before they could be drowned. But one woman whose house was washed away held her baby in her arms, fighting the wild current. A whirlpool threw her onto solid ground but knocked the child out of her arms. The baby disappeared into the rushing current.

The flood did not begin to recede until 3:00 A.M. By dawn, thousands of volunteers moved into the ruined canyon to search for survivors and assess the damage. They found the once peaceful valley of orchards and ranch houses gutted by the flood, pockmarked by mud holes, while vultures circled lazily overhead in search of the dead.

1928: Pennsylvania Mine Explosion. An electrical spark apparently caused an explosion and fire at the Mather coal mine in Mather, Pennsylvania, on May 19. A total of 195 miners were killed in the accident.

U.S. coal reserves are among the largest in the world. The coal industry will survive through the next century. No statistics on the miners' survival rate.

1928: Lake Okeechobee Hurricane. A deadly hurricane packing winds of up to 160 miles per hour struck the Caribbean from the Atlantic Ocean on September 10, ravaged Puerto Rico and other islands, and then headed for the Florida coast.

When the hurricane finally hit the Lake Okeechobee area near West Palm Beach, Florida, on September 16, residents had had plenty of warning. Volunteers from the Miami area drove along the lake's shore before the hurricane, calling out to people to evacuate the area. For many, however, there was nowhere to go. More than six hundred people packed themselves into two grand hotels that had been built on the lake's shore. Thousands of others living in the low-lying areas around the lake simply stayed at home, even though many of them had nothing more than flimsy shanties for shelter.

The storm struck the coast at West Palm Beach and then drove inland toward Lake Okeechobee. Fierce winds spilled the lake waters into low-lying fields, collapsing twenty-one miles of mud dikes designed to protect against flooding. Hundreds of shantytowns, built to house workers who farmed the rich, loamy soil of the region, were washed away. Their inhabitants were drowned in floodwaters that in places reached the second story of their houses.

The furious winds hurled lake water up into the air, creating walls of water that raced through the area, toppling even the stronger buildings at Lake Okeechobee. Before the storm was over, every building in the area except the two big lakeside hotels had been demolished.

In swampy terrain, people trying to escape the raging floodwaters climbed trees, holding their children or carrying them on their backs. On reaching the upper branches of the trees, though, they discovered snakes had taken refuge there as well. Many people not killed by the hurricane died of bites by poisonous water moccasins.

Following the storm, there were so many dead floating in waterways that rescue workers roped the bodies together, then towed long lines of bloated, unrecognizable corpses behind their boats to land. In West Palm Beach, where residents worried about the spread of disease, bodies of seven hundred hurricane victims brought there were hastily buried in a mass grave. Other decomposing bodies were reportedly piled together in swamps and then burned. Funeral pyres, in the days and nights after the disaster, could be seen for miles around.

Twenty-five hundred people died in the Lake Okeechobee area alone, and some five thousand people in all were killed by the storm, including about one thousand in Puerto Rico. An estimated 350,000 people were left homeless. The federal government later sponsored a five-million-dollar flood-control program for the area and built an eighty-five-mile rock levee, thirty-four feet high, along the southern shore of Lake Okeechobee.

1929: Saint Valentine's Day Massacre. On the morning of February 14—Valentine's Day—some of the leading figures in "Bugs" Moran's underworld gang were waiting for the coffee to boil in a Chicago warehouse that served as a front for their bootlegging operation. They were startled to see a detective's blue car screech to a stop at the curb.

Two men dressed in police uniforms and wearing badges got out of the car, along with two plainclothes "officers." They were armed with sawed-off shotguns and submachine guns. But what Moran's men did not know was that this apparent police raid was actually an execution ordered by Al "Scarface" Capone, Moran's rival.

Disguised in the police uniforms, Capone's men forced the Moran gang members to face a white wall, arms above their heads, and then opened fire. Altogether they fired more than one hundred shots, riddling the rival gangsters with up to twenty bullets each. One man tried to crawl away; instantly a machine gun blast tore off the top of his head. Six men lay dead; a seventh survived for several hours, but refused to say anything to the police.

After completing the cold-blooded execution, the killers escaped by leading two of their own out of the building, hands above their heads as though they were under arrest. Then they all made their getaway by car, leaving the dead bodies sprawled across the warehouse floor. Only a snarling police dog that belonged to the Moran gang survived the massacre.

The massacre is one of the gangster legends of the "Roaring Twenties."

1929: Deadly Cleveland Hospital Fire. Fire in the X-ray room of the Cleveland Clinic in Cleveland, Ohio, on May 15 produced poisonous gases that spread throughout the hospital. A total of 121 people were asphyxiated by the fumes.

Some people thought they were going there to get well.

1929: Stock Market Crash. The trading floor of the New York Stock Exchange was packed with frantic stockbrokers on October 24 as stock values plummeted and traders rushed to sell. Huge crowds gathered outside the exchange, and a steady stream of curious observers, among them Winston Churchill, former chancellor of Britain's Exchequer, watched the frenetic activity on the floor from the visitors' gallery above.

Share prices continued their dizzying downward spiral until 1:00 P.M., when the leading bankers decided to boost investor confidence by pooling their corporate money and investing over twenty million dollars in key stocks. The market rallied, and by the end of the day, after a record twelve million shares had changed hands, exchange prices had recovered approximately two-thirds of their losses. It appeared that a national catastrophe had been narrowly averted.

Over the next few days, the market alternately sagged and rallied, until October 29, "Black Tuesday," when the stock market collapsed completely. As soon as the exchange opened, stockbrokers who had patiently waited for share prices to rise began selling off their remaining investments fifty thousand shares at a time. This triggered a selling frenzy, and as hundreds of stockbrokers and investors simultaneously tried the same maneuver, share prices tumbled downward again. Trying to avoid complete ruin, stockholders now frantically dumped their shares for whatever they could get, and by the end of the day, sixteen million shares had been traded. More than fifteen billion dollars in paper fortunes simply vanished in one day.

The assets of thousands of shareholders, big and small, were wiped out by the crash. Ruined bank presidents and financiers shot themselves, a Saint Louis stockbroker swallowed poison, and Winston Churchill woke up Wednesday morning to discover that a man had plunged to his death right outside his window. Humorist Will Rogers wryly remarked that "you had to stand in line to get a window to jump out of, and speculators were selling space for bodies in the East River."

The crash devastated the national economy, precipitating the Great Depression of the 1930s. A vicious cycle began in which consumers could not afford to buy goods, thereby forcing manufacturers to lay off workers; the now-unemployed workers bought even fewer goods, and still more manufacturers went bankrupt. The unemployment rate skyrocketed: The seven million who were unemployed in 1930 became fourteen to sixteen million unemployed by 1933 (one in four workers) as the shock waves of the stock market crash swept over the entire nation.

But what a great time to get into the market. Prices would never be lower.

1930: Prisoners Killed by Ohio Penitentiary Fire. The nightly lockup of the forty-three hundred inmates at the dangerously overcrowded Ohio State Penitentiary in Columbus had just been completed on April 21 when two rebellious inmates apparently set fire to the prison's wooden roof. While a stiff wind rapidly spread smoke and flames, a head guard steadfastly refused to unlock cells until ordered to do so. Orders are orders, right?

The delay doomed hundreds of prisoners, now screaming in their cells as burning ceilings collapsed around them. By the time guards finally started opening cells, smoke filled the building and many collapsed with the keys in their hands. Guards and convicts alike then risked their lives by volunteering to go into the inferno to smash open cell doors with sledgehammers. Though thousands of inmates did finally get out, 322 prisoners burned to death or were smothered by smoke.

1930: Crash of the *R-101*. The hydrogen-filled British dirigible *R-101* broke up and crashed in flames during a storm at Beauvais, France, on October 5. The crash killed forty-eight crewmen and passengers.

Dirigible engineers have not fully investigated the potential fire hazards. More to come.

1931: Diphtheria Invades the United States. A severe outbreak of diphtheria swept across the United States, killing some seventeen thousand children.

1931: Manchurian Mine Explosion. Fire broke out deep beneath the earth February 8 at the Fushun coal mines in Japanese-occupied Manchuria, fifty miles east of Mukden (now Shenyang). The fire set off a gas explosion that ripped through the shaft, killing some three thousand miners outright or burying them alive. Among the dead were forty Japanese foremen. Relatives of the trapped miners assembled at the mine, weeping as they waited in anguish for news of what had happened underground. Despite repeated official reports by the Japanese of no casualties in the disaster, only a very few Chinese miners are believed to have been rescued from the mine.

If there are no casualties, there is no need to "save face."

1931: Yangtze Flood Kills Millions. Heavy summer rains swelled China's Yangtze River (now Chang Jiang) in early August, causing the thirty-two-hundred-mile-long river to overflow its banks and create enormous lakes of floodwater throughout the country. Sixteen of China's provinces underwent massive flooding, and some twenty-eight million people were affected.

Peasants watched in horror as the floodwaters rose and dikes holding back rivers and canals began breaking. Soon whole villages lay underwater while canals swollen by weeks of heavy rain overflowed onto fields. So heavy was the flow of water that in some places it continued rushing out of dikes for four weeks after they had broken.

The muddy waters of the Yangtze and Hwai rivers rose through streets of cities and towns over a wide area. The region between Nanking (now Nanjing) and Hankow (now part of Wuhan) became a single vast lake strewn with the floating corpses of thousands of drowned people and animals. Survivors meanwhile rode in boats over the rooftops of their homes.

Despite the horror of the flooding and deaths from drowning, the worst was yet to come. Millions faced starvation because floods almost completely wiped out rice and other crops in many areas. In addition, survivors were forced to drink water from the flooded rivers, and as a result, dysentery and typhoid fever became epidemic.

Altogether an estimated 3.7 million people perished from disease, starvation, or drowning. One observer called it "probably the greatest natural calamity which the world has suffered in recent centuries."

"Water, water, everywhere . . ."

1932: Kidnapping of Lindbergh Baby. At 7:00 P.M. on March 1, Charles Lindbergh, Jr., the twenty-month old, blond, curly-headed son of the world-famous hero and his wife, Anne, was put to bed in the nursery of the Lindberghs' new home in a secluded section of Hopewell, New Jersey. At 8:00 P.M. his nursemaid, Betty Gow, looked in on him, and at about the same time, Anne and Charles sat down to dinner. At ten o'clock Betty entered the nursery for a final check and discovered the toddler was gone.

Lindbergh told the butler to call the police while he went

outside into the windy night with a rifle to look around, but found no one. Later the police found two sets of footprints, two holes made by a ladder outside the baby's room, and about seventy feet away, the broken makeshift ladder itself. In the baby's room was a poorly written note demanding fifty thousand dollars ransom in small bills.

After the news of the kidnapping was broadcast, a massive search ensued. At that time, kidnapping was a state offense, and unfortunately, the FBI was not called in. The Lindbergh estate was inundated by several hundred reporters and photographers, and the story eclipsed all other news. The inflated, frequently inaccurate and fabricated stories of the circumstances of the kidnapping increased some newspaper circulations by an estimated 20 percent.

Lindbergh, adamant that nothing should jeopardize the return of the baby and the payment of the ransom, instructed the police to negotiate with the kidnappers rather than arrest them.

A Dr. J. F. Condon, who lived in the Bronx borough of New York, on his own accord ran an ad in a New York newspaper offering to be the intermediary between the kidnappers and Lindbergh. Oddly enough, he was contacted by the kidnappers, and after one meeting and several phone calls with one of the culprits, he and Lindbergh paid the ransom on Saturday night, April 2, outside a cemetery in the Bronx. In return they were given instructions as to the baby's whereabouts. The next day Lindbergh searched for the boat off Cape Cod on which the baby was allegedly kept, but could not find it. Seventy-two days later, little Charlie's decomposed body was found in the woods about five miles from the estate. He had died of a fractured skull.

Although there had been at least twenty-five hundred kidnappings in the three years prior to 1932, this crime was looked upon as the most heinous. The New Jersey state legislature authorized the governor to offer a twenty-five-thousand-dollar reward for information leading to the kidnappers' arrest and conviction. In June the United States Congress passed a bill declaring kidnapping across state lines a federal offense, commonly known as the Lindbergh Law.

Police efforts now turned to the pursuit of the kidnappers and to tracing some of the ransom money (the serial numbers of the bills had been recorded), which was showing up in New York City banks occasionally. The FBI in October 1933 at last joined with the New Jersey and New York police forces on the case, not without some jealous hostility among the officials.

In 1934 Bruno Richard Hauptmann was arrested in New York City after police traced some of the ransom money to him. Hauptmann insisted the money belonged to an acquaintance who had left it with him before leaving for a visit to Germany, where he subsequently died. What little evidence the police had was circumstantial at best, but in their zeal, they indicted him.

The trial was a spectacle, attended by celebrities and society alike, and played up by sensational journalism. The Hearst newspapers paid for Hauptmann's defense (after talking his wife out of retaining their original lawyer who was convinced of his innocence) by an incompetent, alcoholic lawyer, so their reporters could get exclusives.

The mass of evidence to prove Hauptmann's innocence was suppressed while much was invented, even planted, and witnesses were bribed and coerced.

The verdict was guilty, and Hauptmann, declaring his innocence to the end, was executed in 1937.

The identities of the true kidnappers remain a mystery to this day.

1932–1937: The Dust Bowl. In May of 1934, President Franklin D. Roosevelt noticed a thin film of dust on his desk in Washington, D.C. It was prairie soil, blown by the wind all the way from the Great Plains states west of the Mississippi River—what became known as the Dust Bowl.

A drought that began in 1932 combined with poor farming practices to help turn the once productive farming regions of the Great Plains to barren wastes. Huge dust storms, known as "black blizzards," scoured the plains with winds up to eighty miles per hour, tearing up dried, powdery topsoil and whipping it into black, swirling storm fronts one thousand feet high.

Towns were shrouded in darkness during these storms as dust drove cars off the road, derailed trains, and in some places piled in drifts thirty feet deep. Crops disappeared, cattle died, and people grew sick in the prolonged disaster. Thousands of farmers were driven off their land, and in May 1934, dust actually dimmed the daytime sky as far away as New York and Baltimore. The drought finally ended in 1938, after half a million people had been forced to abandon their homes.

And out of this disaster came the classic novel by John Steinbeck, *The Grapes of Wrath*.

1933–1945: The Holocaust. Adolf Hitler promised during a speech in 1920 that he would see to "the removal of the Jews from the midst of our people." Within a month after he became chancellor of Germany in 1933, Hitler began a persecution of Jews that would eventually lead to his "Final Solution," a horribly cold-blooded attempt to systematically kill millions of Jews living within the borders of Nazi-controlled territory.

The first Nazi concentration camps were set up in 1933, originally for imprisonment of political enemies, but soon after, Nazis began to send Jews and other minorities to them. In 1935 Nazi Germany denied citizenship to Jews and forbade them to marry non-Jews. By the beginning of World War II in 1939, Jews were forbidden to own land, practice most professions, or associate with non-Jews. Those not already in concentration camps were forced to live in Jewish ghettos.

The mass murder of Jews began with the German invasion of the Soviet Union in 1941. As German troops advanced, they rounded up Russian Jews and forced them to dig mass graves. Nazi machine gunners then slaughtered as many as five hundred Jews at a time and dumped them into the graves. By the end of 1941, the Nazis had massacred 1.4 million Soviet Jews.

The Wannsee Conference of Nazi leaders in January 1942 formalized Hitler's "Final Solution" to the "Jewish problem": The Jews of Europe were to be relocated to concentration camps, where they would be exterminated or used as slave laborers. Auschwitz, Dachau, Treblinka, and other concentration camps became places of unbelievable cruelty and death as Jews, packed into boxcars like livestock, arrived by the trainload from all over Europe. Starvation, overcrowding, and disease killed thousands on the trains before they even reached the camps; some trains arrived with half the prisoners dead and many of the rest in comas. Those strong enough to work were used for slave labor; the old or sick were marked for immediate extermination.

Thousands of people at a time were herded into chambers marked "Baths and Disinfecting Rooms," which soon filled with poison gas. The corpses were often piled to the ceiling as the prisoners stampeded over one another in a desperate attempt to escape the gas. Other prisoners then were forced to load the bodies into nearby crematoriums. At Auschwitz, sixty crematoriums were in operation; up to six thousand people were executed per day. Black smoke and the stench of burning flesh filled the air.

As the Holocaust proceeded, the Nazis struggled to find the most efficient means of disposing of the millions of corpses. At Treblinka, Nazi guards forced one prisoner to dig up corpses and burn them. He wrote: "Wherever a grave was opened, a terrible stench polluted the air. . . . It turned out that women burned easier than men. Accordingly, corpses of women were used for kindling fires."

Prisoners who were not executed died of starvation, overwork, torture, and beatings. At Dachau the Nazis conducted gruesome medical experiments on prisoners: injecting them with malaria infection, holding them underneath ice-cold water, and castrating them. Skin from executed prisoners was dried and used to make gloves, handbags, and other articles.

The defeat of Nazi Germany in 1945 finally ended the horror of the death camps, and when the Allies liberated the Belsen concentration camp in April 1945, the secret of Nazi atrocities was at last revealed to a stunned world. One British officer described how "the inmates had lost all self-respect, were degraded morally to the level of beasts. Their clothes were in rags, teeming with lice, and both inside and outside the huts was an almost continuous carpet of dead bodies, human excreta, rags, and filth."

An estimated total of 5.7 million European Jews were exterminated during the Holocaust; 2 million died at Auschwitz alone. An estimated 3 million non-Jewish Poles and Slavs—also considered by Hitler to be genetically "subhuman"—perished as well.

One wonders, if Hitler had been accepted into art school as he so devoutly desired, what his twisted mind would have produced.

Without doubt, the Holocaust was one of the most incomprehensible and painful chapters in the history of man's inhumanity to man.

1933: The Suspicious Reichstag Fire. In mid-February Marinus van der Lubbe, a mentally retarded Dutch communist, arrived in Berlin and began boasting in public bars that he intended to set fire to the Reichstag building, home of the German parliament. Several Nazis were said to have overheard these threats and immediately reported them to Hermann Goering, minister without portfolio and Adolf Hitler's right-hand man. Thus began a sinister plot to burn down the Reichstag, a plot that in all likelihood involved the Nazis themselves. Though exact details of the plan remain a mystery, evidence gained at the Nuremburg trials after World War II clearly pointed to the Nazis as those responsible.

Goering supposedly was very interested in the report. Though Hitler was in power as German chancellor, the Nazi party had not gained a majority in recent elections, and a new election was to take place in two weeks. Goering is said to have realized that the raving communist might offer the perfect opportunity to discredit the Communists in time for the elections. So Goering did not have Van der Lubbe arrested, and instead, allowed him to continue broadcasting his incendiary intentions.

Finally, about 9:00 P.M. on February 27, Van der Lubbe entered the Reichstag and apparently tore off his shirt, lighted it, and used the flaming cloth to start the building burning. Meanwhile, Karl Ernst, leader of the Nazi Brownshirts, and three or more of his followers are believed to have secretly entered the Reichstag through a tunnel that led from Goering's official residence. Working quickly, they used cloth soaked in gasoline to start fires in several other places, and then slipped out through the same secret passageway. A policeman passing outside the Reichstag minutes later smelled smoke. Inside, he found Van der Lubbe naked to the waist, and fires burning in various parts of the building.

There was no proof of Nazi involvement at that time, of course, but it was unlikely one man could have set so many fires in so short a time. And not long after, Hermann Goering arrived on the scene, screaming that every Communist official must be shot and every Communist Reichstag member be hanged that very night.

Word of the fire spread quickly, and within minutes a Nazi party member had telephoned Joseph Goebbels at home to apprise him of the situation. Goebbels, propaganda chief for the Nazi party, was at that moment entertaining Adolf Hitler as a dinner guest, and apparently treated the urgent message as a crank call, saying that he refused to believe such a thing. After a few minutes, however, Goebbels and Hitler set off for the Reichstag.

Hitler joined in with Goering's tirade, sternly declaring that he would crush the Communists with an iron fist.

The fire was brought under control at around 10:30 P.M., and by midnight the once glorious Reichstag building was a smoldering, heavily damaged wreck.

The following day, the Nazis swung into action. Hitler persuaded the aged and infirm German president, Paul von Hindenburg, to sign a decree declaring a state of emergency that suspended constitutional rights and personal liberties. Goering ordered the arrest of one hundred Communist Reichstag members, and within a few days, more than four thousand Communist and left-wing leaders were imprisoned.

While the anti-Communist hysteria still did not enable the Nazis to reach a majority in the election, Hitler did manage to convince the Reichstag to pass his Enabling Act on March 23. This single act transfered all legislative power to Hitler's Reich Cabinet, thereby establishing Hitler as dictator of Germany. Hitler had won, and it would only be a matter of time before he set in motion his ruinous plans for German glorification and world conquest.

Marinus van der Lubbe meanwhile confessed to treason and arson and was summarily executed.

1933: Dirigible Crash off New Jersey Coast. The airship USS *Akron,* having proved its airworthiness in thunderstorms before, took off from Lakehurst, New Jersey, for a routine flight on the stormy evening of April 4. A crew of seventy-seven manned the 785-foot dirigible, the largest built up to that time, and the pride of the U.S. Navy.

Throughout the night, blustery winds and violent thunderstorms buffeted the airship. Finally, at 12:30 A.M., a bolt of lightning apparently damaged the huge vessel, and sent it crashing into the sea twenty miles off the coast of New Jersey. Radio contact was lost, and only the eerie light of calcium fires from the burning hulk signaled its presence to a passing tanker.

There was little hope for any crewmen who may have survived the crash. Fierce winds continued to blow the floating wreckage away from shore, and continuing electrical storms hampered rescue communications. Only four of the crew members were eventually picked up from the cold, storm-tossed waters.

1933: French Train Crash Kills Holiday Travelers. Holiday travelers leaving Paris for a Christmas in the country crowded aboard the Nancy Express on December 23. A dense fog soon brought rail traffic to a halt, however, forcing the Nancy Express to stop behind a stalled suburban commuter train fifteen miles east of Paris.

Meanwhile, the Fast Train from Paris to Strasbourg barreled toward the stopped Nancy Express at sixty-five miles per hour. In the heavy fog, the engineer of the Strasbourg train did not see the taillights ahead of him until it was too late and rammed into the rear of the stopped Nancy Express.

The heavy locomotive crushed the wooden cars of the Nancy train to splinters, telescoping and completely destroying the last four cars, and strewing the bodies of the dead and dying along the tracks. Another oncoming train saw the warning lights ahead and managed to stop just in time.

The wreck killed 230 people aboard the Nancy Express.

1934: Fire Destroys Hakodate, Japan. On March 21 gale-force winds knocked over a chimney in Hakodate, Japan, starting a great fire that leveled the city. The fire began late in the evening and spread quickly through the city, which was tinder-dry after a winter drought.

The fire burned throughout the night and devastated six square miles of Hakodate. The business district and some twenty thousand homes were obliterated. Residents lucky enough to escape the flames flocked to the harbor, where many were evacuated in steamships. Bodies littered the streets, however, and some 1,500 died in the terrible fire. Among the dead were 120 parents and children who died after taking refuge in an elementary school.

1934: Fire at Sea—the *Morro Castle*. The luxury vacation liner *Morro Castle,* returning to New York from a cruise to Havana, Cuba, seemed to be a ship headed for disaster. A long history of smuggling drugs, liquor, and illegal aliens by crewmen had preceded the voyage, and now complaints by the crewmen over low pay and inedible food had approached a near mutinous stage.

On the fateful last night of the cruise, the captain ate a specially prepared dinner in his cabin—then died of an apparent heart attack shortly afterward. When the weak-willed second officer took command, he found the ship heading into a fierce storm. Meanwhile, many passengers and crewmen were belowdecks celebrating the voyage's last night by getting drunk. Then, at 2:30 A.M. on September 8, a mysterious fire broke out in the ship's writing room.

Passengers, many of them asleep, drunk, or seasick, were slow to respond to alarms, and the fast-moving fire trapped a number of them in their cabins. The second officer, now acting as captain, was reportedly slow and uncertain in reacting at critical points in the emergency. He apparently waited so long to send out an SOS that nearby ships saw and reported the fire before the *Morro Castle* requested help. When the order to abandon ship finally came, many crewmen reportedly showed little concern for the passengers, saving themselves instead.

Lifeboats were launched with but a few people in them, leaving most passengers trapped on board the burning ship. Eventually the fire forced these unfortunate souls to jump overboard, and many drowned in the rough waters before they could be picked up by rescuers. By morning the burning hulk of the *Morro Castle* beached herself on the shoreline at Asbury Park, New Jersey, a grim testament to a disaster at sea that claimed the lives of 133 people.

Obviously the crew needed just a little more training.

1935: Earthquake Razes Indian City. The sixty thousand people of Quetta in northwestern India (now Pakistan) were roused from sleep at 3:00 A.M. on May 31 by a loud rumbling and cracking sound. Seconds later a series of quakes rolled through the city like tidal waves and demolished 80 percent of its buildings.

Thousands died in their beds. Others who were more fortunate could be heard screaming prayers to the Hindu god Rama as they ran out of their collapsing homes. Confusion reigned in the dark streets, however, as buildings crashed down around the hapless survivors.

Fires and floods in the wake of the main shocks, measuring up to 7.5 on the Richter scale, added to the devastation that extended throughout the entire region. In fact, severe quakes were felt as far away as Kandahar, Afghanistan—125 miles north of Quetta—where whole towns and cities lay in ruins. In all, over fifty thousand people died in the disaster.

1935: Hurricane Devastates Florida Keys. Hurricane warnings had gone out forty-eight hours in advance of the rampaging storm that hit the Florida Keys on September 2. But the World War I veterans employed in three road-building camps in the keys were told to wait for an evacuation train to take them to safety. As furious winds hurled timbers through the air, and waters rose dangerously high, the train finally reached the camp—and kept right on going at full speed.

As the stranded veterans watched the train roar past, fifteen-foot waves slammed over the wooden huts of their encampment, leveling every building. Those who tried to form human chains to make their way to higher ground were washed into the gulf. One group of survivors dug holes underneath railroad ties and buried their heads. "This was the only way we could find to keep our brains from being crushed out" by flying debris, one said.

Rescue workers arrived three days later to find bodies floating in the floodwaters, buried deep in mud, or hanging from trees. Four hundred people—most of them veterans—were dead.

War may be hell, but so, apparently, is road building.

1936: Five Million Chinese Die in New Famine. Millions of Chinese in the rich agricultural region of Szechwan (now Sichuan) Province faced starvation in 1936 as the result of a civil war and subsequent unrest. Roving bands of "famine bandits" were reported plundering farms and towns, while millions slowly died of hunger. Some starving Chinese even sold their wives and children in exchange for food and small amounts of money.

Once again the old in-adversity-sell-your-wife routine.

1937: Massive Flooding in Ohio River Basin. Dikes along the rain-swollen Ohio and Scioto rivers broke in January 1937, resulting in flooding that extended for one thousand miles along the Ohio River basin and included twelve states. The floods killed 137 people and caused $418 million in damages. The Red Cross organized a massive relief effort, including setting up three hundred emergency hospitals and raising $25 million in disaster relief funds.

1937: Texas School Explosion. Classes for some seven hundred children at the New London, Texas, school were almost over on the afternoon of March 18 when an explosion suddenly ripped the newly constructed brick building apart. The blast, apparently caused by a gas leak, lifted the roof off the building and toppled the walls.

Children were hurled about like matchsticks, the lucky ones surviving by being blown completely out of the building or by jumping out of windows as the structure collapsed. Many, however, were torn apart by the force of the explosion or crushed by falling debris.

Meanwhile, parents waiting to take their children home after school watched in horror as the building was blown to pieces before their eyes. Hearing cries for help from children trapped beneath the rubble, parents began tearing at the huge pile of bricks, cement, and twisted steel with their bare hands. Local oil field workers soon arrived with heavy equipment, and eventually an estimated 3,000 people took part in moving the debris. But it was too late for 294 students and teachers who had been killed by the explosion.

1937: *Hindenburg* Disaster. The 804-foot-long dirigible *Hindenburg,* filled with dangerously flammable hydrogen gas for buoyancy, caught fire and crashed in a gigantic ball of flames at an airfield in Lakehurst, New Jersey, on May 6. Thirty-five of the ninety-seven people aboard were killed, and the disaster ended forever the era of commercial airship transportation.

The *Hindenburg,* the world's largest dirigible, was built and promoted by Nazi Germany as a feat of German technology. In size and capabilities, it was a marvel for its time, carrying a maximum of ninety-seven passengers and sixty-one crewmen, having a top speed of eighty-four miles per hour and a range of eight thousand miles. But Germany's warlike stance had cut off access to supplies of strategically important, nonflammable helium gas. *Hindenburg*'s operators instead used seven million cubic feet of explosive hydrogen gas to float the dirigible.

The landing of so large a craft was a major event at Lakehurst, and in the early evening of May 6, a crowd of reporters and spectators eagerly awaited the *Hindenburg*'s arrival. Finally, after delays caused by a passing thunderstorm, the giant dirigible loomed overhead in preparation for landing. Hovering at two hundred feet, the *Hindenburg* dropped mooring lines to the ground crew, and the landing appeared to be proceeding smoothly.

Suddenly, at 7:25 P.M., a small flame shot out of the dirigible's tail fin. In seconds, flames consumed the Nazi swastika emblazoned on it and then engulfed the entire rear of the huge, cigar-shaped dirigible. Horrified onlookers screamed and ran for safety as the blazing airship plunged groundward tail first, tilting at a forty-five-degree angle. Flames spread quickly forward, devouring letter by letter the name *Hindenburg* as the dirigible's outer fabric skin was consumed. With the supporting hydrogen burned away, the huge inner skeleton of metal girders fell to the ground with a terrible crash. In just thirty-two seconds the *Hindenburg* had been reduced to a boiling mass of smoke, flames, and twisted wreckage.

Inside the *Hindenburg*'s passenger compartment, slung under the dirigible's body, the first sign of impending disaster was heard as nothing more than a loud pop. Within seconds, though, horrified passengers and crewmen were surrounded by flames. As the *Hindenburg* sank downward tail first, some were thrown from the gondola. Others jumped for their lives. They hurtled downward, many with hair or clothing on fire, to the sandy ground far below.

Life-and-death decisions had to be made in seconds. One man and wife jumped to safety, while another man went to look for his wife before doing so. He died in the flames. One woman refused to jump, pulled a coat over her head, and later escaped with just minor burns. A mother of three told her terrified children, "Be brave, children," and dropped them out the window before jumping herself. She and one son lived.

While some were killed by fire or the fall, others had near miraculous escapes. A fourteen-year-old cabin boy jumped off the *Hindenburg* only to find himself surrounded by burning wreckage settling to the ground. Nearly overcome by the terrible heat, the boy was soaked by a sudden torrent of water released by a ruptured water tank above him. Seconds later he found a clear path through the flames and walked out virtually unscathed.

The actual cause of the disaster has never been determined. A spark from the engines or static electricity from the atmosphere could have ignited leaking hydrogen gas. There is even a possibility of espionage. Politics had become highly charged in 1937 as World War II approached, and rumors of threats against the *Hindenburg* had surfaced even before the airship left Nazi Germany.

Or maybe they should have paid a little more attention to the differences in the physical properties of helium and hydrogen.

1938: The Meteor that Almost Squashed Pittsburgh. On June 24 a five-hundred-ton meteor entered the earth's atmosphere and began burning up as it hurtled groundward at a shallow angle. Suddenly many people in Pittsburgh, Pennsylvania, were surprised by a bright light passing overhead, followed by a powerful explosion. By some quirk of fate, the big meteorite hit just outside Pittsburgh, narrowly missing the city of a half million people. Scientists later calculated that if the meteorite had come straight down—instead of at an angle—Pittsburgh would have been destroyed, and science fiction would have become a reality.

1938: Great New England Hurricane. While radio stations were preoccupied with broadcasting the latest ranting speech by Nazi Germany's Adolf Hitler on the afternoon of September 21, a hurricane that had unexpectedly veered off its seaward track struck the shores of Long Island in full force.

The deadly storm, packing winds of up to 186 miles per hour, ripped through the towns and villages of Long Island without warning. Forty-foot tidal waves slammed the shore, while the powerful winds left only six houses standing in Westhampton.

Tearing through Connecticut, Massachusetts, and Rhode Island next, the hurricane destroyed thousands more buildings. Stately mansions at Newport were wrecked, while at one Rhode Island seaside hotel, big waves suddenly poured into the first floor, drowning the unsuspecting patrons sitting in the lounge. The *Bostonian* express train plowed through high water flooding the tracks, and at one point even had to nudge a house that had fallen onto the tracks out of its way.

Before it was over, the wayward hurricane had destroyed nearly fourteen thousand buildings, done an estimated five hundred million dollars in damages, and killed some five hundred people.

When it rains, it pours.

1939: DDT Is Developed. The Swiss chemist who developed DDT in 1939 received a Nobel Prize for his discovery, and his new, highly effective insecticide eventually was widely used against malaria-carrying mosquitoes and other insect pests. Years later, however, scientists discovered DDT had caused an ecological disaster that far outweighed the good it was capable of doing. They found that DDT broke down very slowly in the environment, that it was killing off wildlife, and was adversely affecting humans as well. Use of DDT in the United States was finally restricted in 1972.

A little too much good for our own good.

1939: Chilean Earthquake. Hundreds of people watching an American movie in Chillán, Chile, were suddenly crushed to death when a powerful earthquake brought the theater crashing down upon them. In just three minutes, at a little before midnight on January 24, twenty of Chile's coastal towns and cities were reduced to utter ruin. In addition to Chillán, the quake almost obliterated the cities of Concepción and Talca. Estimates of the dead reached a staggering fifty thousand, with sixty thousand more injured.

Fires gutted most of the few buildings that remained standing. Pilots who flew over Chillán said it looked like a "vast ant heap." Chillán's many historic landmarks, including the home of Chile's founding father, Bernardo O'Higgins, were all demolished. Even the hospital lay in ruins; doctors worked outdoors, with thousands of dead and dying surrounding them.

As if the disastrous quake itself were not enough, survivors had to endure with little or no shelter the torrential rains that hit on January 28. Then new quakes shook the ruined cities again on the thirtieth, but there was virtually nothing left to destroy.

And once again, geology determines our fate.

1939: Submarine *Thetis* Sinks. Forty-one civilian observers and sixty-two crew members crowded aboard the newly built British submarine HMS *Thetis* for its first diving test in Liverpool Bay on June 1. Then, to everyone's surprise, the sub refused to submerge.

Trying to locate the source of the problem, an officer opened the check valves on a torpedo tube that should have been filled with water. He had no way of knowing that dried paint had plugged the check valve tube, or that the outer torpedo tube door was wide open. Believing the torpedo tube to be dry, he opened the inner door and let in a flood of water that quickly submerged the submarine's bow. Meanwhile, the sub's stern floated above water, which was the way rescue ships found her when they arrived the next morning.

The captain and three others got out of *Thetis* by means of an escape hatch, but the sub sank suddenly while rescuers were trying to put a cable around the floating stern. Ninety-nine persons aboard were lost.

1939: Flood and Famine in China. Heavy rains beginning in late August and lasting until November 1939 resulted in widespread flooding throughout much of northern China. Shantung and Hopei provinces were hit hardest.

Tientsin (now Tianjin), a city of 1.3 million in Hopei Province, was completely flooded beginning in late August. Residents there fled the rising waters in small boats or by swimming to safety with a few possessions on their backs. Most escaped to higher ground, but much of Hopei Province remained under ten feet of water for several months.

While a total of some twenty-five million were made homeless, the worst aspect of the flood was destruction of food supplies. A deadly famine spread over the region during the next few months, eventually killing some two hundred thousand people.

1939: Soviet Steamer Wrecks in Japan. It was the end of the fishing season, and some eleven hundred Soviet fishermen and their families were heading home aboard the Soviet steamship *Indigirka* on December 12 when a blizzard overtook their ship along the coast of Japan. Driven off course by high winds and heavy seas, the steamer ran aground near a small Japanese islet off Wakkanai.

The ship sent out a single SOS as waves crashed over it, but the heavy snow made it impossible for the ship to identify its position. Meanwhile, with its hull ripped open and its engines smashed, the disabled steamer capsized and drifted to shore with hundreds of passengers frantically clinging to her sides. Ten crew members boarded a lifeboat in an attempt to bring back help, but the violent waves and driving snow made rescue efforts nearly impossible. Not until the following day were the survivors rescued from the wreck.

The bodies of the drowned and frozen passengers from the *Indigirka* washed up along the shoreline for four miles, and in all, some 750 of them died in the wreck.

1939: Turkish Earthquake. A devastating series of earthquake shocks during three hours on December 27 obliterated towns and cities over a wide area in eastern and northern Turkey. Seven shocks, following one after another between 2:00 and 5:00 A.M., wrecked virtually every town in the districts of Erzincan and Kemah.

Erzincan, a city of twenty-five thousand, was completely wiped out: The only building left standing was the prison. Thousands of terrified survivors fled for the open fields to escape falling buildings and camped out in makeshift tents, suffering through the brutal cold of a severe winter blizzard. Convicts, freed from the city's prison, valiantly risked their lives in the bitter cold to free those trapped in the debris and to find shelter for survivors.

Throughout Turkey, some fifty thousand died, and tens of thousands more were injured. Powerful quakes were also felt that night in Los Angeles and Central America, and the shocks even broke a seismograph in London.

Another landscape rearrangement courtesy of Mother Nature.

1940: Katyn Forest Massacre. In an effort to halt resistance to the Soviet invasion and occupation of Poland in 1939, Soviet dictator Joseph Stalin imprisoned some 14,500 Polish military officers and prominent citizens in three internment camps located deep within Soviet territory. In April 1940, more than four thousand of these men were taken to the Katyn Forest near Smolensk. With their hands bound, they were murdered on the spot in cold blood, each being killed by a single shot fired into the nape of the neck.

When Hitler's troops overran the area in April 1941, they discovered the officers' mass grave and denounced the deed and Stalin to the world. Stalin, however, vehemently denied the accusation and blamed the Nazis. The bullets used were eventually proven to be of Russian manufacture, but Stalin continued to blame Hitler.

Finally, in 1990, the Soviet Union acknowledged its responsibility and publicly apologized for the cruel massacre. While the whereabouts of the remains of the other ten thousand or so imprisoned Poles was not specifically mentioned, the official Soviet statement indicated that all 14,500 had been killed by Stalin's orders.

This ranks Stalin right up there with the rest of them: Mithridates, Caligula, Genghis Khan, and Ivan the Terrible.

1940: Rhythm Night Club Fire. An old Natchez, Mississippi, church in a predominantly Afro-American neighborhood had been converted into the popular Rhythm Night Club dance hall before it went up in flames on April 23. As three hundred patrons danced to the music of Walter Barnes's Chicago Orchestra, fire broke out at the front of the club and spread rapidly, feeding on the dried Spanish moss that decorated the walls. Terrified patrons stampeded toward the single exit, trampling others to death before fire finally blocked the door. A few escaped by breaking through windows that had been boarded up to keep gate-crashers out. But the majority of the trapped victims huddled by the bandstand, where the coroner found their burned and smothered bodies "piled up like cordwood." The blaze killed 198 people, including 10 of the 12 orchestra members.

Another instance of one door and blocked exits. There's a lesson to be learned here.

1940: Battle of Dunkirk. Nazi tanks and troops sweeping through Belgium in May isolated British and French forces defending northern France. When the German army sliced through northern France from the south and linked up with forces from Belgium, the Allied armies were suddenly trapped with their backs to the English Channel. In danger of being forced to surrender or of being cut to pieces by the surrounding Germans, the mostly British force had to attempt to evacuate across the English Channel from the small port of Dunkirk, France.

The British government amassed a ragtag armada of ships and private boats, and on May 29 the desperate evacuation of 340,000 troops began. The German air force launched savage attacks on Dunkirk's port facilities as British and French destroyers boarded troops from quays. Within a few hours the port facilities were demolished, making it inaccessible to the large ships. Then the armada of 222 navy ships and 665 private vessels—yachts, tugs, fishing boats, and ferries—appeared off the sandy beaches outside Dunkirk. Troops either swam out to these boats or were ferried out in small lifeboats, while British antiaircraft guns fired at attacking squadrons of planes.

More than nine hundred German planes bombarded the evacuation force in one of the greatest air attacks ever to take place. Though vastly outnumbered, British Spitfire fighter planes launched savage counterattacks. The furious battle raged until June 4, but nearly all the troops were safely evacuated to Britain. The British had to leave behind virtually all their tanks, artillery, and other munitions, however, and for some months after Dunkirk, were hard-pressed to even reequip the soldiers they had saved, much less repulse a threatened German invasion.

Nice job all 'round.

1940: The London Blitz. The German Luftwaffe, preparing for a planned major invasion of Britain, began bombing raids against British ports and other military targets soon after the fall of France in June 1940. In August they began the London blitz, regular bombing raids against the city that continued long after the Nazis had been forced to abandon any attempt at invading Britain.

The first daily bombing raids against London were targeted against the East End, where the docks, armament works, and tank assembly plants were located. Unfortunately for the cockney workers and their families living there, flimsy East End tenements were packed in among the factories, and bombs raining down on the factories also destroyed hundreds of homes at a time. During big raids, it was common for bombs, fires, and falling buildings to claim one thousand lives a night. Six times that many were injured.

East Enders frantically sought refuge from the deadly attacks, but the government failed to provide them with adequate underground shelters. Hundreds crowded into an abandoned railway tunnel, but the lack of sanitation facilities soon led to the spread of disease among the refugees.

Distraught and angry that the upper classes in London's untouched West End cared little for their sufferings, the battered East Enders were on the verge of open rebellion when on September 10 a stray German bomber accidentally hit the West End, damaging Buckingham Palace and narrowly missing the royal family. Morale in the East End suddenly shot up, boosted by the knowledge that the king and queen now shared their plight. Even the queen admitted, "I'm glad we've been bombed. It makes me feel I can look the East End in the face."

In mid-September the Luftwaffe began to bomb all of London indiscriminately. No longer was the battered East End the sole target, and people throughout London were forced to leave their homes each night and seek refuge underground. They crammed by the hundreds into department store basements, bedded down in underground tube platforms, and huddled in churches. There they spent the nights, rocked by bombs exploding overhead, and ventured out at dawn to survey the damage. The grinding regularity of the raids exhausted the Londoners, but that only seemed to make them more determined to resist the Nazis.

While shelters generally provided a safe, but crowded, haven from German bombs, not all of them were capable of withstanding a direct hit. On September 14 hundreds of people had crowded into the crypt of the Church of the Holy Redeemer in Chelsea. But during the raid that night, a Nazi bomb blew up the crypt in a horrific tragedy. One badly injured victim reported that the scene resembled a massacre: People had been literally blown to bits, and arms, legs, and seared flesh were strewn about, grimly juxtaposed with the schoolbooks, toys, and other everyday items.

By November 5, more than fourteen thousand civilians had been killed during the raids on various parts of Britain, and twenty thousand had been seriously wounded. More than 80 percent of these casualties occurred in London, which up until this point had borne the brunt of the Luftwaffe's devastating power. From November 14 through December, however, the Luftwaffe shifted their bombing raids to provincial cities, and heavy casualties were reported in Coventry, Southampton, Bristol, Birmingham, Sheffield, Liverpool, and Manchester.

The German bombers returned to London on December 29, dropping thousands of incendiary bombs to start a conflagration the likes of which had not been seen since the Great Fire of 1666. Much of the old city was destroyed, and though the dome of Saint Paul's Cathedral caught fire, volunteers managed to extinguish the flames in time to save the church.

The raids continued in 1941, including a massive incendiary raid on May 10, and went on sporadically throughout the rest of the war. Just after the Normandy invasion put Allied troops on the beaches of German-occupied France in 1944, the Nazis began a new offensive against London, this time using the V-1 flying bombs to attack the city during peak rush hours. By September the more advanced German V-2 rockets were also fired at targets in Britain, but by this time the tide of the war had already turned against the Nazis. And not a moment too soon for Londoners.

We've advanced from bows and arrows to rocket bombs in our determination to destroy one another. Civilization can be proud of itself.

1941: Midwest Blizzard. On March 15, mild, almost springlike weather in North Dakota and neighboring states suddenly disappeared as strong winds moved in and the temperatures plunged, at one point dropping fourteen degrees in just fifteen minutes. By 9:00 P.M. Saturday, thousands of motorists throughout the region found themselves stranded by eighty-five-mile-per-hour winds that forced cars off the road and churned a light snow into whirling clouds.

With temperatures now barely above zero, two thousand people in Moorhead, Minnesota, were stranded at a high school basketball game and had to spend the night at the school. Throughout North Dakota, whole families of farmers who had gone to town on Saturday night were stranded at theaters and stores.

They were the lucky ones. Motorists stranded out on the highways had to choose between staying in their cars or trying to make their way on foot through the furious winds and driving snow in search of other shelter. Some of those who stayed in their cars froze to death or died of carbon monoxide poisoning. Among those who sought out other shelter, some spent the night in sheds and nearly died from frostbite. But others died before they even managed to get out of the wind, freezing to death after collapsing from exhaustion, or suffocating in the clouds of dirt and snow whipped up by the wind. Meanwhile, farmhouses were besieged by frostbitten refugees seeking shelter.

Visibility throughout much of North Dakota was no more than ten feet. Four fraternity brothers at the University of North Dakota linked arms and searched the roads near their fraternity house, rescuing twelve stranded people. Elsewhere, a seventy-year-old man was found frozen to death fifty feet from his house, his arms wrapped around a telephone pole to steady himself against the wind. Another elderly man became lost between his house and barn. He tried to protect himself from the wind by burying himself in a stack of straw, but froze to death nonetheless.

A Northern Pacific locomotive hit two teenage girls who had wandered onto the tracks in the blinding snow outside of Pembina, North Dakota. Visibility was so poor that the conductor did not realize what had happened until later when he found the body of one of the girls still caught on the front of the train.

In northern Michigan, also hit by the storm, more than thirty people were ice-fishing on Lake Superior when the storm hit. Suddenly the temperature dropped twenty-five degrees, and heavy winds churned up twenty-five-foot-high waves on the open water. Thirty of the fishermen were stranded for hours when a large section of the ice they were fishing through broke away from shore and drifted out into the storm-tossed waters. Poor visibility and enormous waves made rescue by plane or boat impossible. Luckily, though, a shift in the wind drove the ice back to shore. The fishermen spent the night on shore in makeshift wind shelters they built from ice and driftwood. All of them survived the night.

The storm tore furiously eastward across Michigan until the winds abated on March 16. By that time 151 people had been killed by the terrible wind and cold.

1941: Yugoslavian Fort Explosion. A massive explosion wrecked Fort Smederovo, located near Belgrade, on June 9 when an ammunition dump in the fort blew up. Some fifteen hundred people were killed by the blast.

1941: Attack on Pearl Harbor. Sunday, December 7, promised to be clear and calm as the morning sun rose over the Hawaiian islands—another picture-perfect day in the Pacific paradise. At Pearl Harbor, the big U.S. naval base on Hawaii, the early morning sun warmed the assembled might of the U.S. Pacific fleet—ninety-four warships, nearly the entire fleet, lay anchored close together in Pearl Harbor, while on the nearby airfields, almost four hundred warplanes were parked, wingtip to wingtip, to guard against sabotage. Virtually no one suspected that disaster was about to strike, but then, at the time, the United States was not even at war.

At 7:55 A.M., a sneak attack by 181 carrier-based Japanese bombers, fighters, and torpedo planes suddenly changed all that.

Sweeping down over Pearl Harbor, the Japanese planes wreaked havoc upon the anchored warships and their unsuspecting crews. As bombs rained down and explosions rocked the big battleships, sailors desperately fired antiaircraft guns at the attacking planes, even as their ships sank beneath them.

The battleship *Oklahoma* took three torpedoes in her port side and capsized within twenty minutes, while a Japanese bomb scored a direct hit on the magazine of the *Arizona,* sinking her quickly and dooming more than one thousand crewmen trapped belowdecks. Those lucky enough to escape the flaming *Arizona* found themselves surrounded by slicks of blazing fuel oil, while Japanese planes strafed them from above.

Nearby, the *West Virginia* exploded in a burst of flame and sank rapidly, trapping hundreds of men belowdecks. It took two weeks to put the fires out, but three hundred trapped sailors were rescued from the ship's hull eighteen days later.

By 10:00 A.M., 18 ships had been sunk, beached, or badly damaged, and 188 warplanes at the airfields had been destroyed on the ground. The death toll in the attack was high: 2,403 sailors and soldiers were killed—more than half of those from the ill-fated *Arizona*—and 107 civilians were killed or wounded. The United States declared war on Japan the next day. Our allies were overjoyed.

1941: Three Thousand Die in Peruvian Mud Slide. Torrential rains in a mountainous area of Peru unleashed an avalanche of mud and rocks a half mile wide and 150 feet deep on December 13. Cascading down the mountainside, the wall of mud slashed through the town of Huaraz and continued on to the Santa River, which was partly diverted by the mass of debris.

The mud slide utterly destroyed the entire residential area of Huaraz, a town of nine thousand located 185 miles northwest of Lima. Some three thousand people were crushed, buried, or drowned, and corpses lay scattered throughout the mud and debris for six miles around the town. The mud mass also caused the Santa River to overflow its banks, washing out bridges and train tracks. Violent earth tremors before dawn the next day further terrified survivors and delayed rescue efforts.

1942: Bataan Death March. Following their victory over the last remnants of the U.S. forces on the Philippine island of Bataan, the Japanese forced an estimated seventy thousand American and Filipino prisoners of war to march sixty-five miles from Balanga to Camp O'Donnell, which had become a Japanese prisoner-of-war camp. The incredible cruelty of many of the Japanese guards made the Bataan Death March one of the grimmest episodes of the war in the Pacific.

When the march began on April 9, the prisoners—who had been holding out against the Japanese for months—were already weak with starvation, malnourishment, malaria, dysentery, and other diseases. Yet their Japanese captors drove them on, day after day. Those who could not keep up the pace were often beaten with clubs or buried alive. Guards beheaded prisoners for even minor infractions.

The prisoners were given virtually no food or water, and some Japanese guards beat back civilians who offered to feed the starving captives. One survivor of the march wrote: "They'd halt us intentionally in front of these wells so we could see the water and they wouldn't let us have any. Anyone who would make a break for water would be shot or bayoneted. . . . There were bodies lying all over the road in various degrees of decomposition . . . black, featureless corpses."

The tale of atrocities grew more horrible each day. On April 12 the Japanese slaughtered four hundred Filipino officers and noncoms by hacking them to death with swords. In another incident, one survivor told of seeing Japanese guards throw a prisoner in front of ten oncoming tanks. "When the last tank left, there was no way to tell there'd ever been a man there. But his uniform was embedded in the cobblestone." Japanese guards even looted the prisoners' few remaining personal possessions; a guard chopped off one man's finger when he refused to give up his wedding ring.

By the time the last survivors of the march reached Camp O'Donnell, an estimated five thousand to ten thousand Filipinos and six hundred Americans were dead; sixteen thousand others died of malnutrition and disease within a few weeks after arriving at the camp.

The Japanese did not play by the rules, nor did they understand the meaning of humane treatment of prisoners.

1942–1943: Bloody Battle of Stalingrad. As four hundred thousand German troops surrounded the Soviet city of Stalingrad on August 23, 1942, six hundred German bombers began a furious bombing attack to prepare the way for the assault on the city itself. Forty thousand people died and another 150,000 were wounded as the German bombs leveled the city of nearly half a million people, and a mass evacuation began as Stalingrad went up in flames.

On September 2 the German troops moved into the city, now occupied mainly by Russian troops. Instead of withdrawing as they had in the past, the Russians fought from house to house, even sewer to sewer. The Russian generals told their troops: "Every German soldier must be made to feel that he is living under the muzzle of a Russian gun."

They succeeded in that. Week after week the furious battle continued in the rubble of Stalingrad. As a BBC correspondent reported October 11, "This is not a battle for a locality or a river, but for street crossings and houses. . . . France was defeated in thirty-eight days. In Stalingrad it took the Germans thirty-eight days to advance from one side of the street to the other." Some Russian troops barricaded in an apartment house struggled heroically for fifty-eight days against constant attacks by artillery and tanks. By November 12 the beleaguered Russians had nearly lost the city. Then finally a massive Soviet counterattack began on November 19. It stunned the Germans, and within days the Soviets had encircled Stalingrad.

As the bitter Soviet winter came on, the German troops found themselves cut off and surrounded, confronting relentless enemies on all sides—the Russians, starvation, and temperatures of forty below zero. On January 31, 1943, the remnants of German units at Stalingrad—some ninety thousand men—surrendered. The bloody battle had been costly indeed. An estimated three hundred thousand German troops lost their lives at Stalingrad, and hundreds of thousands of Russians died there as well. But this battle marked an important turning point in World War II, as the Soviets at last gained the offensive against the Germans.

German military strategists must have slept through their lectures on Napoleon.

1942: Colliery Blast Kills 1,549. The colliery at Honkeiko, Manchuria, exploded on April 26, killing a vast number of miners. Though only sketchy reports were available on the blast, the disaster is believed to be the worst explosion in history at a mining operation and its assorted buildings.

1942: Dieppe Raid. An attack force of some six thousand Allied troops—80 percent of them Canadian—crossed the English Channel during the night of August 19 in what was the first major Allied attack on Nazi-occupied France. The raid's main objective was to test German defenses against amphibious landing techniques.

A flotilla of torpedo boats, gunboats, destroyers, and tank-landing craft took part in the landings, which were made at dawn at six points along the French coast near Dieppe. A heavy naval bombardment and some ten thousand Royal Air Force bombers supported the landing force. One witness reported that "British bombers filled the sky like bees around a hive."

In nine hours of bloody fighting, however, the German defenders completely overwhelmed the landing force, and four thousand of the six thousand Allied troops were killed before the Allied flotilla retreated back across the channel.

Heroic efforts, by the dawn's early light.

1942: *Queen Mary* Rams Cruiser. Because of a desperate need for shipping during World War II, authorities converted the famed British luxury liner *Queen Mary* into a troop transport. During one such voyage in October, the British light cruiser *Curaçao* provided escort protection against German U-boats. But as the two ships maneuvered off the Irish coast on October 2, a tragic miscalculation put the two ships on a collision course. Crewmen aboard the cruiser were suddenly horrified to see the *Queen Mary*'s huge bow coming right at them at full speed. With a terrible crash, the liner sliced completely through the *Curaçao,* carrying the two halves forward before they fell away. Some of the cruiser's four hundred crewmen were tossed into the icy Atlantic waters and were probably drawn into the liner's propellers. Meanwhile, the mangled halves of the cruiser swamped and sank in a matter of minutes, taking hundreds more sailors down with them and bringing the death toll to 338 officers and men.

1942: Tens of Thousands Die in Bengal Hurricane. Packing winds of up to 150 miles per hour, a hurricane slammed into the Bengal Province in India on October 16, killing forty thousand people.

1942: Cocoanut Grove Fire. On Saturday evening, November 28, over one thousand people packed the Cocoanut Grove, a popular Boston nightclub with three cocktail lounges and a cabaret area. The boisterous, standing-room-only crowd, twice the building's rated capacity, consisted of the usual Saturday night patrons plus many football fans who had attended the Holy Cross–Boston College game earlier that day.

Surrounding the revelers were decorations designed to enhance the Cocoanut Grove's tropical atmosphere. Walls were lined with dark leather, the ceilings with cloth, and artificial palm trees were everywhere. All of these trappings were dangerously flammable.

By about 10:00 P.M., the Saturday night revelry was in full swing. Downstairs in the basement Melody Lounge, few noticed a busboy as he set about replacing a light bulb removed by a prankster. To see what he was doing, the busboy lit a match, but it scorched his fingers. The dropped match landed on one of the artificial palm trees, which immediately burst into flames. And so began the terrible fire.

Nearby a woman screamed "Fire!" and panicked revelers suddenly rushed en masse toward the narrow stairs leading up to the first-floor exit. The fire spread quickly, and soon the leather walls and cloth ceiling burned furiously around the now hysterical crowd. Racing up the stairwell, the flames quickly spread to the ground floor. Hundreds of desperate people clogged the narrow staircase to the club's main exit, unaware that a mass of frantic patrons ahead of them had jammed the revolving door to the street.

Seeking another way out, hundreds of others raced past boarded-up windows to the side emergency exit, only to find it bolted shut. As those in the back of the crowd surged forward to escape the flames, they crushed to death a hundred people at the door. Another hundred needlessly burned to death downstairs in the Melody Lounge after the crowd frantically massed forward against a door that opened inward. Other unfortunates tripped and fell and were trampled to death by the stampeding mob.

A few levelheaded and lucky patrons smashed basement windows and crawled through the shattered glass to safety. The club manager and ten others took refuge in the basement icebox and survived. And then there was the heroic chorus boy, a teenager, who led thirty-five of his coworkers up to the roof, where they safely crossed over to an adjacent building.

When the blaze was finally put out, 491 people lay dead in the smoldering building, many of them heaped in piles several feet deep at the clogged exit doors. Almost two hundred others sustained serious injuries. Less severe burns and smoke inhalation also took their toll, and very few of the survivors escaped the tragic blaze unharmed.

Panic kills again. And stricter fire laws ensued.

1943: Bizarre Air Raid Shelter Accident in London. As German bombers approached London on March 3, people from the East End hurried through the darkened streets toward an air raid shelter at the Bethnal Green underground train station. Soon long lines of people were filing quickly down the dimly lit flight of nineteen stairs into the station.

In the crowd was a middle-aged woman carrying a baby and heavy packages. She had made it nearly the whole way down the stairs when she suddenly tripped and sprawled across a landing. Pushed by others behind them, people behind her could not stop, and fell over her, one by one. Within moments three hundred people had fallen on top of one another, struggling and screaming for air. The sheer weight of the human beings piled on top of one another on the landing and stairs quickly suffocated 173 people, including 60 children. Ironically, the woman whose fall had triggered the calamity survived, though the baby she carried was among those smothered.

Among the casualties of war.

1943: Warsaw Ghetto Uprising. By the summer of 1942, Nazi Germany had deported some 265,000 Jews from the Warsaw ghetto to the Treblinka extermination camp. Several Jews had escaped Treblinka, however, and had returned to the ghetto with word of what was really happening to those being herded onto trains to the Nazis' so-called rural labor camps.

With that, leaders of the fifty thousand to sixty thousand Jews remaining in Warsaw prepared to resist. After four days of street fighting in January 1943, the Nazis temporarily halted the deportations. Then, on April 19, the first day of the Jewish celebration of Passover and the day before Hitler's birthday, two thousand Nazi troops descended on the ghetto, supported by tanks and heavy artillery.

The Jews had planned for such an event, and tens of thousands of them hid in basements, sewers, and makeshift bunkers while a Jewish resistance force estimated at between 750 and 1,200 fighters took to the streets in open rebellion. The rebels, armed only with revolvers, hand grenades, and a very few rifles and machine guns, launched constant surprise attacks on the Nazis. A witness described a rabbi celebrating the traditional Passover seder, "his reading punctuated by explosions and the rattling of machine guns."

For four weeks the rebels held out against terrible odds in the rubble of the ghetto. The streets were strewn with the bodies of Jews, left lying where they had been gunned down. German troops set fire to building after building, forcing Jews to leap to their deaths from high windows. One survivor wrote, "When we threw those hand grenades and saw German blood pouring over the streets of Warsaw, after we saw so much Jewish blood running in the streets . . . there was rejoicing."

The heavily armed Nazis eventually broke the revolt, but not before hundreds of Nazi soldiers had been killed. On May 16 the Nazis demolished the great Warsaw synagogue, declaring "The Warsaw ghetto is no more." Some seven thousand Jews died in the fighting, while all of the ghetto's remaining population of fifty thousand or so were shipped away to the death camps.

Another bloody chapter in the history of World War II.

1944: Asphyxiation on Italian Train. A forty-seven-car freight train, pulled by two steam engines, slowly pulled out of Balvano, Italy, at about 5:00 A.M. on March 2. As the train labored to gain speed up a steep grade, hundreds of illegal passengers clambered aboard the freight cars, looking for an easy ride over the mountains. The weight of these riders only increased the burden of the two engines, already handicapped by the low-grade coal they were forced to burn because of the war.

The train finally slowed to a halt just after entering a long tunnel on the steep grade up Mount Armi. At this point, the engineers aboard the two locomotives argued about what to do.

One wanted to stoke the engines with the poor-grade coal and continue through the tunnel, while the other engineer thought it best to let the train roll backward out of the tunnel.

The argument ended in a matter of seconds, however, as the low-grade coal continued to belch forth thick black smoke laden with deadly carbon monoxide, killing the engineers and the firemen. As the smoke billowed back through the tunnel, the hundreds of illicit riders were overcome by the choking fumes, and within minutes 426 people had died.

He who hesitates is lost.

1944: The Bombay Explosion. When a munitions ship at Bombay, India, caught fire on April 14, military personnel desperately tried to get the blaze under control. Despite their efforts, the fire touched off the cargo of munitions, and two massive explosions rocked the entire city.

The blast smashed windows out of buildings—raining broken glass down on the crowded streets—and spread fire to the docks, warehouses, and a nearby residential area. The blaze raged for thirty-six hours, driving thousands from their homes and killing 1,376 people.

1944: "The Greatest Show on Earth" Ends in Tragedy. Despite the ninety-degree temperatures roasting Hartford, Connecticut, nearly seven thousand people—mostly women and children—sat under the big top on July 6 enjoying a matinee of the Ringling Brothers and Barnum & Bailey Circus. After a spellbinding act featuring wild animals, the spotlight in the 550-foot-long circus tent turned to the high-wire act of the Flying Wallendas.

With the audience's attention diverted, circus workers began herding the lions, tigers, bears, leopards, and jaguars into cages and metal chutes, which for the moment blocked many of the tent's exits. Suddenly the leader of the circus band spotted a small fire on the tent's sidewall. Because the canvas had been treated with a mixture of paraffin and gasoline, the fire grew rapidly. Thinking quickly, the band leader had his musicians play "The Stars and Stripes Forever," which was used as a signal for serious trouble in the circus world.

Within seconds, a column of flame surged furiously some forty feet up the side of the big top. By now the audience had seen the fire as well, and panic began to spread as fast as the smoke and flames. The band kept playing as fire roared to the top of the tent and began consuming, one by one, the six center poles. Crowds poured off the bleachers and pressed toward the exits, where they had to get by animal cages and climb over the metal chutes. Those who fell were trampled by the stampede coming from behind.

Part of the crowd pushed toward the back of the tent—farthest from the flames—but winds quickly spread the fire, and in less than a minute the entire roof of the tent was consumed. Burning sheets of canvas collapsed and fell over hundreds of people at a time. Meanwhile, parents on the highest bleachers began throwing their children down onto the escaping hordes of people at ground level. Some of these unfortunate children were picked up and saved, while others were trampled to death.

Inside the tent, the scene was one of incredible chaos, with the mingling sounds of raging fire, bleachers crashing to the ground in flames, roars of wild beasts, and people screaming out of fear and pain. "It was like you'd opened hell's doors," one survivor said.

Circus midgets heroically risked their lives, crawling under the tent flaps over and over again to bring out people still trapped inside. And then there was the boy with a clubfoot who used his Boy Scout knife to slash a hole in the tent wall, providing a means of escape for some three hundred people. One woman, torn from her children during the scramble to escape, had to be restrained as she tried to run back into the flaming tent, screaming, "My God, my God, my kid is in there."

Ten minutes after the blaze began, all six center poles had collapsed and the entire tent was in flames. Hundreds of people were still trapped in the inferno, but miraculously, all of the circus performers had escaped by this time, even members of the band who had bravely played on as long as they could. Eventually all but 168 unfortunate victims, two-thirds of them children, got out, though another 174 people were badly burned or otherwise injured. The cause of the tragic fire was never discovered.

1944: Port Chicago Munitions Explosion. During World War II the town of Port Chicago, located on California's San Francisco Bay, became a busy port for loading munitions ships. Two ships tied up at the docks, *Quinault Victory* and *E. A. Bryan,* were being loaded with ammunition at night on July 17 when suddenly both of them exploded with a deafening roar.

Flames shot high up into the air, and the blast was felt miles away in San Francisco, Oakland, and other places in the Bay area. The fifteen hundred residents of Port Chicago were startled from their sleep by the explosion, and every building in the town sustained at least some damage.

The town's wharves were obliterated, and the 321 men who had been loading the ships were all killed instantly.

Munitions are lethal. Bows and arrows don't explode.

1944: Major Hurricane Hits New England. In towns throughout much of New England on the morning of September 14, trucks with loudspeakers blared urgent warnings about the approach of a powerful hurricane. Having begun in the West Indies six days before, the storm was following the same track as the killer hurricane of 1938.

Then the storm, packing winds of up to 140 miles per hour, barreled through New Jersey and on up into New England, uprooting trees, tearing roofs off buildings, and hurling moored ships onto dry land. The tide in some areas rose to seven feet above normal.

One man drowned as he tried to beach his rowboat during the furious storm. Another was electrocuted when he touched a steel fence charged by a fallen power line. But many of the hurricane's 389 victims perished at sea. A navy destroyer, two coast guard vessels, and countless smaller boats foundered in rough seas and heavy rains. The deadly storm caused some fifty million dollars in damages, including widespread crop destruction.

Progress is being made. We are now getting warnings.

1944: Terror in Cleveland. A violent blast stunned Cleveland on the afternoon of October 20 as liquid gas storage tanks belonging to the East Ohio Gas Company caught fire and exploded. Flames surged high into the air as millions of cubic feet of liquified natural gas ignited. Lesser explosions rocked the city when gas mains burst into flames, and manhole covers were blown high into the air.

Fire spread with terrifying speed over a fifty-block section of Cleveland, filling the air with thick, black smoke. Threatened by the rapidly advancing inferno, horrified drivers in one area abandoned their cars and jumped into Lake Erie to escape the flames. Meanwhile, sound trucks with loudspeakers drove through the burning streets of the East Side neighborhood, announcing, "Get out! Run eastward! The neighborhood is on fire!"

Although almost everyone managed to get out, by the time the fire burned down that evening, 135 people had died, while some 3,600 were left homeless.

The home front isn't so safe either.

1944: Trains Collide in Tunnel. About five hundred people were killed when two trains collided and caught fire while in a tunnel near Aguadilla, Spain, on November 7.

1945: Firebombing of Dresden. Nazi Germany was already losing the war on February 13 when the historic city of Dresden held a carnival to bolster the sagging spirits of its 1.2 million residents. At 10:15 that night 244 British bombers suddenly swarmed overhead, beginning a three-hour series of firebombing raids that rained 650,000 incendiary bombs on the city, leaving it in flames.

The bombing created huge fire storms as hot air rose rapidly, sucking in cold air at tremendous speeds. Tornadoes of fire at temperatures of over eighteen hundred degrees Fahrenheit melted brick buildings and sucked people into the swirling flames. The next day, February 14, Valentine's Day, 450 American bombers continued the raids and the destruction.

A grim retribution for past Nazi brutality and a calculated effort to spread terror in Nazi Germany, the two days of attacks destroyed an area three times that leveled in London by German bombing. Over ninety thousand homes were burned to the ground, and the estimated death toll was at least 135,000.

Revenge is bittersweet.

1945: Bloody Fight for Iwo Jima. In what some described as the most desperate fighting in the Pacific theater, U.S. Marines took control of the tiny volcanic island of Iwo Jima in February, following a series of savage battles against fanatically determined Japanese defenders. The island soon became a strategic U.S. airbase, used to launch bombing raids on the Japanese homeland.

About seventy thousand marines began their amphibious landings on February 19 and were met by intense mortar and artillery fire from the twenty thousand Japanese defenders. The Japanese had heavily fortified the island, creating a labryinth of underground tunnels in the one dominating physical feature of the island, the five-hundred-foot-high extinct volcano, Mount Suribachi. Pillboxes, blockhouses, tank traps, and minefields were everywhere on the island.

Desperate fighting continued for days. American forces struggled to move themselves and heavy equipment through the loose, black, cindery sand covering the island. The enemy meanwhile laid down devastating barrages from Suribachi with mortars, artillery, and machine guns.

Finally, after thousands of casualties, American forces captured the island's airfields and eventually fought to the top of Suribachi, nicknamed "Mount Plasma" by the U.S. Marines because of the heavy losses incurred in taking it. Cleanup operations continued into June, and so, too, did the losses. Americans suffered about twenty-seven thousand casualties, while estimates of Japanese casualties were put at twenty thousand.

1945: Airplane Hits the Empire State Building. Fortunately, because it was a Saturday, most offices in the giant New York city skyscraper—the world's tallest building at this time—were closed on the morning of July 28. But a partial staff of fifteen, mainly young women office workers, was at work on the seventy-ninth floor in the War Relief Office of the National Catholic Welfare Conference.

About 9:45 A.M. the pilot of a twin-engined B-25 bomber received permission to switch his landing from New York City's LaGuardia airport to the Newark, New Jersey, airport because of dense fog over Manhattan. The pilot apparently lost his bearings in the poor visibility and dropped down so low over Manhattan that a shocked secretary watched the bomber pass right by her thirty-eight-floor window. The plane was climbing steep and fast, but not steep or fast enough. Hurtling through the mist, it flew directly into the Empire State Building, smashing through the heavy masonry wall between the seventy-eighth and seventy-ninth floors.

The skyscraper trembled at the impact and the thunderous roar of the airplane's exploding fuel. Burning fuel and chunks of the plane flew into the building, setting fires that spread to six floors. One of the plane's engines shot straight through the building and out the other side; the other engine tumbled down an elevator shaft to the sub-basement. Eleven people in the building, mostly workers in the Catholic War Relief Office, were killed by the crash and fire, as were the three military men in the plane.

Where is King Kong when you need him?

1945: United States Drops Atomic Bombs on Hiroshima and Nagasaki. The fanatical Japanese government had refused an ultimatum to surrender, even in the face of certain defeat, as recently as July 26. Now, on August 6, when U.S. President Harry Truman announced the dropping of an atomic bomb on Hiroshima, Japan, he warned the Japanese that if they again refused to surrender, they "may expect a rain of ruin from the air the like of which has never been seen on this earth." The president's words described with ghastly accuracy what had happened just after 8:00 A.M. that day when the American B-29 *Enola Gay* flew over Hiroshima, a city of 390,000, and dropped the nine-thousand-pound atomic bomb dubbed "Little Boy."

The bomb exploded with the force of seventeen thousand tons of dynamite. A thunderous roar, flash of white light, and searing hot wind preceded the massive column of the mushroom-shaped cloud that rose over the city. Within seconds a heat wave scorched everything in its path and laid waste to everything within a two-mile radius.

Thousands died instantly, their skin burned black. The blast smashed trains, tossing them through the air as if they were weightless. Trees burned like matchsticks. Metal and stone melted, and buildings collapsed in showers of debris and broken glass. One survivor described victims burned so badly, "you couldn't tell whether you were looking at them from the front or the back."

Within a three-mile radius of the explosion, two-thirds of all buildings were utterly destroyed, and ninety thousand buildings wrecked. Fires broke out throughout the ruined city. Burned victims ran screaming through the streets, skin hanging in strips from their bodies. Many of those who managed to survive the blast found themselves encircled by fire.

At least seventy-five thousand died from the immediate effects of the blast. But even more deaths resulted from the black rain of radioactive debris that fell over the city a half hour afterward. For five minutes the rain fell out of the cloudless morning sky. Within weeks, the lethal doses of radiation tortured thousands of people with nausea, fever, bleeding, and finally death. Pregnant women had miscarriages or gave birth to deformed or brain-damaged babies. Many who did not die of radiation sickness contracted cancer within the next few years; rates of leukemia were fifty times normal in Hiroshima by 1948. The number of deaths caused by long-term effects of radiation, along with the immediate destruction of the bombing, are virtually incalculable, though estimates range as high as 250,000.

By that night, the fires had sputtered out. As one survivor put it, "there was nothing left to burn. Hiroshima had ceased to exist."

Still the Japanese refused to surrender. Three days later, on August 9, the United States dropped a second bomb, the ten-thousand-pound plutonium bomb "Fat Man," on Nagasaki. At least forty thousand Japanese were killed, and forty thousand others injured. The bomb leveled more than a third of the city's fifty-five thousand buildings.

The incredible destruction of the two attacks finally forced the Japanese to surrender, thus ending the long years of fighting in World War II. A month later, as horrified observers toured the ruins, one described how "this chalky desert, looking almost like ivory in the sun, surrounded by a crumble of twisted ironwork and ash heaps, was all that remained of Hiroshima."

And, thus, in victory and sadness the world entered the Atomic Age. We had finally created the ultimate weapon to destroy ourselves.

1945: Thousands Die in Chinese Riverboat Wreck. The wreck of a river steamer near Hong Kong on November 8 killed 1,550, most of them soldiers who had been crowded aboard the craft.

1946: Last Major Polio Epidemic in the United States. After four years of large, and increasing, numbers of cases of polio, the U.S. epidemic peaked in the summer of 1946 when 25,191 new cases were reported in twenty-three states. The crippling disease, which struck mainly children, was virtually wiped out by the introduction of effective vaccines a few years later.

1946: Winecoff Hotel Fire. Like most hotels in Atlanta, Georgia, at this time, the 194-room Winecoff had no sprinkler system or fire escapes, and each floor of the fifteen-story brick building was accessible only by elevators and the central spiraling staircase—there were no other means of exit. Incredibly, despite these deficiencies, the Winecoff had recently passed a routine fire safety inspection and was classified as "fireproof."

Most of the hotel's 280 guests were asleep at about 3:15 A.M. on December 7. At that time an elevator girl alerted the night manager, Comer Rowan, that she had smelled smoke while passing the third floor. Rowen sprinted up the central staircase and was horrified to see flames reflected in a mirror hanging in the mezzanine. Rowan raced back to his desk and called the fire department. Then, working the switchboard frantically, he began ringing the guests' rooms to warn them. He had only managed to call a few rooms when the switchboard went dead.

By this time the fire was out of control, raging through the hallways on almost every floor. Huge flames shot up the elevator shafts and stairwell. Denied these exits, hotel guests had no way to escape the flames, and many climbed out on window ledges. Soon the facade of the building was alive with terrified people, some wildly waving their arms and screaming for help, others attempting to climb down makeshift ropes of knotted bedsheets.

As heat in the building grew more intense and black smoke billowed out of windows, several desperate people, unable to wait for firemen to set up safety nets, flung themselves to the pavement below rather than face death by fire. Firemen scrambled up their ladders to rescue those they could reach, but their fully extended ladders reached only to the tenth floor. Hapless guests on the top five floors had no other choice but to jump and hope they would land in nets held by firemen. Many did not.

Thousands of spectators gathered during the six-hour ordeal. They watched in horror as frenzied victims lost their grip on the window ledges or hurtled downward when makeshift bedsheet ropes gave way. A woman on the eighth floor flung her four-year-old son into the air, screaming for someone to save him. Miraculously, the boy was caught unharmed by a bystander, but the mother plunged to her death.

What spectators and firemen could not see, however, were the dozens of hotel guests who had chosen to barricade themselves in their rooms, hoping against hope that firemen would reach them before fire did. The heat in the inferno reached fifteen hundred degrees Fahrenheit, enough to melt doorknobs and telephones. Almost all victims who remained inside were consumed in the flames or asphyxiated by the smoke.

The Winecoff fire, the worst hotel fire in U.S. history, killed 119 people before it was over. Ninety other guests suffered serious injuries but nonetheless survived the tragic blaze.

Apparently "fireproof" means different things to different people.

1946: Seismic Wave Hits Hawaii. At 2:00 A.M. on April 1, a subsea earthquake in the Aleutians generated a one-hundred-foot-high seismic wave that swept over a wide area of the Pacific. Traveling at an estimated five hundred miles per hour, the wave first struck the California coast with waves about eleven to twelve feet higher than normal. Five hours later, a series of seismic waves about fifty feet high crashed without warning onto the shores of the Hawaiian islands. The Hawaiian seaport of Hilo was hardest hit by the waves, and throughout the islands 179 people were killed, and one thousand buildings were destroyed.

1946: Airliner Crashes on Takeoff at LaGuardia. United Airline pilot Lucky Baldwin tried to abort his takeoff after the wind shifted suddenly at LaGuardia on May 30, but instead the plane careened through a fence, bounced up in the air after hitting a car on Grand Central Parkway, and finally crashed in flames in a field a short distance away. "Lucky" Baldwin and five others escaped, but forty-two passengers died in the crash.

1946: La Salle Hotel Fire. Chicago's twenty-two-story La Salle Hotel, promoted as "the largest, safest, and most modern hotel west of New York," went up in flames just after midnight on June 5.

The fire started in the basement Silver Grill Cocktail Lounge at 12:15 A.M. and spread quickly, feeding on rugs, sofas, and wood paneling. Hotel guests at first tried to put the blaze out with bottles of seltzer, but the flames soon engulfed the first five stories while smoke poured through elevator shafts and hallways on upper stories.

A courageous switchboard operator died at her post while telephoning guests room by room to warn them. More than one thousand guests got out safely by means of fire escapes or jumping into nets, and a Seeing Eye dog led out a blind woman from the eleventh floor. Sixty-one hotel guests died in the blaze, either from suffocation or by leaping to their deaths from upper stories.

1947: Texas City Tragedy. The billowing tower of black smoke on April 16 drew more than two hundred curious onlookers to the docks in Texas City, an industrial and port city on the gulf coast of Texas. The smoke rose from a fire aboard the French freighter *Grandcamp,* docked just seven hundred feet from the Monsanto chemical plant. The *Grandcamp* had just been loaded with explosive ammonium nitrate fertilizer, as had the U.S. freighter *High Flyer,* which was two berths away. Rumors aboard the American freighter held that a cargo of ammunition was also aboard the *Grandcamp*.

The fire had been raging for over half an hour when, shortly after 9:00 A.M., there was a deafening roar. The explosion of the *Grandcamp* sent three-hundred-pound chunks of red-hot steel flying through the air. Bystanders had their clothing, even arms and legs, ripped off by the powerful blast, which shook buildings over one hundred miles away. The force of the explosion even knocked two planes out of the air, heaved a steel barge one hundred yards inland, flattened nearby buildings, and flung people out of doors and windows a mile away.

Seconds later another series of explosions rocked Texas City as the Monsanto chemical plant exploded. Buildings damaged by the *Grandcamp* explosion crumbled from the repeated blasts, burying hundreds of people under the rubble. As the fire spread to oil refineries adjacent to the now-destroyed Monsanto plant, the sky became black with heavy smoke billowing four thousand feet above the town.

Texas City's volunteer fire department, already on the scene to battle the fire aboard the *Grandcamp,* was all but wiped out when the blast destroyed its equipment and killed forty-five volunteers. Fire trucks from surrounding areas responded quickly to the disaster, but the violent blasts had damaged water mains, and fires burned out of control throughout the city. Ambulances braved the ongoing subsidiary explosions at the waterfront area as they tried to reach hundreds of dead and dying victims there. Rescuers had to wear gas masks to protect themselves from the poisonous chlorine and nitrogen dioxide gases escaping from damaged storage tanks.

Emergency hospitals were set up in city hall and the high school gymnasium as Red Cross and Salvation Army volunteers arrived with food, clothing, and medical supplies. Much-needed plasma was flown in from Philadelphia, and extra doctors and nurses arrived from Houston. Throughout the day and into the night doctors and volunteers worked to save hundreds of injured people in the ravaged town.

Fire fighters at last appeared to have the disaster under control when at 1:11 A.M. the *High Flyer* exploded with a blast so strong, it registered on a seismograph in Denver. Once again the blast wiped out everyone in the waterfront area, including dozens of paramedics and volunteers administering aid.

By the next morning, the once thriving industrial city lay in smoldering ruins, 522 people were dead, and over 3,000 were injured.

It was the worst explosive disaster ever in a U.S. port.

1948: Gandhi Assassination. The seventy-eight-year-old Mohandas Gandhi was at this time the most important man in India. Revered by his Hindu followers as a man of peace, he had led the massive nonviolent protests that helped bring about India's independence from British colonial rule, achieved just the year before, in 1947. Now he was campaigning for tolerance between Hindus and Muslims, as religious strife threatened to divide the newly independent nation.

A crowd of five hundred welcomed Gandhi just after 5:00 P.M. on January 30 as he prepared to give his daily prayer message in a New Delhi garden. When Nathuran Vinayak Godse stepped forward from the crowd, Gandhi gave him the traditional Hindu gesture of welcome, but the Hindu fanatic pulled a gun and fired from three feet away, striking Gandhi three times in the chest and abdomen. The great leader collapsed into the arms of his two granddaughters, and died not long afterward, surrounded by candles grieving supporters believed would light his way to eternity. His assassin, apparently opposed to toleration of Muslims, was later hanged.

Once more, intolerance rears its ugly head.

1948: German Chemical Plant Blows Up. Part of the massive I. G. Farben chemical plant at Ludwigshafen, Germany, was demolished on July 28 when a plant producing lacquer exploded with a mighty blast. A total of 184 plant workers were killed, and 6,600 others were injured.

1948: Six Thousand Die in China Troop Ship Disaster. Sudden changes in the front lines were a fact of life in the protracted civil war between China's Nationalist government and Chinese communists. Thus, when communist armies advanced in Manchuria, the Nationalist Chinese government moved to evacuate elements of its Fifty-second Army from Yingkou, Manchuria, to more secure positions. Early in November thousands of these troops and some refugees were loaded aboard a merchant ship bound for an unspecified port farther south in Nationalist territory. But somewhere along the way the ship exploded, possibly after hitting a mine. Some six thousand people, most of them soldiers, were killed in this single tragic incident far from the battle lines.

1948: Second China Ship Disaster Kills Thousands More. Thousands of paying refugees and hundreds of stowaways seeking to escape the advancing communist forces crowded aboard the coastal steamer SS *Kiangya* at Shanghai on December 4. Cruising on the Whangpoo River with about thirty-four hundred people aboard some fifty miles south of Shanghai, the ship apparently hit an old Japanese mine left over from World War II. The explosion ripped through the stern, hurling sleeping passengers into the air. Within moments the ship sank in shallow water, killing most of the passengers in the lower decks immediately.

On the top deck, over a thousand terrified passengers struggled for a place to stand on the swamped deck as the water rose to their waists, and some passengers were shoved into the sea.

Because the *Kiangya*'s radio had been disabled by the explosion, three hours passed before the tragedy was discovered and help arrived. By that time some 2,750 people had drowned.

1949: Earthquake Ravages Ecuador. A powerful earthquake destroyed over a half dozen cities and towns in a fifteen-hundred-square-mile area of Ecuador on August 5. Centered on the slopes of the Andes Mountains about sixty miles south of Quito, the first shock was followed by a second six minutes later.

The quakes sent landslides roaring down the mountain slopes, burying many victims and even entire villages, and causing rivers to overflow their banks. Fissures opened in the ground and swallowed men working in fields. A one-thousand-foot-high hill split in two, and four towns in the area were almost completely obliterated. The city of Ambato was hard hit, and some two hundred children died there when the cathedral collapsed upon them. In all, some six thousand people died in the disaster.

1949: Fire in Chungking, China. An incredible eighteen-hour fire devastated the city of Chungking (now Chongqing), China, on September 2 and 3. The Nationalist Chinese, struggling to hold their country against overwhelming Chinese communist forces, had planned to make Chungking their new capital before the disaster. The blaze started at 4:00 P.M. in the slums of the city and, fanned by strong winds, quickly engulfed the residential area. Before fire fighters could contain the relentless fire, it raced through the business section, the waterfront, and other parts of the city. The flames consumed or seriously damaged over ten thousand buildings, trapping and burning to death hundreds of people. Many others trying to escape the fire's intense heat probably drowned in the rivers that flow through the city. Some one hundred thousand residents were left homeless, and about seventeen hundred died. A suspected communist was later executed by the Nationalists on charges of having set the fire.

The Nationalists wouldn't need a capital, anyway.

1949: Chinese Refugees Undertake Deadly March to Freedom. Thousands of Chinese Muslims fleeing the advancing Chinese communist armies embarked in mid-November on a dangerous trek from China's Sinkiang Province (now Xinjiang Uygur) across the Himalayas to India.

The brutal seven-hundred-mile journey to Leh in Kashmir took them through high mountain passes, where six-foot snows and bitter winds proved deadly for the refugees. Chinese communist border patrols had earlier deprived the refugees of extra clothing and most other possessions, and forced a long delay in their passage that caused refugees to use up half the food brought for the journey. Thus when the fifty caravans traversed the eighteen-thousand-foot-high passes in the Himalayas, they lacked food and protection against the cold. The bitter weather and high altitude killed both the refugees and hundreds of horses. By the time survivors reached Leh toward the end of December, some five hundred refugees had died.

1949: German Mine Explosion. A short-circuited electrical cable deep in a Soviet-controlled uranium mine in the German Democratic Republic (East Germany) led to catastrophe for thousands of miners on November 29. At the mine in Johanngeorgenstadt, near the Czechoslovakian border, sparks given off by the short-circuiting cable apparently ignited explosives stored nearby. Suddenly the mine erupted in a massive explosion, wrecking it and blowing apart the only elevator cage by which miners could have escaped. It is believed that about thirty-seven hundred miners perished, making it one of the worst mine disasters in history. The Soviet press, however, denied there had been any loss of life. Nothing ever goes wrong in a communist state.

1950: Two French Airliners Crash, Same Night, Same Place. An Air France DC-4 crashed near Bahrain in the Persian Gulf on the night of June 12, killing forty-seven people. Incredibly, later that night, a second Air France DC-4 crashed near the very same location.

Supernatural forces?

1950: Chinese Flood Leaves Ten Million Homeless. The early August flood in Anhui Province in eastern China was the worst ever experienced by the province up to that day. Floodwaters from the Hwai River and its tributaries inundated a huge area, including much of the province's northern region. Rampaging waters washed away some 890,000 houses, forcing about half the population in this area to flee for safety. Deaths numbered 489, and a staggering ten million persons were left homeless, as 3.5 million acres of flooded farmland were so badly damaged, they would not produce crops again until the following year. Meanwhile, Jiangsu and other provinces also suffered flooding as the Hwai and Chang Jiang (Yangtze) rivers overflowed their banks. One reporter described the area around the city of Hwaiyuan in Jiangsu Province as "a vast ocean of water stretching beyond the horizon."

Over the centuries China seems to have had more than its share of floods and famine, not to mention earthquakes and fires. Mother Nature has been relentless in that part of the world.

1952: Blizzard Hits Sierra Nevadas. The passenger train City of San Francisco, bound for San Francisco from Reno, Nevada, was stranded in the Sierra Nevada Mountains on January 14 in the midst of a treacherous blizzard, the worst storm in a half century. A massive snowslide blocked the tracks, stranding 226 passengers and crew near the remote Donner Summit.

While passengers waited for rescue crews, the locomotive ran out of diesel fuel, cutting off heat and light for a time. Elsewhere in California and Nevada, the blizzard blocked roads, and scores of automobiles, with stranded motorists inside, were covered by drifts. A Greyhound bus filled with high school students was missing for two days, and two persons were killed by a snowslide at a mountain resort.

Near the northern California coast, where the weather was warmer, the same storm system brought torrential rains and extensive flooding, while seventy-five-mile-per-hour winds toppled trees and ripped signs from buildings. Twenty-six deaths were blamed on the storm.

1952: Killer Fog Chokes London. The heaviest and most destructive fog in the history of London—a city famous for its fog—descended on the damp, cold night of December 5. A complete absence of breezes allowed the thick mist to settle hard on the city. Meanwhile, Londoners trying to keep warm in the frigid weather only made the noxious soup worse: Tens of thousands of chimneys throughout the city belched sulfurous smoke from coal fires within the houses.

In the past, the fog had always blown away, and everyone expected it to do so again. But a high-pressure system caused an unusual thermal inversion, in which a layer of hot air trapped cold near the ground. (Air near the ground is usually warmer than that above.) So coal smoke and factory fumes did not rise as usual, instead mixing with the fog to create an incredibly thick, yellowish smog that soon reduced visibility to almost zero for twenty miles around the city.

The fog was so bad that many motorists found themselves stranded, because they could see no more than five yards ahead.

Some people abandoned their cars and made their way on foot, while others who kept on driving despite the poor visibility risked winding up in one the many accidents reported throughout the city. All of the city's thirty-eight ambulances were on the streets at once; often the smog was so heavy that an official had to walk ahead of the ambulance as a guide.

By 2:00 P.M. on December 6, the city had gone almost completely dark. Crowds huddled under streetlights; incredibly, the fog was so thick that even pedestrians had trouble finding their way along streets. Airports were completely shut down, and following the wreck of one commuter train, passengers formed a human chain to grope their way along the streets to the next train station. The thick fog meanwhile offered unexpected protection for robbers and other petty criminals, who were quick to take advantage.

Soon the smog even invaded the inside of buildings and flats, filling rooms with a damp, yellowish mist. One movie theater was so fog-ridden that the film could only be seen from the front rows. At a livestock exhibition, eight prize heifers choked to death from the smog, after the failure of efforts to save them by making gas masks soaked in whiskey.

By December 7 the human toll began to rise as the very young, very old, and those with heart and respiratory problems succumbed to the choking smog. The "fog sickness" led to nausea, hacking coughs, and bluish skin resulting from lack of oxygen. Hospitals soon overflowed with the sick and dying; many more died in their smog-ridden flats.

Finally the winds returned, blowing the poisonous air out to sea on December 8. By that time, though, the unexpectedly high number of deaths in London had created a ten-day delay in burying the dead. Some four thousand people died as a direct result of the smog, and some officials estimated total deaths, including those who died later of respiratory complications, were as high as eight thousand. One Parliament member commented, "It's almost on the scale of mass extermination."

Britain introduced its Clean Air Act four years later.

1953: North Sea Floods. Spring tides, a full moon, and gale-force winds of eighty-five miles per hour combined to generate flood tides that devastated the east coast of England and the Netherlands coastal areas from January 31 to February 1. The wind-driven tidal surge crashed through seawalls and inundated English coastal villages, flooding some areas as far as three miles inland and forcing some fifty thousand people to abandon their homes.

Raging flood tides breached the seawalls on Canvey Island in the Thames Estuary, submerging the town under nine feet of water. Rescuers in small boats frantically worked to save the town's thirteen thousand inhabitants, while wind and waves smashed apart houses.

Meanwhile, the terrible winds and heavy seas battered the dikes in the Netherlands, where one-third of the land lies below sea level. Water swept through sea islands and low-lying areas of the Netherlands and Belgium, knocking down houses and tearing up roads. Altogether, floodwaters claimed 1,835 lives in England, the Netherlands, and Belgium.

1953: New England Tornado. Ninety people were killed and thousands left homeless by a tornado that struck Worcester, Massachusetts, and neighboring towns on June 9. About four thousand buildings were demolished.

1953: Christmas Eve Train Wreck. An unlikely series of events conspired to create a Christmas Eve tragedy near Waiouri, New Zealand. A minor eruption of the volcano Mount Ruapehu on December 24 created a flash flood in the River Wangachu. The surging waters in turn steadily undermined the footings of a railroad bridge over the river, until the weight of a passenger train crossing the bridge finally collapsed it. The locomotive and first six passenger cars fell into the river on Christmas Eve, killing 155 people.

1954: Yangtze River Floods. As the worst rainfall in one hundred years pounded central China in late July and early August, over a million people worked in an incredible effort to hold back floodwaters. As the Yangtze (now Chang Jiang) and Hwai rivers rose steadily, the Chinese desperately built and repaired dikes to contain the flooding.

At one point, when an earthen wall was giving way, over ten thousand people stood in the breach with mats on their backs until the wall could be reinforced. Meanwhile, the Yangtze rose to over ninety-six feet, and high winds lashed the waves perilously close to the top of 98.5-foot-high dikes protecting 1,255,000 people in the tri-city area of Hankow (now Hankou), Hanyang, and Wuchang.

While the three cities escaped the threat of floods, other areas along the flood-prone rivers were not as fortunate. Some forty thousand people ultimately died in a vast flooded area estimated to be about the size of the state of Indiana.

1954: Iranian Flash Flood Kills Worshipers. Some five thousand pilgrims had come to pray at a Muslim shrine located at the bottom of a steep gorge at Farahzad, Iran, having trekked to the secluded site by donkey. On the evening of August 16, a storm began to gather, but the sound of thunder gave little warning of the massive calamity that was about to occur.

By midnight, a heavy downpour roused pilgrims from shelters adjacent to the shrine. About two thousand of them rushed to the shrine to pray for protection. Their chanting was so loud, it could be heard over the roar of the storm.

Suddenly a ninety-foot-high wall of water poured down between the narrow walls of the gorge, smashing the shrine and carrying away the pilgrims. Rescuers later pulled the bodies of some two thousand people from the mud and debris.

1954: Japanese Typhoon. Some sixteen hundred people perished when a violent typhoon ripped its way across Japan on September 26, collapsing buildings, causing avalanches, and foundering boats at sea.

In spite of severe weather warnings, the train ferry *Toya Maru,* carrying over 1,250 people and a number of railroad cars, attempted its usual crossing between the islands of Hokkaido and Honshu. Soon waves broke over the ferry's low-slung bow and stern, and one of the two engines stalled. As the crippled ferry was swept toward shore, several railroad cars broke loose, crushing passengers as the cars rolled on the pitching and heaving deck. The ferry then struck a reef and overturned, tossing passengers into the raging waters. About eleven hundred people died in this wreck alone. Four other ferries were sunk during the typhoon.

Maybe they didn't hear those weather reports.

1954: Hurricane Hazel's Long Path of Destruction. Beginning in the Caribbean on October 12, Hazel first swept over

Haiti before next making landfall at Myrtle Beach, South Carolina. Packing winds of up to 130 miles per hour, the hurricane followed an unusual inland path northward through North Carolina, Virginia, Washington, D.C., Maryland, New York, and into Canada before dying out. The storm caused one billion dollars in damages and killed 411 people.

Now we are naming these zephyrs.

1955: Train Plunges into Mexican Canyon. Passenger trains running from Guadalajara, Mexico, to the coastal resort town of Manzanillo had been crowded all weekend because of the Easter holiday. The night express on April 3 was no exception as hundreds of residents of Guadalajara jammed into the train, eager to start their holiday vacations on Mexico's Pacific coast beaches.

Tragedy struck when the train was just fifty miles from Manzanillo, however. As the train traveled along the side of a deep canyon, part of it derailed. Nine passenger cars filled with horrified vactioners plunged six hundred feet to the bottom of the canyon, killing three hundred people. Rescue workers were unable to reach the wrecked cars until after dawn because the canyon walls were so steep.

1955: Gold Fever in Argentina. Gold fever ran rampant after a large nugget of gold was found in Minas Gerais State in Argentina. Excited prospectors began digging a trench under the spot where the nugget had been found, apparently hoping to strike a vein of gold, but though they dug deeper and deeper, they found nothing. Finally, on April 21, when the prospectors had tunneled forty feet down, the inadequately shored walls of the trench collapsed, burying alive thirty of them.

Gravity triumphs over greed.

1955: Bloody Le Mans Car Crash. Spectators were packed twenty to thirty deep behind a dirt safety wall at France's Le Mans racetrack on June 11, eagerly watching the Grand Prix race in which the celebrated Brazilian race driver Juan Fangio was competing. Two hours into the race, spectators turned to watch three sleek cars racing toward them at 125 miles per hour. An instant later, one of the cars bumped another and spun out of control. It should have been a relatively minor collision, but instead of bouncing off the dirt wall and back onto the track, the out-of-control Mercedes catapulted over it, somersaulted in midair, and plowed into the screaming crowd.

Spectators had no time to react. The hurtling wreck cut a horrendous, bloody swath through the crowd. Flying debris sliced through dozens of victims, decapitating two children while their parents watched in horror. The bodies of other victims were badly burned after having been doused with gasoline from the now-burning wreck.

Officials let the race continue while rescue workers went about their grim job at the crash site. Eighty-three persons, including the driver of the car, died that day at Le Mans, and some one hundred others were injured.

1956: Midair Crash over the Grand Canyon. The heartrending words came over the radio, "Salt Lake! United 718! We're going in!" A crewman of a United DC-7 airliner frantically shouted his message at 11:32 A.M. on June 30, just seconds after his plane had collided in midair with a TWA Super Constellation over the Grand Canyon. Then the radio went dead and nothing more was heard from either plane.

The two airliners had taken off from Los Angeles within three minutes of each other, and both pilots had decided to give passengers a scenic view of the Grand Canyon. A thundercloud reduced the pilots' visibility, however, and the TWA Super Constellation was reportedly flying at the altitude assigned to the United plane.

Suddenly the United plane rammed into the Super Constellation's fuselage, tearing it open; the instantaneous depressurization apparently killed everyone aboard the TWA flight instantly. As bodies and debris from the Super Constellation rained down on the Grand Canyon, the United plane hurtled downward, too, finally smashing into a rocky butte less than a mile from the wreckage of the Super Constellation. All 128 passengers and crewmen aboard the two planes were killed.

1956: The Luxury Liner *Andrea Doria* Sinks. At 11:22 P.M. on the evening of July 25, the luxury liner *Andrea Doria,* pride of the Italian merchant navy, was rammed on the starboard side by the Swedish steamship *Stockholm* in heavy fog off the Nantucket coast. Crewmen and passengers on the *Andrea Doria* were suddenly knocked off their feet, several passengers were crushed to death by the impact, and several others were pinned under wreckage, making escape impossible.

The *Stockholm,* now with a forty-foot hole in her bow, survived the collision, but water poured into the gashed *Andrea Doria,* making her list badly. Rescue ships, including the huge liner *Ile de France,* came to the sinking ship's aid, rescuing over sixteen hundred passengers and crewmen.

At 10:14 the following morning, the *Andrea Doria* capsized and sank. Fifty-two persons died in the collision, which occurred despite the fact both ships had radar. Actresses Ruth Roman and Betsy Drake, wife of Cary Grant, were both rescued from the sinking ship.

Was anyone watching the radar?

1956: Dynamite Explosion Wrecks Colombian City. Trucks loaded with dynamite suddenly exploded on August 7 while traveling through Cali, Colombia. The blast killed about twelve hundred people and demolished eight blocks in the city.

They should have filled in those potholes.

1956: Hungarian Revolution. Emboldened by Soviet leader Nikita Khrushchev's February denunciation of Joseph Stalin's oppressive rule, Hungarian citizens began protesting the Stalinist regime in their own country, calling for governmental reforms and free elections.

On October 23 thousands of demonstrators gathered in Budapest to hear a speech by the Communist party leader Ernö Garo. Garo denounced the demonstrators, calling them fascists, and soon the AVO (state security) guard began firing into the crowd. Soldiers and workers at a nearby munitions plant, who had been called in by the government to back up the AVO, instead sympathized with the demonstrators and began passing out arms to the frightened and angry crowd.

After a night of fierce hostilities, revolutionary leader Imre Nagy was appointed to the post of minister president. Thus, the revolutionaries seemed to have won their cause. Nagy formed a coalition government, and on November 1 he cabled the United Nations for recognition as a neutral state.

At 4:00 A.M. on November 4, however, Soviet tanks rumbled into Hungary without warning and attacked major towns, reaching the parliament building in Pest by 8:00 A.M. Within an hour,

Communist leader János Kádar announced over the radio that he was now minister president and that he had appointed Communists to all major posts.

Fierce fighting broke out all over the country, with the Soviets having the advantage of heavy artillery and planes. Soviet troops were ruthless in their attacks and killed thousands of Hungarian citizens, most of them unarmed. The revolt was effectively crushed by November 14. Nagy and others were arrested after being promised humane treatment, but were later executed.

So much for freedom.

1957–1958: Worldwide Asian Flu Epidemic. A new strain of flu virus appeared in Singapore and Japan in May 1957, and in less than a year spread throughout the entire world. Though there were comparatively few deaths from the flu, the disease is thought to have been one of the most widespread in history.

Now that our planes are flying faster, we can spread disease much more quickly.

1957: Soviet Nuclear Disaster in Ural Mountains. Though long kept secret by Soviet authorities, a huge nuclear disaster occurred at a nuclear weapons plant near Sverdlovsk, U.S.S.R., when a tank of radioactive waste exploded. An estimated fifty million curies of radiation were released, and an area the size of Rhode Island was so heavily contaminated that it had to be abandoned until 1974. Soviet authorities finally acknowledged the accident in 1989.

Who, us?

1957: Missouri Nursing Home Fire. In just fifteen minutes on February 17, flames raced through the Katie Jane Memorial Home in Warrenton, Missouri. Over 150 elderly persons, visitors, and staffers were in the 2½-story brick building when the fire broke out in a first-floor hallway at 3:45 P.M. Staffers and passers-by repeatedly braved the inferno to rescue elderly patients, but the intense heat soon ended their efforts. Several people then jumped from windows onto mattresses in the final minutes before the fire department arrived. After the fire, officials revealed the home had inadequate fire escapes, no sprinkler system, and was not fireproof. Seventy-two people died in the tragic blaze.

Where were all the fire inspectors?

1957: Hurricane Audrey. This hurricane slammed into Texas, Louisiana, and Mississippi on June 27, packing 105-mile-per-hour winds and killing some 550 people. Twenty-foot waves accompanied the furious storm. Near Galveston Bay, a seventy-eight-ton fishing boat crashed into an oil-drilling platform, drowning at least seven people. The resort town of Holly Beach, Louisiana, was wiped off the map, while in nearby Cameron, about 90 percent of the buildings were destroyed. Along eighty miles of Louisiana coast, only one of every twenty-five houses was left standing. Meanwhile, many people were left stranded, some of them clinging to roofs and trees for up to eighteen hours in flooded areas.

1957: Fiery Train Wreck in West Pakistan. A speeding express train rammed into a stopped train loaded with oil at Gambar, West Pakistan, on September 29. The crash ignited the oil, sending three hundred people to fiery deaths.

No signals?

1958: Starkweather Killings. Life was not going well for Charles Starkweather, a nineteen-year-old from Lincoln, Nebraska. Toward the end of 1957, he lost his job as a trash collector. In January 1958 his landlord locked him out of his rooming house for nonpayment of rent, and then he was asked to leave his parents' home after a fight over an accident with the family car. In addition, the parents of his fourteen-year-old girlfriend, Caril Fugate, told him to stay away from her.

Starkweather, apparently cracking under pressure, went on a killing rampage from January 27 to 29, during which he reportedly murdered ten people. First to die were Fugate's mother, her stepfather, and their three-year-old daughter. After wantonly murdering six more people, Starkweather, accompanied by his girlfriend, Caril, fled to Wyoming in a stolen car.

On January 29, near the town of Douglas, Wyoming, a passerby named Joe Sprinkle stopped to help two cars stalled on the roadside. Sprinkle was horrified to find the blood-spattered body of Starkweather's tenth victim in the front seat of one car. Worse yet, Sprinkle found the teenage murderer there as well.

Starkweather attacked him, but as the two men wrestled for control of a rifle, a deputy drove up. Starkweather escaped in Sprinkle's car. Driving at 110 miles per hour, he crashed through a roadblock as police fired at him. Police continued after him in a high-speed chase, however, and Starkweather finally gave up. Both Starkweather and Fugate were convicted in the murder spree.

Students study this case in criminal justice classes.

1958: Assassination of Iraqi King Faisal. Iraqi army leaders staged a coup in which King Faisal and other members of the royal family were assassinated on July 14. The military opposed Faisal's attempts to help end civil wars in Lebanon and Jordan, and soon aligned Iraq with anti-Western Arab nations. Within days, U.S. troops were sent to Lebanon to help restore order there.

The military takes over when peace threatens their power.

1958: Chicago Parochial School Fire. A devastating fire quickly engulfed Our Lady of the Angels Parochial School on December 1, killing ninety-three children and teachers. While over sixteen hundred children were attending classes, the fire apparently erupted in a basement stairwell at 2:42 P.M. Flames spread so rapidly that fire fighters later found the bodies of over twenty children still seated at their desks, with books and homework assignments stacked neatly in front of them. Children who had time to escape were panic-stricken. Some jumped or were pushed from windows, while others were trampled to death in the rush to exits. One father who lived nearby ran to his daughter's classroom and passed six children through a window before being driven out by the smoke and fire. The sixth child was his daughter. Other hysterical parents had no choice but to watch helplessly as flames devoured the building where their children remained trapped and dying.

1958: Bogotá Department Store Fire. Almacen Vida, a department store in Bogotá, Colombia, was suddenly filled with smoke and flames on December 16, after a string of Christmas lights short-circuited and started a blaze. Eighty-two people trapped in the store were killed.

1959: Fire Finds "Room at the Top." Flames shot one hundred feet into the air as fire raged through a block of shops and commercial buildings in the London suburb of Ilford, England, on March 16. Fire fighters did not even arrive until 7:50 P.M., twenty minutes after the blaze had begun, and by that time the fire was burning almost out of control.

For nearly five hours the massive flames consumed shops, apartments, warehouses, and a department store. Though firemen confined the blaze to the one block, the intense heat shattered plate-glass windows of stores across the street and burst water mains.

The scene reminded many of the London Blitz during World War II as firemen from the fifty trucks responding to the alarms attacked the blaze. Fortunately there were no deaths, though property damage ran into the millions of pounds, and people living in apartments above the burned-out shops lost their homes. Among the businessmen who lost everything was a restaurateur. He had been finishing up renovations on his premises, which would have included a new rooftop garden called "Room at the Top."

1959: Typhoon Vera. The most destructive typhoon in Japan's history struck on September 26. Nagoya, Japan's third largest city, and the surrounding areas were especially hard hit, with some five thousand people killed, fifteen thousand injured, and four hundred thousand left homeless.

Nagoya, an industrial city of 1.3 million located 180 miles southwest of Tokyo, was celebrating the seventieth anniversary of its becoming a municipality in September, but the festivities would soon come to an abrupt end. A "super typhoon" called Vera had gathered in the Pacific near Iwo Jima and was now moving steadily toward the Japanese islands. Unlike most Japanese typhoons, Vera did not swerve away from the main island of Honshu, but drove full force directly for it. Winds of up to 160 miles per hour accompanied the storm as it headed toward Nagoya on the island of Honshu.

The force of the storm was devastating. Seventeen-foot waves slammed the shoreline from Tokyo to Nagoya. In Nagoya Harbor, fishing boats were thrown around furiously; some were washed into city streets as massive waves and torrential rains inundated the city. Wind and waves even tore the British freighter *Changsha,* which weighed 7,412 tons, from her moorings and threw her up onto the beach.

As wind and water wracked the city, log pilings from the

harbor were ripped loose by the waves and sent crashing into buildings along the flooded streets. Rising floodwaters poured into houses, forcing whole families to climb up onto roofs to survive. There they endured the full fury of the violent storm. One apartment building collapsed, leaving eighty people pinned in the ruins. Nearly six thousand houses collapsed during the first onslaught of the storm.

Nagoya Harbor soon filled with drowned bodies, debris, and wrecked boats. Seven ships were washed ashore. A golden dolphin on the facade of the 350-year-old castle was torn loose and carried off by the flood. Meanwhile, the storm cut off transportation and communications, grounding airplanes, forcing cancellation of trains, and downing telephone lines. Landslides and floods washed out roads as the storm moved northward up the island of Honshu. Provinces of Toyama, Yamagata, Akita, and Niigata were soaked before the deadly storm moved on to rage across southeastern parts of the island of Hokkaido.

The next day in Nagoya, bodies floated everywhere, and some twenty-five thousand people were left stranded on the roofs of their houses. While waiting to be rescued, some dived into the dirty floodwaters to retrieve scraps of food from their gardens. Though helicopters eventually rescued the stranded multitudes, it was too late to prevent the spread of disease. Soon those who had survived the storm began falling ill with tetanus, dysentery, and gas gangrene.

By the time the waters receded, property damage from the storm was estimated to be $750 million. Thousands of acres of farmland were flooded, and millions of dollars worth of crops had been destroyed.

1960: The Terrible Tragedy of Thalidomide. The drug Thalidomide had been marketed as a nonprescription sleeping pill for a number of years in Europe when in 1960 it was linked to tragic birth defects. Chief among them was the deformation called phocomelia, in which babies were born armless, their hands protruding directly from their shoulders like seal flippers. There were other equally severe defects of the legs, eyes, ears, and even the intestines. In all, some eight thousand children were born with deformities before the drug was taken off the market.

1960: South Africa Mine Disaster. A cave-in on January 22 trapped and killed 417 coal miners working deep underground in the Coalbrook mine, located near Johannesburg. Workers ignored the first sign of trouble, a small rockfall at 4:30 P.M. in a shaft about six hundred feet below ground. Three hours later, an exploding ventilation fan set off a bigger rockfall. Soon after, another explosion sealed off the shaft, entombing the miners. Signs of the extensive cave-in could even be seen up on the surface, where roads cracked open and sank a foot or more in places. Rescue workers eventually tunneled through about a mile of debris to reach the victims.

1960: Twelve Seconds of Destruction in Morocco. Agadir, a peaceful seaport and resort city of forty-eight thousand people in Morocco, was demolished by a deadly earthquake at 11:45 P.M. on February 29. Lasting just twelve seconds, the quake jerked the ground four feet to one side, then snapped it back in the other direction. At the same time, a massive tidal wave swept inland, reducing to rubble everything that lay before it.

The sudden, wrenching force of the quake collapsed buildings onto thousands of terrified people who never had a chance to escape. Some houses burst apart, spewing forth wreckage, broken glass, and debris. Water mains broke, and power and communications were lost. Fires spread throughout the city, but there was no one to put them out in the chaos that reigned once the ground stopped trembling. In those twelve seconds of the quake, about 80 percent of the city was destroyed, and some twelve thousand people were killed.

It has been estimated that a million earthquakes occur every year. Most of them are minor.

1960: Hurricane Donna Ravages U.S. East Coast. Donna first wrecked Puerto Rico on September 6 and then devastated Florida with 150-mile-per-hour winds. Moving northward next, the hurricane lashed the eastern seaboard until September 12, when it finally died out off the coast of Canada. The storm killed 143 people, 22 of them in the United States.

1960: Cyclones Strike Bay of Bengal. October proved to be a disastrous month for coastal areas along the Bay of Bengal. On October 10 a cyclone and storm wave demolished coastal towns and villages, killing about four thousand people. Then, on October 31, another storm-and-wave one-two punch slammed into the area, killing some ten thousand people and destroying nine hundred thousand houses.

1960: Soviet Rocket Explodes on Launchpad. One hundred sixty-five technicians and others were killed on October 24 in a fiery explosion at Baikonur Space Center in the U.S.S.R. A repair crew reportedly tried to replace a malfunctioning component on the first stage of a new Soviet missile and accidentally ignited the rocket's second stage. People nearby the exploding rocket "just burst into flames like candle wax." Soviet authorities did not release details of the accident or the death toll until 1990.

After all, investigations take a while in the Soviet Union.

1960: Collision of Airliners Over Staten Island. A United DC-8 airliner apparently strayed off course on the misty morning of December 16 and rammed into a TWA Constellation jetliner over Staten Island, New York. Both planes had been making landing approaches when the collision occurred. There were no survivors among the 126 passengers and crew of the two planes, and 8 people were killed on the ground in Brooklyn by falling pieces of the planes.

1961: Terrorists Sink *Dara*. Officers of the British streamship *Dara,* which made regular runs between Bombay, India, and Basra, Iraq, wore stab-proof vests to guard against attacks by Arab terrorists. But the danger finally came in the form of a bomb instead of a dagger.

The *Dara,* with 716 aboard, had reached the Persian Gulf at dawn on April 8. Suddenly a time bomb planted by Omani terrorists exploded belowdecks. Fire raced through the entire ship, killing many of the passengers and crewmen while they slept, the intense heat burning some bodies down to mere skeletons. Fires continued burning for two days before the ship finally sank. The death toll was 236, many of whom were Arabs, who made up the majority of passengers and crew.

Terrorism, a cowardly ploy.

1961: Bay of Pigs Invasion. CIA-backed Cuban exiles attempted to overthrow Fidel Castro's communist government by an ill-fated invasion of Cuba at the Bay of Pigs on April 17. Far from inspiring the oppressed in Cuba to rise up against Castro, the fifteen-hundred-man invasion force was quickly defeated by Cuban regulars. The incident then turned into a major foreign policy disaster for the new administration of U.S. President John F. Kennedy.

The operation began on April 15, when three Cuban air bases were bombed by B-26 planes flown by pilots who claimed to be Cuban air force fliers opposed to Castro's regime. They then sought and received asylum in the United States. Two days later, on April 17, the Cuban exiles began landings on Cuba's coast, the main invasion being at the Bay of Pigs. The exile army was no match for Cuban regulars, especially when President Kennedy withdrew U.S. military support from the exiles at the last minute. By April 19, Castro's forces had control of the situation and took some eleven hundred invaders prisoner.

While the imprisoned exiles were eventually ransomed by the Cubans and released, the appearance of indecision within the Kennedy administration led two years later to the 1963 Cuban Missile crisis, a showdown between Kennedy and Soviet leader Nikita Khrushchev. That crisis brought the two nations to the brink of nuclear war before the Soviets finally agreed to withdraw nuclear missiles from Cuba.

1961: Deadly Circus Fire in Brazil. The worst circus fire in history killed 323 people and injured as many as 800 others when a nylon circus tent caught fire in Niteroi, Brazil, on December 17.

On that afternoon, some twenty-five hundred people gathered under the Gran Circo Norte-Americano's big circus tent at Niteroi, a suburb near Rio de Janeiro. Among them were fourteen hundred children enjoying a Christmas-week celebration, and their attention was riveted on trapeze artist Antonietta Estavanovich and her partner, who were then swinging high above the audience. As Estavanovich was about to leap midair from her trapeze to her partner, she suddenly spotted the fire beginning at the base of the tent. The cause of the fire has never been determined; explanations ranged from arson to the sparks thrown off by a nearby freight train.

Estavanovich had to force thoughts of the rapidly spreading fire out of her mind and somehow kept her concentration as she completed her daredevil stunt. Both she and her partner then dropped to safety nets and made their way out of the tent unharmed.

Almost half of those in the audience were not so fortunate. The fire spread furiously, roaring up the sides of the tent and across its roof, consuming the supporting poles within moments. Thousands of children and adults stampeded wildly for the exits, which immediately became jammed with struggling people. A number of them were trampled to death in the crush. One man saved himself and his children by climbing underneath the stands, making his way out by bypassing the jammed exits. Elsewhere in the tent, a Boy Scout used his pocket knife to cut a hole in the canvas and then led a number of children and adults to safety.

Amid the chaos, a terrified circus elephant named Elisa escaped and ran amuck, charging into the burning tent. The enormous hole she tore in the tent wall made an easy way out for hundreds of people who immediately scrambled through it to escape the fire. Tragically, the elephant was killed by the blaze, but the other circus animals all survived. They were housed in a smaller tent that did not catch fire.

Just three minutes after the fire broke out, the big tent collapsed. Nearly three hundred children clustered in the middle of the tent were suddenly covered by the burning roof material. They had no way to escape, and all either suffocated or were burned to death.

Not long after, the circus tent lay in ashes. Then began the grim jobs of treating the six hundred to eight hundred seriously injured and of identifying the 323 dead. To relieve overcrowding at the morgue, officials resorted to using the sports stadium, where they laid out bodies for identification. Two thousand people lined up outside, looking for the bodies of lost children and relatives. The death toll at Niteroi surpassed even that of the tragic Ringling Brothers and Barnum & Bailey Circus fire that killed 168 people at Hartford, Connecticut, in 1944.

1962–1964: The Boston Strangler. In June 1962 a man entered the apartment where fifty-five-year-old Anna E. Slesers lived alone, took a cord from the housecoat she was wearing, and strangled her. Thus began the string of brutal murders ascribed to the Boston Strangler.

His victims were all women who lived alone, and no one

knows how he gained access to their apartments, because there was never any sign of forced entry. Once inside, the maniacal killer overpowered his victims and strangled them with their clothing or ordinary household items.

The killings terrorized Boston until 1964, and were eventually attributed to Albert Henry DeSalvo, a mental patient who bragged of them while in a hospital for the criminally insane. He confessed to killing thirteen women. On January 18, 1967, he received a life sentence for an armed robbery committed in late 1964, but due to lack of evidence, he was never tried for the Strangler killings.

His story made a good book and a movie, though.

1962: Peruvian Avalanche. Summer melting loosened part of a glacier on the extinct volcano Huascaran, a 22,205-foot peak in the Peruvian Andes. About 7:00 P.M. on January 11, millions of tons of ice, snow, and earth suddenly crashed downward, destroying everything on its way through the Llangauco Valley to the Santa River. Villagers at Ranrahirca heard a sudden roar and saw a cloud of snow and dust approaching, but there was no time to escape. Within minutes the landslide completely destroyed the town. Afterward, one doctor reported, "We have nothing to do because there are no injured. They are all dead." Only fifty of Ranrahirca's five hundred inhabitants survived. Elsewhere the story was much the same. At least six villages were destroyed and four thousand people killed, leaving in ruin the scenic mountain area known as the "Switzerland of South America."

Mother Nature (or should that be "Father Nature"?) is just as dangerous as she is beautiful.

1962: Powerful Earthquake Shakes Iran. Some ten thousand people were killed by a powerful earthquake felt throughout much of western Iran on September 1. Thirty-one villages were demolished, and at one, Dan-Isfahan, almost three-quarters of the forty-five hundred residents perished.

Mother Earth relieving the pressure on herself again.

1963: Death Aboard the USS *Thresher* Submarine. It was a blustery morning on April 10 when the brand-new nuclear attack submarine USS *Thresher* made a routine test dive during sea trials some 220 miles off Cape Cod. After about ninety minutes underwater, the *Thresher* sent a message to an accompanying rescue vessel that she was in trouble.

The forty-three-hundred-ton submarine was on the bottom in eighty-four hundred feet of water, and unable to rise. A piping system in the engine room had failed, flooding the vessel and sending it down onto the ocean floor. The *Thresher*'s next "message" was the horrifying muffled sound of a submarine being crushed and broken up by the enormous water pressure at that depth, over 1½ miles beneath the surface. All 129 seamen and civilian technicians on board succumbed.

1963: Twenty-two Thousand Die in East Pakistan Cyclone. A powerful storm demolished Chittagong, East Pakistan (now Bangladesh), on May 28 and 29, knocking down some one million primitive houses made of dried mud.

1963: Hurricane Flora's Fury. Haitian villagers and farmers had little advance warning of the deadly hurricane that struck their island on October 3. The storm battered the island with two-hundred-mile-per-hour winds and torrents of heavy rain for over twenty-four hours. Villagers watched in horror as their homes and possessions were washed away. Winds ripped up entire forests and turned small streams into deadly, raging rivers. Coffee, rice, and banana plantations were totally destroyed, and rubble was strewn over nearly half of the island. Some five thousand Haitians lost their lives, and one hundred thousand were left homeless.

Next, the hurricane attacked Cuba, where it lashed the island for four days. Flash floods caused the most severe damage. Some families stayed in homes that had never before been reached by floodwaters, only to see them washed away by the record floods caused by this furious storm. Most crops and cattle were destroyed; over 90 percent of Cuba's coffee crop was gone. Worst of all, almost two hundred thousand homes were destroyed, and some one thousand Cubans were killed.

1963: Deadly Floods in Italy. About two thousand people living in the Piave River basin in Italy were killed on October 9 after a torrent of water spilled over a dam and flooded the valley. An avalanche that fell into the lake behind the dam caused the massive surge of water.

1963: Indiana Ice Show Explosion. Some forty-three hundred people at the State Fairgrounds Coliseum in Indianapolis were watching skaters perform to Dixieland music on October 31 when suddenly a fifty-foot section of box seats blew up. People, parts of the stands, and chunks of concrete were hurled upward as a ball of flame rose thirty feet into the air. Caused by an exploding tank of bottled cooking gas in a concession stand, the blast lifted up the box seat section and dropped it down on bleachers filled with people. Amid screams and cries for help, the band continued to play and thereby helped to avert wholesale panic. Many prominent citizens and wealthy patrons in the expensive box seats, including a number of women wearing mink coats, were among the 65 dead and 340 injured.

1963: Japanese Mine Explosion. Above ground at Omuta, Japan, on November 9, it was a crisp autumn day. Deep underground, over twelve hundred miners were busy digging coal in the Mikawa Mine. Suddenly a spark ignited coal dust and gas fumes in the air, setting off a massive explosion. The blast was so powerful, it not only shattered mine installations below ground, but destroyed mining offices on the surface. People heard and felt the explosion miles away.

The explosion turned the mine into a death trap. Many were killed instantly by the blast or were buried in cave-ins, while others were felled by a deadly fireball touched off by the explosion. Then poison gas filled the tunnels, making rescue efforts almost impossible and sealing the fate of those miners left below. In all, 447 miners lost their lives in what was Japan's second deadliest mine disaster up to that time.

The volatility of coal gas is one of nature's little ironies.

1963: Kennedy Assassination. On the morning of November 22, forty-six-year-old President John F. Kennedy was en route from Fort Worth to Dallas, Texas, aboard Air Force One. It was his first visit to Texas, a politically influential state, since winning the 1960 presidential election. During the brief flight, he worked on the speech he planned to deliver following a ten-mile presidential motorcade through the city.

Meanwhile, an ex-marine sharpshooter who had once attempted to defect to Russia was also preparing for Kennedy's motorcade. Lee Harvey Oswald, twenty-four years old, was working as a filing clerk at the Texas School Book Depository, located in downtown Dallas along what would be the route of Kennedy's motorcade. Oswald had been affiliated with a number of left-wing causes, including a pro-Castro group, and this morning arrived for work carrying a package wrapped inconspicuously in brown paper. Inside was a disassembled high-powered rifle, complete with telescopic sight.

Later that morning, Oswald made his way to the depository's sixth floor. There he rearranged cardboard cartons to create a spot where he would be hidden from view but would still have a clear line of sight on the passing motorcade.

The motorcade got under way at 11:55 A.M., moving slowly through the Dallas streets. Kennedy's limousine, a large blue Lincoln Continental convertible, was wide open to the sunny Dallas weather; a protective clear plastic bubble had been brought in case of rainy weather, but was not needed. The Kennedy car was preceded and followed by numerous other vehicles in the motorcade, including police motorcycle escorts and cars filled with security people, politicians, and journalists. Texas Governor John Connally and his wife enjoyed the honor of riding with the president and Mrs. Jacqueline Kennedy.

Increasingly large crowds of cheering spectators greeted the motorcade as it approached the center of Dallas. People stood twelve-deep on the sidewalks while others cheered and waved from open windows. At times people pushed onto the street to get a better look, forcing the motorcade to an even slower pace. Twice the president angered his Secret Service agents by stopping to shake hands with children along the way.

While workers at the book depository left for lunch or to get a look at the president, Oswald slipped away to his sixth-floor vantage point to wait for the motorcade to approach. There he assembled the rifle, loaded it, and took aim at the street below.

It was 12:30 when the motorcade passed the book depository and turned left, traveling at barely eleven miles per hour. Cheering crowds prompted the governor's wife, Nellie, to remark, "You surely can't say Dallas doesn't love you, Mr. President." Smiling, Kennedy responded, "No, you can't."

Kennedy had just raised his arm to wave when suddenly rifle shots rang out from the building above. The first bullet penetrated the back of the president's neck and passed through him to hit Connally, who was injured in the ribs, lung, and wrist. The president grabbed his throat just as the second bullet hit, tearing away the back of his skull. Jacqueline Kennedy screamed, "Oh, no!" just as he fell, lifeless, into her lap.

A bodyguard instantly pulled Mrs. Kennedy down and shielded her from further gunfire as the car sped away, leaving the confused and hysterical onlookers behind. At Parkland Memorial Hospital, doctors tried vainly to save the president, giving him transfusions, oxygen, and anesthesia, but it was too late. At 1:00 P.M. he was declared dead.

Dallas police quickly discovered the rifle and ammunition clip that Oswald had left behind and obtained a description of him from witnesses. Oswald was arrested within two hours, but not before he shot and killed a policeman who had tried to stop him for questioning.

Oswald was charged with the two murders, but he did not live to stand trial. Two days later, as Oswald was being transferred to the county jail, a Dallas nightclub owner named Jack Ruby stepped from the crowd and shot him dead. Oswald's murder only added to speculations about the tragic assassination of Kennedy, which, despite various rumors of plots and escaped accomplices, the Warren Commission finally ascribed to Oswald alone. In the 1980s, however, reports surfaced indicating the assassination may have been engineered by Cuban leader Fidel Castro, reportedly in retaliation for a failed U.S.-backed attempt on his life.

1964: Murder of Kitty Genovese. Of all the tragedies that can befall a neighborhood or a city, one of the worst is the kind of fear or the apathy that overtook a quiet neighborhood in the borough of Queens in New York City on March 13. Twenty-eight-year-old Catherine ("Kitty") Genovese, the manager of a bar, was coming home from work in this middle-class neighborhood at 3:20 A.M. when a man attacked her in the street.

"Oh my God, he stabbed me!" she screamed. "Please help me!" Lights came on in apartments all along the block, and one man screamed to the attacker to leave her alone. But not one of the thirty-eight witnesses came to her aid or even called the police. Before Genovese could crawl to her apartment, the attacker returned and stabbed her again. Witnesses heard Genovese scream, "I'm dying." Scared off by the lights in windows, the attacker drove away, but incredibly, returned a third time and stabbed Genovese to death.

Not a soul ventured out to help the young woman, and police were not called until 3:50 A.M. They arrived within two minutes, but by then it was too late. Witnesses later told police they were afraid to get involved. One man said, "I was tired. I went back to bed."

Am I my brother's keeper?

1964: Deadly Earthquake Shakes Alaska. Many residents of Anchorage, Alaska, were on their way home at 5:37 on the evening of March 27 when a monster earthquake struck the area, crumbling buildings and opening huge fissures in the earth. The quake registered 8.6 on the Richter scale, making it the worst in the United States up to that time. It was a day to remember, and ironically, it was Good Friday. It wasn't to be a better Saturday, either.

For five long minutes the ground shook with frightening violence, and people fought desperately for their lives. Some ran from the collapsing buildings to seek safety in the streets. Others clung frantically to anything they could reach to keep from being swept into the crevices opening up in the ground. A group of one hundred people formed a human chain, holding on to one another to try to survive. One witness reported that roads undulated with oceanlike waves, causing cars and trucks to roll and slam into each other.

In the city of Seward, a tidal wave knocked buildings from their foundations, followed by fires that burned much of what remained of the business district. The powerful tidal wave came ashore over a wide area, tossing giant redwood logs onto roads and through buildings. Cars and trucks were thrown as though they were toys onto heaps of rubble. Meanwhile, a family camping on the beach lost all four of their young children when the deadly wave carried them out to sea. In all, the quake took 118 lives.

1965: Thirty-five Midwest Tornadoes Kill 271. Many people were out of doors on the pleasant Sunday of April 11 when the earliest warnings of tornadoes were circulated. As unlikely as it may have seemed then, the warnings could not have been more accurate. Beginning later that afternoon, no less than thirty-five deadly tornadoes struck the midwestern states of Iowa, Wisconsin, Michigan, Illinois, Ohio, and Indiana during a rampage of death and devastation that lasted ten hours.

Survivors said the tornadoes sounded like low-flying jet planes approaching. And everywhere there was the sound of breaking glass. Many residents of rural communities were crushed as their homes collapsed around them, while others were tossed by the two-hundred-mile-per-hour winds into their fields and buried in mud. One family of seven miraculously survived as their home was torn apart around them. In another case, a man taking a shower was picked up and deposited stark naked onto the street, dazed and embarrassed but unhurt. His house, meanwhile, was completely destroyed.

Of the thousands of persons injured, many were motorists whose cars or trucks were lifted from the roadway, then tossed to the ground. In Indiana, particularly hard hit, tornadoes decimated a trailer park, killing several people and injuring many others.

1965: African Ferry Capsizes in Crocodile-Infested River. Three heavy trucks were carrying about two hundred people, many of them women and children, to their homes in Liwonde, Malawi, on the evening of May 23, following a rally attended by the tiny African republic's prime minister. The journey to Liwonde required a ferryboat crossing of the Shire River, which was infested with crocodiles and hippopotamuses.

With the three trucks and several cars aboard, the ferry edged out onto the river. Some distance from the shore, the ferry's guide cable suddenly snapped and the boat swung about in the current and overturned, dumping trucks, cars, and people into the river. Screams filled the air as people bobbed to the surface, frantically trying to stay afloat. Meanwhile, crocodiles slithered through the murky water toward the scene of the commotion.

Just fifty-two people managed to swim ashore, escaping both drowning and being eaten by hungry crocodiles. Local authorities expressed little hope of ever finding any remains of the 150 or so others who had been aboard the ferryboat.

1965: Fifty-three Die in Titan II Missile Silo Fire. "If it hadn't been for God, I don't guess I'd ever gotten out," said one of the two workers lucky enough to escape the fire in a Titan II missile silo near Searcy, Arkansas. Fifty-five civilian workmen had been modifying the silo housing on August 9 when the blaze erupted, possibly in a diesel generator, and filled the silo with heavy black smoke. The Titan II missile was in the silo, minus its atomic warhead but loaded with highly explosive rocket fuel.

The two men who escaped happened to be near the top of the silo, while those who were trapped had been working on lower levels. One of the survivors reported hearing fellow workers crying out for help in the dense smoke and intense heat. "It was horrible," he said. "I couldn't see. I just felt my way out."

Rescue workers were unable to stay in the silo for long because of the extreme heat. Air force personnel at the missile silo's control center reportedly saw that it would be impossible to rescue the trapped workmen and sealed their control center as they left, cutting off all possible escape for those inside. Although this doomed the workmen, it reportedly helped smother the fire before the silo got hot enough to ignite the rocket fuel.

No one is ever paid enough to make decisions like that.

1965: Los Angeles Riots. It was a hot, muggy evening on August 11 when police stopped a black motorist in the Watts area of Los Angeles on suspicion of drunken driving. Racial tensions had been on the increase throughout the United States for some years by this time, and as the patrolmen questioned the motorist, a crowd began to gather.

Soon onlookers were screaming insults at the police and hurling rocks, but the escalation of violence was not to stop there. Watts quickly erupted into full-scale riot as the violence spilled over into other sections of the neighborhood. Black residents began stoning city buses and looting local shops and businesses, while gangs of black youths fired shots at police and accused them of brutality. In one incident, angry rioters threw a Molotov cocktail into the car of a white motorist and then pulled him out onto the street, beating him savagely.

More than four hundred policemen cordoned off a twenty-block section of the city to contain the rioting, but the violence continued until August 16. Thirty-four people were killed, many of them bystanders, and over forty-one hundred were arrested. Some two hundred buildings were completely destroyed, and over six hundred damaged, with property damage in the area totaling forty million dollars. Watts was one of many destructive race riots in inner-city ghettos that exploded in the United States during the 1960s.

The rage within erupts.

1966–1969: China's Abortive Cultural Revolution. During his final years in power, China's leader Mao Tse-tung became determined to strengthen China's revolutionary spirit and assure that the country's basic institutions, and his own place in history, would survive. Mao's plan became known as the Cultural Revolution, and included replacing political leaders with unacceptable ideological views, strengthening the Chinese Communist party, and promoting a revolutionary zeal among China's youth.

Mao began by mobilizing much of China's urban youth into groups called the Red Guards. These young people were encouraged to attack the bourgeois elements in Chinese culture and government, ostensibly to strengthen them. Unfortunately, the Red Guards soon ran amok. In the anarchy that followed, there were random acts of violence in which many people were physically attacked and sometimes killed. The widespread disorder and uncontrollable violence that raced through the nation's cities eventually brought about the collapse of the movement by 1969.

Give them an inch and they'll take a mile.

1966: Lima Soccer Riot. On May 25 passions were running high two minutes before the end of an Olympics qualifying soccer game between Argentina and Peru at Lima stadium in Peru. Argentina led 1–0 when a Peruvian player scored the tying goal. Home team fans in the crowd of forty-five thousand went wild—but then the referee disallowed the goal. Now the Peruvian fans roared their anger, and some leaped over barriers to try to attack the referee. When he suspended the game, the angry mob broke through the barriers, rushing onto the field, but the players and officials escaped into a locker room.

Police, trying to disperse the unruly mob, fired tear gas and released attack dogs. The crowd then surged toward the exits, trampling many among them underfoot, while others were asphyxiated by the crush of bodies falling on top of them. Some 248 persons were killed in the melee. The rioting fans then swarmed onto the streets, where they looted and burned nearby buildings.

It's a game, people, just a game.

1966: Chicago Nursing Student Slayings. At 11:00 P.M. on July 13, six nursing students were asleep in their town-house-style dormitory in South Chicago. There was a knock on the door, and when one of the nurses opened it, she was greeted by Richard Speck, a twenty-four-year-old ex-convict and drifter who was armed with a knife and a revolver.

Waking the other sleeping nurses, Speck herded them into a back bedroom, where he cut up a bed sheet with this knife and tied up the trembling, terrified young women. In the meantime, three more nurses arrived at the dormitory, and they, too, were bound. Speck promised the women he would not harm them, then he led one of them from the room, closing the door behind him. Later he returned alone, and led another out of the room.

Incredibly, he cold-bloodedly killed eight of the nurses, one by one, either by stabbing them with the knife or by strangling them with bed sheets. One nurse, Corazon Amurao, while still bound, rolled under a bed and hid there until the killer left. She survived to identify Speck in court, where he received the death penalty and joined the ranks of our more spectacular serial killers.

1966: University of Texas Tower Killings. About 11:00 A.M. on Monday, August 1, an architectural honor student named Charles Whitman walked onto the observation deck atop a twenty-seven-story office tower at the University of Texas, Austin. The student, a former marine marksman, carried with him a footlocker filled with three rifles, a sawed-off shotgun, two pistols, ammunition, and food and water.

Whitman apparently killed his wife and his mother before heading for the campus. On the way up the tower, he calmly killed the elevator operator and a mother and her two children. After reaching the top of the tower, where he had a clear view of the campus, Whitman began shooting at the unsuspecting students below.

Suddenly a student toppled from his bicycle. Another student, standing in the doorway of a bookstore, fell dead. Realizing they were being shot at by a sniper, students began screaming and running for cover. All the while Whitman just kept firing his rifle, even trying to hit those who went to aid wounded students lying out in the open.

Meanwhile, a combined force of state, city, and campus police returned fire and began moving in on the tower. Whitman was finally killed by an off-duty patrolman who managed to sneak up behind him. In his hour-long shooting spree, Whitman killed twelve people and wounded thirty-three.

The games some people play.

1966: Avalanche in Aberfan. On October 21 some 250 children awaited the start of classes in the schoolhouse at Aberfan, a coal-mining town in Wales. One of the children recalled, "We were laughing and playing . . . waiting for the teacher to call the register." Then came the sound of two million tons of rock, coal, and mud thundering down the side of an eight-hundred-foot-high coal slag heap located directly in back of the school. The avalanche crushed a dozen miners' cottages and partly crushed and buried the schoolhouse with all the children inside.

Mothers and fathers came running, knowing that the village school was directly beneath the giant slag heap. Some schoolrooms had been leveled while others were only partly demolished, and in the first minutes about one hundred children were gotten out safely. But for the parents of the rest of the children, the anguishing ordeal of Aberfan was just beginning.

The cause of the disaster, the man-made mountain of coal waste, shale, and other materials left over from processing coal, was known as a "tip." Some two hundred tons of waste was carted to the tip every working day from a colliery in the village. While such tips were common in coal-mining areas, the tip in Aberfan had been weakened by heavy rains and a natural underground spring.

People in Aberfan had long worried about the dangers of a sudden avalanche burying the school. But nothing had been done in the past, partly because workers feared the colliery's closing and the subsequent loss of jobs. In the days before the tragedy, a number of people reported seeing movement in the slope, and ironically, a maintenance man from the mine was up on top of the slag heap inspecting it when the avalanche gave way.

In the aftermath, some two thousand rescue workers, including miners from neighboring villages, gathered to help dig through the mud and rock to find trapped children. Worried parents worked among the rescuers, desperately searching for their children. Meanwhile, bulldozers were brought in to help clear big pieces of rubble, and periodically all digging would cease while everyone listened for the sound of muffled cries from beneath the mud and debris of crushed buildings.

Digging went on through the night under searchlights and into the next day, and a total of 134 children got out alive. The bodies of 116 children and 29 adults who were killed in the avalanche were taken to two village chapels, which served as temporary mortuaries during the tragedy.

The children were finally buried in a mass grave marked by a one-hundred-foot cross. Queen Elizabeth visited the grave, adding her condolences to the flood of sympathy messages sent from around the world.

1966: Flooding in Italy Ruins Art Treasures. Heavy November rains swelled the River Arno until it flooded the historic city of Florence from November 4 to 6, damaging millions of dollars worth of art treasures in the city. Venice, Rome, and Naples were also inundated by the November rains. A total of 113 people lost their lives.

1967–1969: Famine in Biafra. An attempt to secede from Nigeria led to civil war and a severe famine. An estimated 1.5 million children in secessionist Biafra died. Another political famine.

1967: Soviet Reactor Meltdown. The world's first nuclear reactor meltdown at sea apparently occurred aboard the nuclear-powered icebreaker *Lenin* while it was under way somewhere in the Arctic. Though Soviet authorities did not even report the accident, U.S. experts estimate that about thirty crewmen were killed.

Another nonerror by the Soviets.

1967: *Apollo I* Fire. A horrific flash fire in the *Apollo I* command module on January 27 killed three U.S. astronauts on the launchpad at Cape Kennedy. The astronauts had been taking part in a rehearsal for a launch of the rocket that would eventually take the first men to the moon.

At 6:31 P.M. on January 27, American astronauts Virgil (Gus) Grissom, Edward White, and Roger Chaffee were strapped into their seats within the *Apollo I* command module, perched atop the huge two-stage Saturn I rocket. Though they were only ten minutes away from the simulated lift-off, there were no medical crews or fire equipment standing by, because the rocket had not been loaded with fuel. Closed-circuit television cameras relayed pictures of the astronauts, already five hours into their rehearsal, to nearby observers.

Suddenly there was a bright flash, and the observers' television monitors went black. Sparks from an electrical short had ignited the pure oxygen atmosphere maintained inside the command module, and in an instant everything combustible inside the capsule burst into flame, killing the three astronauts instantly. Emergency crews tried frantically to reach the trapped astronauts but were driven back by heat and dense smoke. It was four minutes before they were able to force open the hatches.

Had they not been killed immediately, the three-man crew would probably still have died, as they had no way to get out of the burning capsule quickly enough. NASA officials estimated that under the best of circumstances, it would have taken them ninety seconds to open the hatch and evacuate the spacecraft. But what probably sealed the astronauts' fate was the fact that they were wearing pressurized space suits and were breathing pure oxygen at the time of the tragedy. Thus, the fire probably burned from within their suits as well as from without.

Grissom, White, and Chaffee were the first U.S. astronauts to be killed on the job, although, ironically, they died on the ground. Previously three astronauts had died in aviation accidents, but the tragic fire marked the first time astronauts had been killed while actually aboard a spacecraft.

An investigative board was appointed to study the tragedy, which effectively put a halt to the Apollo space program for twenty-one months. Investigators eventually found the short to be the immediate cause of the accident, but also blamed other contributing causes. These included the use of pure oxygen in the command module (a less combustible mixture was later substituted) and the amount of combustible material in the spacecraft, such as paper, Velcro cloth, and nonmetallic insulation for wires. It was suggested that, in their rush to prepare Apollo for its flight, NASA officials had overlooked crucial precautions.

Actual test flights finally began in December 1968, and after a series of successively more ambitious flights, the United States triumphantly landed the first men on the moon on July 16, 1969.

1967: Torrey Canyon Oil Spill. The giant oil tanker *Torrey Canyon* was en route to England from the Persian Gulf on March 18 when she smashed onto rocks off the British coast in the English Channel. The rocks ripped open more than half the tanker's bottom, including fourteen of the sixteen oil compartments. Some thirty thousand tons of oil began pouring into the sea, the start of what was to became the world's worst oil spill up to that time.

Cleanup efforts included spraying detergent on the oil-clogged waters (a procedure that proved even more deadly to marine life than the oil) and bombing the disabled ship, on the orders of British Prime Minister Harold Wilson, to burn any remaining oil in her tanks. The oil refused to burn, however, and within days more than seventy thousand additional gallons escaped into the sea. Efforts to clean the British and French coastlines continued for months. The disaster resulted in the death of one officer and the loss of tens of thousands of marine animals and sea birds.

Our first great ecological disaster. More to come.

1967: Brussels Department Store Fire. The explosion of a gas cylinder in Brussels's largest department store, L'Innovation, touched off an enormous fire on May 22. The blaze began at lunchtime, when between three thousand and four thousand shoppers and salespeople crowded the store. People panicked and hordes of shoppers stormed the exits, trampling over unfortunates who fell. Flames spread so quickly that customers became trapped on upper floors. Dozens of them rushed to windows, and many jumped to their deaths before safety nets could be set up. Others managed to reach the roofs of nearby buildings. One survivor rushed back into the blazing inferno and reappeared soon after, leading out several small children. But before the fire was put out, 322 people had died. Buildings surrounding L'Innovation burned to the ground in the tragedy as well.

1967: Aircraft Carrier USS *Forrestal* Fire. The third largest United States aircraft carrier, the USS *Forrestal*, was in its fifth day of service off Vietnam when, at 10:53 A.M. on July 29, an A-4E Skyraider fighter plane preparing for lunch accidentally dropped a fuel tank, spilling 250 gallons of highly flammable fuel on the flight deck. Flames spread rapidly over the four-acre deck, setting fire to rockets, bombs, and fuel tanks. Exploding 750-pound bombs blew four giant holes in the flight deck, while forty-mile-per-hour winds spread the fire to the hangar deck.

Emergency crews aboard the *Forrestal,* which carried a full complement of over four thousand sailors, fought valiantly against the blaze. Risking their lives, sailors threw bombs and rockets overboard before the munitions could detonate. Surrounded by exploding bombs, one sailor drove a forklift to push burning planes into the ocean. Nearby ships quickly joined the effort, spraying water onto the burning deck. Nevertheless, some eighty sailors drowned after being forced to jump overboard by the advancing flames, and others burned to death belowdecks in their quarters.

By the time the blaze was extinguished ten hours later, the death toll had reached 134. Twenty-six planes were destroyed, and thirty-one damaged. Total damages were estimated at eighty-five million dollars.

1967: Lisbon's Killer Rainstorm. More than 450 people died and thousands were left homeless on November 26 when a freak rainstorm flooded Lisbon, Portugal, and surrounding areas. The rains began in the morning and became a torrential downpour between 6:00 P.M. and midnight, dumping 3½ inches on the city during that time. Lisbon's sewers soon backed up, and six feet of water poured through the streets. In a Lisbon movie theater, 150 people found themselves stranded in balconies when the water suddenly filled the orchestra section. Eventually the floodwaters cut off power, downed telephone lines, stalled and overturned cars, cut roads, and stranded trains. Rising to thirteen feet deep in parts of Lisbon and nearby Quintas, floodwaters even knocked down some houses.

1967: Silver Bridge Collapses During Rush Hour. On December 15 the combination of rush hour and Christmas shopping created heavy traffic on the Silver Bridge, a 1,750-foot suspension bridge spanning the Ohio River from Kanauga, Ohio, to Point Pleasant, West Virginia. About 5:00 P.M. some drivers heard an ominous groaning sound, then suddenly the span supporting the roadway on the Ohio side of the river twisted and fell, followed by other spans and the bridge's two great towers. Some sixty cars and trucks plummeted with the mass of steel and concrete into the near-freezing Ohio River some eighty feet below.

"There isn't any bridge anymore," one stunned observer said. "The whole bridge is in the river." Meanwhile, people could be heard screaming for help from the nightmarish tangle of wreckage out in the water. Because darkness came soon after the collapse, rescue workers had trouble finding survivors in the swift-moving river, and forty-six persons died as a result of the disaster.

Soon afterward, investigators speculated the collapse had been caused either by the overloading of the forty-year-old bridge or by the use of bridge supports fashioned from double steel eyebars instead of the standard woven steel cables.

Evidently some bridges were not built to be driven over.

1968: Tet Offensive in the Vietnam War. Communist guerrillas shattered a truce arranged for the Vietnamese New Year—Tet—by launching coordinated surprise attacks on targets in over one hundred cities from the Mekong Delta to the South Vietnamese highlands. At least some of the guerrillas infiltrated the cities before the attack, smuggling in arms and ammunition as they did so.

In Saigon, guerrillas waited until nighttime to attack various targets in the city, creating widespread confusion and disarray among the U.S. and South Vietnamese forces before being defeated. Communists briefly captured part of the American embassy, failed in an attempt to take the presidential palace, attacked Saigon Airport, and seized a Saigon radio station. Elsewhere, the Vietcong scored their greatest victory in the offensive by capturing the city of Hue, which they held until late February.

While Vietcong casualties were put at twenty times those of U.S. and South Vietnamese troops, the offensive nevertheless was a major psychological victory for them and demonstrated that they posed a continuing military threat.

This fifth column worked very well back in the United States as well, for President Lyndon Johnson soon after announced that he would not be a candidate for reelection.

1968: The My Lai Massacre. Some seventy U.S. infantry troops stormed the tiny Vietnamese village of My Lai on March 16 with orders to wipe out the hamlet. My Lai, located 235 miles northeast of Saigon, was a Vietcong stronghold, and its villagers reportedly had planted land mines and other booby traps to kill U.S. troops.

U.S. forces began shelling the village just after dawn. Then a battalion led by Lieutenant William Calley moved in and went from hut to hut, torching and dynamiting everything in sight. As the villagers tried to flee, the troops mowed them down with M-16 rifle fire. Within twenty minutes the troops had massacred some 450 men, women, and children, burned all the huts, and killed all the livestock. Virtually the only survivors were those who had been buried under the bodies of the dead. Calley was later sentenced to twenty years at hard labor following a court-martial.

Just following orders, sir.

1968: King Assassination. "It really doesn't matter what happens now," said the Nobel Prize-winning civil rights leader Martin Luther King, Jr., the night before his assassination. "I've been to the mountaintop. . . . So I'm happy tonight. I'm not fearing any man."

Death threats followed the thirty-nine-year-old King to Memphis, Tennessee, as he arrived on April 3 to direct a nonviolent resistance movement by thirteen hundred striking sanitation workers. The two-month-old strike had led to rioting two weeks before, and King was determined to keep the demonstrations nonviolent. The civil rights leader was also preoccupied with plans for a massive camp-in in Washington later in the month to "channelize the smoldering rage of the Negro and white poor."

"We've got some difficult days ahead," he said. "Like anybody, I would like to live a long life. . . . But I'm not concerned about that now. I just want to do God's will. And He's allowed me to go up to the mountain . . . and I've seen the promised land."

At 6:00 P.M. the next evening, King stood on the second-story balcony of his room at the Lorraine Motel, talking with colleagues Jesse Jackson and Ralph Abernathy, Jr. He asked a musician who was there to sing "Precious Lord, Take My Hand" at a rally that evening. Then, as King leaned over the railing to speak to Jackson in the parking lot below, a rifle shot rang out from the bathroom window of a rooming house across from the motel.

One witness described the shot as "a tremendous blast that sounded like a bomb." The bullet tore through the right side of King's neck, penetrating his spinal cord and hurling him back against the wall. Blood poured from King's jaw. As King's colleagues pressed towels to his wound, some thirty-five policemen in the area rushed to the scene. Meanwhile, the assassin, James Earl Ray, escaped from the rooming house, leaving his high-powered rifle behind.

Emergency surgery failed to save King. Within an hour, the man who had led the U.S. civil rights movement, preaching nonviolence and peaceful coexistence, lay dead in a Memphis hospital.

The assassination stunned the black community and the nation as a whole. President Lyndon Johnson appealed to Americans to "reject the blind violence that has struck Dr. King, who lived by nonviolence." But rage over King's assassination erupted into rioting by blacks in over 125 cities. Hardest hit were Washington, Chicago, Baltimore, and Kansas City, Missouri. More than fifty thousand troops were sent out to control the disturbances. Forty-six people were killed, and at least twenty-six hundred were injured. Property damage from looting, arson, and vandalism was estimated at forty-five million dollars.

Meanwhile, police identified Ray, a forty-year-old white man who was an escaped convict, as the assassin. Ray had apparently followed King and taken a room situated to give him a clear shot at the door to King's room. Ray was later caught, convicted, and sentenced to ninety-nine years in prison.

Violence begets violence, amid a nonviolent movement.

1968: U.S. Submarine *Scorpion* Lost. The last message from the U.S. submarine *Scorpion* was a brief account of location and speed received on May 21. The 3,075-ton nuclear-powered attack submarine was homeward bound to Norfolk, Virginia, after three months in the Mediterranean, and had been told to observe radio silence during the return voyage.

Tragedy struck shortly after *Scorpion* sent her message. Faulty pipe joints apparently began leaking badly, and that, along with an inadequate deballasting system, caused the 252-foot submarine to start sinking uncontrollably in the deep waters off the Azores. As she drifted downward, enormous water pressure began to build up, pushing against her hull until finally, at a depth of two thousand feet, it crushed the *Scorpion* like an egg. All ninety-nine officers and men on board were killed instantly.

Despite a massive search by the U.S. Navy, the wreckage was not located until six months after the sub was reported missing. Remains of the *Scorpion* were finally located in ten thousand feet of water by a hi-tech search ship using submersible cameras.

1968: Iranian Earthquake Kills Twelve Thousand. The normally peaceful lives of farmers in the agricultural areas of northeastern and eastern Iran were shattered on August 31 by an earthquake measuring 7.8 on the Richter scale. The violent shaking lasted for about four minutes, and was felt over a wide area of the sparsely inhabited countryside.

When the quake struck, the farmers' mud-brick huts collapsed easily, trapping thousands of villagers in the rubble of their own homes. Many villages were completely obliterated. Men and women, weeping as they dug through the rubble with their bare hands, searched for friends and loved ones. In addition to the twelve thousand killed, the earthquake injured thousands, and left more than one hundred thousand homeless.

1969: Venezuelan Plane Crashes. The fiery crash of a Venezuelan Air Lines DC-9 into a populous suburb of Maracaibo, Venezuela, on March 16 killed 155 people, making it the worst airline disaster up to that time.

The flight was en route from Caracas, Venezuela, to Miami, Florida, with a stopover in Maracaibo. During the takeoff from Maracaibo, the plane unexpectedly lost altitude, hit a high-tension wire, hurtled into the suburban neighborhood, then exploded into flames as it tore through the trees, cars, buses, and homes in its path. A family of five sitting at the dinner table was instantly crushed when the plane hit their home. Meanwhile, burning fuel was spread over a five-block area, setting fire to about twenty other houses. All eighty-four passengers and crewmen aboard the plane were killed, along with seventy-one victims on the ground.

1969: Bloody Cult Murders. Late on Friday evening, August 8, intruders cut the telephone line outside film director Roman Polanski's secluded mansion in Beverly Hills, California. Inside the house were Polanski's twenty-six-year-old pregnant wife, actress Sharon Tate, hairdresser Jay Sebring, movie director Voyteck Freykowski, and coffee heiress Abigail Folger. Minutes later they became the victims in a bizarre murder orgy involving four members of a hippie drug cult.

Once inside the house, the killers stripped Ms. Tate down to her panties and bra, and put a hood over Sebring's head. One end of a nylon rope was tied around Tate's neck, the other end around Sebring's neck, and the middle looped over a beam in the ceiling. The two victims were found in this position next morning, stabbed to death. Freykowski and Folger were killed outside on the lawn, apparently while trying to escape. A fifth victim, eighteen-year-old Stephen Parent, was stabbed at the wheel of his car in the driveway. Murderers wrote the word "Pig" with the victims' blood on the door of the house.

The cult struck again the following night, this time brutally killing supermarket chain owner Leo LaBianca and his wife in their home near the Tate mansion.

Finally, in December, police arrested a hippie cult leader named Charles Manson and three women who were members of his group. All were later convicted of the crimes.

This was one of the more maniacal crimes of our time. It also gave hippies a bad name.

1969: Hurricane Camille. One of the South's most devastating hurricanes, Camille, slammed into Gulfport, Mississippi, on August 17. Packing winds up to two hundred miles per hour, Camille uprooted trees, knocked over houses, and dumped torrential rains onto the stricken areas. After sweeping north to Hattiesburg, Mississippi, Camille veered east and wreaked havoc on Alabama.

By the next day, August 18, the storm had reached Virginia, where flash floods and high winds killed sixty-seven people. Meanwhile, the storm's departure did not end troubles in Mississippi: Thousands of poisonous cottonmouth snakes headed to high ground during the flooding and infested people's yards and homes.

Camille's two-day spree of destruction killed 258 people and caused an estimated $1.5 billion in damages. These storms are getting more and more expensive.

1970: Peruvian Earthquake. The calm of a leisurely Sunday afternoon on May 31 suddenly vanished when a quake measuring 7.75 on the Richter scale struck northern Peru. While Peru's capital of Lima was largely spared, destruction elsewhere in the north occurred on a massive scale.

Chimbote, a coastal city of eighty thousand, was almost completely destroyed; 80 percent of its buildings crashed to the ground during the quake. One survivor there looked out on a sea so agitated, it "seemed to be boiling." Meanwhile, in the Andes north of Lima, the tremors released enormous landslides of water, rock, and mud.

On Mount Huascaran, an avalanche of ice and rock crashed into a lake, spawning a new avalanche of mud and rock that then poured down over the resort town of Yungay. The city was so completely buried that only the tops of palm trees and a statue of Jesus could be seen. The caption of a newspaper photograph of the buried city read: "Yungay was here."

Incredibly, all but some three thousand of the city's forty-one thousand residents were killed in the seconds it took the avalanche to sweep through the city. A survivor radioing for help said, "We had been terrified by the quake, and most of us were praying in the streets amid the wreckage of the city when we heard the infernal thunder of the *huayco* [avalanche] coming down from Huascaran. For God's sake, send us help. We have no medicine, no food. . . . All night the women have cried and prayed; some men were cursing, raising their fists to heaven." Four days later, some twenty-five hundred survivors from Yungay were rescued from a mountaintop cemetery where they had been stranded by the torrent of mud.

Across northern Peru, great mud slides broke dams, flooding whole valleys and wiping towns completely off the map. Seemingly, whatever the earthquake itself missed destroying, the landslides completed. Roads were flooded or buried in mud and debris, and those living in mountainous areas were left completely isolated.

It was the earthquake that leveled the resort town of Huaras, 180 miles north of Lima. About 95 percent of the houses collapsed during the quake, and one witness there reported, "Survivors wander around in a daze, like sleepwalkers, looking for food and water. Many children were choked to death by the dust that hung over the city. All we have is thirst, hunger, the stench of dead bodies, and despair." Finally survivors had to resort to throwing the dead, wrapped in blankets or sheets of newspaper, into mass graves, because coffins were in short supply.

Throughout the earthquake-ravaged area, the count of the dead rose day by day as new victims were located in the rubble. Altogether, between fifty thousand and seventy thousand are believed to have died, while another one hundred thousand were injured and eight hundred thousand left homeless. At least five thousand children were orphaned in the worst disaster recorded in the history of Peru, a nation plagued by an average of eight major earthquakes each century.

1970: Yarra River Bridge Collapses. One of the world's longest bridges, spanning the Yarra River near Melbourne, Australia, suddenly collapsed while still under construction on October 15, killing thirty-five men working on the structure. Apparently a 367-foot box-girder span on the uncompleted west side of the bridge gave way, causing the collapse.

1970: French Dance Hall Fire. Some 165 patrons were enjoying the music of a rock band at 1:45 A.M. on November 1 when fire suddenly turned the Cinq Sept dance hall in Saint-Laurent-Du-Pont into a death trap. Apparently started when a youth tossed a cigarette in jest, the blaze spread rapidly among the dance hall's plastic and paper decorations. A few lucky patrons managed to escape, but most were trapped behind emergency exits that had been padlocked and boarded up to insure that everyone paid admission. One exit was torn open from the outside, and some panicked survivors, their clothes on fire, were pulled from the tangled mass of people jamming the doorway. Rescue workers later discovered piles of victims' bodies pressed against other blocked exits. The death toll eventually reached 144.

Another shining example of locked emergency exits, and for what greedy reason?

1970: Hundreds of Thousands Die in East Pakistan Cyclone. A deadly cyclone and fifty-foot tidal wave struck the unprepared Ganges River Delta area of East Pakistan (now Bangladesh) on the evening of November 12, in one of the worst disasters of modern times.

Although the storm had been predicted, its intensity and potential danger had not been reported. As a result, few villagers left coastal areas, thinking the storm would be no worse than one that had hit the previous month. That turned out to be a fatal error in judgment, particularly for those living on the numerous offshore islands that rise barely twenty feet above sea level.

Packing winds of 150 miles per hour, the storm swept in from the Bay of Bengal, ripping apart houses and uprooting trees on numerous small offshore islands and in coastal mainland areas. Many places were flooded under as much as twenty feet of water for eight hours. Survivors reported clinging to the tops of trees or to rooftops, holding on desperately for hours in the terrible wind and rain while waiting for the water to recede.

Then the winds stiffened and the storm hit the mainland. One survivor recalled hearing a great roar before looking out into the black sky. All he could see was a distant glow that seemed to come closer and closer. It was the crest of the giant tidal wave that moments later crashed over the heavily populated coastal islands, washing away most of the buildings and inhabitants on them. In fact, most of the storm victims were either drowned by the incoming wave or washed out to sea when it retreated. The offshore islands were devastated; more than twenty thousand people were lost on just one of them. On another, the storm swept away an eighteen-foot-high seawall built to protect against just such a disaster.

The staggering death toll could only be approximated—somewhere between three hundred thousand and five hundred thousand people were killed. After the storm, bodies clogged rivers and coastal areas. One villager, attempting with great difficulty to cross a river in his small boat, rescued two young girls from among the hordes of floating dead. Elsewhere, as many as five thousand corpses were buried at a time in some mass graves. When there were just too many dead to bury, villagers with bamboo poles tried pushing the bodies out to sea. Those bodies washing back onto the beaches were simply pushed out again.

Vultures gorged themselves on the rotting flesh of humans and livestock littering the landscape, and water in the Ganges Delta rice paddies reportedly turned bloodred. Soon after the storm, cholera and typhoid epidemics spread rapidly among the survivors, adding still more deaths to the toll.

Communications with many of the worst-hit areas, including

more than one hundred small offshore islands, were completely cut off for several days, making relief efforts all but impossible.

1971: Mount Etna in Sicily Erupts. Etna's eleventh eruption during the twentieth century lasted from April 5 to June 9, opening a half-mile-long crack in the volcano's side. The resulting lava stream wiped out farms and vineyards on Etna's lower slopes, but narrowly missed destroying two villages in its path.

Etna keeps right on ticking.

1971: Soviet Space Disaster. After spending more than three weeks in space, Soviet cosmonauts Georgi Dobrovolsky, Vladimir Volkov, and Viktor Patsayev were near their goal of setting a new space endurance record. Only the return journey to earth remained, and on June 29 they separated their *Soyuz 11* spacecraft from the Salyut space station. Everything appeared to be proceeding normally, and the cosmonauts broke contact at the prearranged time during reentry. Sometime after that, however, one of the spacecraft's seals apparently failed, and pressure inside the *Soyuz 11* dropped suddenly. While the spacecraft continued with a seemingly normal reentry, the pressure drop allowed air bubbles to form in the cosmonauts' bloodstreams—a deadly condition called "caisson disease." When the unsuspecting Soviet recovery crew opened the capsule a short time later, they were shocked to find all three cosmonauts had died.

Going where no man has gone before is not the safest occupation. More to come.

1971: North Vietnam Floods. Heavy rains caused severe flooding in North Vietnam in late August, killing over one hundred thousand people. At Hanoi, dikes were reported holding back swollen rivers that were over thirty feet above street level.

1971: Overly Realistic Japanese Landslide Experiment. Every year naturally occurring landslides kill people in Japan, and on November 11 scientists from Japan's Agency of Science and Technology hoped to learn more about these disasters by creating one artificially. They chose a steep, sixty-foot-high hill near the city of Kawasaki and, with about twenty-five scientists and journalists gathered at a safe distance, began wetting down the hillside with fire hoses to mimic the effects of a severe rainstorm. Suddenly the hillside gave way in a far greater avalanche than the scientists had expected, and a nine-foot-deep torrent of mud and boulders swept downward to engulf the shocked onlookers. Fifteen of them, including four government scientists, were killed, and nine others injured. A TV cameraman in the group filmed the entire incident.

No doubt shown later on Japan's "Funniest Home Videos."

1971: Korean Hotel Fire. Fire broke out in a second-floor coffee shop at the Taeyonkak Hotel in Seoul, South Korea, on Christmas Day and killed 162 people—over half the 296 people in the hotel. The twenty-two-story building was just two years old, though certain basic fire safety precautions were lacking.

1972: Logan County, West Virginia, Flood. On February 26, after three days of torrential rainstorms, a coal mine slag heap serving as a dam in Logan County, West Virginia, suddenly burst and sent a destructive wall of water rushing through the narrow, winding valley below. Several small coal-mining towns were flooded by the rampaging waters, which washed out six major bridges and completely destroyed the towns of Lorado and Lundale. Witnesses on high ground described a wall of water twenty feet high slamming houses into each other and carrying them away. Water briefly rose up to the tops of telephone poles in places and also cut roads throughout the area. One of the worst floods in West Virginia history, the disaster claimed 107 lives.

Coal mine slag heaps are very unreliable.

1972: Iran Goes from Drought to Blizzard. A four-year drought in Iran ended in early February, but not in the way most people wanted. An incredible week-long blizzard dumped between ten and twenty-six feet of snow over much of the country, creating massive drifts and making rescue efforts difficult or even impossible in certain rural areas.

The relentless storm overwhelmed one southern Iranian village with twenty-six-foot drifts, which left four thousand people trapped in their homes helplessly awaiting rescue. Elsewhere, a party of mountain climbers was apparently caught unprepared and disappeared near Teheran, as did the five-member search party that went to its rescue. Of the thousands missing at the height of the storm, an estimated one thousand people died.

1972: Rhodesian Coal Mine Explosion. An explosion of unknown origins ripped through one of three shafts at the Wankie Colliery in northwestern Rhodesia (now Zimbabwe) on June 6, trapping hundreds of miners below ground. Heavy machinery was flung to the surface by the powerful blast, and a cable car flew through the air as if shot from a cannon. Although one seriously injured man and the bodies of three others were found at the bottom of a three-hundred-foot shaft, cave-ins caused by the explosion trapped the other 464 miners in tunnels. Rescue workers wearing oxygen masks dug feverishly through the debris in an attempt to reach trapped miners before it was too late, but only thirty-seven of the men were brought out alive.

By the end of the twenty-second century, our coal resources will be depleted and we won't have these mine disasters anymore.

1972: Hurricane Agnes Ravages East Coast. From June 21 to 26, Hurricane Agnes swept northward up the U.S. East Coast from Florida all the way to New York, collapsing houses and unleashing torrents of rain. About 116,000 houses were destroyed by the storm, and 118 people were killed.

1972: Managua, Nicaragua, Earthquake. At 11:10 P.M. on December 23, a series of destructive earthquakes started rocking the capital city of Managua, Nicaragua, in which some 374,000 people lived. Registering a maximum of 6.25 on the Richter scale, the quakes demolished the Presidential Palace, churches, hotels, and other large buildings, ruptured water mains, and started fires that soon destroyed over 70 percent of the city.

Thousands of victims were killed by collapsing buildings or were burned to death by the fires. The reclusive American billionaire Howard Hughes, lodged in a Managua hotel during the earthquake, escaped unharmed, however. Two days after the disaster, the bodies of the dead remained trapped under the rubble, and government officials cut off food supplies in an effort to force the evacuation of the entire city before disease claimed even more lives. An estimated ten thousand people died in the earthquake and fires.

1973: Eruption on Heimaey Island, Iceland. Dormant for some five thousand years, the island's volcano began spewing ash and lava on January 23. Fortunately, the fifty-two hundred residents of this tiny island were safely evacuated in hours. Over the next months, however, hundreds of homes and other buildings were set afire by falling "lava bombs" or were crushed under tons of ash. To keep lava from destroying Heimaey's valuable harbor, workers cooled lava with jets of seawater. This helped control the flow until eruptions ceased in July. But another plan, using explosive charges on lava streaming into the harbor, could have ended tragically. Experts realized just in time that explosives might mix large amounts of hot lava and cold seawater too quickly. Such rapid mixing could have caused a disastrous two- to four-megaton explosion.

Thoughtful planning on someone's part.

1973: Staten Island Gas Storage Tank Explodes. The world's largest liquefied natural gas storage tank, located on Staten Island, New York, exploded with a tremendous blast about 1:00 P.M. on February 10. Forty workers were killed when the eleven-story-high, 272-foot-diameter tank blew up, shooting flames hundreds of feet into the air.

1973: Mississippi River Floods. In April, floodwaters swelled the Mississippi River to its highest level since 1844. From northern Illinois to the Louisiana delta, some seven million acres of land lay underwater as the river nearly doubled its normal rate of flow.

Fear of still more damage to homes and property rose with the floodwaters, as they tested the strength of those levees still standing. Convicts, students, servicemen, and civilian volunteers worked side by side sandbagging levees. Still, important levees crumbled at West Alton, Missouri, where the Missouri and Mississippi Rivers converge. A huge lake then enveloped Alton, driving five hundred people from their homes. Meanwhile, water nine feet above flood stage forced hundreds to evacuate in Saint Louis. As the levee weakened in the town of Montz, Louisiana, thirty-six families were evacuated while the Army Corps of Engineers desperately constructed a new levee.

The greatest concern was downriver in New Orleans, where ships on the Mississippi floated on floodwaters high above the roads at the base of levees. Raging waters made ships hard to control, and if one of them rammed a levee, the entire city might be inundated. The danger of just such a disaster loomed for seventy-seven days until the waters of the Mississippi finally began to recede.

1973–1974: The Zebra Killings. The random pattern of the "Zebra" murders (named for a special police radio channel designated Zebra) terrorized the white community in San Francisco, California, between October 1973 and April 1974. Police had little to go on in the racially motivated slayings by unknown black assailants, who by April had killed twelve whites and wounded six others.

The break in the case came on April 27, 1974, when San Francisco Mayor Joseph Alioto met with an unidentified informant in the mayor's office. The following Wednesday, one hundred heavily armed police arrested seven black men, three of whom—Manuel Moors, J. C. Simon, and Larry C. Green—were indicted for the random shootings.

1974: Turkish Airline Crash. Moments after a Turkish Airlines DC-10 took off from Paris on March 3, witnesses heard an explosion and saw debris falling from the jet. Though they had no way of knowing it at the time, a rear cargo door had broken open at an altitude of 12,500 feet, causing explosive depressurization of the plane.

The stricken DC-10 jet crashed into a forest twenty-six miles north of Paris, and as it plummeted toward earth, debris and bodies of six passengers fell from the plane. The impact of crashing into the ground at an estimated 475 miles per hour completely demolished the plane. Officials later found wreckage strewn all over the forest crash site, and clothing, shoes, bits of paper, pieces of the plane seats, and other debris hanging from the trees.

All 346 passengers and crew died in the crash.

1974: Tornado Alley. A deadly storm system spawned over 148 tornadoes in the U.S. South and Midwest from April 3 to 4, killing 315 people. The death toll was highest in Kentucky, Indiana, and Ohio, though tornadoes hit in thirteen different states. Half the town of Xenia, Ohio, was demolished.

1974: Hurricane Fifi. About five thousand people were killed when Hurricane Fifi rampaged along the coastal areas of Honduras from September 19 to 20. The storm wrecked many houses and caused widespread flooding, leaving some sixty thousand people homeless.

1975: London Subway Crashes. It was a typical morning rush hour at 8:46 A.M. on February 28 as a six-car train packed with commuters pulled into its final stop at London's Moorgate station. But inexplicably the train accelerated as it neared the end of the tunnel, smashing through a protective barrier and crashing into the wall.

The first fifteen seats in the front car were compressed into just a two-foot mass of mutilated metal. The second and third cars jumped track and were smashed into a twisted wreckage, the heavy wheels of one car having ripped through the car in front to crush the passengers.

People in the rear of the train were hurled to the floor and smashed against seats. In the pitch-black tunnel, injured and panicked survivors screamed for help. Finally rescuers reached the train and began leading out the injured who had been at the back of the train. Then began the horrible task of cutting through the wreckage to the bodies in the first car. One woman the rescuers found was still conscious, but they had to amputate her foot in order to get her out. Forty-one commuters died in the crash that morning. For which the railway no doubt apologized profusely.

1975: Vietnam Orphans Plane Disaster. After years of warfare in Vietnam, a U.S. government plan to evacuate two thousand Vietnamese orphans to the United States got under way just weeks before South Vietnam's final surrender. On April 4 the first flight, a U.S. Air Force C-5A transport, took off from Saigon with 243 orphans, 46 attendants, and 16 crewmen aboard. Soon after takeoff, however, a rear door blew out and struck the tail, damaging the plane's steering system. Struggling to control the big four-engine plane, the pilot managed to turn back toward Saigon and then somehow steered clear of populated areas before crash-landing in a rice paddy. The impact instantly crushed 50 orphans strapped into the cargo hold. Other victims, some only eight months old, were found buried in the rice paddy's muddy bottom. Ultimately, bodies of 172 orphans, attendants, and plane crewmen were pulled from the wreck. Another "rear door" accident.

1976: Khmer Rouge Commits Atrocities in Cambodia. On a warm evening in September, a young Cambodian boy sat down to eat a meager dinner with his family. They all lived together in a tiny, thatch-roofed hut, grandparents, mother and father, he and his brother. Suddenly bullets spit through the thin wooden front door, striking the elderly grandmother in the face and neck and killing her instantly. She fell forward, her face against the table. The boys' father was struck in the shoulder and chest; he fell moaning onto the dirt floor.

The boys sprang back from the table in fright just as a huge boot kicked through what remained of the door, and three soldiers entered the room. The family knew all too well that the intruders were Khmer Rouge, the hated and feared communist guerrillas who had taken over their country and were massacring thousands of Cambodian villagers. While the young boys watched, the soldiers savagely kicked their injured father to death, shot their grandfather through the eyes with their machine guns, and dragged their sobbing mother away as she begged to remain with her children. They never saw her again.

A bloody five-year civil war had by 1975 taken the lives of some seven hundred thousand Cambodian civilians, roughly a tenth of the nation's population. More than 3.4 million people had been left homeless. Then, after Khmer Rouge insurgents finally toppled the Lon Nol regime, communist leader Pol Pot declared himself prime minister in 1976.

Under his ruthless leadership, there began widespread executions which killed hundreds of thousands more of his countrymen. He called it a purge, claiming that he was ridding the nation of those still loyal to the Lon Nol government. But observers called it a bloodbath, the wholesale slaughter which began with army officers, government officials, and their wives, but then seemed to spread randomly to villagers, farmers, even elderly peasants and children.

But Pol Pot did not stop there. He ruthlessly ordered the cities evacuated, breaking up families and putting everyone to work at hard labor in prisonlike communes in the countryside. Communications with neighboring countries were broken off, and foreigners were told to leave the nation at once.

Those who got out of Cambodia had chilling stories to tell. They spoke of victims whose throats were slit, of others who were repeatedly bashed on the head with hoes and shovels, of people, many of them children, buried alive in the muddy Cambodian swamps. "They killed a person just like killing an ant," cried one woman as she described the deaths of her husband and four children at the hands of unsmiling, robotlike Khmer Rouge soldiers.

Throughout the countryside, the savage Khmer Rouge overseers forced men, women, and children to labor in the fields from dawn until well after dark. Those who were sick or malnourished relied on untrained medics, who reportedly "treated cholera with Pepsi-Cola and typhoid with coconut milk." Thin, watery gruel was the only meal of the day. Dancing was not allowed, nor were reading, singing, or discussing politics. Those who broke the Khmer Rouge rules faced immediate execution, usually by being clubbed to death with pick handles. Others were buried to their necks in the soft soil and then beaten to death. The heads of the dead were chopped off and jammed onto pointed stakes, warnings to the living of the harsh penalty for disobedience.

Pol Pot's disposition toward violence brought his nation into serious border fighting with Vietnamese communists in 1978. The Vietnamese finally invaded Cambodia and, by 1979, had ousted Pol Pot's government, installing their own Vietnamese-backed regime in its place. By this time, though, the country had already been cruelly decimated. An estimated three million Cambodians were brutally slaughtered or died of malnutrition and disease during the bloody five years of Khmer Rouge rule.

Pol Pot never had a course titled "Civil Rights and Liberties." He ranks right up there with Genghis, Stalin, and Ivan.

1976: Guatemalan Earthquake. Around 3:00 A.M. on February 4, a powerful earthquake toppled simple adobe homes and large buildings alike into the streets of Guatemala City, Guatemala. The powerful earthquake, registering 7.5 on the Richter scale, brought down the city's old Hotel Continental and other large buildings in the downtown area, but Guatemala's extensive slum section was probably hardest hit. Many victims were crushed or buried alive when their poorly constructed adobe homes caved in on them.

Meanwhile, the quake created a swath of destruction fifty miles wide across this Central American nation. Many rural towns and villages were leveled, while avalanches set off by the quake and its many aftershocks blocked roads for days. In one remote town, survivors buried the dead by the truckload and resorted to eating rats until help finally arrived. The disaster claimed an estimated twenty-three thousand lives.

Mother Nature has been picking on Central America lately.

1976: Chemical Explosion at Seveso, Italy. A chemical mixture used in production of a powerful herbicide exploded at the ICMESA chemical plant near Milan, Italy, on July 10. The explosion blasted away a safety valve, releasing a massive, cone-shaped cloud of chemicals containing dioxin, one of the most toxic substances in existence.

The cloud drifted over the town of Seveso, contaminating both farmland and houses with dioxin. Some six thousand residents suffered direct exposure to the deadly chemical. Within days, thousands of birds dropped dead from the sky, small animals died, and the people of Seveso began to suffer from vomiting, diarrhea, headaches, dizziness, and sores on their skin.

But it was not until two weeks after the explosion that plant officials called for evacuation of the contaminated areas. No decontamination was possible, and the potential long-term effects of the poisoning include leukemia, liver and kidney damage, heart problems, skin diseases, and nervous disorders.

We wage chemical warfare on ourselves.

1976: Tangshan Earthquake. One of the most severe earthquakes in history struck the heavily populated coal-mining city of Tangshan, China, on July 28. The quake completely destroyed the city, located about one hundred miles northeast of Beijing, and exacted a staggering death toll. Over 240,000 people were killed, and some estimates run as high as 750,000.

At 3:42 A.M. the night sky over Tangshan was illuminated by strange red and white lights, probably caused by the impending earthquake. Then, with no other warning, there came a rumbling "muffled explosion like thunder" and violent shocks measuring 8.2 on the Richter scale. Victims suddenly found themselves thrown against walls and ceilings of their homes. Thousands of houses crumbled instantly, roofs caved in, and chimneys toppled. Bridges fell and a railroad train was swallowed up whole. Nothing was spared. Below ground, the honey-comb of coal mine shafts running underneath Tangshan caved-in, burying alive an estimated twelve thousand miners then at work on the night shift.

The terrible upheavals lasted a full two minutes. As one survivor recalled, "It was like an ocean, an ocean, everything moving." Afterward, virtually no building was left standing. Twenty square miles of city, where 1.6 million people once lived, was reduced to a rubble-strewn wasteland.

One hundred miles away in Beijing, the quake was less severe, but nevertheless many older buildings collapsed. Beijing's six million residents were driven out into the streets by the earthquake. Danger of aftershocks kept them from returning to their homes, and Beijing became a city of makeshift tents and lean-tos fashioned from plastic tablecloths and cotton bed sheets.

China's official press agency waited a full day before announcing the massive earthquake, citing only "great losses to people's lives and property." Many details were never released by Chinese officials, who, some outside observers felt, were embarrassed by their failure to predict the quake. The Chinese had, in recent years, claimed great advances in earthquake detection.

The earthquake's epicenter was at Tangshan, which was located atop one of northern China's numerous fault zones. Inactive for many years, the Tangshan area had been largely ignored by experts. In just two minutes, though, the fault zone provided a grim reminder of its presence. Scientists later concluded that this massive earthquake was related to several major earthquakes that occurred in 1976 along an arc stretching from Italy, through parts of the Soviet Union, and southward to the Pacific Ocean.

Among the mysteries surrounding the quake is how Chinese officials were able to issue an advance warning for a second powerful earthquake that hit Tangshan sixteen hours after the first. This one measured 7.4 on the Richter scale and caused more widespread destruction.

The threat of aftershocks, which continued to jolt the region long after the two big quakes, kept millions of Chinese living outside in makeshift shelters for up to sixteen days. Torrential rains that followed the earthquakes only added to the survivors' misery. Meanwhile, in keeping with their reluctance to disclose details about the tragedy, Chinese officials refused all offers of international aid.

In a closed society, nothing ever goes wrong. So why would they need help?

1976: Legionnaires' Disease Outbreak at Philadelphia. In July some seventy people attending a state convention of the American Legion at Philadelphia, Pennsylvania, became sick with a strange respiratory disease soon after returning home. Twenty people eventually died of the disease, which thereafter was popularly known as Legionnaires' disease.

1977–1980: Love Canal. Some twenty thousand tons of toxic substances were buried in leaky drums underneath an elementary school in the Love Canal section of Niagara Falls, New York. A chemical corporation had disposed of the highly toxic waste over a period of twenty-five years. Then, when the canal was filled in, the school was constructed above it. In the 1970s, children reported seeing a gooey black substance oozing up out of the soil on playgrounds and the school baseball diamond.

Meanwhile, the Environmental Protection Agency determined in 1977 that the hazardous wastes at Love Canal were causing the area's unusually high rates of cancer, birth defects, chromosome damage, and miscarriages. One woman noted "It's really something around here now to have a normal baby that's healthy. . . ."

In 1978 the state of New York relocated some 227 families from the area. Other Love Canal residents were cautioned about the dangers associated with water contamination, and were urged not to eat vegetables grown in their gardens. They were warned that water seeping into basements could be producing hazardous vapors within their homes.

In 1980 President Jimmy Carter declared the Love Canal situation an emergency, making three to five million dollars in federal funds available to relocate families in the ten-block area surrounding the contaminated site.

Love conquers all.

1977: Double Disaster at Tenerife. A terrorist bomb, planted by a Canary Islands separatist group at the Grand Canary Island airport, diverted all air traffic to the Tenerife Island airport, Los Rodeos, on March 27. The diversion doubled the usual air traffic on Tenerife, one of the Canary Islands located off the coast of Morocco. Among the planes diverted to Tenerife were a KLM 747 and a Pan-American 747.

The chartered jumbo jets were filled with vacationing tourists: The 364 passengers aboard the Pan-American jet from Los Angeles were to board the *Golden Odyssey* for a twelve-day Mediterranean cruise; the KLM jet carried 14 crew members and 235 passengers, mostly Dutch tourists vacationing in the Canary Islands. But the passengers had no way of knowing that the narrow airstrip on the mountainous island of Tenerife had a reputation among pilots as a difficult place for landings and takeoffs. Meanwhile, dangers inherent in the heavy air traffic conditions were sharply increased by fog and rain. Vertical visibility was near zero, and horizontal visibility was only three hundred yards.

After several hours of waiting for takeoff, the KLM jet finally taxied to the end of the runway at 4:40 P.M. and turned around into the takeoff position. Meanwhile, the Pan-American jet taxied onto the runway. If all had gone according to plan, the Pan Am jet would have turned down a diagonal runway and into the line of jets waiting to take off. But before his plane had cleared the main runway, the Pan Am pilot saw headlights glaring through the fog. "At first we thought it was standing there at the end of the runway," he said. "Then we realized they were coming toward us."

At that moment the KLM flight was barreling down the runway, gathering speed for takeoff and heading straight for the Pan Am jet. It was too late for either pilot to do anything to avert the catastrophe in those last seconds. The Pan Am pilot tried to turn off the runway, though that only put the plane's fuselage directly into the path of the oncoming jumbo jet. Desperately he radioed, "We're still on the runway."

The KLM jet slammed into the side of the Pan Am 747, ripping the top off the grounded plane. Then it bounced wildly along the runway for six hundred yards before exploding, as one witness put it, "in a big ball of fire" with "tongues of flame leaping everywhere." All 249 passengers and crew died instantly.

On the Pan Am flight, 46 passengers barely had time to escape the burning wreck before the fuel tanks exploded. Some emerged from holes torn in the plane with all their clothing burned from their bodies. One witness described them as "walking singly, mechanically, without any sort of reaction, like puppets."

Moments later the wrecked Pan Am jet also blew up, a grim finale to the double disaster that incinerated the remains of 334 other victims. Altogether the collision took the lives of 583 people, making it the worst ever disaster in aviation history.

The terrorists seem to have made their point, after all.

1977: A Saturday Night of Death at a Kentucky Nightclub. Shortly before popular singer John Davidson was to begin his act at the Beverly Hills Supper Club on Saturday, May 18, a frantic busboy grabbed the microphone and announced that the club was on fire.

People in the huge nightclub, which had a capacity of five thousand and was located in Southgate, Kentucky, across the Ohio River from Cincinnati, Ohio, reacted in two completely different ways. Some fled for the exits in panic, while others remained seated exactly where they were. Some of those who panicked died in their haste to get out, while many who refused to believe the warning became trapped by the thick smoke and rapidly spreading flames. Singer John Davidson was among those who escaped.

In all, 164 people died in a tragedy that might have been averted had restaurant workers been more alert. The fire had actually started some two hours earlier with an overheated wire inside a wall, causing one room to become so hot that a wedding party had to be moved elsewhere in the club. Wedding guests assumed at the time that the air-conditioning system was faulty.

1978–1979: Revolution in Iran. The public demonstrations that rocked the major cities of Iran in 1978, and in which hundreds of people lost their lives, were orchestrated and encouraged by an Iranian exile living in France, Ruholla Khomeini, known also by his title of ayatollah ("sign of God"). Iranians demanded major changes in their government, not the least of which was the abdication of the shah.

In January 1979 the shah was finally forced to leave the country, and shortly thereafter the Ayatollah Khomeini took power and declared Iran an Islamic republic. Fundamentalist reforms included a return to the veiling of women and repeal of modern divorce laws. All Western influence was denounced, and many government officials, especially the Western-educated elite, fled the country. Then, in November 1979, Khomeini's followers took sixty-six U.S. citizens hostage, keeping forty-two of them prisoners until January of 1981, a move that quickly directed worldwide outrage and censure toward the government of Iran.

During these years of revolution and change, the Iranian economy suffered, and many in the country became increasingly disillusioned by the conditions in Iran. Brutal torture, arbitrary arrests, and executions were commonplace as the government sought to silence or punish those who spoke against its increasingly restrictive measures.

More mayhem and murder in the name of God. Times change, but men do not.

1978: Ted Bundy Brutally Murders Sorority Women. Early in the morning of January 15, thirty-one-year-old Theodore Bundy slipped through an unlocked door of the Chi Omega sorority house at Florida State University in Tallahassee. Bundy carried a club and wore a stocking over his head.

Moving from room to room, Bundy eventually attacked four women in their sleep. He first bludgeoned to death two roommates, beating them repeatedly with the club; he then raped and strangled to death a third woman; and then went on to strangle a fourth. Bundy returned from the sorority house to his home, less than a mile away, without being caught.

Bundy, a former law student who was believed responsible for killing at least thirty other women in a murder spree that had begun in 1974, committed one more horrible murder before being caught—the grisly mutilation and murder of a twelve-year-old Florida girl in 1978. When Bundy was finally put to death in 1989, a crowd of two hundred at the Florida State Prison cheered.

Just like they cheered at the guillotine executions during the French Revolution.

1978: Earthquake in Northeastern Iran. For ninety seconds on Saturday evening, September 16, the earth roared beneath Tabas, an ancient oasis town in northeastern Iran. This main shock, registering 7.7 on the Richter scale, hit without warning. Mosques, minarets, and mud-brick houses suddenly collapsed, turning the town into what one reporter described as a "flattened sand castle." Most of the town's thirteen thousand residents died in the quake, and bodies were everywhere in the rubble. Meanwhile, the scene of destruction was much the same at one hundred other villages in the surrounding countryside of northeastern Iran. In all, an estimated twenty-five thousand people died as a result of the quake.

1978: Jonestown Mass Suicide. The Reverend Jim Jones, who claimed to be a reincarnation of Lenin and Jesus, established the People's Temple in the jungles of Guyana as a socialist utopia. When he moved his ministry from California, Jones brought with him some eleven hundred deeply devoted—too devoted—followers to the jungle commune, but before long, reports of brainwashing, bondage, and other bizarre practices at the commune began to filter back to the United States. Finally California Representative Leo Ryan assembled a team and flew to Guyana to investigate, despite warnings that his life might be in danger.

Ryan and the others, including journalists, arrived in Jonestown on November 17, after Reverend Jones grudgingly granted permission for the visit. Ryan's tour proceeded smoothly until the next day, when he informed Jones that a family of six wanted to leave the commune. Jones became very angry, but finally allowed the family to go with Ryan. As Ryan and the others boarded two planes to leave, however, members of the People's Temple suddenly began shooting, killing Ryan and four others in cold blood.

Shortly afterward at Jonestown, Jones summoned his community over a loudspeaker to gather outside the central pavilion. It was a familiar scene for the members of the Temple. Approximately once a week Jones awoke everyone for a bizarre drill, during which the people acted out a mass suicide by poisoning—Jones's twisted idea of how to respond if his commune were threatened. But this time the drill was real. When Jones received news of the ambush and realized Guyanese police might invade Jonestown, he commanded, "Everyone has to die. If you love me as much as I love you, we must all die or be destroyed from the outside."

In the hot, humid tropical evening on November 18, hundreds lined up as large soup kettles were filled with a strawberry-flavored punch laced with tranquilizers and cyanide. Jones ordered mothers to bring their children to die first. Aides injected poison into the infants' mouths and then laid them on the ground to die. Parents spooned poison into their older children's mouths and then took it themselves as Jones wandered through the crowds, urging, "Hurry, hurry, hurry." Ushers led away those who had drunk the poison, helping them to lie facedown in rows on the ground. Within five minutes the victims suffered convulsions and died, blood streaming from their mouths and noses.

Families lined up together to receive the poison. Many joined hands or embraced as they fell. Only a few resisted; one woman pleaded to live, but the crowd shouted her down, saying she had no right to choose to live. Those who struggled were held down and given injections of cyanide. Guards armed with guns and bows and arrows supervised the mass suicide.

As the rows of bodies built up many layers deep, with faces frozen in contortions of pain, Jones lifted a gun to his head and fired. He fell out of his throne on the stage and slumped over dead.

Authorities arrived the next day to the sickening stench of more than nine hundred bodies decaying in the tropical heat. The count of the dead grew day by day, as authorities underestimated how many corpses were piled on top of one another. One witness said the corpses did not even resemble humans; instead they appeared to be "some sort of grotesque dolls."

Altogether, 910 lay dead, including 260 children, in the ruins of Jones's tropical utopia. "I understand love and hate," Jones had bragged to Ryan the day before. "They are very close."

You are right about the "hate" part, Jim.

1979: Three Mile Island Nuclear Accident. Audiences flocked to see the new hit movie *China Syndrome,* a fictional tale of a nuclear accident in which the near-meltdown of a power plant reactor threatened to destroy "an area the size of Pennsylvania." Meanwhile, on March 28, just twelve days after the film opened, a series of mechanical and human errors created an all too real nuclear accident at the Three Mile Island nuclear power plant in Pennsylvania.

The calamity began at 4:00 A.M. when flashing warning lights and blaring alarms suddenly confronted two control room workers in the Unit II reactor on Three Mile Island, located eleven miles south of Harrisburg, Pennsylvania. A water pump feeding the plant's steam-generating system had malfunctioned, and the two men desperately tried to regain control of the complex reactor systems before it was too late.

When the pump shut down, the reactor continued producing heat, raising pressure in the reactor's primary steam system until safety devices automatically shut the reactor down. While that stopped the nuclear reaction, the heated core continued to pump out residual heat, building up still more pressure in the primary steam system. That tripped open a safety valve in the hot water reserve tank for the primary system, thus draining off water and relieving the high-pressure problem. But the valve stuck open, and radioactive water soon began flooding onto the floor of the reactor containment building.

Next, as more water drained out of the primary system, the water level in the reactor itself became dangerously low. An emergency pumping system kicked on to keep the core from being exposed and thereby becoming overheated. But someone at the plant reportedly shut it off once the water level was restored. Of course, the safety valve was still stuck open, and apparently the water level dropped enough this time to expose the core. Residual heat in the core then apparently melted fuel rod jackets, allowing fuel pellets to further contaminate primary system water.

Thousands of gallons of highly radioactive hot water now flooded the containment building, while a dangerously explosive bubble of radioactive gases formed at the top of the reactor. Meanwhile, a sump pump unexpectedly turned on, draining some of the radioactive water from the containment building into an unsealed auxiliary building. When tanks there overflowed, radioactive steam escaped into the atmosphere through vents.

Over the course of the next few days, authorities tried to avoid public panic as they struggled to find out exactly what was going on inside the containment building. As the crisis intensified, the plant continued venting radioactive steam and water, though authorities insisted the radioactivity remained at a harmless level. An official of Metropolitan Edison, the plant's owner, declared, "We didn't injure anybody through this accident, we didn't seriously contaminate anybody, and we certainly didn't kill anybody."

Finally, on April 9, the Nuclear Regulatory Commission declared an end to the crisis. The reactor had been safely shut down, but the disaster, the worst nuclear accident in American history, shattered public confidence in nuclear power and brought the building of nuclear power plants in the United States to a virtual standstill. (See also: "1986. Chernobyl Nuclear Power Disaster.")

The operative word here is "seriously," as in ". . . we didn't seriously contaminate anybody. . . ."

1979: American Airlines Jet Crashes on Takeoff. At 3:00 P.M. on May 25, an American Airlines jet left the runway at Chicago's O'Hare International Airport. As it began to gain altitude, an engine fell off and the plane crashed to the ground after narrowly missing a gasoline refinery, killing all 271 people aboard. It was the worst U.S. air disaster up to that time.

1979–1981: Twenty-eight Murders in Atlanta. On July 28, 1979, the bodies of two black youths were found in separate wooded areas in southwest Atlanta, Georgia. One of the youths, fourteen years old, had been killed by a bullet; the other, just thirteen years old, had been strangled. Over the next year, 1980, ten more black youths were strangled to death and dumped in wooded areas.

Parents and young children in Atlanta's black community were terrorized, especially as the killings continued and their frequency increased in early 1981. Then, in the predawn hours of May 22, 1981, a policeman on stakeout under a bridge on the Chattahoochee River heard "a big, loud splash," while another policeman saw a car move away slowly from the bridge. Two days later, the body of the last victim—number twenty-eight—floated to the surface a mile downstream. The driver of the car, twenty-three-year-old Wayne B. Williams, was eventually tried and convicted of the last two murders.

1979: What Happened at Sverdlovsk? Unconfirmed reports reached the West of a terrible epidemic of anthrax in the Soviet city of Sverdlovsk in 1979, supposedly caused by an accident at what was believed to be a secret germ warfare research facility. Soviets steadfastly denied that accusation, but what appeared to be the real story—a public health disaster—was not released until 1986. Apparently cattle feed contaminated with anthrax spores had infected some livestock, which was later sold and consumed in Sverdlovsk. Worse yet, stray dogs had eaten scraps of the infected meat discarded in open garbage cans. In all, some ninety-six people in Sverdlovsk came down with anthrax, and sixty-four died. Soviets hurriedly decontaminated all areas possibly infected with the deadly disease and slaughtered stray dogs in the city.

1979: Hurricane David. Some two thousand people were killed between August 30 and September 7 when Hurricane David swept over the Dominican Republic, Puerto Rico, and southeastern United States.

1979: Hurricane Frederick Follows on the Heels of David. On September 12, just days after Hurricane David ripped through the Caribbean, Hurricane Frederick devastated Mobile, Alabama, causing some $2.3 billion in damages along the Alabama and Mississippi coast. Only five people were killed, however.

1979: Antarctic Sight-seeing Plane Crashes. What began as a routine one-day sight-seeing flight over Antarctica on November 28 ended in eerie frozen silence when the excursion plane crashed into the side of the snow-covered volcano Mount Erebus. The Air New Zealand DC-10 carried 257 passengers and crewmen on what had become a routine round-trip flight from New Zealand to Antarctica and back. All was proceeding normally, and as the pilot approached Mount Erebus, he radioed his intent to drop from ten thousand feet to two thousand feet in order to get a closer look at the active volcano. In the next few seconds, however, something went terribly wrong. There might have been a navigational error, or the plane might have become caught in the strong wind currents common around the volcano. Whatever the cause, the DC-10 slammed into the side of the volcano, and everyone aboard was killed.

One way or another, the volcanoes consume their victims.

1980: Deadly AIDS Epidemic Invades the United States. So far we do not know the origins of the HIV-1 virus which causes AIDS, or how it came about in the first place, but we do know how it is transmitted: mother to fetus, infected blood, and sexual contact.

In theory, it should be possible to find out when and where the first case occurred. In practice, this is quite difficult. AIDS, Acquired Immune Deficiency Syndrome, began to be noticed in the late 1970s and early 1980s in several widely separated locations including Belgium, France, Haiti, the United States, Zaire, and Zambia. Medical investigators in the United States traced it backward as far as 1959 to a blood sample, but were not able to go beyond that. Doctors suspect it may have existed unnoticed for many years.

The virus, HIV-1, attacks and weakens the cellular arm of the immune system, leaving the body susceptible to a number of fatal infections. Cancer, especially Kaposi's sarcoma, and pneumonia are leading causes of death among AIDS patients.

The Center for Disease Control in Atlanta, after extensive research, concluded that a homosexual airline steward, who died of cancer in 1984, was the individual responsible for bringing AIDS to North America. He reportedly infected partners in at least ten U.S. cities. Even though doctors warned him that he was infecting everyone he slept with, he stubbornly continued his sexual escapades.

Most AIDS victims in the United States are gay men and intravenous drug users. Less numerous are babies born to AIDS-infected mothers and cases caused by transfusions of blood tainted with the AIDS virus.

Although several medications have been identified to ease AIDS symptoms and prolong life, no cure has been discovered. By the end of 1991, according to the U.S. Institute of Medicine, some 175,000 people will have died of AIDS in the United States alone. It is estimated that ten million people worldwide have been infected.

1980: Harry Truman and Mount Saint Helens. The first sign of impending disaster was detected on March 27 when an ominous bulge developed on the north slope of Mount Saint Helens, a volcano located just forty miles north of Portland, Oregon, in the state of Washington. At about the same time, steam and ash began emitting from the volcano. Then, on the morning of May 18, the birds were uncannily silent.

Most residents of the area around the volcano had already been evacuated, but some few people still refused to leave, among them a crusty eighty-four-year-old named Harry Truman. Living with his seventeen cats in a home about five miles from the volcano, Truman announced his intentions to a nationwide television audience by saying, "No one knows more about this mountain than Harry, and it don't dare blow up on him." Meanwhile, some others—scientists, journalists, and the merely curious—had already filtered into the area, hoping to see an eruption.

At 8:39 A.M. on May 18, they did. Some 1,700 feet suddenly blasted off the top of the 9,677-foot volcano cone in an explosion that was felt one hundred miles away. A mile-wide crater opened on the top of the mountain as 1.5 cubic miles of broken rock shot twelve miles into the air, and a cloud of hot ash sprayed upward to an altitude of sixty thousand feet. The eruption was five hundred times more powerful than the atomic bomb dropped on Hiroshima, and the equal of the eruption that destroyed Pompeii in A.D. 79.

The thick cloud of ash filling the air darkened skies completely as far as eighty-five miles away. No lava was released, but ejected ash and hot gases melted snow, and massive mud slides poured down the mountain at fifty miles per hour. Meanwhile, the force of the blast flattened the surrounding forests, swatting down trees like so many matchsticks, and at least a dozen fires broke out.

A television cameraman on a ridge at the bottom of the mountain found himself flanked by floods of hot mud flowing on either side of him. "I am walking toward the only light I can see," he said while recording impressions of his frightening situation. "I can hear the mountain rumble. At this very moment, I have to say: 'Honest to God, I believe I am dead.' The ash burns my eyes. . . . Ash is coming down on me heavily. It's either dark or I am dead." Ten hours passed before he was rescued by a helicopter.

A group of campers thirty miles from the mountain were cooking breakfast when they heard the eruption. Suddenly trees crashed down and hot ash and boulders rained down around them. Having survived that, they walked through fifteen miles of steaming hot desert, barely able to breathe in the ash-filled air.

"The sky turned as black as I've ever seen," another witness said. "Ash and pumice fell on us like black rain."

Destruction was spread over a wide area. In the nearby town of Toutle, mud slides wrecked 123 houses and knocked down bridges. Mud filled Portland Harbor, and the Columbia River was blocked for twenty miles by fallen trees. Across the Northwest almost six thousand miles of roads were covered with ash the consistency of wet cement, while an ash cloud five hundred miles long and one hundred miles wide moved eastward over Montana and Idaho.

On the mountain itself, the scene was one of almost total desolation. One journalist wrote that the "terrain appeared otherworldly, a madly undulating landscape. The trees looked as if they they had been strewn across the foothills by a careless child." After touring the area, President Jimmy Carter said, "The moon looks like a golf course compared to what's up there."

Some sixty people died as a result of the eruption, including, sadly, Harry Truman. Last seen watering his lawn the day before the eruption, he remains buried beneath a thick blanket of solidified mud that completely covered his house.

Apparently Harry didn't know as much about the mountain as he thought he did.

1980: MGM Grand Hotel Fire. Most of the guests in the Las Vegas, Nevada, MGM Grand Hotel were asleep about 7:00 A.M. on November 21. That's when a fire broke out in the kitchen of the twenty-six-story hotel and spread explosively through the massive casino area. The floor above also caught fire, and thick black smoke filled hotel corridors, trapping thousands of guests on the upper floors. Many screamed for help from balconies, while others simply stayed in their rooms, stuffing wet towels under their doors to keep the smoke out. Meanwhile, over one thousand terrified guests dressed only in their pajamas were plucked from the building's roof by helicopters, as black smoke swirled upward from the fire below. The fire was put out soon afterward, but the eighty-four deaths made this the second worst hotel fire in U.S. history, after the 1946 Winecoff Hotel disaster.

1980: Earthquakes in Southern Italy. Many families were just sitting down to Sunday dinner on November 23 when, at 7:30 P.M., a tremendous earthquake struck southeast of Naples. Buildings swayed "like the waves of the sea," one terrified eyewitness said.

In Balvano, one hundred persons attending evening mass were crushed when the earthquake collapsed the front wall of the church. In Naples, twenty families were trapped when their apartment building caved in on them, while at the city prison, guards had to use tear gas and submachine guns to control panicking inmates.

Fires broke out in the ruined cities as hundreds of thousands of people prepared to sleep in cars or out on the streets, despite freezing temperatures. Many less fortunate souls remained trapped beneath rubble. Dozens of smaller tremors struck during the next six hours, claiming still more victims. Overall, some five thousand people died in the disaster.

1981: The Yorkshire Ripper. For five years West Yorkshire, England, was terrified by a man known only as the "Yorkshire Ripper," who, between October 1975 and November 1980, brutally murdered thirteen women. As with his infamous namesake, Jack the Ripper, his first victims were prostitutes, but soon there was no woman in West Yorkshire who was not afraid to go out at night.

They had good reason. The Ripper would strike his victims from behind with a hammer, then mutilate their bodies with a variety of implements, including kitchen knives, carving knives, and screwdrivers. Gloating over his crimes, he sent letters to police describing his murders in grisly detail. A tape announcing his intent to kill his twelfth victim was broadcast on the radio.

Finally, on January 2, 1981, Peter Sutcliffe was arrested as he sat in a car in a district of Sheffield where prostitutes congregated. The softspoken, thirty-four-year-old truck driver, who lived quietly with his wife, confessed to killing the thirteen women and claimed to be on a divine mission to eliminate prostitutes.

The religion excuse again.

1981: Sadat Cut Down in Hail of Gunfire. As part of Egypt's commemoration of the 1973 war against Israel, Egyptian President Anwar al-Sadat reviewed an enormous military parade in Cairo on October 6. Suddenly a group of soldiers who were Egyptian Muslim fundamentalists broke out of the parade line and walked directly toward the reviewing stand. While jets roared overhead in a scheduled flyover, the soldiers threw hand grenades and began firing rifles into the crowd of dignitaries.

Onlookers watched in horror as Sadat collapsed, hit by two bullets. Ten other people were killed and about forty more wounded before two of the attackers were killed and two others captured. With the reviewing stand awash in blood, President Sadat was whisked away to the hospital, but it was too late. The man who two years before had taken the bold step of leading the first Arab nation to a negotiated peace with Israel died within several hours. Five Muslim fundamentalists implicated in the assassination plot were executed after trials in 1982.

1982: Massacre at Chatila. Just three months after the Israeli army had invaded Lebanon, and only a few weeks after the Palestine Liberation Organization had been evacuated to Syria, a band of Lebanese Christian militiamen entered the Palestinian refugee camp of Chatila in West Beirut on September 16 and, as Israeli forces reportedly guarded the perimeter, began a wholesale slaughter of the unarmed refugees.

Dozens of young men were shot at point-blank range through their cheeks, while several others were lined up against a wall and shot in the back in a ritual execution. At least one young man had been brutally castrated. Women and children, too, were killed, and their bodies bulldozed into piles.

Authorities estimated that at least three hundred were killed in this brutal massacre, although it could not be determined how many more were buried in the mass graves dug by the militiamen.

1982: Explosion Wrecks Soviet Convoy in Afghan Tunnel. A large Soviet military convoy heading toward Kabul, Afghanistan, was wrecked on November 2 when the lead vehicle collided with a fuel truck inside the 1.7-mile-long Salung Tunnel. The explosion and fire killed over one thousand people—possibly seven hundred of them Soviet soldiers.

Never tailgate a fuel truck.

1983: Egyptian Riverboat Catches Fire. A total of 357 people were killed on May 25 when the riverboat *10th of Ramadan* caught fire while crossing Lake Nasser. The steamer had 627 passengers and crew aboard when a gas bottle in the engine room apparently exploded and spread fire throughout the rest of the ship.

1983: Korean Airliner Shot Down. On September 1 Korean Air Lines Flight 007 from New York to Seoul apparently strayed off course and flew toward a top secret Soviet facility at Sakhalin Island off the Pacific coast of Siberia, leading to a tragic international incident.

Immediately after Soviet radar picked up the airliner, eight Soviet fighter planes scrambled and began shadowing the wayward liner. Soviet officials claimed the Boeing 747 had no navigation lights and ignored warnings to change course. Finally, as the airliner approached Sakhalin Island, a Soviet fighter fired a heat-seeking air-to-air missile at the jumbo jet. The KAL flight disappeared from radar screens at 3:38 A.M. as it plunged into the Sea of Japan. All 269 passengers—including Representative Larry McDonald, a Georgia Congressman and chairman of the John Birch Society—were killed. The Soviet action against an unarmed civilian flight provoked international outrage.

1983: Truck Bomb Kills 241 U.S. Soldiers in Beirut. Following the successful Israeli invasion of Lebanon, U.S., French, and Italian troops were sent to Beirut, Lebanon, as a peace-keeping force and to oversee the evacuation of PLO forces that had been bottled up in the city.

The PLO forces were evacuated successfully. But just after dawn on October 23, an Islamic terrorist drove a Mercedes truck loaded with twenty-five hundred pounds of dynamite into the headquarters of a U.S. Marine peace-keeping force stationed in Beirut, Lebanon. Approximately three hundred marines were sleeping in the compound as the truck crashed through sandbag barricades and barbed-wire fences. Bent on his deadly mission, the Free Islamic Revolution Movement terrorist waited until he had rammed the truck into the lobby of the fourth-story building before exploding its load.

The blast created an enormous ball of fire and demolished the building, hurling bodies fifty feet into the air and gouging out a thirty-foot-deep crater in the ground. Bodies were everywhere. Survivors trapped beneath the rubble screamed, "Get us out. Don't leave us." Almost at the same moment, an identical attack destroyed a French military barracks two miles away, killing fifty-eight.

And the religious wars continue.

1983: Terrible Fire at Spanish Discotheque. Fire raced through a popular discotheque in Madrid, Spain, on December 17. Eighty-three people were killed by the smoke and flames.

1984–1985: African Famine. The children in the Ethiopian relief camp were too weak to cry. They lay on scraps of cloth and paper, or on the bare desert sand itself, squinting with hollow eyes at the harsh African sun, while swarms of flies buzzed around their hollow faces and distended bellies swollen by hunger. Nearby, the elderly, too, lay still in the oppressive heat, unable to feed themselves and sometimes barely conscious. Only one doctor and a handful of Red Cross volunteers worked in the refugee camp, where thousands of Ethiopians sought relief from the catastrophic famine that had struck their land.

Nearby, at the edge of the dusty river that trickled through the area, Africans dug shallow graves for their dead. The grave diggers were barely strong enough to move the fine, dry sand, and the number of bodies soon outnumbered the finished graves. An expert might have warned them that they were digging the graves perilously close to the camp's only water supply. With the terrible heat and quick decomposition of bodies, the spread of disease was already a problem, but the people knew no other way.

These and millions of other refugees flooded relief camps throughout a wide area of Africa during 1984. A drought and bitter famine afflicted much of the sub-Sahara, a wide, semiarid belt lying just south of the Sahara Desert and stretching all the way across Africa from the Atlantic coast to the Red Sea. Here, in countries such as Mali, Mauritania, Niger, Chad, Burkina Faso, and Ethiopia, Africans were dying by the hundreds of thousands.

The tragedy had been coming for years. People in this region had long survived by herding cattle and farming grain, relying on the summer rains to sustain them. Even during the best of times, their lives were hard, and people raised large families to work the land. When medical advances lowered the infant mortality rate, the population of the area grew even faster. To support the growing population, farmers cleared grazing lands to plant crops and stripped the area of what few trees were left to get wood for cooking.

And then the droughts began. Crops failed, livestock perished, and nearly a quarter million people died of starvation. In 1984 annual rainfall in the area reached an all-time low. Rivers and lakes dried up and disappeared completely. Suddenly the farmers found their livestock dying and their fields dry and useless, while dust storms blew away irreplaceable topsoil. Hundreds of thousands of starving people fled the barren land for relief camps that sprang up across the continent.

Images of hopeless refugees starving to death evoked enormous sympathy from many richer countries of the world, and aid began to pour into Africa. On July 13, 1985, the Live-Aid rock concert was performed simultaneously in England and the United States, and beamed by satellite throughout the world. More than seventy million dollars was raised to help Africa's famine victims. Unfortunately, the needed shipments of food, medicine, and supplies did not always reach the people. Too often, corrupt officials, local mismanagement, or the disruptions of war prevented shipments from reaching the relief camps.

By the time increased rainfall brought a halt to the tragic famine at the end of 1985, some two million Africans were dead. But as history has shown, droughts and famines are common in Africa. As one relief worker observed, "In this part of the world, we do not just think that people will die of hunger. We assume it."

1984: Brazilian Oil Pipeline Ruptures. Fire spread rapidly through a shantytown on the outskirts of Cubatao, Brazil, on February 25 after a pipeline ripped open and spread flaming oil among the crude huts. Over five hundred people were killed, and three hundred huts were destroyed.

1984: Assassination of Indira Gandhi. Personal security guards flanked Indian Prime Minister Indira Gandhi as she walked to her office in New Delhi on October 31. Gandhi apparently felt there was no reason to suspect the loyalty of two Sikhs among the guards: She had dismissed recent death threats made by militant Sikhs, who were angered by her opposition to Sikh demands for greater autonomy in the Punjab region.

The two Sikh guards suddenly pointed their weapons and fired point-blank, riddling the unsuspecting Gandhi with revolver and submachine-gun fire. Crying out, the prime minister collapsed on the street with blood pouring from at least eight bullet wounds in her abdomen and thigh. Security guards captured the two assassins and rushed the gravely wounded prime minister to the hospital. Gandhi, daughter of Indian independence leader Jawaharlal Nehru and the leading political figure in India, died four hours later. Three Sikhs were later hanged for the assassination.

Et tu, Brute?

1984: Gas Explosion Outside Mexico City. A liquefied gas storage facility outside Mexico City, Mexico, exploded in flames on November 19, incinerating the surrounding shantytown and killing 334 people. Authorities evacuated some one hundred thousand people after the blast, which was apparently touched off by the explosion of a gas truck at the facility.

1984: Killer Gas Leak in Bhopal. Late at night on December 3, thousands of people in Bhopal, India, woke up gasping for air and vomiting, their eyes and throats burning. Though they had no way of knowing it, they were being poisoned by the dangerous chemical methyl isocyanate. A forty-five-ton storage tank at the nearby Union Carbide Company insecticide plant had sprung a leak just after 2:00 A.M., spewing a cloud of the toxic gas over twenty-five square miles of Bhopal.

The gas leaked for forty minutes, but it was two hours before the factory siren was sounded to warn anyone. By then it was too late: Hundreds had already died, and thousands struggling to breathe had crowded into hospitals. Dead dogs, cats, water buffalo, cows, and birds filled the streets. Children and the elderly succumbed most quickly to suffocation, and close to two thousand people ultimately died as a result of the choking fumes.

1985: British Soccer Stadium Fire. On May 11, just before halftime of the soccer season's final match at Bradford, England, some ten thousand fans watched in horror as a flash fire swept through one of the wooden grandstands.

The sudden blaze sent the three thousand spectators in that grandstand scrambling frantically to escape the inferno. Many made their way to rear exits, only to find them padlocked. Meanwhile, the fire burned both from below the stands and from above in the wooden roof as well. Falling debris set spectators' hair and clothing on fire, and one middle-aged man leaped onto the field entirely engulfed in flames. A number of elderly people were literally thrown over the front of the grandstand to get them out of danger, and both policemen and spectators helped to smother fires burning in victims' clothing. "It was an absolute holocaust," said one soccer fan who had burned his hands while dragging two children to safety.

The terrible fire, spread by a strong wind, lasted just four minutes, but in that time it killed fifty-three people and injured over one hundred.

Those soccer games can get pretty heated.

1985: Another Bangladesh Tragedy. A cyclone packing eighty-mile-per-hour winds lashed the disaster-ridden southern coast of Bangladesh on May 24 and 25. Flooding and sea waves whipped up by the storm washed thousands of people out to sea; at least one island disappeared, along with approximately three-fourths of its inhabitants. Salt water from the Bay of Bengal surged inland, damaging croplands and drowning thousands of cattle in an area little able to afford such loss of valuable food supplies.

After the storm, rescuers found the seas around offshore islands littered with floating bodies. Among them were the survivors, clinging desperately to makeshift bamboo rafts in waters infested by sharks and crocodiles. As many as ten thousand people were believed to have died in this Bangladesh disaster.

Cyclones find Bangladesh very attractive. A resettlement inland might help.

1985: Dam Bursts in Northern Italy. A wall of mud and water 150 feet wide swept through a mountain resort area in northern Italy on July 19, after an earthen dam farther up the Fiemme Valley broke. The torrent of water killed over two hundred people, wiped out the village of Stava, and knocked over trees along a two- to three-mile path.

1985: Miraculous Escape in Japan Air Lines Crash. Five hundred twenty people were killed on August 12 in the worst single-plane disaster up to this time when Japan Air Lines flight 123 crashed in a mountainous wilderness north of Tokyo.

The plane, bound from Tokyo to Osaka, was filled to capacity as the Japanese celebrated Bon, a traditional holiday honoring the spirits of ancestors. All but four of the plane's 524 passengers and crewmen were closer to the fate of their ancestors than they knew.

The Boeing 747 SR (for short-range) had an uneventful take-off from Tokyo's Haneda Airport at 6:12 P.M. But within thirteen minutes, the plane's rear bulkhead ruptured; it had been weakened by faulty repairs made seven years before. Suddenly fifteen feet of the plane's rudder broke loose and fell into Tokyo Bay. At 6:25 the crew radioed "Immediate trouble" and requested permission to turn back to Tokyo. Three minutes later, as the plane veered wildly off course, a crewman radioed that the plane had become "uncontrollable."

In the rear of the passenger compartment, off-duty stewardess Yumi Ochiai felt her ears pop as the cabin lost pressure. Suddenly she saw "the whole cabin filled with a white cloud" as cushions swirled around the plane. Oxygen masks dropped down while stewards instructed terrified passengers to put on life preservers and lean forward, head down, to prepare for a crash.

Ochiai remembered catching a glimpse of Mount Fuji out the window as the plane suddenly went "hira hira"—a Japanese word meaning the slow, twisting fall of a leaf. Then the plane dropped at an almost vertical angle. A witness on the ground described the plane as "flying just like a staggering drunk."

At 6:57 P.M., thirty-two minutes after the first sign of trouble, the 747 crashed into the deep forest of Mount Osutaka, sixty-two miles northwest of Tokyo. Ochiai felt two or three "sharp impacts" as seats and cushions fell all around her and trapped her underneath. She heard children wailing before she blacked out.

The plane uprooted trees as it crashed through the forest and was ripped into pieces as it skidded over the mountainous landscape. Fuel tanks burst into flames while pieces of the wrecked plane and bodies were strewn about the crash site.

Rain was falling and it was already dark when the first helicopters hovered over the wreckage. Rescuers had virtually no hope of finding any survivors because the destruction was so complete. The first rescue teams did not reach the remote ridge until morning, where they found the area littered with scraps of metal, smoldering trees, and hundreds of bodies torn to pieces by the impact of the crash.

But one rescuer spotted something moving among the wreckage. Miraculously, fourteen hours after the crash, he found Ochiai, seriously injured with broken bones, but still very much alive. Next rescuers found a twelve-year-old girl trapped in a tree. Incredibly, she suffered only cuts and bruises. Finally they located a mother and her eight-year-old daughter, both of whom were suffering from broken bones. All four survivors had been sitting in the rear of the plane.

Because of the death toll, the JAL crash became the worst single-plane disaster in history. Only the 1977 collision of two planes at Tenerife resulted in more deaths.

1985: Mexico City Earthquake. The morning rush hour was just beginning on Thursday, September 19, when an earthquake measuring 7.8 on the Richter scale brought terror to the streets of downtown Mexico City. The violent shocks, which began at 7:18 A.M. and lasted for two minutes, collapsed over 250 buildings and crushed thousands of people inside them.

Only 39 of 140 people inside the Hotel Principiado survived when that twelve-story structure collapsed. One of them was a two-year-old child who crawled out of the rubble. Schoolchildren waiting on street corners cried for their parents as the ground shook and clouds of dust from the rubble obscured the streets. And in the nearby state of Jalisco a cathedral collapsed on twenty-six people attending morning mass.

The disaster continued in Mexico City the next day when a second quake of 7.5 on the Richter scale struck at 7:37 P.M. Over seven thousand people were killed by the quakes, and tens of thousands were left homeless.

1985: Colombian Mud Slide Disaster. When the snow-capped volcano Nevada del Ruiz, dormant since 1595, erupted on November 13, officials thought there would be no danger for residents of Armero, a town some thirty miles away. But the intense heat rapidly melted snow and ice on the volcano's cone, triggering a seething avalance of mud known as a *lahar*.

Sometime after an eruption at 9:00 P.M., residents of Armero heard a tremendous roar as a wall of mud, following the course of the Lagunilla River, sped toward them. Suddenly the *lahar*, laden with stones, uprooted trees, and other debris, crashed into Armero, overwhelming everything in its path. Much of the town was left completely submerged, while elsewhere only the tin roofs of houses could be seen. Mud-caked, battered survivors huddled on a patch of high ground, waiting for rescue.

Meanwhile, another *lahar* overflowed the Guali River, sweeping away houses and bridges at the town of Mariquita, while a third *lahar* inundated Chinchina. Overall, officials estimated some twenty-five thousand people died in the disasters.

1985: Fiery Plane Crash at Gander Kills Returning U.S. Troops. A chartered DC-8 jetliner that landed for refueling at Gander, Newfoundland, early on December 12 carried a very special group of passengers—250 soldiers from the U.S. 101st Airborne Division who had just completed a six-month tour of duty with an international peace-keeping force in the Sinai Peninsula, and who were now on their way home for Christmas.

Its tanks filled with highly flammable jet fuel, the plane lifted off from the Gander runway shortly before dawn. But it suddenly faltered, barely reaching one thousand feet in altitude, then fell and plowed through a mile of rocky forest of beech and spruce trees. When the wrecked plane finally skidded to a stop, it exploded in a fireball, strewing bodies everywhere among the plane's wreckage. All 258 persons aboard were killed, including the 250 members of the 101st Airborne Division.

1986: U.S. Space Shuttle *Challenger* Explodes. The open-air grandstands at Florida's Cape Canaveral were filled for the launch of the space shuttle *Challenger* on Tuesday, January 28. Hundreds of onlookers, as well as friends and family members of the seven *Challenger* crew members, listened to the flawless countdown and felt the powerful vibrations as the shuttle's huge engines ignited, then strained against the launchpad. They clapped and cheered as the twelve-story-tall shuttle and launch rocket assembly thundered upward, rising majestically through the clear, cold Florida sky. In less than a minute, the craft was ten miles above the earth traveling at nearly two thousand miles per hour.

Then, just after 11:39 A.M., when *Challenger* was barely a minute into its flight, the excitement of the audience swiftly turned to disbelief, then to horror, as the distant shuttle was suddenly enveloped in a roaring orange ball of flame. A teacher in the crowd of onlookers screamed, "Oh God, don't let happen what I think just happened."

Tragically, it had. *Challenger*'s external fuel tank had violently exploded in flames and blown the shuttle to bits. The two booster rockets broke away from the fireball, and bits of debris began falling through the sky amid puffs of smoke and steam.

Back at Cape Canaveral a NASA official hurried through the stands to the parents of schoolteacher Christa McAuliffe, who was on board. "The spacecraft has exploded," he said quietly.

Nearby, the children of *Challenger*'s pilot, Michael Smith, began to scream, "Daddy! I want you, Daddy!" Moments later, an official voice came over the loudspeaker to confirm the disaster which they had watched unfold: "Obviously, a major malfunction."

For more than an hour, flaming bits of debris rained down into the Atlantic Ocean off Florida, while the contrail from the deadly blast hung unmoving in the crisp air, a grim reminder of the tragedy that had occurred.

Throughout the nation, there was widespread mourning for the astronauts and for McAuliffe, a New Hampshire schoolteacher and the first ordinary citizen to travel in space. She had planned to teach several on-board lessons for televised broadcasts to schoolchildren all over the United States.

It was the worst accident in the history of the American space program. NASA officials spent weeks analyzing photographs (some impounded from journalists at the scene), debris recovered from the ocean, and mountains of computer data about the explosion of Shuttle Mission 51-L, before finally concluding the cause of the explosion was the failure of an O-ring seal on the right booster rocket.

1986: Swedish Prime Minister Assassinated. On the evening of February 28, Swedish Prime Minister Olof Palme and his wife left a Stockholm movie theater after seeing the film *Brothers Mozart*. The sidewalks were glistening with snow, and the couple decided to walk home to their apartment. The popular Swedish leader did not have a bodyguard. He enjoyed walking among the people, often stopping to chat with constituents.

At 11:30 P.M. a man approached the couple as they strolled along the main thoroughfare. Suddenly pulling out a gun, the assassin shot the prime minister twice, once in the chest and once in the abdomen. Then, just as quickly, he ran into a back street and escaped. When police arrived soon afterward, they found Palme lying in a pool of blood on the snow-covered sidewalk. The prime minister died minutes later at a nearby hospital. His assassin, a forty-two-year-old Swede with an extensive police record, was caught, convicted, and sentenced to life imprisonment.

Another head of government is gunned down. A dangerous career even in peaceful Sweden.

1986: Chernobyl Nuclear Power Disaster. Operators at the Soviet Union's Chernobyl nuclear power plant, located fifty miles north of Kiev, were conducting a simple test to determine how long a turbo-generator could continue producing power after a reactor shutdown. But an extraordinary series of mistakes turned the experiment into the worst nuclear power accident in history. One observer said, "The mystery remains that so many apparently well-trained people should hit on the precise blend of indiscretions that would make an apparently safe reactor blow up."

The catastrophe began on the afternoon of April 25, when operators made the first of six serious misjudgments by turning off the emergency core cooling systems. As the experiment began to go wrong, the operators violated one safety rule after another in a desperate attempt to control the reactor. By midnight they had disconnected three separate safety systems designed to shut down the reactor in case of an emergency.

That emergency came after 1:00 A.M. on April 26, when cooling water in the reactor was so low that the reactor suddenly overheated in a matter of seconds. What water remained turned into superheated steam, creating a massive explosion that ripped through the reactor, blasting the one-thousand-ton concrete lid of the containment vessel through the roof. Gases produced by reactions within the crumbling reactor set fires throughout the building, and the one-hundred-ton graphite core of the reactor began burning as well.

Flames shot one hundred feet into the air over the blazing reactor, while remains of the core burned at five thousand degrees Fahrenheit. Massive doses of radioactivity—several million times the dose released during the 1979 accident at Three Mile Island in Pennsylvania—were carried by the wind across the Ukraine, the Baltic, and onward through Poland, Sweden, and Norway.

The Soviet government did not publicly announce news of the catastrophe until April 28, when officials at a Swedish power plant detected enormous doses of radiation and thought it must be coming from a leak in their own plant. The Soviet statement was terse: "An accident has taken place at the Chernobyl power station, and one of the reactors was damaged. Measures are being taken to eliminate the consequences of the accident. Those affected by it are being given assistance. A government commission has been set up."

Meanwhile, the open reactor core burned out of control. "No one knows how to stop it," one expert said. "It could take weeks to burn itself out."

The Soviets evacuated residents in the area of heaviest fallout from the catastrophe; altogether some one hundred thousand people were forced to leave their homes. Within thirty-six hours of the accident, more than three hundred people were treated for serious radiation sickness—mostly plant officials or firemen attempting to control the blaze. Victims suffered headaches, fever, and vomiting, and those exposed to high levels of radiation died within six weeks.

In the weeks following the disaster, helicopters dumped sand and lead into the burning reactor, sealing it gradually. A second major fire erupted in the reactor building May 23, but that, too, was eventually contained.

The real cost of the disaster in terms of human lives will probably never be known. As rains washed heavy doses of radiation into the ground across the Ukraine and through much of Europe, officials conservatively estimated the long-term effects of the radiation will eventually mean ten thousand or more deaths from radiation-related cancers.

They were just conducting a simple test and made a few human errors.

1986: The Killer Gas Cloud. Quiet farming villages in a remote part of the African nation of Cameroon became the scene of a bizarre, and extremely deadly, natural disaster on the evening of August 22. A few lucky villagers were asleep and never knew what hit them. But for the rest of the 1,734 people living in villages scattered around a large volcanic lake, there was a horrible bout with terror and a painful, choking death.

That evening most of the unsuspecting villagers were eating supper or preparing for bed when a geyser of very hot, poisonous volcanic gas erupted up through the bottom of Lake Nios, which was actually an old volcano cone that had filled with water. The gas was hydrogen sulfide, colorless but deadly, and it quickly blanketed the villages.

Some villagers tried to outrun the deadly cloud of hot gas and were later found facedown in the muddy roads leading from the towns. Others did not get nearly so far, choking to death on the poisonous fumes just outside their homes. Many had stripped off their clothing because of the brutal heat of the gas cloud. But in the end not one of the 1,734 villagers managed to escape death.

It's not just man-made gas that's lethal.

1986: Soviet Ships Collide in Black Sea. Over twelve hundred passengers and crew were aboard the Soviet vacation liner *Admiral Nakhimov* on August 31 when it was hit by the Soviet freighter *Pyotr Vasyov* two miles from shore in the Black Sea. Torn open, the *Admiral Nakhimov* sank quickly, along with 398 passengers and crew. Incredibly, both captains were aware of the other ship's intersecting course before the collision and were in radio contact, but neither ordered evasive maneuvers. Stubbornness prevailed. Both captains were tried, convicted, and sentenced to fifteen-year jail terms.

1986: Puerto Rican Resort Hotel Fire. The Dupont Plaza, a twenty-two-story resort hotel, was filled with holiday tourists at 3:30 P.M. on New Year's Eve when a deadly fire broke out in the hotel's ground-floor ballroom.

In the casino, blackjack players and crapshooters continued playing when somebody first reported seeing smoke, but a sudden unmistakable burst of smoke finally sent them running for exits, only to find themselves trapped behind clouds of the toxic smoke and superheated air that filled the hotel corridors. One man broke out a window, and he and others escaped by leaping from the second-story window to the pavement below. Some other hotel guests managed to escape to safety by crawling on their hands and knees. Other guests, trapped on the upper floors, clambered through the darkened, smoke-filled stairways to the roof, where they were rescued by helicopters.

Investigators later reported the fire, which claimed ninety-six lives, had been started by an arsonist.

Who, like Nero, probably stood watching and smiling.

1987: British Ferryboat Sinks. One hundred thirty-four people died on March 6 when the ferryboat *Herald of Free Enterprise* capsized and partially sank on its side in shallow waters off Zeebrugge, Belgium. The ferryboat's cargo doors apparently were not fully closed when it left Zeebrugge.

1987: Collision of Philippine Ships. Some fifteen hundred passengers packed the ferry *Dona Paz* on December 20, anxiously anticipating their Christmas holiday in Manila. Meanwhile, the *Victor,* an oil tanker carrying eighty-three hundred barrels of oil, set sail for Masbate Island.

For some unknown reason, the ships collided at 10:00 P.M. The passengers felt a sudden jolt, followed by the sound of an explosion, and suddenly the sea was covered with flaming oil. As smoke filled the *Dona Paz,* panicked passengers rushed up to the decks, where they faced a desperate choice. All those who leaped into the water were consumed by the flaming oil; those who stayed aboard were quickly enveloped by the smoke and went down with the ship. Nearly everyone aboard the two ships perished.

1988: *Exxon Valdez* Oil Spill. The oil tanker *Exxon Valdez* ran aground in Alaska's pristine Prince William Sound on March 24 and began leaking oil in what became the worst oil spill in U.S. history. Ineffective efforts to contain and clean up the spilled oil resulted in considerable ecological damage and at least temporarily wrecked the local fishing industry.

1988: U.S. Downs Iranian Airliner. On July 3, radar technicians aboard the U.S. Navy warship *Vincennes* spotted an unidentified aircraft approaching on their radar screens. The American warship was patrolling the Strait of Hormuz in the troubled Persian Gulf, attempting to protect vital oil shipping from attack by Iranians and Iraqis, then at war with each other.

An attack by Iranian gunboats on a helicopter from the *Vincennes* less than an hour earlier had put the American warship in a defensive posture, and it radioed a demand for identification. Receiving no answer, the warship then warned the aircraft seven times on military and civilian radio frequencies to approach no closer. When no reply was received to any of these warnings, the captain concluded that the approaching aircraft was a hostile Iranian F-14 jet.

The aircraft, however, was an Iranian Airbus A300 airliner. When it dropped altitude and increased speed, apparently in preparation for landing in Dubai, the *Vincennes* interpreted this as a hostile action, and fired two surface-to-air missiles. All 290 aboard the plane were killed.

Radar screens do not tell all you need to know.

1988: North Sea Oil Rig Explosion. A platform above the frigid waters of the North Sea one hundred miles from shore is not a good place to be when a fire breaks out. But for the 232 men aboard the British oil rig *Piper Alpha,* that was a chance they were willing to take, perhaps because the risk of fire seemed so small.

At 9:31 P.M. on July 6, a gas leak on the rig let out a shrieking sound for about thirty seconds. That was the only warning the men had. Suddenly an explosion ripped through the rig, shooting flames seven hundred feet high, instantly destroying the sleeping quarters where about half the crew were resting.

As the rig was engulfed in flames, surviving crewmen panicked. Lifeboats had been destroyed in the explosion, so the men leaped blindly into the ocean fifty feet below. The last radio message sent from the rig was a frantic "We're abandoning the rig. Jesus Christ, we've got to get out of here. There's no more time, we've got to get out."

Twenty minutes later a second explosion tore the rig apart. A total of 166 men, including three rescue workers, died in the explosions, the flames, or of exposure in the cold North Sea waters.

1988: Death at the Air Show. Warm, sunny weather and the lure of dramatic stunts by skilled jet pilots drew more than three hundred thousand spectators to an air show at the American air base in Ramstein, West Germany, on August 28. All eyes turned skyward for the show's finale, in which ten Italian air force jets swooped toward one another trailing red, white, and green smoke.

Suddenly the crowd gasped with horror as three of the jets collided only one hundred feet above the ground. Two of the jets hurtled into a nearby wooded area and crashed in flames. The third jet plowed through a field crowded with spectators, mowing down terror-stricken bystanders and sending fiery wreckage sailing through the air. Some fifty people, including the three pilots, were killed by the crash, and more than five hundred spectators received serious burns.

1988: Armenia Earthquake. At 11:41 A.M. on December 8, a devastating earthquake measuring 6.9 on the Richter scale struck the Soviet republic of Armenia. The worst quake to hit the area in eighty years, it struck at a time when schools and public buildings were full of people. The quake lasted for about a minute, and in that brief space of time, snapped stone and concrete slabs as though they were dry twigs. Schools, factories, hospitals, apartments, and houses all collapsed, trapping tens of thousands of victims beneath tons of rubble.

The quake's epicenter was located twenty-five miles northeast of the Armenian town of Leninaken, in an area where many small faults lay only twelve miles below the surface. Geologists call the region a "structural knot" of interactions of plates. Many smaller quakes had plagued the area; yet construction practices were still primitive. For thirty miles around, every building taller than two stories was toppled by the tremors.

In Leninaken, where the city clock stopped at the time of the quake, the scene was one of ghastly devastation. Homeless survivors huddled around bonfires or searched the city for family and friends. Others fled the city on foot, carrying with them the few belongings they had managed to salvage. Meanwhile, rescue workers searched through the piles of smoking rubble, trying to free the thousands trapped by the deadly quake.

Near the scene of a collapsed school, where more than fifty young bodies had already been removed, rescue workers could hear a small girl crying for her mother and asking for water. They managed to lower some water to her but were unable to rescue her. The problem, there and elsewhere, was the lack of heavy equipment to move the rubble. The Soviet health minister observed, "Every hour of delay means another twenty dead out of every thousand buried."

Meanwhile, over nineteen thousand injured Leninaken residents clogged area hospitals. Although doctors were rushed in from other Soviet republics, many of the injured died due to a critical shortage of antibiotics.

The story was much the same in other Armenian cities and towns. At Spitak, forty-five miles north of Leninaken, the quake leveled everything, killing almost everywhere there. A Soviet television commentator noted, "Ninety-nine percent of the population is gone. Spitak . . . doesn't exist anymore."

Meanwhile, Soviet President Mikhail Gorbachev cut short a

visit to the United States to return and supervise recovery efforts. Soviet television, in keeping with the new Soviet policy of openness, gave unprecedented coverage of the disaster.

The reports were grim. An estimated sixty thousand people were killed by the quake, and some four hundred thousand more were left homeless. The magnitude of the disaster, however, did bring an outpouring of international aid, including doctors, medical and other emergency supplies, and even rescue teams, complete with dogs trained to sniff for bodies buried in debris. The U.S. contribution was the first large-scale assistance sent to the Soviet Union since World War II.

1988: Three-Train Collision in London. Over forty people were killed and over one hundred injured on December 12 when a crowded passenger train rammed into a stopped commuter train in south London, England. An empty freight train then slammed into the wreckage of the first two. Over fifteen hundred people were on the two passenger trains.

1988: Terrorist Bomb Causes Lockerbie Airplane Crash. On December 21, Pan Am flight 103, originating in Frankfurt and bound for New York, was flying north from London carrying 258 passengers—36 of them Syracuse University students returning home for the holidays. As the Boeing 747 reached its cruising altitude of thirty-one thousand feet, however, a tremendous blast blew the jet to pieces, and the flaming wreckage plunged into two rows of houses in the Scottish village of Lockerbie. Pieces of luggage, shredded clothing, and other debris were strewn over an eighty-mile area. All 258 passengers aboard were killed, as well as 12 other victims who died on the ground.

One leading theory of the cause of the explosion is that a plastic explosive was placed aboard in a piece of luggage by a Palestinian terrorist. Only time, new evidence, or a confession will reveal the truth.

1989: British Soccer Tragedy. Fans crowded the fifty-four-thousand-seat soccer stadium at Sheffield, England, on April 15, eagerly awaiting a game between Liverpool and Nottingham Forest. Stands behind the Liverpool goal were particularly packed when, for some unknown reason, the crowd there suddenly surged forward just before the game began. People who lost their footing were trampled and crushed, while some others suffocated in piles of falling bodies.

Worse yet was the situation down at the edge of the field where a sturdy fence had been put up to keep rowdy fans off the playing area. As the crowd surged, some of the children and others standing at the fence were brutally mashed against the wire mesh. Police later had to use wire cutters to free the bodies. Meanwhile, cheering fans in other parts of the stadium had no idea of what was taking place until officials stopped the game after six minutes of play. Only then, as police frantically pulled bodies out of the crush, did the extent of the tragedy become clear—93 people had been killed and over 180 injured.

1989: Tiananmen Square Massacre. After thousands of Chinese students had occupied Beijing's Tiananmen Square for weeks in a peaceful rally for government reforms and greater freedoms, Prime Minister Li Peng ordered the military to reclaim the square by force. On June 4, tanks rumbled in on the Avenue of Eternal Peace and soldiers fired their AK-47 rifles into the crowd.

Demonstrators fought back by swarming around government trucks, toppling them, and then setting them afire with fire bombs. Hundreds of thousands of Beijing residents flocked to the Square, only to be driven back to their homes by the soldiers.

After hours of fighting, the government effectively suppressed the students' protest. Though the total number of casualties probably will never be known, estimates of the dead run into the hundreds, with many others wounded. China instituted harsh new laws limiting freedoms in the wake of the unrest.

In China you do not demonstrate, peacefully or otherwise.

1989: Soviet Gas Pipeline Explosion Wrecks Trains. A leaking gas pipeline turned a valley near the Soviet city of Asha into a vast pool of gas vapors on June 3. The gas remained undetected until two passenger trains entered the valley and sparks from one of them apparently ignited the gas. The resulting blast had the force of ten thousand tons of TNT and felled trees for three miles around. A total of 460 people died in the explosion.

1989: San Francisco Earthquake. At 5:04 P.M. on October 17, while millions of television viewers watched the live coverage of the World Series from San Francisco's Candlestick Park, an earthquake measuring 6.9 on the Richter scale suddenly rocked the stadium. The cameras began to shake, and sportscaster Al Michaels was able to shout, "We're having an earthquake—!" before the power was cut and transmission ceased. Stunned viewers were left staring at their blank television screens.

Centered seventy-five miles south of San Francisco near the small university town of Santa Cruz, the fifteen-second quake was the most powerful in the San Francisco area since the great earthquake of 1906. Great rifts opened up in the earth, houses were shaken off their foundations, and once steady streets and sidewalks buckled and shifted. A worker at Fisherman's Wharf said that the street in front of his store "just exploded out of the ground, like someone had hit it with a giant fist from underneath." An eleven-year-old Oakland girl who was pelted by food flying out of her refrigerator likened the experience to "being in a blender."

In San Francisco's Marina district, built largely on landfill, the devastation was complete. The sandy soil used for fill behaved as though it were a liquid during the quake, and houses and apartment buildings there just crumpled on top of their unsteady foundations. A woman who lived on the second floor of her building was astonished when she stepped out of her door and found herself at street level.

Fires broke out in various places, the largest consuming a whole city block in the beleaguered Marina district. Most of the water mains had been damaged by the jolt, and firemen pumped water from the bay to fight the raging fires.

A fifty-foot section on the upper deck of the two-tiered bridge spanning the bay between San Francisco and Oakland collapsed, killing a driver whose car careened over the edge and onto the deck below. The rush hour traffic screeched to a halt in front of the fallen concrete as terrified motorists felt the bridge jerk and sway ominously beneath them.

In Oakland the powerful jolt collapsed a mile-long stretch of the double-decker I-880 freeway, flattening cars on the lower deck to a height of six inches in places and killing dozens. Miraculously, however, there were survivors. Six-year-old Julio

Berumen was pinned in the backseat of a car beneath a concrete slab and his mother's dead body. Rescue workers were unable to pry him loose and were forced to amputate his crushed right leg to extract him from the smashed vehicle. Then, four days later, after all hope of finding survivors had disappeared, rescuers found Buck Helm, a fifty-seven-year-old shipping clerk, seriously injured but alive in the crumpled wreck of his Chevrolet Sprint.

In all, the quake killed some sixty people, injured more than three thousand, and did more than a billion dollars in damages.

A historic event. Maybe the first quake we watched on live TV.

1990: Fifty-two-Car Pileup in Green Bay. "It was like driving in a milk bottle," one witness reported after seeing the opaque mixture of fog and smoke from three paper mills that had drifted across a section of Interstate 43 in Wisconsin. The early morning crash apparently began when two cars and a truck collided in the mist, where visibility suddenly dropped to ten feet. For the next five minutes, ensuing traffic plowed into the pileup. The result: three people killed and thirty injured.

1990: Forty-one Killed When Bus Falls onto High-Voltage Line. A bus loaded with passengers skidded off a railroad overpass near Kharagpur, India, on March 27, fell onto high-voltage lines below, and caught fire. Miraculously, twenty-one people were lucky enough to escape the inferno.

1990: Fire Aboard North Sea Ferry. On April 8 some 170 people died in a blazing fire on the Norwegian ferry *Scandinavian Star* during an overnight trip from Norway to Denmark. The burned-out ship was later towed to port.

1990: Deadly Train Fire in India. On April 17 a gas cylinder aboard a crowded commuter train apparently exploded, setting fire to two passenger cars as the train neared Kumrahar, India. The flames killed some eighty passengers and injured one hundred others.

1990: Iranian Earthquake. It was after midnight on June 21, and most of the people in Iran's northern provinces were sleeping. Suddenly a savage earthquake ripped through the whole region, flattening more than one hundred cities and towns. Landslides buried small towns beneath tons of rock and earth and cut roads and communications throughout the affected area. Thousands of homes, apartments, and other buildings collapsed, crushing tens of thousands of people trapped within them, and leaving hundreds of thousands of others homeless.

The earthquake, which measured 7.7 on the Richter scale, ravaged an area along the Caspian Sea that is a rich agricultural region. Adding to the initial quake's destruction were over one hundred aftershocks that shook the area over the next thirty-six hours. Aftershocks knocked down more buildings, killed many who were already trapped in collapsed buildings, and caused landslides that took still more lives, including those of rescue workers.

One survivor, who lost his entire family, recalled that during the main shock "the earth was trembling, like nature kicking the cradle. I saw the mountain slide toward the village. . . . But I lived, and all the young ones were taken from me, all because of this rock. . . ." Another told of a boulder as big as a building which crashed into his home, instantly killing four of his six children. The terrible toll of dead, wounded, and homeless swelled to enormous numbers. More than fifty thousand were believed killed. One man said he lost ninety-two relatives in the deadly quake.

Elsewhere, a little girl woke up and found herself trapped inside her collapsed home. She heard her grandfather screaming, but there was nothing she could do until she was rescued hours later. By then, however, both her grandfather and little brother were dead. Then the aftershocks hit "again and again," she said, "until there was nothing left of the village."

Amid the wasteland of ruined cities and towns, people dug through heaps of rubble, trying to find survivors. Children cried for missing parents, and corpses lined the streets. An area that had once been lush and prosperous was turned to mile after mile of smoking rubble, "as if a giant's boot had come down in the middle of the night and flattened homes, businesses, factories, roads—everything."

Warm temperatures gave hope to rescuers that many trapped victims would be able to stay alive until the mountains of rubble could be cleared away. In fact, thousands who had been buried alive did survive hours, even days, without food and water. But most were not so lucky. One village woman watched hopefully only to see rescue workers unearth her dead daughter and then, minutes later, a second dead child. Less fortunate still were those who never learned the fates of lost family members—many corpses had to be buried hurriedly in mass graves to prevent the spread of disease and the pollution of water supplies.

1990: Mecca Tunnel Stampede. Tragedy overtook thousands of faithful Muslims who had journeyed to the holy city of Mecca on July 2. As throngs of pilgrims crossed a pedestrian bridge at 10:00 A.M., a railing suddenly gave way. Seven worshipers fell onto a crowd of people below, who were just then emerging from a six-hundred-yard tunnel that serves as a pedestrian passageway for the pilgrims.

People at the end of the tunnel stopped, but the impatient hordes waiting at the tunnel's mouth could not see what had happened and kept pushing forward. Soon the long tunnel was jammed with some fifty thousand people, all pushing and becoming more agitated.

No one knows exactly why the tunnel lights suddenly went out at that moment, but the darkness added to the general panic. The ventilation system also stopped working, on a day when the temperature outside was 112 degrees. Panic turned to hysteria, and the stampede began. Hundreds of people were crushed to death underfoot, and many others died from suffocation in the pileup of bodies. In all, 1,426 Muslim pilgrims died during the tragedy.

1990: Massacre in Liberia. About thirty government troops reportedly blasted through a church door in Monrovia, Liberia, on July 30 and proceeded to fire into a crowd of two thousand women and children who had taken refuge in the church. The refugees were members of two tribes that supported rebel forces then threatening to topple Liberia's government. Estimates of the number killed in the massacre ranged from two hundred to over six hundred.

1990: Deadly Chain-Reaction Crash in Tennessee. A thick fog blanketing Interstate 75 in Calhoun, Tennessee, on December 11 caused a horrifying pileup involving eighty-three vehicles on both sides of the median. Car after car smashed into the accumulating wreckage, along with dozens of tractor trailers. Injured and terrified drivers, unable to see anything in the thick fog, could only hear the sounds of crashing metal, breaking glass, and exploding gas tanks. Some twelve people died in the crash, and more than fifty others were injured.

1991: Soccer Riot in South Africa. An estimated thirty thousand spectators gathered in the gold-mining town of Orkney on January 13 to watch a soccer match between two popular black teams from Soweto. Fans reacted angrily when the referee upheld a questionable goal by one team, and soon began to riot. Many people trying to escape the melee were trampled to death. At least forty people were killed, and fifty others were injured.

1991: Iraqi Scud Missile Hits U.S. Barracks. The Persian Gulf War marked the wartime debut of the Patriot missile system, a technological marvel designed to knock out incoming missiles before they hit their targets. During six weeks of fighting, the Patriots chalked up a near perfect record against the ungainly and inaccurate Iraqi Scud missiles. But all that changed on the evening of February 25.

Over one hundred soldiers were inside a makeshift U.S. military barracks located in Dhahran, Saudi Arabia, when at 8:23 P.M. the air raid siren warned of an approaching Scud. Seconds later, the Scud broke apart directly above the barracks, making an intercept by the Patriot missiles impossible. If the enemy is going to destroy your missile, beat them to it.

Burning debris rained down on the building, which immediately burst into flame. Many of the soldiers suddenly found themselves trapped inside the burning building, which was reduced to a charred shell within an hour. Twenty-eight were killed, and at least eighty-nine were wounded in this, the deadliest Scud attack of the war.

1991: Italian Ferry Collides with Tanker. Carrying seventy-two passengers and sixty-seven crew members, the Italian ferry *Moby Prince* left port at Livorno, Italy, on April 10, bound for Sardinia. Thick fog blanketing the harbor made for poor visibility, and the ferry suddenly smashed into the side of an anchored oil tanker. The tanker caught fire, and witnesses on shore said they saw a huge flame shoot up into the air. Curiously, the tanker's cargo of 442,000 barrels of light crude oil did not catch fire, but fuel leaking from both vessels did, spreading a huge wall of flames across the water and making rescue efforts difficult and dangerous. Eventually all of the tanker's crewmen were rescued, but only one person on the ferry survived. Some 138 people died, making the collision Italy's worst maritime disaster since World War II.

1991: Cyclone Kills Thousands in Bangladesh. A devastating cyclone packing 145-mile-per-hour winds roared off the Bay of Bengal and battered Bangladesh for more than eight hours on April 30. Twenty-foot waves crashed into the coast, washing away entire villages and flooding the low-lying areas under three feet of seawater. At least seventy thousand people were killed by the storm and the disease and malnutrition that followed. Millions were left homeless.

1991: Rajiv Gandhi Assassinated. On May 21, Rajiv Gandhi was campaigning in the state of Tamil Nadu in southeast India. He had become prime minister in 1984, but lost the election in 1989 and was hoping to regain the position. A woman approached Gandhi and, as she bent toward him, detonated the belt full of explosives she was wearing. The explosion killed her, Gandhi, seventeen policemen, and a number of bystanders.

The woman was no doubt a member of the Liberation Tigers of Tamil Eelam (LTTE), a terrorist group struggling to gain an independent homeland for the Tamils of Sri Lanka. When Gandhi was prime minister, he had signed an agreement with the government of Sri Lanka to settle the island's ethnic troubles. The agreement necessitated that the LTTE lay down its arms. When it refused, Rajiv sent the Indian Peace Keeping Force (IPKF) to subdue the LTTE. The Indian troops eventually left under pressure from a new government in Sri Lanka and a new Indian prime minister. The possibility of Rajiv Gandhi's becoming prime minister again evidently drove the LTTE to the only solution they deemed possible, assassination.

Rajiv had become prime minister after his mother, Indira Gandhi, was assassinated in 1984. He followed in his mother's footsteps a little too well.

1991: Severe Flooding in China. Heavy rains beginning in late May inundated a wide area of southeast China, flooding cities and sweeping away whole villages. Workers in Shanghai frantically dug ditches around the city to drain off the rising floodwaters, and while their measures succeeded in preventing major damage to that city, millions of people in the outlying villages were left homeless. The situation was still so severe in July that Chinese authorities appealed for international aid, citing crop damage as a major problem. At least seventeen hundred died as a result of the flooding.

1991: Jet Explosion Kills 223 Over Thailand. Sixteen minutes after taking off from Bangkok airport on May 27, an Austrian Lauda Air jetliner exploded in a fireball and crashed into the jungle. Shredded clothing and luggage littered the trees surrounding the wreckage, which was still burning when rescuers first arrived. Niki Lauda, former champion race car driver and owner of Lauda Air, reported that the cause of the explosion was unknown. Everyone aboard the plane was killed.

1991: Lightning Kills Spectator at U.S. Open. When a violent thunderstorm approached during the U.S. Open Golf Championship in Chaska, Minnesota, on June 13, approximately forty thousand spectators dashed for cover. A group of six men made the mistake of seeking shelter under a willow tree and were struck by a lightning bolt some minutes later. One man died instantly, while the others suffered minor injuries and shock. This incident is believed to be the first case of death by lightning during a U.S. golf championship, and gives new meaning to the term "sudden death" playoff.

1991: Yugoslavia Begins to Disintegrate. On June 25, Slovenia and Croatia, two of the six federated republics of Yugoslavia, declared their independence. It was the beginning of the destruction of the Balkans as centuries-old religious and ethnic rivalries stoked by ambitious political leaders sundered the country.

On June 15, 1389, the Serbians were vanquished by the Turks at "the Field of the Blackbirds" in Kosovo. The defeat has stuck in their craw ever since. The Serbs—along with the Bosnians, whom the Turks conquered by 1463—were ruled for centuries by the Ottoman Empire. The Serbians maintained their Eastern Orthodox religion, but the Bosnian nobility, and thus the Bosnian populace, converted to Islam under political and economic pressure. Not until 1878 were Serbia and Montenegro completely freed from Turkish rule. Predominantly Muslim Bosnia-Herzegovina, on the other hand, was occupied and then annexed by Austria-Hungary.

After World War I, a South Slav (Yugoslav) federation comprised of the Kingdoms of Serbia and Montenegro plus Croats and Slovenes was formed. The Serbs hoped to dominate. The union, however, was fraught with political dissension and national and religious conflicts. At the beginning of World War II, Hitler invaded Yugoslavia and the country was divided between Germany, Italy, Bulgaria, and Hungary. An independent Croatian state, which included Bosnia, was established and ruled by Ante Pavelic, a ruthless nationalist Croat and an avowed Serb hater who had joined forces with the Fascists. In Bosnia, the Fascist Croats massacred the Serbs, Jews, and Gypsies so savagely that the hatred lasts until this day. A small Bosnian Muslim force called the "Handzar" also brutalized and "ethnically cleansed" the Serbian regions of Bosnia. In turn, Croats and Muslims were massacred by Serbian nationalists who owed allegiance to Serbian resistance leader General Dragoljub Mihailovic.

Meanwhile, Communist forces, led by the Croat Marshal Tito (real name Josip Broz), were growing under their slogan of uniting all Yugoslavia. By the summer of 1944, the Communist "Partisans," as they were called, had taken control of the mountainous areas. In 1945, at the end of World War II, Tito became ruler of a united Yugoslavia after an election in which his was the only party to run. Yugoslavia was proclaimed a Federal People's Republic comprised of six republics—Serbia, Slovenia, Croatia, Montenegro, Macedonia, and Bosnia-Herzegovina—and two autonomous provinces, Vojvodina and Kosovo. Bosnia, in the center of Yugoslavia, was a mixture of Croats, Serbs, and the mostly Muslim Bosnians. In 1948, after being ejected from the Cominform, the organization of Communist parties of nine European nations, Yugoslavia turned toward the western nations. Tito's more liberal policies, called "Titoism," enabled the Yugoslavs to have more freedom and a greater participation in government than those living in other

Communist countries. Tito held the republics together with an iron hand that adequately suppressed extreme nationalism and separatism. When he died in 1980, however, ancient ethnic and religious conflicts once again began to surface among the Muslim Bosnians, Eastern Orthodox Serbs, and Roman Catholic Croats.

In 1987, Slobodan Milosevic, a zealous Serb and the leader of the Communist party, became head of Serbia, the largest republic in Yugoslavia, and began a campaign to reclaim what he called Serbia's former glory. He rose in power and rallied the Serbs by asserting that Serbs had been persecuted throughout history and now was the time for self-rule. He inflamed nationalists with remembrances of the ancient battle of Kosovo and declared, "No one should dare to beat you." Eventually, his militant nationalism forced out the leadership of the autonomous provinces of Vojvodina and Kosovo, which came under direct rule of Serbia.

In 1990, all six Yugoslav republics held free elections. In Croatia and Slovenia, leaders committed to nationalism and secession were elected. In Bosnia, Alija Izetbegovic, a Muslim nationalist leader, became president. Milosevic grew concerned about a looser federation that would divide ethnic Serbs among the other republics and lessen his power. In June 1991, Croatia and Slovenia seceded from the federation and declared independence. Fighting broke out almost immediately between Croats and Serbs in Croatia. In February 1992, Bosnians voted for independence; the Serb minority rejected it and began a campaign to force the Croats and Muslims out of the Serbian areas of the province. The ensuing destruction of the former Yugoslavia and displacement of its people erupted in some of the bloodiest fighting in Europe since World War II. Bosnia bore the brunt of it. The Croatians, who planned to integrate into their own country the areas of Bosnia having a Croatian majority, conquered about a third of the territory, forcing Serbs to leave and causing Muslims to flee in a reign of terrorist ethnic cleansing. Bosnian Serbs captured the other two-thirds of the country, imprisoning inhabitants and expelling Muslims and Croats from the area. Atrocities on all sides were horrifying as cities were besieged and destroyed, towns burned, residents massacred, women repeatedly raped, and children killed. Refugees by the thousands tried desperately to flee into other European countries. Serbs, using the fear of an Islamic regime in their midst, set up detention camps where prisoners were brutally beaten, starved, and executed. Other Croat and Muslim civilians were forced to live in inhumane conditions in an effort to drive them from their homes and into their own ethnic territory. According to the Bosnian Serb leader Radovan Karadzic: "There is no ethnic cleansing, but ethnic shifting."

An estimated 250,000 people died in this fratricidal mania and two million were displaced. Propaganda poison from all sides inflamed the already paranoid populations. The Serb and Croat paramilitary forces claimed they were fighting a holy war against militant Islamic insurgents. Conversely, the Muslims, finding their villages burned and families slain, turned murderously violent against their former neighbors. It was the utter, inconceivable, deliberate brutality and viciousness during the fighting that horrified the western nations.

U.N. troops were sent into Bosnia as early as 1991, and in the following year more troops were stationed to protect the airport at Sarajevo. Altogether, thirty-three nations provided a contingent of troops to UNPROFOR: the U.N. Protection Forces for humanitarian and military purposes. In 1992, a plan was proposed by the American Cyrus Vance and British Foreign Secretary Lord Owen to divide Bosnia into ten autonomous provinces. The Bosnian Serbs would have to withdraw from much of the territory they had claimed; they rejected the proposal in 1993. In the meantime, fighting continued in Bosnia, where the Croats and Muslims, who were once loosely allied against the Serbs, turned against each other. In the summer of 1993, a second peace plan proposed to divide Bosnia into three ethnic republics. It, too, was rejected, this time by the Bosnian Muslims, who demanded return of territory that had been seized from them. In March 1994, negotiators were able to get Bosnian Muslim and Croat leaders to agree to end hostilities. Plans to divide Bosnia again were proposed whereby one area was designated for a Muslim and Croat federation and another for Bosnian Serbs. The Bosnian Serb leader Karadzic condemned it, and the Bosnian president demanded return of Muslim land as well as the freedom for thousands of refugees to return. All the while, fighting continued. Finally, in December 1995, Presidents Franjo Tudjman of Croatia, Alija Izetbegovic of Bosnia-Herzegovina, and Slobodan Milosevic of

Serbia signed a peace treaty formalizing an accord reached at Dayton, Ohio, a month before. Bosnia was divided into two regions, one to be controlled by Serbs and the other by a Muslim-Croat federation. The three leaders then pleaded for an estimated six billion dollars to help rebuild the country they had destroyed.

Political and ethnic tensions remain alive in the Balkans at the turn of the century. In April 1998, violence broke out in northwestern Bosnia when Bosnian Serbs attacked Bosnian Croats heading to a Catholic mass. The Croats retaliated by setting buildings on fire and overturning U.N. cars. The U.N. refugee agency office was burned to the ground, and the headquarters of U.N. police monitors was attacked. The return of refugees to their hometowns has also been hampered by continuous ethnic and religious conflicts. The wounds of war are very deep, and the memories of past humiliations very long.

"It ain't over till the fat lady sings." And she's dead.

1991: Jet Carrying Moslem Pilgrims Crashes in Saudi Arabia. Shortly after takeoff from Jidda on July 11, the pilot of a DC-8 carrying 247 Nigerians home from a pilgrimage to Mecca reported a fire in the plane's landing gear. Then the jet nose-dived into the airport runway and exploded in flames, scattering wreckage and charred bodies across a wide area. All 261 passengers and crew were killed.

1991: Horror in Milwaukee. On July 22 a terrified young man in handcuffs flagged down a police patrol car cruising a high-crime neighborhood in Milwaukee, Wisconsin. He told police he had been lured to a nearby apartment, handcuffed, and threatened with a knife.

When police went to the apartment of thirty-one-year-old Jeffrey Dahmer, they were greeted by an overpowering stench that filled the hallway. The scene inside Dahmer's apartment was horrifying. Boxes filled with parts of human bodies, four human heads, and seven human skulls littered the room. A barrel of acid stood nearby, and there were photographs of mutilated corpses.

Police immediately arrested Dahmer, a quiet, average-looking white male who worked in a chocolate factory. Dahmer reportedly at first confessed to killing, mutilating, and sometimes eating parts of at least eleven victims—all young men, and most of them black. Dahmer told police he lured victims to his apartment with promises of money in exchange for being allowed to photograph them. Then he drugged them, strangled them, and mutilated their corpses. Continuing the grim saga, he said he often boiled the victim's heads, keeping the cleaned skulls, and admitted taking snapshots of victims while they were alive, after killing them, and after mutilating them.

Three days after being taken into custody, Dahmer reportedly gave police information about six additional victims killed during the past ten years. Police subsequently found the scattered remains of his first victim—a hitchhiker he picked up in 1978—in a wooded area near Dahmer's boyhood home.

It would be wise not to trust those nice "boy next door" types too much.

1991: The Cold War Thaws. On September 27 President George Bush proposed a reduction in nuclear weapons to which the Soviets agreed, thus ending four decades of the bitter "Cold War" between the two superpowers. One step forward for humankind. We may yet turn our swords into plowshares.

But is it just the superpowers we must be concerned about? The little guy can be just as dangerous.

1991: Bloodbath in Texas. Luby's Cafeteria in Killeen, Texas, was crowded at lunchtime on Wednesday, October 16, when suddenly a Ford pickup accelerated across the parking lot and crashed through the restaurant's window. Out jumped a young man with a semiautomatic pistol, pockets loaded with ammunition. He began shooting into the stunned crowd and shouting, "This is what Bell County did to me . . . it's payback time!" For ten minutes, the killer fired methodically, mostly at point-blank range with both a Glock 17 and a Ruger P89, until police wounded him and he finished himself off with a bullet to the head. The count was twenty-three dead—fourteen women and nine men—and twenty-eight wounded, making it the worst mass murder rampage in U.S. history.

The gunman was identified as thirty-five-year-old George Hennard, a resident of nearly Belton. An ex-Navy man, he had been in the merchant marine as a seaman on cargo ships until he lost his license after a marijuana bust in 1989. Hennard apparently had a hatred of women, often referring to them as vipers and harassing female passersby and neighbors with obscenities and threatening letters. The rage within him exploded that day at Luby's Cafeteria.

A week later, after intense lobbying by the National Rifle Association, the U.S. Congress defeated a measure to ban thirteen different assault weapons and the ammunition clips that make them even more destructive.

1992: Los Angeles Riots. The not guilty verdict in the Rodney King beating trial came in on April 29. Stunned by the acquittals, Los Angeles exploded in chaos as riots broke out in communities all over the area. South Central L.A. was hardest hit.

On March 3, 1991, twenty-five-year-old Rodney King was viciously beaten by four Los Angeles police officers after a traffic stop. The incident was caught on videotape from the balcony of a nearby apartment. The officers were indicted and critics demanded Police Chief Daryl Gates be dismissed. The acquittal of the officers unleashed torrents of rage in black communities, where it was believed justice had not been served. Stores were burned to the ground; businesses were ransacked by looters of every race; fights, knifings, and shootings broke out; cars were overturned; and anarchy reigned as rioters took the law into their own hands in protest.

Soon, riots erupted in other cities across the country. In San Francisco, the Pacific Stock Exchange was closed and the Giants-Phillies baseball game was canceled as vandals smashed store windows and overturned cars. In New York, workers went home early, stores were shut, and crowds of protesters gathered at Madison Square Garden, City Hall, and Columbia University. In Atlanta, people battled with police and burned a bookstore. In San Diego, autos were vandalized and motorists and police assaulted. Protests spread through Seattle, Denver, Bridgeport and Hartford in Connecticut, and Jersey City.

The National Guard was called out, and President Bush sent 5,000 federal troops to Los Angeles. After three days, while Americans watched in horror on television, the riots subsided. The death toll in L.A. alone was 58, with 4,000 injured and 5,348 arrested. In South Central Los Angeles, scores of businesses were destroyed, nearly all grocery stores were closed, and blocks of buildings lay in ruins. Mail delivery had been canceled. Slowly, the residents emerged with shovels and brooms, determined to clean up the debris and start over.

Rodney King appeared at a televised news conference, appealed for peace, and implored, "Can we all get along? Can we get along?" Words that would be echoed again and again in future years.

1992: Somalia Starves. As two rival warlords, Ali Mahdi Mohammed and General Mohammed Farrah Aidid, fought each other for control of the African nation of Somalia, one-and-a-half million of their countrymen faced starvation. The nation had been in a state of anarchy since the 1991 overthrow of the dictator Mohammed Siad Barrah. A severe drought and brutal civil war caused 800,000 to flee the country into camps in neighboring Kenya, including an estimated 5,000 Ethiopians who had fled from war and famine in their own homeland.

In July, 8,000 tons of food arrived by ship in Mogadishu, the Somalian capital, where brigands forced payment of $4,000 a day as a security fee until they could negotiate off-loading costs. In a nearby warehouse, 7,0000 tons of food remained under control of vandals who refused to release it. The United Nations began an emergency airlift in hopes of relieving the situation. In the meantime, the two factions, along with bands of armed freelance marauders, seemed intent on destroying the country.

The winner takes all. Of course, there won't be anything left.

1992: Hurricane Andrew. On August 23–25, Hurricane Andrew raged across the Bahamas, ripped through southern Florida, and then hit Louisiana, registering winds up to 175 miles per hour along its course. As the winds died down, the remnants of Andrew generated tornadoes and violent rainstorms in the Middle Atlantic states and as far north as Maine. Called the worst natural disaster in U.S. history, the storm caused an estimated $20 to $30 billion in damages and killed 65 people. As many as 250,000 people lost their homes, some 180,000 of them in Florida, where Andrew flattened Homestead, site of a U.S. Air Force base, and adjacent Florida City.

Andrew was on a whirlwind tour.

1992: Riots in India. On December 6, militant Hindus in the northern city of Ayodhya in Uttar Pradesh, India's most populous state, tore down the historic Babri Masjid mosque and sparked nationwide riots that killed more than 3,000 people. Enmity between the Hindu majority and the Muslim minority goes back to the thirteenth century, when Muslim invaders overwhelmed the Hindu kingdoms and established the Mogul Empire. In 1528, the Afghan conqueror Babur ordered his soldiers to construct the Masjid, which is believed to have been built on top of a ruined Hindu temple, the birthplace of the Hindu god Lord Ram. When the mosque was destroyed 464 years later, the conflict between the Hindus and the Muslims, fanned by political factions, erupted into violence in cities as far away as Bombay. The city, with a population of over 12 million, came to a halt as rioters prevented trains, buses, and cars from moving. Destruction was rampant. Aside from the religious ramifications, the riots were also about class struggle and poverty. *The Hindustan Times* asked: "Will our leaders look beyond politics for a change and save the nation?"

1992: Killer Tidal Wave. On December 12, a gigantic tsunami resulting from an earthquake measuring 6.8 on the Richter scale killed 2,500 people in East Nusa Tenggara, about 1,100 miles east of Jakarta, Indonesia. The rumblings never cease in this part of the world.

1993: World Trade Center Bombing. At about noon on February 26, a bomb exploded near the base of Manhattan's World Trade Center. The blast, centered on a ramp of the parking garage directly below the Vista Hotel, knocked out the power plant for the 110-story Twin Towers buildings. Over 50,000 people were trapped in the skyscrapers with no lights, elevators, or heat. Atop Tower 1, the transmitters of all but one television station in New York City lost power. Smoke and soot filled the buildings as fire departments from all five boroughs responded to the incident. Occupants were instructed via telephone and the few radios available in some offices to stay where they were, remain calm, block air vents, and wait. By midnight, rescuers had reached the last of the ninety-nine elevators and led the occupants, who had been stuck there for twelve hours, to safety. At 2:30 in the morning, the emergency was declared under control.

Over one thousand people were injured and six killed in the bombing, and 105 firefighters were injured during rescue operations. The explosion tore through steel-reinforced floors on three levels and left a crater 150 feet in diameter. The control center for the Port Authority Police Department on the first level was destroyed. Elevator shaft walls and concrete walls were demolished, and water from damaged refrigeration, sewer, and fresh water lines poured into basement levels. Over 120 parked cars were destroyed and 102 damaged. Huge chunks of concrete were blown onto the subway station mezzanine.

The closing of the towers forced many firms with offices in the buildings to find temporary accommodations. Approximately 2,500 tons of rubble was removed from the six-floor-deep sublevels, while nearly 3,000 workers repaired the damage to the infrastructure. Tower 2 tenants moved back on March 18, and on March 29, Tower 1 occupants were able to regain their offices.

An hour after the bombing, the first of many calls claiming responsibility began to arrive at police stations. A $2 million reward was posted by the United States for information leading to the perpetrators. In February 1995, twenty-seven-year-old Ramzi Ahmed Yousef was captured in Pakistan and in December 1997, the federal court in Manhattan convicted him of masterminding the bombing plot. Yousef had intended to topple one of the Twin Towers into the other, destroying both and killing 250,000 people. The court also found twenty-six-year-old Eyad Ismoil, a Jordanian, guilty on charges of driving the van loaded with the explosives. Four others were also convicted in the bombing plot.

After the bombing, police received hundreds of bomb-threat calls and several buildings in the city were evacuated as a result. For months, jittery New Yorkers had a lot of practice climbing down the staircases in their buildings.

1993: The Storm of the Century. On March 12–14, the eastern area of the United States suffered through one of the worst winter storms in its history. The blizzard forced the closing of all interstate highways north of Atlanta, Georgia, and every major airport on the coast shut down for at least part of the time. At New York's LaGuardia Airport, winds gusted up to 71 miles per hour. On Long Island, roofs collapsed under the heavy wet snow, and the pounding surf swept 18 houses into the sea. In Alabama, a record-breaking snowfall of more than a foot, along with powerful winds followed by devastatingly cold temperatures, paralyzed sections of the state for two days. The storm there resulted in 14 deaths, numerous injuries, and property damage of over $50 million. Fifteen tornadoes were reported in Florida; six inches of snow fell in the Panhandle. Forty-four storm-related deaths were reported. Over 200 hikers trapped in the storm in the Tennessee and North Carolina mountains were rescued. On North Carolina's Outer Banks, 200 homes were demolished. In New Jersey, two-and-a-half inches of sleet covered twelve inches of snow, bringing the state to a halt. Power outages were widespread as trees fell under the pressure of heavy snow and sleet and downed power lines. The Coast Guard rescued over 160 people at sea in the Gulf of Mexico and the Atlantic Ocean, and a freighter sank in the Gulf. In Canada, a ship sank off Nova Scotia with 33 crew members aboard while winds up to 131 miles per hour slammed into Nova Scotia itself. Over 270 deaths were attributed to the storm, with the total cost of damages exceeding $6 billion.

The famous "Blizzard of '88" also began on March 12.

1993: Tragedy in Texas. On April 19, eighty members of the Branch Davidian religious sect, including twenty-one children, and their leader, David Koresh, died when fire swept through their compound near Waco. The destruction of Mount Carmel, the name given to the compound by the Davidians, ended the fifty-one-day standoff between Koresh and the FBI.

A splinter sect of the Seventh-Day Adventist Church, the Branch Davidians were formed in 1929 under Victor Houteff, who believed that Christ would return to Earth after a small number of Christians had been purified. He also sought to reveal secret information in the scroll secured by Seven Seals described in the Book of Revelations. He founded Mount Carmel in 1935 and from then on recruited members worldwide. After Houteff's death, power struggles resulted in the leadership being taken over by Vernon Howell, who had joined the group in 1981. Howell renamed himself David Koresh (after the biblical King David and Babylonian King Cyrus) and was considered to be the prophet who would open the Seven Seals; Armageddon would occur, and the Branch Davidians alone would rise to Heaven. The sect led a communal life over which Koresh held extreme sexual and physical control while preaching his apocalyptic doctrine.

While awaiting doomsday, the group acquired an estimated eleven tons of mainly illegal weapons. On February 28, agents from the Bureau of Alcohol, Tobacco and Firearms attempted to serve search and arrest warrants against Koresh. They were looking for a range of weapons from AK-47 rifles and antitank guns to grenades and pipe-bomb devices. A shot rang out, and in the ensuing exchange of gunfire, six Davidians and four ATF agents were killed. For the next two months, the government tried negotiations and other tactics to force Koresh to leave the compound. Some children and adults were eventually sent out or left, but Koresh refused to surrender, contending that he was waiting for God to tell him when he should leave and that he was working on a manuscript explaining the Seven Seals. Finally, on April 19, at six in the morning, the FBI decided that Koresh had no intentions of surrendering. They notified the Davidians by telephone and loudspeaker of an imminent tear gas attack and advised them to leave the compound. Two FBI combat engineering vehicles (CEVs) began spraying gas into the building, and the Davidians began shooting. One CEV then began breaking holes in the walls of the building to allow Davidians to escape. Other CEVs inserted more gas into other parts of the compound. The fire started about noon. Some reports state that small fires were started simultaneously at various locations in the building, although some Davidians who escaped claim that the tanks had upset lantern fuel and a lamp, which ignited. Fanned by high winds, the fire quickly became a conflagration engulfing the entire compound. Although Koresh had fervently insisted that suicide was not an option, many of the bodies that were found had gunshot and stab wounds.

Armageddon had arrived.

1993: Secret Serial Killer. In the wee hours of the morning of June 28, New York State troopers chased a pickup truck traveling along the Southern State Parkway on Long Island. The truck crashed into a pole, and the driver was pulled from the cab and handcuffed. After noticing a foul odor coming from the rear of the truck, troopers uncovered the decaying corpse of a woman. The driver, Joel Rifkin, confessed to having picked up the woman in Manhattan the week before. After having sex, he strangled her and was on his way to a nearby airport to dispose of her body. Rifkin then told the police that the bodies of sixteen other women he had murdered over the past three years were buried in woods and dumps in the New York area. Police were able to connect him with thirteen bodies, some dumped along remote highways, three in oil drums submersed in canals. In his garage, investigators discovered a chain saw and a blood-stained wheelbarrow, suggesting a connection with more gruesome methods of disposal. Rifkin preyed on prostitutes who prowled Lower Manhattan and after killing them kept a little keepsake to remember each of them: a driver's license, a credit card, an earring, a shoe, or similar memento.

Rifkin was a landscaper whose luxuriant garden surrounding his house was the envy of the neighborhood. Exceptional fertilizer, maybe?

1993: Train Plunges into Bayou. On the foggy morning of September 22, at about 3:00 A.M., a drifting barge slammed into a railroad bridge over a bayou near Mobile, Alabama. A few minutes later, the Miami-bound *Sunset Limited* started across the bridge. The weight of the train collapsed the damaged structure, sending several cars into the swampy waters. Forty-seven people died in the worst accident in Amtrak's history.

1994: Los Angeles Rocked. At 4:30 A.M., Monday, January 17, Los Angeles area residents were shaken awake by a 6.6 magnitude earthquake. Apartment buildings and department stores collapsed; nine highways, including the Santa Monica Freeway, were ripped asunder; an oil main and gas lines burst, touching off fires; circuits blew, thrusting three million people into darkness; and water mains ruptured. More than 1,000 aftershocks followed. The quake killed at least fifty-eight people and caused an estimated $15 to $30 billion in damages.

Hardest hit was the Northridge area, twenty miles northwest of downtown L.A. Although Angelenos are well aware of the infamous San Andreas fault running 800 miles southeast from San Francisco to San Diego, smaller cracks also weave their way under the California crust. It was one of these fault lines, hidden nine miles below the Northridge suburb, that shuddered and quaked and rearranged the topography that fateful morning.

Californians are still waiting for the "Big One" scientists say could happen any day. That one would be eighty-five times more powerful. Adios, California.

1994: Massacre in the Mosque. At dawn on Friday, February 25, about 700 Muslim men, women, and children thronged the Ibrahim Mosque in Hebron, on the West Bank of Israel, to begin their morning prayers in observance of the holy month of Ramadan. Dr. Baruch Goldstein, an Israeli settler and ultranationalist, also entered the mosque, and from his position in the rear opened fire with a military-issue assault rifle. Ten minutes later, twenty-nine Arabs were dead and some seventy others had been wounded. The murderer himself was beaten to death on the spot.

Goldstein's fanatical mission was not just to kill Arabs but to kill the peace process between Israel and the Palestinians. The P.L.O. withdrew from talks with Israel and riots erupted in the West Bank. Not until the U.N. Security Council condemned the massacre did Syria, Jordan, and Lebanon agree to continue talks with Israel and the P.L.O. and come back to the conference table.

Mission not accomplished.

1994: Genocide in Rwanda. Beginning on April 6, one of the bloodiest slaughters in history erupted in Rwanda, when members of the Hutu tribe, inflamed by decades of hatred and resentment, embarked on a crusade to exterminate their rival, the minority Tutsi tribe. It is estimated that between 500,000 and 1,000,000 died in the massacres. Men and boys, women and children, were indiscriminately cut down and left by the roadsides, thrown into rivers, or herded into churches and classrooms and shot, hacked, or bludgeoned to death with machetes, Uzis, hoes, or whatever instrument of death was available.

The frenzied massacres began just after President Habyarimana, a Hutu, was killed when his plane was shot down over Kigali, the Rwandan capital. Habyarimana was returning from a peace conference in Tanzania; he hoped to further a truce between the Hutu and Tutsi. The Hutu blamed the crash on Tutsi rebels of the Rwandan Patriotic Front; the United Nations suspected the Hutu presidential guard.

The kingdoms of Ruanda-Urundi were formed many centuries ago by the Tutsi, originally from Ethiopia. The Tutsi subdued the short, stocky, dark-skinned Hutu, who were farmers. The Hutu became vassals to the aristocratic Tutsi in a feudal-like system, farming the fertile valleys and supplying the food to the tall, slender, lighter-skinned Tutsi, who owned and raised cattle. By the fourteenth century, Ruanda-Urundi had become a powerful nation in eastern Africa ruled by a Tutsi king. The Hutu did not always accept a Tutsi ruler, and there were minor revolts through the years. This symbiotic relationship lasted until the late nineteenth century, when the nation came under the German sphere of influence, then under Belgian administration after World War I.

In 1959, there was a rebellion in Rwanda against the Belgian-backed Tutsi dominance and many Tutsi fled, including the tribal king. Hutu parties won elections in both Rwanda and Burundi and in 1961, Rwanda declared itself a republic. Elections held in September of 1961 under U.N. supervision were won by Hutu in Rwanda and Tutsi in Burundi. The U.N. proposal that the two countries become federated was rejected by them, and in 1962, Rwanda became independent of Belgium. In a 1973 power grab, Habyarimana became president and began agitating against the Tutsi. Meanwhile, the economy deteriorated and famine spread. After several bloody massacres by the Hutus, exiled Tutsi in neighboring Uganda formed the Rwandan Patriotic Front, whose stated goal was to overthrow the Habyarimana government. In 1990, they invaded Rwanda and fought the Hutu until August 1993, when the Rwandan government and the Tutsi leaders signed the Arusha Accord in Tanzania. The accord decreed that the Tutsi would be permitted to join in a national-unity government and that both Hutu and Tutsi soldiers would form a new army to implement the peace. Hutu hardliners, however, refused the idea of reconciliation and started plotting against Habyarimana, resulting in the genocide that followed. The Hutu hunted down not only Tutsi but moderates in their own government. Vicious Hutu death squads in street clothing routinely killed any Tutsi they came upon.

In one twenty-four-hour period, 250,000 desperate people crossed into Tanzania, forming a new city. Some were Tutsi refugees but many were Hutu who feared revenge from the Tutsi RPF in control of the eastern part of Rwanda near Kigali. By August, nearly 2.5 million people, including 1 million Hutu refugees, had fled to Tanzania, Zaire, and Burundi. They remained in overcrowded refugee camps where there was no sanitation and typhoid, dysentery, and cholera ran rampant. In July, the RPF claimed victory and gained control of Rwanda. A new government that included Hutu and Tutsi was formed. The RPF, in a flourish of conciliation, appointed a moderate Hutu as president. General Paul Kagame, the Tutsi military mastermind, became vice president and the real power behind the government.

In 1998, it was revealed that U.N. Secretary General Kofi Annan's office had been aware of the Kigali government's plan to exterminate the Tutsi, having been notified by General Roméo Dallaire, commander of the U.N. forces in Rwanda. Nothing was done to intercede, however, since the report was deemed to be speculative. Annan apologized to the Rwandans for not trying to prevent the genocide, claiming that the "world failed Rwanda at that time of evil." Rwandans wanted those responsible for the slaughter punished, and the International Criminal Tribunal for Rwanda, founded in November 1994, was urged to speed up the pace of the trials of suspected murderers. More than 125,000 people are awaiting trial in Rwanda. In April 1998, the government began executing by firing squad the 116 already found guilty and sentenced to death. The executions were carried out in public, according to Justice Minister Ntezilyayo, because "justice must be seen to be done."

1994: Airline Crash in Japan. Japan's second-worst air disaster occurred on Tuesday, April 26, when a China Airlines

A300-600R en route from Taiwan crash-landed and burst into flames at Nagoya. The crash killed 264 people.

1994: Air Crash in Pittsburgh. On September 8, a USAir Boeing 737 was on its airport approach when it crashed into the woods northwest of Pittsburgh, killing all 132 people aboard.

The cause of the crash has not been definitely determined, but it could possibly have been a rudder malfunction.

1994: The *Estonia* Capsizes. Near midnight on September 27, the seas were rough as the passenger and car ferry *Estonia* was making its way across the Baltic to Sweden. Most of the passengers, mainly Swedes and Estonians en route from Tallinn to Stockholm, were asleep when the ferry suddenly listed. At 1:22 A.M., and again at 1:24 A.M., the ship sent out a distress signal; by that time, the boat was already healed over at an angle of forty-five degrees. Five minutes later, the ship sank twenty-five miles off the southwest coast of Finland. The massive rescue operation, coordinated by the Finnish Rescue Service, included helicopters from Sweden, Denmark, and Finland, as well as five passenger ships from the area and several freighters. The gale-force winds and high seas impeded the recovery procedures as rescuers fought to save lives and pluck passengers from the fifty-degree waters. Of the 1,049 persons on board, only 137 survived. Swedish authorities described the sinking as "the greatest catastrophe for Sweden in modern times." It was also one of the worst maritime disasters of this century and the worst in peacetime Europe since World War I. Flags flew at half-mast in Estonia and Sweden, and a hotline was established for relatives and friends of those aboard the ship who waited word of survivors.

An investigation into the cause of the sinking was begun immediately. It was concluded that a weak door lock on the ferry's bow visor, a hinged door that swung upward to enable cars to enter and exit, was the culprit. The rough seas pounding on the bow broke the lower lock, setting off a chain of events in which other locks broke and loosened the visor, allowing water to pour in.

1994: Suicide Bomber Blasts Bus. On the morning of October 19, a young Palestinian from the West Bank entered the

Number 5 bus in busy downtown Tel Aviv. He carried a twenty-two-pound package of TNT. As the bus was passing through the busy shopping district, he got up and detonated the bomb. Blown to smithereens were the bomber, the bus, and twenty-one passengers. So violent was the force of the explosion that the bus was fragmented and body parts were hurled through store windows. The perpetrator was identified as Sallah Abdel Rahim Nazal Souwi, a member of Hamas, the Palestinian terrorist organization bent on disrupting the peace talks going on between P.L.O. leader Yasser Arafat and Israeli Prime Minister Yitzhak Rabin. Only a few days before, Arafat, Rabin, and Israeli Foreign Minister Shimon Peres had been named Nobel Peace Prize recipients.

The talks continued, but not the twenty-one passengers, unfortunately.

1995: Kobe Earthquake Disaster. At 5:46 in the morning on Tuesday, January 17, an earthquake with a magnitude of 7.2 jolted the Kobe and Osaka regions of Japan. Outside of Tokyo, the area is the most populated and industrialized region of Japan, with a population of about ten million. The ground shook for about twenty seconds, causing intense damage over a wide area, including the cities of Kobe, Osaka, and Kyoto.

By nightfall, more than 300,000 people were homeless, over 5,500 dead, 35,000 injured, and 180,000 buildings damaged or destroyed. Central Kobe was largely demolished and, according to older residents, looked like a war zone. Streets were filled with rubble and roads were impassable; a 2,000-foot section of the elevated Hanshin Expressway in Kobe had collapsed. Direct damage was estimated at $147 billion, making it the greatest economic loss created by a natural disaster in recent history.

Loss of life from the earthquake was the worst since the Great Kanto Earthquake of 1923 *q.v.* The Emperor didn't resign this time either.

1995: Barings Bank Collapses. In February, the British bank that helped finance the Louisiana Purchase in 1803 and underwrote the Napoleonic Wars collapsed under debts totaling $1.3 billion. The investment bank Barings, PLC, established in 1762, was brought down almost single-handedly by Nick Leeson, a twenty-eight-year-old trader in Barings' Singapore branch with a $320,000 salary plus a million-dollar bonus offer. The losses were incurred by Leeson's unauthorized dealings in derivatives based on the future direction of the Japanese Nikkei stock index, which he concealed in a fraudulent account. Leeson was betting that the Nikkei index would rise and had already racked up significant losses when Japan was hit by the earthquake in Kobe and its stock market plummeted. Barings was left to cover the losses, which outweighed the bank's cash reserves. The collapse, one of the largest in British banking history, caused the pound sterling to drop and sent stocks tumbling in many countries as investors tried to recover assets.

Leeson faxed his resignation to Barings and headed for England, but Singapore's fraud squad officials caught up with him in Frankfurt, Germany, where he was arrested and later extradited. Eight months later he pleaded guilty in Singapore to two counts of fraud and forgery after implicating several colleagues in the fiasco. Leeson was sentenced to six and a half years in jail and promised to repay Singapore over $100,000 for prosecution costs. Upon hearing a rumor that Leeson was going to profit from a book and movie deal, his Singapore attorney vehemently denied any deal, stating, "Our client is not a crook."

We've heard that one before.

1995: Nerve-Gas Attack on Tokyo Subway. Passengers jammed the Tokyo subways during rush hour on Monday morning, March 20. Before their commute was over, 5,500 had been injured and 12 killed by the nerve gas sarin.

Developed in Germany in the 1930s, sarin had been used as a chemical warfare agent by the Nazis during World War II. Open containers of a liquid version of the gas had been placed in five different cars on three subway lines where it vaporized, sending fumes spreading through the cars. Thousands of people poured out of the subways retching and gasping for breath, some with eyes stinging, temporarily blinded by the gas. There was no panic as they lined up to wait for treatment. At St. Luke's International Hospital in downtown Tokyo, nurses washed victim's eyes and administered oxygen as patients lay in beds lining the corridors. Of the 4,600 people who were treated in hospitals, 603 remained overnight.

Police and military personnel wearing protective gear combed through trains and subway stations looking for more of the gas or clues to the culprits in the case. Subway service was restored by the afternoon except for one line, and by evening rush hour the trains were packed again.

The police suspected Aum Shinrikyo, a religious cult that had been associated previously with sarin production. A similar nerve-gas incident had occurred in 1994 in a residential area of Matsumoto, where 7 people died and 2,000 were injured. Japanese officials raided the cult's compound and arrested its leader, Shoko Asahara, and sixteen other members. Asahara had preached a combination of Buddhism and Hinduism laced with prophecies of mass destruction. Later inquiries determined that the cult had carried out nine other biological attacks that had failed. Their germ warfare wasn't virulent enough, even though members had traveled afar on microbe hunts in hopes of acquiring deadly germs.

Evidently Asahara was determined that his prophecies would become reality.

1995: Oklahoma City Bombing. It was a beautiful morning on Wednesday, April 19, in Oklahoma City as workers in downtown office buildings settled down to their jobs. In the Alfred P. Murrah Federal Building, some employees had just left their children at the second-floor day-care center before going to work at one of the government agencies housed in the building. On other floors, people were waiting for their appointments with employees of the Housing and Urban Development Agency, Veterans Affairs, the Social Security Administration, or one of the other federal bureaus. Suddenly a horrendous explosion sent the north side of the nine-story building crashing to the ground in a heap of concrete and steel. A minute later, stunned employees in adjacent buildings looked out of their own shattered windows upon a scene of utter devastation. Half the Murrah Building was gone, people covered in blood were staggering out of the other half, and bodies were lying dead or injured on the ground. The blast had dug a crater eight feet deep and twenty feet wide; the crater was filled with debris two stories high. Burning wreckage and cars were scattered over the streets for blocks while black smoke streaked the skyline.

Rescue work was a slow process. The building was so damaged that merely searching for victims was a hazardous procedure. The floors of the building had "pancaked" and fallen one on top of the other. An hour after the explosion, more than 50 people had been rescued; the injured were carried to a triage center set up on the street. Many were in a state of shock and disoriented. Hospitals all over the city called for medical personnel to report in, and the Red Cross sent out an alert for blood donations. Just when the fire department was about to reach more people, rescue efforts were stopped for an hour and a half while the bomb squad investigated the possibility of an unexploded bomb, which proved false. A hook and ladder was raised on the damaged side of the building to help evacuate workers trapped on the upper floors. All the while, the whole building was in danger of collapsing. Hardest to face was the fact that about 30 children had been in the day-care center and were yet to be rescued. A deputy fire chief said, "It's very emotional inside there right now. I've seen firefighters coming out with tears in their eyes, very frustrated they can't get in there sooner." Days later, when everyone had been accounted for, the death toll reached 169 with 500 injured, many of them seriously. The bombing was the most destructive terrorist attack ever in the United States. Governor Frank Keating said, "Obviously, no amateur did this. Whoever did this was an animal."

The bomb that destroyed the Murrah Building was composed of 4,800 pounds of ammonium nitrate fertilizer mixed with fuel oil and loaded into twenty blue plastic drums. Combined with this mixture were metal receptacles full of hydrogen or acetylene designed to increase the explosive power. The drums were then placed in a rental truck, driven to the Murrah Building, parked in front, and detonated by remote control. A small piece of a truck axle found in the rubble was the first clue that put investigators on the trail of suspects. As luck would have it, very shortly after the bombing, the highway patrol stopped Timothy McVeigh for driving without a license plate and for carrying a concealed weapon. Further investigation into McVeigh's background revealed his connection to right-wing paramilitary organizations, particularly one sometimes known as the Patriots. McVeigh had been introduced to the anarchist doctrines of the group by his former army buddy Terry Nichols.

Since childhood, McVeigh had apparently had an inordinate interest in guns and weapons and aspired toward a career in the Special Forces. He joined the army out of high school and received the Bronze Star for serving in Desert Storm. When he failed to qualify for Special Forces training, however, he resigned from the army and began to drift. His own right-wing leanings intensified when he met up again with Nichols. When the FBI checked out Terry Nichols's farm, they found thirty-three firearms, a 60-millimeter antitank rocket launcher, three empty fifty-pound bags of ammonium nitrate, and four blue plastic drums similar to those used in the bombing. Nichols turned himself in but wouldn't talk. He did say, however, that McVeigh had called him three days before the bombing and had said that "something big is going to happen." Nichols and his brother, James, were held in custody and charged with conspiracy to make bombs, but not accused of complicity in the bombing. In August, a grand jury indicted Timothy McVeigh and Terry Nichols, as well as another former army buddy, Michael Fortier, who was charged with transporting stolen guns, perjury, and helping McVeigh case the building. In June 1997, McVeigh was convicted of murder and conspiracy and sentenced to death. In June 1998, Terry Nichols was sentenced to life in prison for conspiracy and involuntary manslaughter. Fortier, who became the government's star witness against the other two and claimed he didn't believe McVeigh was actually going to go through with the bombing, was sentenced to twelve years in prison for failing to notify authorities about the plot.

The Murrah Building was razed. In its place is a grassy park, a memorial to the 169 who died there.

1995: Rabin Assassinated. On Saturday night, November 4, Israeli Prime Minister Yitzhak Rabin was walking to his car after attending a peace rally in Tel Aviv when a gunman suddenly appeared behind him and shot him twice. Rabin was rushed to Ichilov Hospital, where he died in surgery.

The assassin, captured immediately, was identified as Yigal Amir, a law student at Bar Ilan University who was known to be connected with extremist groups and right-wing causes. Amir, angered by militant Muslim attacks on Israel, confessed that he was acting under orders of God and that

"I have no regrets." He is now spending the rest of his life in prison.

Although according to Jewish custom the dead are buried within one day, the prime minister was buried two days later to allow time for world leaders to arrive for the funeral services. President Clinton called Rabin "a martyr for his nation's peace" and Secretary of State Warren Christopher said that "history will record Prime Minister Rabin as one of the towering figures of the century."

1995: Tragic Fire in Dabwali, India. On December 23, approximately 1,200 children, parents, and teachers were gathered inside a tentlike structure within a walled courtyard to celebrate the annual festivities marking the end of the school year. As the ceremonies were about to close, a fire broke out and swiftly raged through the building. Over 500 people died in the conflagration and more than 250 were injured.

1996: Slaughter of the Innocents. About 9:30 A.M. on Wednesday, March 13, a gunman burst into the gymnasium of the primary school in Dunblane, Scotland, and began shooting. A few minutes later, thirteen kindergarten children and one teacher lay dead. Three more died later in a hospital; twelve others and two teachers were wounded. The murderer saved the last bullet for himself. It was the worst massacre by a lone gunman in modern British history.

Identified as Thomas Hamilton, the gunman had evidently been planning the killing for a long time. A loner, social misfit, and gun enthusiast, Hamilton had frequently asked questions about the layout and classes at the school, according to testimony presented at the inquest. He had been forced to resign as a Boy Scout leader years before under suspicion of improper behavior toward young boys and harbored a deep resentment toward the town for labeling him a pervert and ruining his reputation. The grudge festered within him and he set about getting revenge.

The evil that men do lives on and on. . . .

1996: Everglades Crash. On May 11, ValuJet Flight 592 nose-dived into the Florida Everglades a few minutes after taking off from Miami. The plane, carrying 110 passengers and crew, hit the ground with such force that it disappeared completely into the swamp and remains buried there.

Investigators later determined that the plane was carrying illegally stored oxygen generators that apparently fanned a fire and caused the crash.

1996: Flight 800 Tragedy. It was a hot evening on July 17 when TWA Flight 800 took off from New York's JFK airport loaded with passengers headed for Paris. Minutes later, the Boeing 747 exploded and crashed into the Atlantic Ocean off of Long Island, sending all 230 passengers and the crew into a watery grave.

At first the cause of the explosion was rumored to be a bomb, a missile, or a meteorite. Aircraft parts were fished out of the ocean and reassembled in a hangar on Long Island in the greatest crash investigation in U.S. history. After a lengthy and intensive inquiry, investigators concluded that the nearly empty 12,890-gallon central fuel tank had exploded. Air conditioners that had been cooling the plane had turned the remaining liquid fuel in the tank into unstable combustible vapors. A minute spark from adjacent electrical wiring was probably all it took to touch off the disaster.

1996: Midair Crash Over India. The Saudi Arabian Airlines 747-100 had just taken off from the airport at New Delhi, India. Incoming was a Kazakhstan Air Lines Ilyushin 76 cargo jet. Seven minutes later, the two collided over Charkhi Dadri, sixty miles west of New Delhi. The impact killed 289 passengers and 23 crew members aboard the 747 and 37 people on the Ilyushin. The November 12 accident was the world's most disastrous midair collision.

Apparently the sky is limited.

1997: Grand Forks Deluge. Townspeople had been sandbagging emergency levees for weeks, but on April 18, the Red River of the North broke through the dike and inundated the towns of Grand Forks, North Dakota, and its sister city, East Grand Forks, Minnesota. More than 58,000 people, nearly the entire population, had to evacuate. In downtown East Grand Forks, the city hall, fire department, library, schools, churches, and shops were all underwater. In Grand Forks, already flooded, a fire raged through the downtown section, completely destroying it. There was no drinking water, no heat, and no electricity. The river water mixed with sewage, algae, oil, and fungus and turned into sludge. The debris from the homes and buildings later filled ten acres of the town landfill. Although no one died in the flood, the damage exceeded one billion dollars. Over 11,000 businesses and homes were damaged and 700 houses had to be demolished. In East Grand Forks, almost all the houses were damaged; 500 had to be bulldozed.

In true "the show must go on" fashion, through flood, fire, and pestilence the *Grand Forks Herald,* the local newspaper, kept publishing. Its downtown offices having been destroyed, it moved to a school in a nearby town and never missed a day. For its efforts, it was awarded the Pulitzer Prize for public service.

1997: Air Crash in Guam. On August 5, a Korean Air 747-300 was making a nighttime airport approach in heavy rain when it crashed three miles short of the runway at Agana, Guam's capital. Of the 231 passengers aboard, 207 were killed, and 21 of the 23 crew members died.

1997: Death of a Princess. At 12:15 A.M. on Sunday, August 31, a black Mercedes 280 SL pulled away from the rear entrance of the Ritz Hotel in Paris, sped along the expressway by the Seine, and entered the tunnel by the Place de l'Alma. Seconds later, the Mercedes crashed head-on into a concrete support column, careened into the opposite wall, and spun around. In the backseat of the crushed vehicle, the British Princess Diana lay dying. Dead beside her was her companion, Dodi Fayed. In the front seat, the only survivor, bodyguard Trevor Rees-Jones, slumped unconscious and critically injured alongside the dead driver of the car, Henri Paul. In the ensuing moments, the paparazzi descended upon the crash scene, followed by the police and the ambulances. Diana was rushed to La Pitié-Salpétrière hospital, where doctors worked on her in surgery but to no avail. By five o'clock she was dead.

Shocked and grieving British mourners gathered at the gates of Buckingham Palace and Kensington Palace, Diana's home. They brought bouquets of flowers, little mementos, hand-lettered signs, and personal notes. Flags were lowered to half-mast, and crowds waited patiently for hours to sign official books of condolences. Queen Elizabeth II, in an unexpected moment, appeared live on television to tell her subjects that "we have all been trying in our different ways to cope."

The sky was bright and cloudless on September 6, as 1,900 invited mourners filled Westminster Abbey for the funeral. They came from all walks of life: royalty, statesmen, artists, actors, commoners whose lives Diana had touched, as well as representatives of over seventy charities. Outside the abbey, thousands of people gathered to hear the service over loud-speakers, while millions more watched on television. After the service, Diana's body was driven to the Spencers' ancestral home at Althorp, where she now rests in the family vault on an island in the lake on the property.

The case of the accident became a matter of contention. The couple had been stalked by photographers all evening and, in a last-ditch effort to evade them, had decided to leave from the rear entrance of the hotel, leaving a decoy car at the front. Their driver was later found to have four times the French legal limit of alcohol in his blood. He apparently lost control of the speeding car while trying to outrun the photographers and may have hit or been hit by another car in the tunnel.

The future heir to the throne of England and his younger brother had lost their mummy.

Wear your seat belts.

1997: Paradise Lost. The Caribbean island of Monteserrat was all but obliterated by the Soufrière Hills volcano, which spewed molten lava, gas, and ashes over the island's villages. The volcano had been asleep for five hundred years when it awoke in 1995 and began to rain its destruction over the thirty-nine-square-mile British colony. By September 1997, ash from the volcano had covered two-thirds of the once-lush island, a favorite destination of tourists. More than two-thirds of the 12,000 people who inhabited the island had left; others fled to relative safety in shelters set up in the northern part of the island. As the volcano continued to smoke and belch hot debris, many of the remaining residents reluctantly accepted relocation to England or neighboring islands, abandoning Montserrat to Soufrière.

And Paradise is Wilderness now.

1997: Luxor Tourists Slaughter. The Temple of Hatshepsut on the west bank of the Nile at Luxor is visited by two million tourists a year. At 9:00 A.M. on Monday, November 17, busloads of sightseers began arriving at the famous temple; three hours later, 62 were dead and 24 were wounded. Gunmen belonging to Gama'a al-Islamiya (the Islamic Group) had originally planned to take as many tourists as possible hostage in order to compel release of their leader, cleric Sheikh Omar Abdel-Rahman, imprisoned in the United States for conspiracy in the 1993 World Trade Center bombing in New York. Attackers hijacked a bus carrying Japanese tourists, then killed them and hijacked another bus full of tourists, killing them also. Gunmen hiding in the temple opened fire on approaching tourists, mowing them down where they stood. Two policemen were killed before the assailants were themselves killed by security forces.

President Mubarak flew to the site the next day and told reporters, "We are going to close all entrances to the area except the main gate" and promised to tighten security at all tourist sites. According to Mubarak, "Such people who kill human beings are not Muslims, Christians, or Jews . . . they are criminals." Over 1,000 people, including nearly 100 foreigners, have been killed since 1992, when militant groups began their struggle to overthrow the secular Egyptian government and set up an Islamic state. By bringing Egypt's huge tourist industry to a halt, they hoped to upset the economy enough to collapse the administration.

Queen Hatshepsut, who reigned from c. 1503–1482 B.C., devoted herself to encouraging commerce.

1998: Famine in Sudan. For fifteen years, a civil war has raged in Sudan between the Sudan People's Liberation Army, fighting for Christian and animist autonomy in the south, and the Arab and Muslim government at Khartoum in the north. An estimated 1.5 million have died because the war effort has left land uncultivated, and cattle have been destroyed by marauding militias. By the summer of 1998, the war, combined with two years of unending drought, put 1.2 million people in danger of starving in southern Sudan and another 1.4 million in government-controlled areas. Skeletal refugees trudging toward relief camps dropped by the wayside, parents were forced to abandon some of their weaker children, children watched their parents die. Leaves and water left in puddles from a few scattered showers became the only sustenance. In some camps, people sat waiting for food airdrops from Operation Lifeline Sudan, established in 1989, which had not been able to airlift food supplies rapidly enough to stave off starvation. The fleet of cargo planes operated by the organization was grounded for several days in June to make repairs to the overworked aircraft.

In July, after urging by the British Foreign Office minister, the Sudanese rebels declared a cease-fire for three months to enable a food delivery system to reach hundreds of thousands of starving people. The government in the north, at the request of Kenyan President Moi, allowed a monthlong truce. Nearly 10,000 tons of food per month were dropped by the U.N. World Food Program into southern Sudan. Government soldiers frequently looted or burned food supplies to keep them out of the hands of the rebels, whose leaders denied the accusation that they diverted relief stocks to feed the troops of the Liberation Army. Occasionally, sacks of corn dropped from a plane burst when they hit the ground, sending masses of old people and children scurrying to grab as many kernels as possible to ward off starvation.

"Our children are dying," said an old man. "Tell the world to come and ask why our people are dying."

1998: Why? Cable Car Clipped by Jet. On February 3, a U.S. Marine EA-6B Prowler on a low-level training mission near Aviano in the Italian Alps severed the wire supporting a cable car, sending the ski gondola and its 20 passengers plummeting 370 feet to their death. Italian authorities claimed the jet was six miles outside the flight corridor and was flying too low. The Marine Corps placed the blame on the crew for flying lower and faster than authorized. Defense lawyers contended that the gondola cables did not appear on the maps issued to the crew. The pilot and navigator were charged with involuntary manslaughter and negligent homicide as well as dereliction of duty, destroying military and civilian property, and faced a court-martial. The pilot was acquitted of the serious charges, which were then dropped against the navigator. The navigator, however, pleaded guilty to conspiracy and obstruction-of-justice charges after admitting he destroyed a videotape taken from the plane's cockpit. He was sentenced to dismissal from the Marine Corps. The pilot, who took the videotape, was sentenced to six months in prison and a recommendation he be dismissed from the Marine Corps.

1998: Taiwan's Worst Plane Crash. On the foggy evening of Monday, February 16, China Airlines Flight 676 was coming in for a landing at Taipei's Chiang Kai-shek airport when it suddenly veered off its approach, hit a residential area, and exploded in flames. The crash killed all 197 on board and 7 on the ground. The passengers were mainly Taiwanese families returning from vacation in Bali. The impact scattered bodies and parts of bodies throughout the area. Only three large pieces of the fuselage, a piece of one wing, and a tailpiece remained of the charred plane.

The director of Taiwan's Civil Aeronautics Administration took moral responsibility for the crash and resigned.

1998: Toxic Sludge Disaster in Spain. On April 25, a reservoir at the Los Frailes iron pyrite mining complex in southern Spain ruptured, disgorging an estimated 1.3 billion gallons of sludge into the Guadiamar River and creating one of Spain's worst ecological disasters. The toxic waste, composed of heavy metal tailings, acidic chemicals, and mineral sediment, contaminated cotton fields and rice paddies along a twenty-five-mile stretch of the river area, causing an estimated 14 million dollars in agricultural losses. The river was diverted by makeshift dikes and a canal into the Guadalquivir River in an endeavor to keep the pollution away from Donana National Park, Europe's largest nature preserve, twenty-five miles southwest of Seville. The park is home to millions of birds, lynx, otters, and other endangered species who live in its 185,000 acres of dunes, marshes, and forests. Some authorities fear the spill has caused permanent damage to the area due to the difficulty of eradicating the metal residues from land and river sediments. During the extensive cleanup, twenty tons of dead fish were retrieved from the river near Donana. In a massive removal effort, the sludge was bulldozed, hauled away, and deposited in an abandoned open-pit mine at a site west of Seville.

Only to ooze out again, perhaps?

1998: Killer Mud Slides. On May 6, after two days of incessant rain, mud and debris hurled through the narrow streets of small towns in southern Italy killing at least 148 people and leaving nearly 2,000 more homeless. In minutes, houses were torn apart, cars were swallowed up in the muck, and bridges were demolished by the fast-flowing torrents. Railroad tracks and roads were piled with mud, cutting off transportation and downing power and telephone lines. Hardest hit was Sarno, where 44 people lost their lives. Mud burst through the hospital, killing doctors, nurses, and patients. Ambulances and cars were piled one on top of the other and a nearby five-story building was pushed 500 yards downhill. Many homes in the region, a thirty-five-mile swath between Naples and Salerno, had been built illegally close to rivers or streams or in terrain prone to landslides. Construction had also denuded vegetation on the hillsides that kept the earth in place.

Save those trees!

1998: Nuclear Duel. On May 11, India's Prime Minister Vajpayee announced that his country had detonated three underground nuclear devices. The news was greeted with joy by Hindu nationalists throughout India as the prime minister announced that India was now a nuclear weapons state and declared, "It is India's due." On May 13, two more devices were tested. India's neighbor, Pakistan, retaliated two weeks later by detonating six nuclear devices of its own. The Pakistanis danced in the streets in celebration and congratulated their scientists on the great achievement as Prime Minister Nawaz Sharif proclaimed, "Today we have settled a score."

When India gained its independence from Britain in 1947, it was partitioned into two countries, predominantly Hindu India and Pakistan, which was carved out of the northwestern part of India as a home for Muslims. The two have been fighting each other periodically ever since over the partitioning and over the northern state of Jammu and Kashmir, which wanted to remain independent. In 1959, there were border clashes with China. In 1962, China invaded India along the Himalayan border, but India was able to push back the Chinese with help from the United States, Canada, and Britain. Since then India has been increasing its defenses and has accused China of aiding Pakistan's nuclear development.

After India's announcement of its detonations, the United States and other countries immediately ordered sanctions and suspended aid, but threats of sanctions did not deter the Pakistani government. India declared a moratorium on testing and Pakistan offered to sign a nonaggression pact if India would.

In the weeks that followed, routine hostilities continued. Pakistan blamed India for the bombing of a movie theater in the ancient city of Lahore that killed three and injured ten. India blamed Pakistan for the deaths of twenty-five men killed at wedding festivities by Muslim guerrillas.

And the beat goes on.

1998: Financial Turmoil in Indonesia. Rumblings of financial disaster erupted in riots in May that brought down the thirty-two-year autocratic reign of President Suharto. Indonesia consists of an archipelago of 17,500 islands with 204 million people, making it the fourth most populous country in the world. The rupiah, the national currency, began to drop in value in the fall of 1997, when Indonesian banks began calling in questionable loans. In order to pay off their debt, borrowers rushed to get U.S. dollars which, in turn, forced down the value of Asian currencies. Suharto, who controlled a family business worth billions of dollars, was hesitant to apply economic reforms that might weaken the financial interests of his six children and his political cronies. The International Monetary Fund, however, insisted he dismantle the monopolies owned by family and friends before Indonesia could receive emergency funds to shore up its banks. In response, the government cut subsidies on fuel, electricity, and food to prevent budget deficits, causing prices to soar as much as 70 percent. In protest, students began to riot in several of the universities. Protesters gathered force among the poor and violence spread throughout the country as mobs ransacked, burned, and looted. The eight million ethnic Chinese who dominated commerce and industry were especially targeted as scapegoats for the failing economy. Their businesses and homes were burned as they scrambled to leave the country in fear of their lives. The capital city of Jakarta was laid waste as hundreds of buildings, including large stores and supermarkets, churches, government buildings, and factories, were set on fire. The week of rioting left over 1,200 dead and caused $250 million in property damage.

On May 21, as students cheered, Suharto, his voice quivering with emotion, gave his speech of resignation, declaring his "deepest sorrow" for "mistakes, failures, and shortcomings." Then he named a successor, Vice President Habibie, to serve until the term ends in 2003. Habibie, a close friend and political ally of Suharto, promised to "attack corruption, collusion, and nepotism."

Yeah, sure.

1998: Bolivia Shakes. At dawn on Friday, May 22, the Quechua Indian farmers in central Bolivia were awakened by a magnitude 6.6 earthquake followed by more than 100 aftershocks. On Saturday, another tremor of 5.6 toppled homes that had already been damaged during Friday's quake. Eighty-four people were killed, 200 were injured, and thousands left homeless.

1998: Afghanistan Earthquake. On May 30, the remote northeastern region of Afghanistan was rocked by a massive 6.9 magnitude earthquake. The quake wiped out an estimated sixty-one villages, killed nearly 5,000 people, injured thousands more, and left another 95,000 homeless. The area had suffered an earlier quake in February that had killed 2,300 and left 15,000 homeless. In the Shari Basurkh district, the epicenter of the quake, sun-baked mud houses, already weakened by the previous quake and recent severe rainstorms, collapsed into dust heaps. In the village of Rostaq, 140 children died when their school collapsed on them. One farmer raced back to his village and found it gone. He and a few friends began digging in the rubble, but the people they uncovered were already dead, including his 12 relatives. Another farmer lost his wife and child and declared, "I have lost everything . . . we must leave everything in Allah's hands, but I wonder why he is punishing the people of this country so much."

Aid was difficult to deliver to this rugged mountainous area. Villagers carried their injured on stretchers made of sticks and rags and waited for the helicopters that flew in medical supplies and evacuated the most seriously injured. Two days after the quake, cargo helicopters loaded with tons of food, blankets, and tents finally reached Faisabad, the area capital, for distribution.

Afghanistan has suffered from years of civil war and internal strife. Now it must cope with two major earthquakes. As one villager said, "We are a tough people. We have learned how to survive."

1998: Fatal Train Crash in Germany. On June 3, Inter-City Express 884 was heading north between Hanover and Hamburg at 125 miles per hour when twelve of the fourteen cars derailed and crashed into a steel-reinforced concrete overpass. Passengers were crushed and mutilated in the wreckage of the cars and the collapsed overpass. One hundred and one people were killed in the wreck and over 100 were injured, making it the deadliest train accident in Germany in over fifty years. The cause of the crash was apparently a damaged wheel that threw the train off the track as it passed over a switch.

1998: More Cyclone Deaths in India. On June 9, a cyclone struck the state of Gujarat on India's west coast, causing a tidal wave that washed away at least eight villages, sweeping people into the sea or burying them in mud. Transformers were damaged and power lines downed, leaving survivors without lights and water. A week later, the official death toll was 1,084 with thousands homeless. According to rescue workers, however, 10,000 to 14,000 people had simply disappeared.

Mother Nature seems bent on raising havoc in this part of the world.

1998: The Terrifying Tsunami. On Friday, July 17, villagers living along the northern coast of Papua New Guinea were eating their dinners when suddenly they were awash in a thirty-foot-high sea of water. A mammoth tidal wave had engulfed the villages. Driven by an undersea magnitude 7 earthquake twelve miles off the coast, the wave sucked entire villages back into the ocean as it reformed and roared inland three times. Houses crumbled and bodies were battered against trees and debris as the water crashed over the palms and stilt-legged homes.

Of the roughly 9,000 people living in the eighteen-mile stretch of land hit by the tidal wave, only about 3,000 were accounted for a week later. Many of the survivors were seriously hurt, with broken backs, multiple fractures, and internal injuries. Drowned and bashed bodies lay askew among the damaged houses and wreckage. The corpses were buried in mass graves or burned in the huts where they lay. Although an accurate count was not possible, it is estimated that more than 6,000 people lost their lives in those few terrifying moments.

1998: More Floods in China. During the summer, the swollen Yangtze (Chang Jiang) River once again spread havoc over China in the country's worst flooding in forty years. Millions of soldiers and civilians patrolled the dikes along the world's third-longest river, plugging up leaks and watching for indications of collapse. Hundreds of villagers and soldiers were swept away north of Wuhan when a levee gave way; 400 more soldiers drowned after a levee broke in another town. By August 6, an estimated 1,300 people had lost their lives as torrential rain continued to pour down over southwestern China. As dikes burst, people were warned to leave their homes, but not all made it in time. The Yangtze reached a record high of 149.2 feet at the city of Shashi in Hubei province, where dikes were about to be dynamited to protect downriver cities before the water began to subside. In Heilongjiang, 20,000 residents were stranded when the floods washed away railroad tracks. Landslides and more flooding closed another railway in the northwestern Xinjiang region and threatened oil fields in Daqing. People who had been submerged in polluted water suffered from skin infections and outbreaks of dysentery, typhoid, and cholera. The Chinese government announced a final death toll of 3,656, but it is estimated that at least 10,000 people were dead or missing as a result of the floods.

China, one of Mother Nature's favorite haunts.

1998: U.S. Embassies in East Africa Bombed. At 10:40 on Friday morning, August 7, a bomb exploded at the U.S. embassy in downtown Nairobi, Kenya, shattering the structure and demolishing the Ufundi Cooperative House building next door. Five minutes later, in a residential district of Dar es Salaam, the capital of neighboring Tanzania, a bomb destroyed sections of its U.S. embassy, killing 12 Tanzanians and injuring 72.

The explosion in Nairobi crushed hundreds in the Ufundi building under a three-story-high pile of concrete and steel. In the embassy, 49 people, including 12 Americans, were killed by the blast as windows shattered, doors blew off, and ceilings fell. Out on the streets, shock waves were felt over a quarter of a mile as burning fragments ignited parked cars and charred buses. Huge chunks of debris rained down on the avenues, injuring passersby.

Rescue workers immediately began to chop away at the rubble with shovels and pickaxes in a desperate effort to rescue the injured, many of whom began crawling out of the rubble with broken bones and bloodied faces. Large cranes arrived to remove huge slabs of concrete while a team of Israeli soldiers aided in the recovery with Rottweilers trained to search for bodies. Teams of foreign medical personnel flew in to assist the Kenyans as thousands of victims were rushed to hospitals for treatment.

The explosion in Nairobi damaged fifty-three buildings, killed 201 people, and injured over 5,000, some very seriously. According to Kenyan President Daniel arap Moi, damage to the Kenyan economy was estimated at $500 million.

Chief suspects in the the bombing were associates of Osama bin Laden, a wealthy exiled Saudi businessman living in Afghanistan, who finances and runs al Qaida, a worldwide terrorist organization. Bin Laden has declared a holy war against the United States.

But not against the Kenyans.

1998: Car Bomb Ravages Omagh. At three in the afternoon on Saturday, August 15, shoppers in the small town of Omagh in Northern Ireland were suddenly blown apart by a 500-pound bomb blast. The explosion killed 28, injured 220, many of them critically, and left the town center in rubble. Among the dead were 9 children and 13 women, most of them shopping for back-to-school clothes.

A half-hour prior to the explosion, a caller using an Irish Republican Army code name warned a newspaper that a bomb would be detonated near the courthouse. Police moved crowds away from that area only to have the car bomb go off at an intersection where many had gathered. Police suspected that a dissident splinter group of the IRA calling themselves the "Real IRA" had planned the bombing in an effort to disrupt the peace accord that had been agreed upon three months earlier. It was the worst carnage in the thirty years of sectarian strife that has cast a pall over Northern Ireland.

And just when everyone thought it was safe to go out in the streets again.

1998: Disease, Disaster, and Despair in Bangladesh. By September, the longest-lasting flood in the history of Bangladesh had marooned inhabitants, destroyed crops, damaged roads and buildings, and bred disease in one of the poorest nations in the world. Inundations from the Jamuna and other rivers normally last only a few weeks in the flood-prone country, but the sea level this year was higher than usual and the waters backed up into the lowlands. The floods covered more than half the country, killed over 900 people, displaced more than 30 million, and destroyed 2.3 million tons of rice. Disease, particularly diarrhea, ran rampant as the murky waters became a dumping ground for all manner of waste material and garbage. Authorities predicted that 3.5 million people would be afflicted with the malady, which would be more prevalent after the floods subsided.

And once again Mother Nature turns on us.

1998: Air Crash in Nova Scotia. On Wednesday, September 2, Swissair Flight 111 was headed from New York to Geneva when the pilot reported smoke in the cockpit of the MD-11 jet and suggested he turn back to land in Boston. Authorities advised him that Halifax was closer and the crew opted to land there. The pilot then began the descent from 33,000 feet, dumping fuel en route in preparation for an emergency landing. Fifty-eight miles southwest of the airport, a "Pan-Pan-Pan" warning was issued by the pilot designating a dangerous condition. Minutes later, at 10:31 P.M. local time, the plane crashed into the Atlantic near Peggy's Cove, Nova Scotia, killing all 229 passengers and crew.

It was later disclosed that Picasso's "The Painter," worth 1.5 million dollars, had been destroyed in the crash. Also on board were over one hundred pounds of cash sealed in plastic and four and a half pounds of diamonds, both in a locked but not fireproof container.

1998: Ship Capsizes Near Manila. At 8:00 P.M. on Friday, September 18, *The Princess of the Orient* set sail from Manila for Cebu City in the central Philippines. A few hours later, the ship began to list during a storm, then capsized about seventy-five miles south of Manila. One hundred ninety-four passengers were rescued from the rough seas, but at least 250 were missing and presumed drowned.

1998: Hurricane Georges Strikes. During the third week of September a hurricane named Georges blew through the eastern Caribbean, the Gulf Coast, and the Florida Keys. The wind and rains devastated areas of Puerto Rico, the Dominican Republic, and Haiti with winds of nearly 150 miles per hour. The Dominican Republic reported 210 dead with over 500 missing. Official figures from Haiti included 94 dead and 60 missing. On September 23, the town of Fonds Verrettes in Haiti was completely wiped out by a surge of water and debris that killed 85 inhabitants and left the rest homeless. In Puerto Rico, over 10,000 people were housed in temporary shelters in the worst disaster to strike the island in about four decades.

Just the usual September weather in the Caribbean.

1998: Nigerian Oil Pipe Explosion. On the night of October 17, a section of an aboveground oil pipeline running between the Nigerian cities of Warri and Kaduna exploded into a fireball, incinerating an estimated 700 people and injuring hundreds more.

Nearly a thousand destitute villagers, including women and children from the impoverished town of Jesse, had gathered in the night armed with metal and plastic cups and buckets in an attempt to sabotage the pipeline and siphon fuel for themselves, a common practice in this wretchedly poor country. Among them were a few black marketeers hoping to profit from the stolen oil. Authorities believe tools used to break open the pipeline caused a spark setting off the explosion.

The ensuing fire burned in the town of Jesse and nearby villages for a week. The local hospitals were overwhelmed with the injured, many of whom were not involved in the incident but were burned in the aftermath as the fire spread. Many of the injured fled the hospitals for fear of prosecution from the authorities, although the town crier was sent to assure them they would not be arrested.

Nigeria is the sixth-largest oil producer in the world, but it exports so much that very little is left for its own indigent peoples.

"The mass of men lead lives of quiet desperation." And when terribly desperate, sometimes cause explosions.

1998: Hurricane Mitch Wreaks Havoc on Millions. On October 26, a category 5 hurricane, one of the strongest of the century with winds up to 180 miles per hour, roared through the Caribbean headed for Central America. By October 28, it was parked over Honduras and Nicaragua, where it dumped more rain in six days than either country normally gets in three years. On October 31, Mitch was downgraded to a tropical depression as it veered over Guatemala and the Yucatan Peninsula, then touched on southernmost Florida before dissipating over the Atlantic. The area's deadliest storm in 200 years killed more than 11,000 people; an estimated 10,000 were missing, and over two million were left homeless.

Hardest hit was Honduras, where Mitch destroyed 70 percent of the infrastructure, devastated crops, and ravaged the capital city of Tegucigalpa. President Carlos Flores Facusse described the scene as "a panorama of death, desolation, and ruin." In neighboring Nicaragua, 3,800 people lost their lives when a rain-swollen crater lake overflowed, sending torrents of mud and debris over several villages and burying alive more than 3,000 people. Minister of Defense Pedro Joaquin Chamorro Barrios suggested, "It would be appropriate to declare the area of the tragedy a national cemetery."

As the wind and rains subsided, workers began the task of rescuing those trapped on roofs of flooded houses or stranded on islands surrounded by muddy waters. Survivors searched in vain for missing family members in the muck and wreckage of their villages. There was no food and no potable water and relief workers feared the death toll could double as people succumbed to disease and starvation.

The economic loss was in the billions. In Honduras, 75 percent of the country was under water, a third of the buildings in the capital were destroyed, most of the bridges were out, and the roads were inundated with debris. Nearly 15,000 homes along the coast were obliterated. Most of the beans, rice, and corn crop was gone. Banana plantations were totally destroyed, leaving thousands unemployed.

Aid from other countries in the form of helicopters, troops, cargo planes with food, water, cots, and plastic sheeting for shelters began flooding in. Doctors and medicine arrived on the scene while military engineers were sent to repair bridges and roads. According to some reports, it will take decades to restore the economy.

As the old song goes, "Yes, we have no bananas . . ." and no corn and no wheat and no rice and no beans and no coffee and no water and no homes . . .

1998: Train Wreck in India. In the early morning darkness of Thursday, November 26, the *Frontier Mail,* headed for Amritsar in northwest India, derailed, sprawling four cars across the tracks. A few minutes later, the oncoming *Sealdah Express* bound for Calcutta crashed into the derailed train. The collision demolished the derailed cars and the express engine. Most of the passengers were asleep at the time of the accident, which killed 205 and injured at least 260.

There are about 300 accidents on India's railroads every year, one of the largest networks in the world. Take the bus.

1998: AIDS Rivals the Black Death. A report by the United Nations published in November stated that of the 33 million people worldwide who were infected with the HIV virus, 22 million live in Africa, most of them in the sub-Saharan region. In thirteen African countries, 10 percent of the adults were infected, and in Zimbabwe, Namibia, and Botswana, the infection rate rose to a quarter of the adults. Infection rates for pregnant women range from 32 to 70 percent in some of the major African cities. The women then pass on the virus to their babies. Health officials reported that most Africans may not know they are infected because testing is not always available.

Although HIV rates are lower in Eastern Europe, Asia, and South Africa, the transmission rate is doubling and sometimes tripling. In Southeast Asia, Cambodia suffers from the highest rate of infection with half the country's 10,000 to 20,000 prostitutes carrying the virus. In 1997 alone, 2.3 million people died from AIDS, making it among the top five causes of death worldwide.

During the nearly twenty years of the Black Death scourge of the 14th century, 25 million people died in Europe. Deaths from AIDS may equal that in the long run.

1999: Sex, Lies, and Audiotapes. On January 7, the U.S. House of Representatives presented to the Senate a resolution impeaching William Jefferson Clinton, president of the United States, for high crimes and misdemeanors. It was the second time in U.S. history that a president had been impeached. The Articles of Impeachment charged Clinton with perjury and obstruction of justice for providing false and misleading testimony to a grand jury in a civil suit brought against him; and for corrupt efforts to influence the testimony of witnesses in the suit and for engaging in conduct designed to delay, impede, cover up, and conceal the existence of evidence in the case.

In August 1994, Kenneth Starr was appointed independent counsel and charged with investigating Whitewater, a real estate deal in Arkansas in which Clinton and his wife had been involved when he was governor of the state. The case was investigated for several years, and while Starr and his staff could find no evidence of wrongdoing on the part of the President, other participants were convicted of misconduct.

In February of that year, Paula Corbin Jones had filed suit against the President, claiming he had made unwanted sexual advances toward her in 1991 when he was governor of Arkansas and she was a state clerk. Out of testimony in the Jones case arose the sex and lies scandal that nearly brought down the presidency, occupied the media for months, and had the rest of the world wondering what all the fuss was about.

In an effort by Jones's lawyers to strengthen their case against the president, former White House intern Monica Lewinsky was subpoenaed in January 1998 to testify. In a sworn affidavit, she told Jones's lawyers she had had no relationship with the President while working in the White House in 1995. Unbeknownst to Lewinsky, her friend and confidante, Linda Tripp, an employee at the Pentagon where they both now worked, had taped private telephone conversations in which Lewinsky related in detail her affair with the President. Tripp gave Whitewater prosecutor Starr the tapes, then wore a hidden microphone and secretly taped a conversation with Lewinsky in which she allegedly told Tripp that Clinton had asked her to conceal their relationship. By that time, the President had already testified under oath in the Jones case and answered questions about several women with whom he had allegedly had sexual contact. He denied the affair with Lewinsky. On January 20, the story broke in the press. On January 26, the president again denied the affair and cover-up and publicly uttered his now famous words, "I did not have sexual relations with that woman. . . . I never told anybody to lie."

Attorney General Janet Reno formally approved Starr's request to expand his investigation into the possibility of obstruction of justice and perjury in the Jones case. For months, the grand jury heard testimony from a wide variety of witnesses including Lewinsky's mother, Vernon Jordan, aides Bruce Lindsey and Sidney Blumenthal, several Secret Service agents, and the President. On April 1, the Jones case was dismissed by Judge Susan Webber Wright; Jones announced she would appeal.

On August 17, the President appeared on national television and confessed to having a relationship with Lewinsky. The next month, Starr sent the final report on his findings to the House of Representatives, which then made it public over the Internet; ten days later, the President's videotaped testimony was made public. Despite the scandal, the President's approval rating remained high and in the November elections, to the consternation of the Republicans, the Democrats picked up five seats in the House. According to exit polls, two-thirds of the voters did not want the President impeached. On November 13, Clinton offered Jones $850,000, but no apology or admission of guilt, if she agreed to drop her suit. The tapes of conversations between Tripp and Lewinsky were released to the public, and two days later on national television, Starr defended his investigation to the House Judiciary Committee. The House approved Articles of Impeachment accusing the President of perjury and obstruction of justice in the Jones case.

In order to remove the President from office, two-thirds of the Senate must vote for removal. On February 12, the forty-five Democrats and fifty-five Republicans in the Senate acquitted the president, mostly along party lines. Clinton apologized to the people, saying "how profoundly sorry I am for what I said and did to trigger these events and for the great burden they have imposed on the Congress and the American people."

As for the first president who was impeached in a vitriolic political campaign against him in 1868, Andrew Johnson was also acquitted . . . by one vote.

1999: Earthquake Ravages Western Colombia. On January 25, a magnitude 5.8 earthquake devastated cities and villages in the heart of the coffee-growing region of Colombia and shook buildings in Bogotá, the capital city 140 miles away. Hardest hit was Armenia, a city of nearly 300,000, and the nearby towns of Pereira and Calarca. Estimates of the dead and missing exceeded 2,000, with 3,500 injured and 200,000 left homeless. Stores, banks, and businesses were destroyed, leaving people with no jobs and no money. Twenty-seven aftershocks were felt in the area. Two days later, another 5.4 magnitude quake rumbled in the northeast, but no damage was reported.

The earthquake had left the city with no running water or toilets, and shortages of food and antibiotics. Relief supplies were difficult to deliver because of the shortage of trucks and vans. Food stores were looted by desperate survivors trying to feed their children, and the usual fears of epidemics after such a disaster ran rampant. According to Colombian Interior Minister Humbert Martinez, $100 million would be needed to rebuild the stricken region.

The coffee crop, however, was not affected.

1999: Chaos at Columbine High. Engraved on a hallway at Columbine High School in Littleton, Colorado, are the words "The finest kids in America pass through these halls." At 11:15 A.M. on Tuesday, April 20, two of the finest—armed with homemade bombs, two sawed-off shotguns, a 9-millimeter semiautomatic carbine, and a Tec-9 semiautomatic handgun—passed through the halls on a deadly mission. When it was completed, the body count totaled fifteen: one teacher, twelve students, and the two perpetrators, who had killed themselves. Another twenty-three lay wounded.

The two students, Eric Harris and Dylan Klebold, belonged to a group known as the Trench Coat Mafia for the long black trench coats and black clothing they wore to school. They liked to play violent video games, parroted Nazi philosophy, and in general felt alienated from most of their classmates. They apparently had spent the day before building pipe bombs in Harris's garage, which, according to his website, was the "easiest way to kill a group of people." Their rage exploded the next day.

The Columbine massacre was the seventh school shooting in less than two years involving students. The first was on October 7, 1997, in Pearl, Mississippi, where nine students were shot. In December of that year, three students were killed and five wounded in West Paducah, Kentucky. In March, 1998, four students and a teacher were killed and ten wounded by an eleven- and thirteen-year-old in Jonesboro, Arkansas. The following month, a teacher was shot in Edinboro, Pennsylvania, at an eighth-grade dance. The next month, an honor student in Fayetteville, Tennessee, killed a fellow student; and two days later in Springfield, Oregon, a fifteen-year-old killed his parents, then killed two and wounded twenty at his high school. One month after the Columbine massacre, a fifteen-year-old boy wounded six students at his high school in Conyers, Georgia.

In an attempt to answer the question of "why?" blame for the Columbine shootings as well as the others was laid on parents and dysfunctional families, school cliques, sadistic music, violent movies and video games, and on the easy access to guns and weapons.

The weekend after the Columbine killings, the National Rifle Association cut back its scheduled three-day meeting in nearby Denver to one day, and canceled its gun show. Outside the convention's hotel, thousands of protesters peacefully demonstrated against the organization.

1999: Twister Flattens Oklahoma Cities. On May 3, winds swept across "tornado alley" with unsurpassed fury in one of the deadliest tornadoes in fifty years. The first warning was issued at 4:45 P.M. Fifteen minutes later, the first of over forty tornadoes, one nearly a mile wide, touched down. At the storm's peak, some of the twisters reached a velocity between 207 and 260 miles per hour, with one tornado reaching 318 miles per hour, a record for winds on earth. The tornadoes raged for five hours, cutting across several states, with the greatest damage in Oklahoma and Kansas.

The destruction was scattered over eleven counties in Oklahoma, declared disaster areas by the President. Buildings lay in rubble, cars and trucks were strewn in twisted heaps, trees and power lines were down, dead cattle littered the fields, and houses were completely or partially gone. In hard-hit Moore, whole neighborhoods were flattened; people returning to their homes could identify them only by the numbers painted on the curbstones in front. In some of the smaller villages, the devastation was complete, with nothing remaining. Altogether over 3,000 houses and forty-seven businesses were destroyed in the state. Forty-four people were killed, and at least 500 were injured. In neighboring Kansas, three died and over 1,000 buildings were destroyed. It was estimated that it would take two to three years to rebuild everything.

To be undone when the winds come sweeping down the plains again?

1999: Head-on Train Collision in India. At 1:55 on the morning of August 2, while most of the 2,500 passengers slept, the *Awadh-Assam Express* and the *Brahmaputra Mail* collided head-on at Gaisal. The official death toll was 286 with almost 400 injured. The Awadh-Assam train had been switched to the "down" line on which the Brahmaputra train was also traveling in the opposite direction. The switch was apparently known to some staff members but no action had been taken to avert the tragedy. The Minister of Railways, Nitish Kumar, resigned stating he had "moral responsibility" for the accident, which was blamed on "negligence and lack of alertness."

Heads up, guys.

1999: Violent Earthquake Moves Turkey. At 3:02 the morning of August 17, inhabitants of cities and villages in northwestern Turkey awoke with a jolt. For forty-five terror-stricken seconds they were heaved about as their world tumbled down around them. Buildings swayed, collapsed, and crashed, injuring, killing, and burying the populace. The earthquake also fueled a fire at an oil refinery, knocking out one-third of the country's gasoline needs and causing $200 million in damage.

The 7.4 magnitude quake was centered in the city of İzmit, sixty miles east of Istanbul. Strong aftershocks continued spasmodically for the next two weeks, including a 5.2 magnitude temblor August 31, again centered in the already devastated İzmit. Three weeks later the official death toll was reported as 15,082. Over 29,000 had been injured and an estimated 35,000 were missing and presumed buried in the rubble. The quake also left 200,000 homeless, most of them in the hardest hit areas of İzmit-Gölcük, Adapazari, and Yalova. On September 14, the area was again shaken by a 5.8 magnitude quake, sending panicked inhabitants running into the streets.

The high number of casualties was attributed to shoddy construction by unscrupulous contractors who shunned building codes and erected flimsy apartment buildings to house the many migrants seeking work in the cities. The survivors also blamed the government for not responding fast enough to the overwhelming catastrophe.

According to seismologists, the earthquakes moved Turkey four feet closer to Europe as the tectonic plates shifted under the Anatolian fault. It may have moved Turkey politically closer to Europe, too. Almost all European countries sent immediate aid, as did Greece and Armenia, whose relations with Turkey over the years have been chilly.

Out of the ashes arises the phoenix of conciliation?

1999: Hurricane Floyd Floods. On September 2, thunderstorms generated over West Africa banded together and began a westward course over the unusually warm waters of the Atlantic, growing into a storm soon dubbed Hurricane Floyd. By the following week Floyd had intensified into an extremely dangerous category 4 hurricane. Meterologist predicted it would make landfall along the southern Atlantic U.S. coastline, continue inland, turn northward up through Virginia and bear along the coast through the New England states. As the 600-mile-wide hurricane with winds up to 155 miles per hour headed for them, residents from Florida, Georgia, and the Carolinas were ordered to evacuate the coast, producing colossal traffic jams, some 200 miles long. Floyd's winds abated as it suddenly shifted northward, sparing Florida and hitting the Carolinas on September 15 and 16. It then veered north along the coast as far as Maine, dropping tons of rain in its wake and causing flooding in many states. When it was over, the eastern third of North Carolina was almost completely under water in the worst disaster ever to hit the state. Inundated also were parts of Virginia, Maryland, Pennsylvania, New Jersey, and New York.

As rivers began to rise, some as much as 27 feet above flood stage, conditions in eastern North Carolina worsened. Whole towns were submerged with the roofs of buildings barely perceptible. Sections of Interstate 95, the main north-south artery, were closed due to flooding as were parts of Interstate 40, along with another 1,000 roads entirely under water. People who had gone to shelters were stranded in those buildings while others were trapped in their homes as the waters kept rising. Helicopters plucked an estimated 420 inhabitants from rooftops and cars while the National Guard and volunteers in boats cruised the streets rescuing people as well as their dogs and cats. Forty-eight people lost their lives, mostly by drowning. The flood destroyed entire crops of corn, soybeans, cotton and tobacco, killed an estimated 2.1 million chickens, 737,000 turkeys, 30,500 hogs, and 880 cattle.

Two weeks later many areas were still submerged. Governor Hunt told President Clinton, "This is the worst flooding I've ever seen." Debris was everywhere: clothing, furniture, restaurant equipment, propane gas tanks, as well as animal carcasses and eighty caskets that had floated up from deluged cemeteries. Many houses and small businesses were beyond repair and most were without flood insurance. As one flood victim summed it up, "They say they don't know when we can go back, but there's nothing to go back to." Early estimates of storm damage amounted to $1.3 billion but could go as high as $6 billion. It would take years to recover from the economic damage alone.

As residents undertook the task of cleaning up their waterlogged and mudfilled homes and stores and the rivers receded, heavy rains began pouring down again.

A few arks would be a wise addition to rebuilding plans.

1999: Temblor Shakes Taiwan. At 1:45 in the morning on September 21, an earthquake measuring 7.6 on the Richter scale struck Taiwan. The quake's epicenter was ninety miles south of the capital, Taipei, near the city of T'ai-chung. Apartment buildings swayed and leaned against each other as other structures collapsed into piles of concrete, burying the occupants. Roads across the island buckled; a reservoir was damaged as well as major pipelines carrying a third of Taiwan's water supply. The earthquake killed an estimated 2,500 people, left 100,000 homeless, and caused over $9 billion in damage. A major aftershock, measuring 6.8, struck five days later, creating more panic among the inhabitants.

1999: Egyptair Flight 990 Crashes. The Boeing 767-300 left New York City bound for Cairo with 217 passengers and crew. A half-hour later the plane dove from its altitude of 33,000 feet to 16,700 feet with a speed up to 716 miles per hour, rose to 24,000 feet, then plunged into the Atlantic off the coast of Massachusetts. It all happened in less than two minutes in the dark of Halloween night, October 31.

1999: Deadly Mud Slides in Venezuela. For days rains had poured down along the northern coast of Venezuela. On Wednesday, December 15, the rain-drenched earth gave way and swept down Mount Avila toward the port city of La Guaira. The avalanche of mud and boulders buried residents living in shacks of clay, tin sheets, wood, and cinder blocks in slum villages perched on the mountainside. Estimates of the dead ran as high as 20,000, although an accurate count may never be known. At least 6,000 people were reported missing and 150,000 were left homeless. In La Guaira, a country club and a yacht marina were completely destroyed. While rescue efforts were under way, many of the inhabitants searched for food in broken ship containers along the shore. Damage to the port, roads, utilities, hospitals, schools, and homes was estimated at close to $2 billion in one of the worst natural disasters in Venezuela's history.

1999: Conflict in Kosovo. The turmoil that has marked the history of the Balkans flared up again when Yugoslavian President Slobodan Milosevic rejected a United Nations peace plan for the embattled province of Kosovo.

Kosovo, populated mostly by Muslim ethnic Albanians, had enjoyed virtual autonomy for decades within Serbian-dominated Yugoslavia. All that started to change, however, when Milosevic became president of Yugoslavia in 1989. New laws stripped the province of autonomy and cracked down on Albanian culture. Ethnic Albanians responded in 1992 by voting to make Kosovo a republic, independent from the newly formed country of Serbia. Serb leader Milosevic immediately declared the vote invalid; Kosovo President-Elect Ibrahim Rugova preached passive resistance.

In 1997, with the province still under Serbian rule, the Kosovo Liberation Army (KLA) turned to violent rebellion. The Serbs retaliated with a campaign of unbridled ethnic cleansing. Military, paramilitary, and Serbian police forces drove more than one million Albanians from their homes, massacring, pillaging, raping, and burning whole villages in their wake. Refugees poured into Albania and adjacent countries, while the United Nations tried to negotiate with Milosevic to end the conflict.

Milosevic refused to stop the slaughter, and on March 24, NATO launched a massive bombing campaign to destroy the Serbian infrastructure, targeting command posts, power plants, government buildings, and military bases. Numerous civilian buildings were inadvertently hit, along with the Chinese Embassy, several ambassadors' residences, and a group of ethnic Albanians huddled near a Serbian army post. On June 3, after two and a half months of continual bombing, Milosevic finally accepted an international peace plan for withdrawing troops and allowing Kosovar refugees back into their destroyed homeland. On June 10, the Serbian troops began leaving and a NATO peacekeeping force of 50,000 troops entered the devastated province, where they were met by the sight of wounded civilians, burned villages, and mass graves—the gruesome evidence of Serbian atrocities.

As the Kosovo refugees began returning to what was left of their ravaged homes and villages, violence continued to erupt. Many of the ethnic Albanians retaliated with a vengeance against the Kosovar Serbs, burning and looting their houses, assaulting and killing them in an attempt to force them out of the province. The remaining estimated 30,000 Kosovar Serbs, now living in fear, began seeking refuge in ethnic Serbian villages or in neighboring Montenegro or Serbia.

In August, Serbian opposition to Milosevic began to mount. Demonstrators, chanting, "Slobo—go," held anti-government rallies calling for Milosevic to resign, but he held his ground.

Kosovo is in ruins and still a province of Serbia, not the republic it would like to be; Serbia's infrastructure has been demolished and its president indicted by the United Nations on charges of crimes against humanity.

It was a victory Pyrrhus would have been proud of.

2000: The Third Millennium Begins. The world waited with bated breath on January 1, as clocks around the globe began tolling the arrival of the new century and the beginning of the next thousand years according to those who follow the Gregorian calendar. The Y2K (year two thousand) problem was uppermost in the minds of those living in our technological societies. When computer programmers began to design software, in order to save space they used only the last two digits in the four-digit number representing a year. Thus a computer read 99 as 1999. When the year 2000 occurred the date would read 01-01-00 and many computers would think it was 1900. This could cause a major shutdown of factories, machinery, power plants, communication facilities, and everything run by computers. To avoid this technological havoc, governments and businesses had been working on the Y2K problem for several years. In 1998 it was estimated that 25 percent of the world's computers were in crisis and 1.2 trillion lines of programs had to be rewritten, then verified and validated. The United States alone spent nearly $100 billion to fix the problem.

In anticipation of major or minor malfunctions, many people began stockpiling food and water, and the Federal Reserve printed an extra $50 billion of cash in expectation of a run on ATMs. As New Year's Eve approached, some people filled up their gas tanks . . . just in case. Fear of terrorist strikes at midnight caused the tightening of security in vulnerable places. Airports were nearly empty as many flights were canceled, trains slowed down just before midnight, and the military was on alert. Those who were sure the apocalypse was nigh, and the world was coming to an end, simply prayed.

On New Year's Day, despite a few minor glitches, ATMs dispensed cash, utilities functioned, planes were still flying in the air, no nuclear weapons were deployed, terrorists did not strike, and as drawn broke around the world, the earth was still rotating on its axis.

It was enough to bring tears to a pessimist's eyes. Of course, we never know what's just around the corner, do we?

SELECTIVE BIBLIOGRAPHY

Albritton, C. *Catastrophic Episodes in Earth History*. London: Chapman & Hall, 1989.

The Annual Register. Various editions from the eighteenth century onward.

Bixby, William. *Havoc*. New York: Longmans, Green and Co., 1961.

Bold, Alan, and Robert Giddings. *The Book of Rotters*. Edinburgh: Mainstream Publishing, 1985.

Canning, John. *Great Disasters—Catastrophes of the 20th Century*. London: Octopus Books, 1976.

Cornell, James. *Great International Disaster Book*. New York: Scribner, 1982.

Editors of the Encyclopedia Britannica. *Catastrophe! When Man Loses Control*. Chicago: Encyclopedia Britannica, 1979.

Felton, Bruce, and Mark Fowler. *Felton & Fowler's Best, Worst, and Most Unusual*. New York: Thomas Y. Crowell, 1975.

Frank, Beryl. *Great Disasters of the World*. New York: Galahad Books, 1981.

Garrison, Fielding H. *An Introduction to the History of Medicine*. Philadelphia: W. B. Saunders, 1917.

Herring, Susan. *From the Titanic to the Challenger*. New York: Garland, 1989.

Horne, Charles. *Great Events by Famous Historians*. New York: The National Alumni, 1904.

Kartman, Ben, ed. *Disaster!* New York: Pellegrini & Cudahy, 1948.

Kingston, Jeremy, and David Lambert. *Catastrophe and Crisis.* New York: Facts on File, 1979.

The London Times. Various editions from the late eighteenth century onward.

Marx, Robert F. *Shipwrecks of the Western Hemisphere, 1492–1825.* New York: World Publishing Co., 1971.

Mousnier, Roland. *Peasant Uprisings.* New York: Harper & Row, 1970.

Nash, Jay Robert. *Darkest Hours.* Chicago: Nelson-Hall, 1976.

The New York Times. Various editions from the late nineteenth century onward.

Oberg, James E. *Uncovering Soviet Disasters.* New York: Random House, 1988.

Shaw, Robert B. *A History of Railroad Accidents, Safety Precautions, and Operating Practices.* Vail-Ballou Press, 1978.

Singleton, Esther, ed. *The World's Great Events.* New York: Collier, 1913.

The Virginia Gazette. Various editions from the mid- to late eighteenth century.

Walker, John. *Disasters.* Chicago: Follett Publishing Co., 1973.

Wetterau, Bruce. *Macmillan Concise Dictionary of World History.* New York: Macmillan, 1983.

———. *New York Public Library Book of Chronologies.* New York: Prentice Hall, 1991.

Williams, Henry. *The Historian's History of the World.* London: Encyclopedia Britannica, 1926.

Wilson, Colin. *A Criminal History of Mankind.* London: Granada, 1984.

TIMELINE OF EVENTS

Air Crashes

1908 Fatal Air Crash in Maryland, 191

1921 Crash of the *R-38,* 215

1930 Crash of the *R-101,* 228

1933 Dirigible Crash off New Jersey Coast, 235

1937 *Hindenburg* Disaster, 239–241

1945 Airplane Hits the Empire State Building, 261–262

1946 Airliner Crashes on Takeoff at LaGuardia, 265

1950 Two French Airliners Crash, Same Night, Same Place, 270

1956 Midair Crash Over the Grand Canyon, 276

1960 Collision of Airliners Over Staten Island, 284

1969 Venezuelan Plane Crashes, 305

1974 Turkish Airline Crash, 314

1975 Vietnam Orphans Plane Disaster, 315

1977 Double Disaster at Tenerife, 320–322

1979 American Airlines Jet Crashes on Takeoff, 327

1979 Antarctic Sight-seeing Plane Crashes, 328

1983 Korean Airliner Shot Down, 333–334

1985 Miraculous Escape in Japan Air Lines Crash, 338–340

1985 Fiery Plane Crash at Gander Kills Returning U.S. Troops, 341

1988 U.S. Downs Iranian Airliner, 346–347

1988 Death at the Air Show, 347

1988 Terrorist Bomb Causes Lockerbie Airplane Crash, 349

1991 Jet Explosion Kills 223 over Thailand, 357

1991 Jet Carrying Moslem Pilgrims Crashes in Saudi Arabia, 361

1994 Airline Crash in Japan, 372–373

1994 Air Crash in Pittsburgh, 373

1996 Everglades Crash, 379–380

1996 Flight 800 Tragedy, 380

1996 Midair Crash Over India, 380

1997 Air Crash in Guam, 381

1998 Taiwan's Worst Plane Crash, 385

1998 Air Crash in Nova Scotia, 392

1999 Egyptair Flight 990 Crashes, 402

Assassinations

44 B.C. Julius Caesar Assassinated, 18–19

1170 Murder of Thomas à Becket, 37

1589 Assassination of Henry III, 73

1792 Assassination of Gustavus III of Sweden, 97

1965 Assassination of President Abraham Lincoln, 135–136

1881 Assassination of Czar Alexander II, 151–152

1881 President James Garfield Assassinated, 152

1900 Italian King Umberto I Assassinated, 175

1901 President McKinley Assassinated, 176–177

1914 The Spark That Ignited World War I, 198

Automobile Crashes

Avalanches

Battles, Conquests, and Other Military Action

490 B.C. Battle of Marathon, 8–10

331 B.C. Battle of Arbela, 14–15

218 B.C. Hannibal Crosses the Alps, 15

216 B.C. Hannibal Decimates Roman Army at Battle of Cannae, 16

70 The Siege of Jerusalem, 25–27

410 Visigoths Sack Rome, 31–32

930 Muslim Rebels Sack Holy City of Mecca, 35–36

1084 Normans Sack Rome, 36

1175–1218 Genghis Khan, the Bloody Terror, 37–38

1204 The Sack of Constantinople, 39–40

1209–1229 Christian Against Christian: Albigensian Crusade, 40–41

1212 Children's Crusade, 41–42

1281 The "Divine Wind" Saves Japan, 43–45

1453 Fall of Constantinople, 55

1520 "Sad Night" at Tenochtitlán, 61–62

1521 Disease and the Spanish Reconquest of Tenochtitlán, 63–64

1524–1525 Peasants' War in Germany, 64–66

1527 The Sack of Rome, 66

1588 The Disastrous Voyage of the Invincible Armada, 71–73

1671 Buccaneer Sir Henry Morgan Sacks Panama, 81–82

1687 Tragic Blast Destroys Parthenon, 83

1836 The Fall of the Alamo, 117–118

1854 Charge of the Light Brigade, 127–128

1862 Battle of Antietam, 131–132

1876 Battle of the Little Bighorn, 147–148

1885 Battle of Khartoum, 157

1915 First Use of Poison Gas by Germans, 200

1916 Battle of Verdun, 203–204

1917–1934 Russian Revolution—the Terrible Toll, 204–206

1940 Battle of Dunkirk, 245–246

Earthquakes

1268 Earthquake in Asia Minor, 43

1456 Earthquake Destroys Naples, 55

1531 Violent Quake Hits Lisbon, 67

1556 Great China Quake Kills Over 830,000, 67

1626 Seventy Thousand Die in Naples Earthquake, 75

1692 Jamaica Hit by Tidal Wave, 85

1693 A Year of Destruction in Italy, 85

1703–1704 Tokyo Earthquake, 85–86

1727 Earthquake Hits Persia, 87

1731 Deadly Earthquake Rocks Beijing, 88

1754 Earthquake Demolishes Cairo, 89

1755 Lisbon Earthquake, 89–91

1755 Severe Earthquake Rocks Boston, 91

1783 Earthquake Hits Italy, 94–95

1797 Ecuadoran Earthquake, 102

1805 Earthquake in Naples and Calabria, 103–104

1811–1812 New Madrid Earthquakes, 105–106

1812 Earthquake Destroys Caracas, Venezuela, 106

1819 Earthquake in Italy Kills Twenty Thousand, 111

1822 Aleppo Earthquake, 111

1835 Darwin Witnesses Chilean Earthquake, 117

1847 Japanese Earthquake, 123

1857 Earthquake and Fire Ravage Tokyo, 128

1868 South American Earthquake, 139

1876 Hundred-Foot Tsunamis Wreck Japanese Coast, 146–147

1886 Earthquake Shakes Eastern United States, 157–158

1887 Deadly Earthquake Shakes Riviera, 158

1891 Earthquake Shakes Up Central Japan, 166

1896 Japanese Tidal Wave, 170

1906 Great San Francisco Earthquake and Fire, 185–187

1908 Messina Earthquake, 190–191

1920 Earthquake Devastates Gansu, China, 214

1923 Great Kwanto Earthquake, 216–218

1935 Earthquake Razes Indian City, 237

1939 Chilean Earthquake, 242

1939 Turkish Earthquake, 244

1946 Seismic Wave Hits Hawaii, 265

1949 Earthquake Ravages Ecuador, 268–269

1960 Twelve Seconds of Destruction in Morocco, 283

1962 Powerful Earthquake Shakes Iran, 287

1964 Deadly Earthquake Shakes Alaska, 292

1968 Iranian Earthquake Kills Twelve Thousand, 305

1970 Peruvian Earthquake, 307–308

1972 Managua, Nicaragua, Earthquake, 312

1976 Guatemalan Earthquake, 317–318

1976 Tangshan Earthquake, 318–319

1978 Earthquake in Northeastern Iran, 323–324

1980 Earthquakes in Southern Italy, 331–332

1985 Mexico City Earthquake, 340

1988 Armenia Earthquake, 348–349

1989 San Francisco Earthquake, 351–352

1990 Iranian Earthquake, 352–354

1994 Los Angeles Rocked, 369–370

1995 Kobe Earthquake Disaster, 374

1998 Bolivia Shakes, 388

1998 Afghanistan Earthquake, 388–389

1999 Earthquake Ravages Western Colombia, 398

1999 Violent Earthquake Moves Turkey, 404–405

1999 Temblor Shakes Taiwan, 402

Environmental Calamities

65 Million Years Ago Extinction of the Dinosaurs, 1–2

6 Million Years Ago Mediterranean Sea Dries Up, 2

85 Thousand Years Ago The Last Ice Age?, 2–3

10 Thousand Years Ago Making of the Sahara Desert, 3–4

1816 Year Without a Summer, 110–111

1967 *Torrey Canyon* Oil Spill, 300

1977–1980 Love Canal, 320

1984 Killer Gas Leak in Bhopal, 337

1986 Chernobyl Nuclear Power Disaster, 343–344

1988 *Exxon Valdez* Oil Spill, 346

1998 Toxic Sludge Disaster in Spain, 385

Epidemics

1490 B.C. Biblical Plagues in Egypt, 6

453 B.C. Plague Ravages Rome, 10

430–427 B.C. Thousands Die in Plague at Athens, 10–12

164 B.C. Deadly Smallpox Epidemic Kills Thousands, 16

79–88 Plague Ravages Roman Empire, 28

125 Plague of Orosius, 28–29

164–180 Plague of Antoninus, 29

250–265 Black Plague Strikes Roman Empire, 30

542 Plague Strikes Constantinople, 35

746–749 Plague Ravages Constantinople, 35

1347–1351 Black Death, 47–48

1347 Saint Vitus' Dance Epidemic, 48–49

1485 Outbreak of English Sweating Sickness, 59

1490s Syphilis Epidemic Begins, 59

1665 Great Plague of London, 78

1672 Black Plague at Naples, 82

1711 Black Plague in Holy Roman Empire, 86

1722 Ergotism Outbreak in Russia, 87

1735–1740 Diphtheria Outbreak Hits New England, 88

1781–1782 Influenza Epidemic, 94

1792 Plague Sweeps Through Egypt, 97

1793–1804 Yellow Fever Wars, 100–101

1793 Yellow Fever Epidemic in Philadelphia, 101

1799–1800 Yellow Fever Ravages Spain and North Africa, 103

1826–1837 Cholera Epidemics Ravage Europe, 114

1851–1855 Tuberculosis Epidemic in Britain, 125

1878 Yellow Fever Epidemic in Memphis, Tennessee, 149

1889–1890 Worldwide Influenza Epidemic, 165

1893–1894 Deadly Cholera Epidemic, 168

1900–1907 Sleeping Sickness Epidemic, 173

1903–1908 Plague Sweeps Over India, 179

1906 Discovery of Typhoid Mary, 183

1910–1913 Last Major Outbreak of Black Plague, 192

1918–1919 Influenza Epidemic, 210–211

1931 Diphtheria Invades the United States, 228

1946 Last Major Polio Epidemic in the United States, 263

1957–1958 Worldwide Asian Flu Epidemic, 278

1976 Legionnaires' Disease Outbreak at Philadelphia, 320

1979 What Happened at Sverdlovsk?, 327–328

1980 Deadly AIDS Epidemic Invades the United States, 328–329

1998 AIDS Rivals the Black Death, 395–396

Famines and Droughts

1200–1202 Egyptian Famine, 38–39

1601–1604 Half Million Russians Die in Famine, 74

1769–1770 Indian Famine Kills Millions, 91

1790–1792 Skull Famine in India, 96

1845–1848 Irish Potato Famine, 120–121

1866–1870 Famine and Fever in Northern India, 138

1876–1878 Famine Strikes India Again, 146

1876–1879 Famine Kills Millions in China, 146

1896–1897 Famine Hits India Again, 169

1921–1923 Famine in the Soviet Union, 214–215

1928–1929 Famine in China, 223

1932–1937 The Dust Bowl, 231–232

1936 Five Million Chinese Die in New Famine, 238

1939 Flood and Famine in China, 243

1967–1969 Famine in Biafra, 298

1984–1985 African Famine, 335–336

1992 Somalia Starves, 364

1998 Famine in Sudan, 383–384

Financial Disasters

1720 The South Sea Bubble, 87

1929 Stock Market Crash, 226–227

1995 Barings Bank Collapses, 374–375

1998 Financial Turmoil in Indonesia, 387–388

Fires and Explosions

538 B.C. Babylon Burns in Great Fire, 8

390 B.C. Gauls Burn Rome, 13–14

64 Great Fire of Rome, 23–24

817 Rome Burns in Great Fire, 35

1106 A Very Bad Year for Venice, 36–37

1212 Fire Burns London, 41

1608 Disastrous Fire at Jamestown, 75

1645 Explosion Rocks Boston, 77

1657 Tokyo Fire, 77

1666 The Great Fire of London, 78–80

1687 Tragic Blast Destroys Parthenon, 83

1729 Constantinople Fire, 87–88

1751 Stockholm Burns, 89

1752 Three Successive Fires Ravage Moscow, 89

1769 Lightning Ignites Powder Magazine, 91–92

1795 Copenhagen Fire, 101–102

1800 British Warship Sinks After Catching Fire, 103

1807 Luxembourg Powder Magazine Explodes, 104

1812 Moscow Burns, 107–108

1814 Washington, D.C., Burns, 109

1824 Cairo Fire, 113

1825 New Brunswick Fire, 113–114

1834 Fire in British Parliament, 117

1836 Theater Fire Kills Seven Hundred in Russia, 118

1841 Erie Steamboat Fire, 119

1842 Train Crash Near Versailles, France, 120

1845 Quebec Fire, 121

1845 Chinese Theater Burns, 122

1845 Fire Ravages New York City, 122

1848 Great Fire in Constantinople, 124

1849 Steamboats Burn in Saint Louis Fire, 124

1851 Fire in the Congressional Library, 126

1851 San Francisco Fire, 126

1852 Fire Hits Montreal, 127

1856 Deadly Gunpowder Magazine Explosion, 128

1857 Earthquake and Fire Ravage Tokyo, 128

1858 Fire Wrecks London Docks, 130

1858 Fire Aboard Passenger Liner, 130

1863 Deadly Church Fire in Santiago, Chile, 133

1865 *General Lyon* Burns at Sea, 135

1865 Fiery Explosion of the *Sultana,* 137–138

1866 Firecracker Burns Portland, 138

1866 Twenty-five Hundred Homes Burn in Quebec Fire, 138–139

1870 Constantinople Fire, 139

1871 Great Chicago Fire, 141–142

1871 Fire Ravishes Peshtigo, 142–144

1872 Boston Fire, 144

1874 Fire Aboard Ship Kills 468, 145

1876 Brooklyn, New York, Theater Fire, 148–149

1881 French Opera House Fire, 152

1881 Vienna Ring Theater Fire, 153–154

1883 Polish Circus Burns as Firemen Fall Through Ice, 154–155

1887 Paris Opera Fire, 158–159

1887 Exeter Theatre Fire, 159–160

1887 Four Hundred Die in Fire Aboard Steamship, 161

1892 Oil City, Pennsylvania, Catches Fire, 166

1894 Forest Fire Incinerates Hinckley, Minnesota, 168–169

1896 Cripple Creek Conflagration, 169–170

1897 Tragic Fire at Paris Charity Bazaar, 171

1898 Sinking of the *Maine,* 171

1899 New York's Windsor Hotel Burns, 172

1903 Iroquois Theater Fire, 179–180

1904 Fire Destroys Baltimore, 181

1904 *General Slocum* Burns, 181–183

1908 Tragic Fire at Ohio Elementary School, 188–189

1910 *Los Angeles Times* Fire, 192–193

1910 Forest Fire in Montana and Idaho, 193

1911 Triangle Shirtwaist Company Fire, 193–194

1914 British Battleship Explodes, 199

1915 Explosion of British Warship, 202

1916 Russian Munitions Factory Blows Up, 204

1917 Exploding Munitions Plant Blasts Silvertown, England, 206

1917 Munitions Ship Explodes at Archangel, 207

1917 Bohemian Munitions Plant Blows Up, 208

1917 British Battleship Blows Up, 208

1917 Nova Scotia Blast, 208

1918 TNT Explosion Rips Pennsylvania Plant, 211

1918 Deadly Fires in Minnesota and Wisconsin, 212

1918 Munitions Train Explodes, 213

1921 German Dye Plant Explodes, 215–216

1924 Babb's Switch Christmas Eve School Fire, 218–219

1926 Explosions Rip Apart Chinese Troop Ship, 220–221

1927 Panic Kills Children at Montreal Movie Theater, 221

1927 Pittsburgh Gas Explosion, 221

1929 Deadly Cleveland Hospital Fire, 226

1930 Prisoners Killed by Ohio Penitentiary Fire, 228

1933 The Suspicious Reichstag Fire, 233–235

1934 Fire Destroys Hakodate, Japan, 236

1934 Fire at Sea—the *Morro Castle,* 236–237

1937 Texas School Explosion, 238–239

1940 Rhythm Night Club Fire, 245

1941 Yugoslavian Fort Explosion, 249

1942 Colliery Blast Kills 1,549, 252–253

1942 Cocoanut Grove Fire, 254–255

1944 The Bombay Explosion, 257

1944 "The Greatest Show on Earth" Ends in Tragedy, 257–258

1944 Port Chicago Munitions Explosion, 258–259

1944 Terror in Cleveland, 259–260

1945 Firebombing of Dresden, 260

1945 United States Drops Atomic Bombs on Hiroshima and Nagasaki, 262–263

1946 Winecoff Hotel Fire, 264–265

1946 La Salle Hotel Fire, 265–266

1947 Texas City Tragedy, 266–267

1948 German Chemical Plant Blows Up, 268

1949 Fire in Chungking, China, 269

1956 Dynamite Explosion Wrecks Colombian City, 277

1957 Missouri Nursing Home Fire, 278

1958 Chicago Parochial School Fire, 280

1958 Bogotá Department Store Fire, 280

1959 Fire Finds "Room at the Top," 280–281

1960 Soviet Rocket Explodes on Launchpad, 284

1961 Terrorists Sink *Dara,* 284

1961 Deadly Circus Fire in Brazil, 285–286

1963 Indiana Ice Show Explosion, 289

1965 Fifty-three Die in Titan II Missile Silo Fire, 293–294

1967 *Apollo I* Fire, 298–299

1967 Brussels Department Store Fire, 300

1967 Aircraft Carrier USS *Forrestal* Fire, 300–301

1970 French Dance Hall Fire, 308

1971 Korean Hotel Fire, 311

1973 Staten Island Gas Storage Tank Explodes, 313

1976 Chemical Explosion at Seveso, Italy, 318

1977 Saturday Night of Death at a Kentuckly Nightclub, 322

1980 MGM Grand Hotel Fire, 331

1982 Explosion Wrecks Soviet Convoy in Afghan Tunnel, 333

1983 Egyptian Riverboat Catches Fire, 333

1983 Terrible Fire at Spanish Discotheque, 334

1984 Brazilian Oil Pipeline Ruptures, 336

1984 Gas Explosion Outside Mexico City, 337

1985 British Soccer Stadium Fire, 337–338

1986 U.S. Space Shuttle *Challenger* Explodes, 341–342

1986 Puerto Rican Resort Hotel Fire, 345

1988 North Sea Oil Rig Explosion, 347

1989 Soviet Gas Pipeline Explosion Wrecks Trains, 350

1990 Fire Aboard North Sea Ferry, 352

1990 Deadly Train Fire in India, 352

1993 World Trade Center Bombing, 365–366

1993 Tragedy in Texas, 367–368

1995 Oklahoma City Bombing, 376–378

1995 Tragic Fire in Dabwali, India, 379

1998 U.S. Embassies in East Africa Bombed, 390–391

1998 Car Bomb Ravages Omagh, 391–392

1998 Nigerian Oil Pipe Explosion, 393–394

Floods and Tidal Waves

2400 B.C. The Great Deluge, 5

1106 A Very Bad Year for Venice, 36–37

1277 Floods Devastate Holland, 43

1574 Victory by Flood in Holland, 70–71

1642 Three Hundred Thousand Die in China Flood, 77

1824 Ten Thousand Drown in Saint Petersburg, Russia, 113

1829 Broken Dike Floods Danzig (Gdansk), Poland, 115

1875 Garonne River Flood, 145

1887 Flooding in China, 160–161

1889 Johnstown, Pennsylvania, Flood, 164–165

1911 China Devastated by Flood, 194

1915 Deadly Floods in China, 202

1916 Ten Thousand Die in Netherlands Flood, 202–203

1927 Mississippi Valley Floods, 221–222

1928 Saint Francis Dam Breaks, 223–224

1931 Yangtze Flood Kills Millions, 229

1937 Massive Flooding in Ohio River Basin, 238

1939 Flood and Famine in China, 243

1950 Chinese Flood Leaves Ten Million Homeless, 270

1953 North Sea Floods, 272–273

1954 Yangtze River Floods, 273–274

1954 Iranian Flash Flood Kills Worshipers, 274

1963 Deadly Floods in Italy, 288

1966 Flooding in Italy Ruins Art Treasures, 298

1971 North Vietnam Floods, 310

1972 Logan County, West Virginia, Flood, 311

1973 Mississippi River Floods, 313–314

1985 Dam Bursts in Northern Italy, 338

1991 Severe Flooding in China, 357

1992 Killer Tidal Wave, 365

1997 Grand Forks Deluge, 380–381

1998 More Floods in China, 390

1998 Disease, Disaster, and Despair in Bangladesh, 392

1999 Hurricane Floyd Floods, 400–401

Massacres and Other Mass Killings and Cruelty

88 B.C Massacre of One Hundred Thousand Romans, 16

87–80 B.C More Romans Die, 17

37–41 Blood and Power: Caligula's Cruel Reign, 22

64 Nero Persecutes the Christians, 24–25

1175–1218 Genghis Khan, the Bloody Terror, 37–38

1191 Massacre at Acre, 38

1282 Sicilian Vespers Massacre, 45–46

1321 Massacre of Jews in France, 46–47

1402 The Rise of the Black Slave Trade, 50–52

1417 Massacre of the Armagnacs, 53

1459 The Many Horrors of Vlad Dracula, "the Impaler", 55–57

1478 Cruel Tortures of the Spanish Inquisition, 57–58

1520 Human Sacrifice Among the Aztecs, 62–63

1546 Massacre of the Waldenses, 67

1562 Massacre at Vassy, France, 68

1570 Massacre at Novogorod, 68

1572 Massacre of Saint Bartholomew, 69–70

1685 The Bloody Assizes, 82–83

1690 Schenectady Massacre, 83–84

1692 Glencoe Massacre, 84

1738 Massacre at Delhi, 88–89

1756 Black Hole of Calcutta, 91

1778 Wyoming Valley Massacre, 92

1792 Russian Persecutions of the Jews, 96–97

1792 The September Massacres, 97–98

1793–1794 Reign of Terror, 98–100

1811 Massacre of the Mamelukes, 104

1820 Manila Massacre, 111

1826 Massacre of the Janissaries, 114–115

1832 Bad Axe Massacre, 116

1864 Fort Pillow Massacre, 134

1864 Sand Creek Massacre, 134

1876 Turkish Massacre in Bulgaria, 145–146

1905 Massacre of Russian Demonstrators, 183

1915 Turks Massacre Armenians, 201–202

1917–1934 Russian Revolution—the Terrible Toll, 204–206

1919 The Massacre of Amritsar, 213

1929 Saint Valentine's Day Massacre, 226

1933–1945 The Holocaust, 232–233

1940 Katyn Forest Massacre, 244–245

1949 Chinese Refugees Undertake Deadly March to Freedom, 269–270

1968 My Lai Massacre, 302–303

1976 Khmer Rouge Commits Atrocities in Cambodia, 316–317

1978 Jonestown Mass Suicide, 324–325

1982 Massacre at Chatila, 333

1989 Tiananmen Square Massacre, 350

1990 Massacre in Liberia, 354

1994 Massacre in the Mosque, 370

1994 Genocide in Rwanda, 370–372

1994 Suicide Bomber Blasts Bus, 373–374

1995 Nerve-Gas Attack in Tokyo Subway, 375–376

1997 Luxor Tourists Slaughter, 383

Mining Disasters

1900 Utah Coal Mine Explodes, 174

1906 Courrières Mine Explodes, 184–185

1907 West Virginia Mine Disaster, 188

1907 239 Miners Killed in Explosion, 188

1909 Explosion and Fire at Illinois Coal Mine, 191

1910 British Coal Mine Disaster, 193

1913 Welsh Mine Explosion and Fires, 196–197

1913 New Mexico Mine Explosion, 197

1928 Pennsylvania Mine Explosion, 224

1931 Manchurian Mine Explosion, 228

1949 German Mine Explosion, 270

1960 South Africa Mine Disaster, 283

1963 Japanese Mine Explosion, 289

1972 Rhodesian Coal Mine Explosion, 312

Miscellaneous Calamities

18 Billion Years Ago The Big Bang, 1

5 Thousand Years Ago Giant Meteor Hits Arizona, 4–5

27 Stadium Collapses in Rome, 20

Third Century War Destroys Library at Alexandria, Egypt, 30

1587 Lost Colony of Roanoke Island, 71

1891 Rescue of British Harpooner, 165–166

1908 Strange Blast in Siberia, 189–190

1938 The Meteor That Almost Squashed Pittsburgh, 241

1943 Bizarre Air Raid Shelter Accident in London, 255

1955 Gold Fever in Argentina, 275

Murders and Infamous Executions

Nuclear Accidents

Railroad Disasters

Revolts, Rebellions, and Riots

Shipwrecks and Other Marine Disasters

1800 British Warship Sinks After Catching Fire, 103

1810 Wreck of British Frigate Kills 490, 104

1811 Two Thousand British Sailors Die in Storms, 105

1837 Mississippi Steamboat Collision, 119

1841 Erie Steamboat Fire, 119

1848 Incredible Tale of the *Omega,* 123

1850 Coastal Steamboat Sinks, 125

1852 *Birkenhead* Sinks Off Cape Town, 126–127

1854 *City of Glasgow* Disappears at Sea, 127

1855 Clipper Ship Sinks in Ice Field, 128

1857 The Tragic Fate of the *Central America,* 129–130

1857 Russian Warship Sinks in Storm, 130

1858 Fire Aboard Passenger Liner, 130

1859 *Royal Charter* Sinks, 130

1860 Lake Michigan Steamer Sinks, 130

1865 *General Lyon* Burns at Sea, 135

1865 Fiery Explosion of the *Sultana,* 137–138

1866 Disappearance of the *Monarch of the Seas,* 138

1870 Ironclad Warship Sinks, 139

1873 The *Atlantic* Sinks Off Nova Scotia, 144–145

1874 Fire Aboard Ship Kills 468, 145

1878 Sinking of Excursion Steamer, 150

1883 The Steamship *Daphne* Capsizes, 156–157

1887 Four Hundred Die in Fire Aboard Steamship, 161

1895 Spanish Warship Founders, 169

1898 Sinking of the *Maine,* 171

1898 Collision at Sea Kills 571, 171

1902 Steamer Sinking Drowns 739, 177

1904 *General Slocum* Burns, 181–183

1907 Night of Death Aboard a "Joy Line" Steamer, 187–188

1912 Unsinkable *Titanic* Lost, 194–196

1912 Japanese Steamer Sinks, 196

1914 Steamer Sinks Off Brazil, 197

1914 Ship Passengers Drown as They Sleep, 197–198

1914 British Battleship Explodes, 199

1915 Sinking of the *Lusitania,* 200–201

1915 Explosion of British Warship, 202

1916 Ramming of Chinese Troop Ship, 204

1917 Sinking of British Transport, 206–207

1917 British Battleship Blows Up, 208

1917 Nova Scotia Blast, 208–209

1918 Collision at Sea Kills 425, 212

1918 Sinking of Steamship *Princess Sophia,* 212

1920 French Liner Sinks, 214

1921 Mayhem Aboard Sinking Chinese Steamer, 215

1926 Explosions Rip Apart Chinese Troop Ship, 220–221

1934 Fire at Sea—the *Morro Castle,* 236–237

1939 Submarine *Thetis* Sinks, 242–243

1939 Soviet Steamer Wrecks in Japan, 243–244

1942 *Queen Mary* Rams Cruiser, 253

1945 Thousands Die in Chinese Riverboat Wreck, 263

1948 Six Thousand Die in China Troop Ship Disaster, 268

1948 Second China Ship Disaster Kills Thousands More, 268

1956 The Luxury Liner *Andrea Doria* Sinks, 276–277

1961 Terrorists Sink *Dara,* 284

1963 Death Aboard the USS *Thresher* Submarine, 287–288

1965 African Ferry Capsizes in Crocodile-Infested River, 293

1967 Soviet Reactor Meltdown, 298

1967 Aircraft Carrier USS *Forrestal* Fire, 300–301

1968 U.S. Submarine *Scorpion* Lost, 304–305

1983 Egyptian Riverboat Catches Fire, 333

1986 Soviet Ships Collide in Black Sea, 345

1987 British Ferryboat Sinks, 345

1987 Collision of Philippine Ships, 346

1988 *Exxon Valdez* Oil Spill, 346

1990 Fire Aboard North Sea Ferry, 352

1991 Italian Ferry Collides with Tanker, 355–356

1994 The *Estonia* Capsizes, 373

1998 Ship Capsizes Near Manila, 393

Storms

1666 West Indies Hurricane, 78

1694 Hurrican Founders British Ships, 85

1719 Killer Snowstorm in Sweden, 86

1737 Cyclone and Earthquake Demolish Calcutta, 88

1769 Lightning Ignites Powder Magazine, 91–92

1776 Caribbean Hurricane Ravages Shipping Trade, 92

1780 The Great West Indies Hurricane, 93–94

1782 Gale Wrecks Barbados, 94

1784 First Hailstorm Deaths in the United States, 95–96

1789 Cyclone Hits India, 96

1798 New England Blizzard, 103

1807 Luxembourg Powder Magazine Explodes, 104

1811 Tornado Wrecks Charleston, 104–105

1822 Deadly Cyclone in India, 111

1831 Hurricane Devastates Barbados, 116

1833 Fifty Thousand Die in Calcutta Cyclone, 116

1840 Natchez Tornado, 119

1841 Hurricane Wipes Out Saint Jo, Florida, 120

1842 Tornado Again Ravages Natchez, 120

1862 Typhoon Kills Thousands in China, 130–131

1864 Calcutta Cyclone, 134–135

1876 Bengal Cyclone Wipes Out One Hundred Thousand, 148

1881 South Atlantic Coast Gale, 152–153

1882 Storm Devastates Bombay, 154

1884 Cyclone Rips Through Southeastern U.S., 157

1888 East Coast Blizzard, 162–164

1888 Hailstorm Kills 250, 164

1891 Caribbean Hurricane, 166

1892 Oil City, Pennsylvania, Catches Fire, 166

1893 Hurricane Kills One Thousand in the South, 167

1893 Killer Hurricane Hits Gulf of Mexico, 167

1896 Deadly Twister Devastates Saint Louis, 170

1898 Blizzard Hits Coastal Northeastern U.S., 172

1900 Galveston Hurricane, 175–176

1917 Tornadoes Ravage Eight States, 207

1922 Heavy Snows Hit Eastern Seaboard, 216

1922 Swatow's Twin Typhoons, 216

1925 Midwestern Tornado, 219–220

1926 Florida Hurricane, 220

1927 Tornado Wrecks Saint Louis, 222

1928 Lake Okeechobee Hurricane, 224–225

1935 Hurricane Devastates Florida Keys, 238

1938 Great New England Hurricane, 241–242

1941 Midwest Blizzard, 248–249

1942 Tens of Thousands Die in Bengal Hurricane, 254

1944 Major Hurricane Hits New England, 259

1952 Blizzard Hits Sierra Nevadas, 271

1952 Killer Fog Chokes London, 271–272

1953 New England Tornado, 273

1954 Japanese Typhoon, 274

1954 Hurricane Hazel's Long Path of Destruction, 274–275

1957 Hurricane Audrey, 279

1959 Typhoon Vera, 281–282

1960 Hurricane Donna Ravages U.S. East Coast, 283

1960 Cyclones Strike Bay of Bengal, 283–284

1963 Twenty-two Thousand Die in East Pakistan Cyclone, 288

1963 Hurricane Flora's Fury, 288

1965 Thirty-five Midwest Tornadoes Kill 271, 292–293

1967 Lisbon's Killer Rainstorm, 301

1969 Hurricane Camille, 306

1970 Hundreds of Thousands Die in East Pakistan Cyclone, 308–310

1972 Iran Goes from Drought to Blizzard, 311

1972 Hurricane Agnes Ravages East Coast, 312

1974 Tornado Alley, 314

1974 Hurricane Fifi, 314–315

1979 Hurricane David, 328

1979 Hurricane Frederick Follows on the Heels of David, 328

1985 Another Bangladesh Tragedy, 338

1991 Cyclone Kills Thousands in Bangladesh, 356

1991 Lightning Kills Spectator at U.S. Open, 357

1992 Hurricane Andrew, 364–365

1993 The Storm of the Century, 366–367

1998 More Cyclone Deaths in India, 389

1998 The Terrifying Tsunami, 389–390

1998 Hurricane Georges Strikes, 393

1998 Hurricane Mitch Wreaks Havoc on Millions, 394–395

1999 Twister Flattens Oklahoma Cities, 399–400

Technological Disasters of the Twentieth Century

1906 Quebec Bridge Collapses, 187

1921 German Dye Plant Explodes, 215–216

1939 DDT Is Developed, 241–242

1947 Texas City Tragedy, 266–267

1948 German Chemical Plant Blows Up, 268

1957 Soviet Nuclear Disaster in Ural Mountains, 278

1960 The Terrible Tragedy of Thalidomide, 282

1965 Fifty-three Die in Titan II Missile Silo Fire, 293–294

1967 Soviet Reactor Meltdown, 298

1967 *Apollo I* Fire, 298–299

1967 *Torrey Canyon* Oil Spill, 300

1970 Yarra River Bridge Collapses, 308

1971 Soviet Space Disaster, 310

1973 Staten Island Gas Storage Tank Explodes, 313

1976 Chemical Explosion at Seveso, Italy, 318

1977–1980 Love Canal, 320

1979 Three Mile Island Nuclear Accident, 325–327

1984 Brazilian Oil Pipeline Ruptures, 336

1984 Gas Explosion Outside Mexico City, 337

1984 Killer Gas Leak in Bhopal, 337

1986 U.S. Space Shuttle *Challenger* Explodes, 341–342

1986 Chernobyl Nuclear Power Disaster, 343–344

1988 North Sea Oil Rig Explosion, 347

1989 Soviet Gas Pipeline Explosion Wrecks Trains, 350

Volcanic Eruptions

5000 B.C. Volcanic Eruption Creates Crater Lake, 4

1628 B.C. The Great Volcanic Eruption on Thera, 5–6

1226 B.C. First Known Eruption of Mount Etna, 6

79 Vesuvius Destroys Pompeii and Herculaneum, 27–28

186 Massive Volcano Erupts in New Zealand, 30

472 Vesuvius Erupts, 32

1169 Mount Etna Erupts, 376

1591 Eruption of Philippine Volcano Taal, 73–74

1631 Eruption of Mount Vesuvius, 76

1638 Indonesian Volcano Explodes, 76

1669 Eruption of Mount Etna, 80–81

1772 Java Volcano Blows Its Top, 92

1783 Iceland Volcanic Eruptions, 95

1793 Deadly Explosion of Japanese Volcano, 98

1794 Ecuadoran Volcano Erupts, 101

1814 Sleeping Philippine Volcano Suddenly Erupts, 108–109

1815 Indonesian Volcano Explodes, 109–110

1822 Eruption of Galung Gung, 112

1872 Spectacular Mount Vesuvius Eruption, 144

1883 Krakatoa Erupts, 155–156

1902 Mount Pelée's Deadly Eruption, 177–179

1902 Guatemalan Volcano, 179

1919 Volcanic Lake in Java Erupts, 213–214

1971 Mount Etna in Sicily Erupts, 310

1973 Eruption on Heimaey Island, Iceland, 312–313

1980 Harry Truman and Mount Saint Helens, 329–331

1986 The Killer Gas Cloud, 344–345

1997 Paradise Lost, 382